# CHARLES RENNIE MACKINTOSH

## ARCHITECT :: ARTIST :: ICON

TEXT BY JOHN McKEAN

PHOTOGRAPHS BY COLIN BAXTER

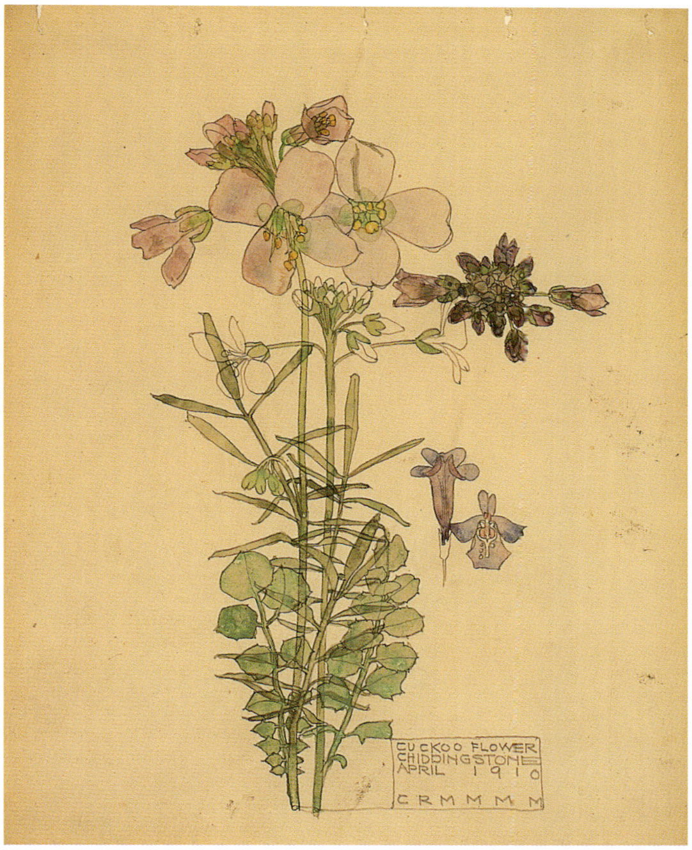


**LOMOND**
www.lomondbooks.com

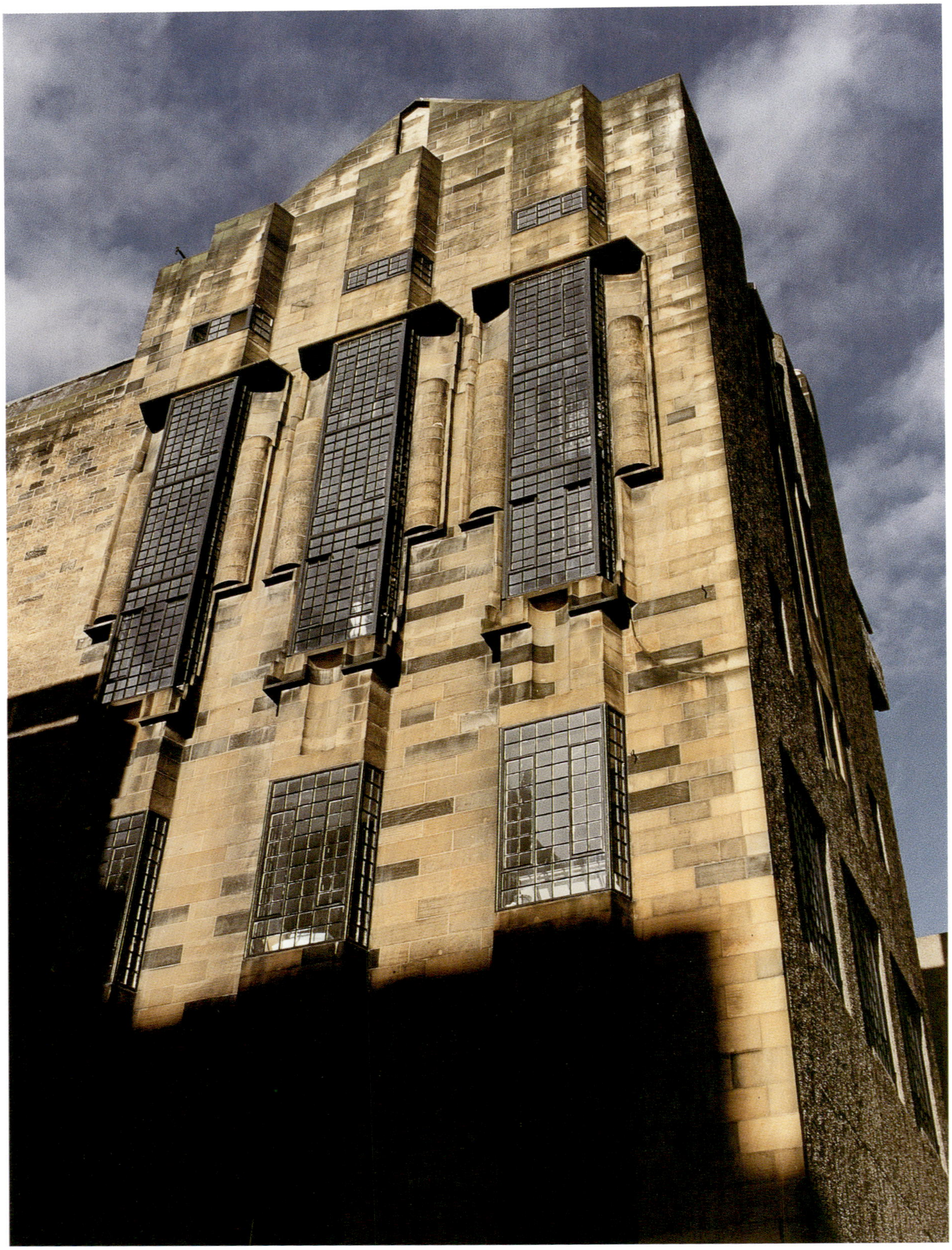

# CONTENTS

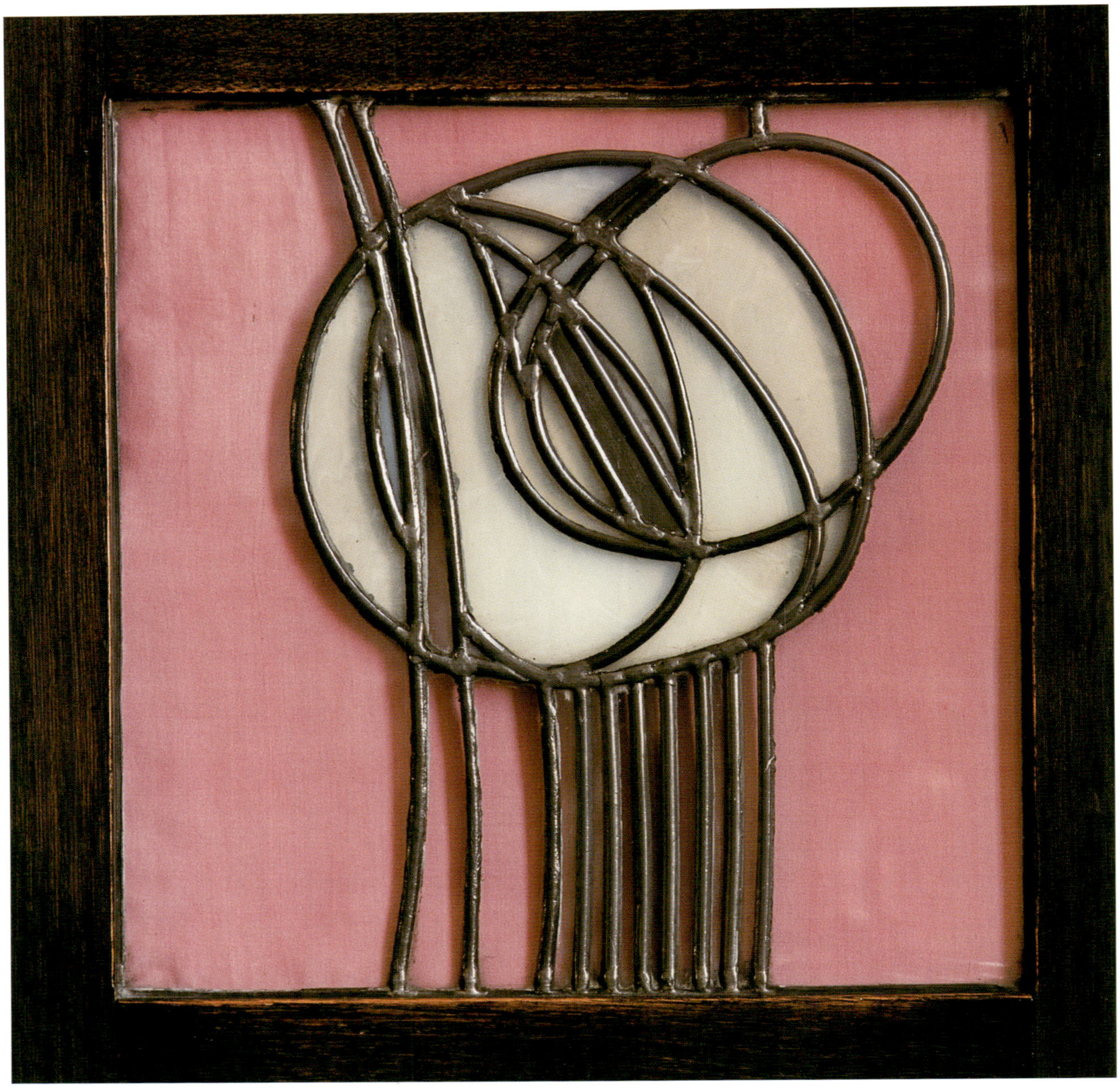

# PREFACE

Nikolaus Pevsner sits on a stool at the bar in a tiny basement Victorian pub in London. A stuffed lion at his shoulder, a great waxy fish in a glass case on the wall, shelves of ancient bottles. He is talking quietly and reticently about Alexander Thomson, Glasgow's great Victorian architect. It is the early 1970s, Thomson is virtually unknown in England and I am honoured Pevsner has agreed to come and chat about the man I've recently been studying. We don't even mention Mackintosh.

Pevsner, the grand old man of twentieth-century architectural history, invented the story of a clean and functional 'modern movement'; he created its 'pioneers', men of the end of the nineteenth century, at the moment of The Glasgow School of Art. Twenty years before our meeting, he suggested to the young Mackintosh researcher Thomas Howarth that they publish a monograph together. He was politely turned down. Howarth produced *Charles Rennie Mackintosh and The Modern Movement*, which became the indispensable documentary record. But its title explained its theme: a tale leading to Pevsner's mid twentieth-century Modernism, with its 'hero' as 'pioneer', tainted but never really deflected by feminine ornamentation and Art Nouveau trivialisation. No one mentions nonsense like symbolism. Similarly, Pevsner's colleague J.M. Richards, still working in the next room to this bar, called The Glasgow School of Art 'a building remarkably ahead of its time.' He continues: 'There have been many misunderstandings about modern architecture. It is not, for one thing, a fashionable style of jazz ornament...'[1]

The pub where we sit is entirely fake (apart from the drink), put together from scraps rescued by Pevsner's and Richards' colleagues a generation earlier. They collected bits of out-of-fashion, into-skip, disposable interiors, which were being chucked to make way for 'Fifties functional'. In this little warren of spaces, there is no embarrassment in repro, no postmodern knowing games about authenticity, no hint of kitsch. The boldly etched mirrors advertise old beers in flamboyant playbill lettering.

Pevsner takes my thesis as he leaves, shortly to return it with a polite, mailed note. In his tiny and clear hand, he expresses appreciation but queries my approach to writing architectural history.

That makes me think back. Ten years earlier, architectural history for me as a student involved the most tedious afternoons in the basement lecture theatre of The Glasgow School of Art. A young but ancient Hugh Ferguson, his back to us, would be at the blackboard as we came in. With coloured chalks, he would copy neatly from an old, dusty Banister Fletcher's *History of Architecture on The Comparative Method*, as we mumbled and fidgeted. He finished, stood aside and we laboriously repeated his diagrams into our own notebooks. As he droned on about ancient civilisations, we waited to get back to the fresh air of the 1960s.

I loved the Art School but, without an invitation, would never have thought of writing about Mackintosh. I am encouraged really by one comment of Pevsner's in his short study (Milan, 1950) which was, in fact, the first-ever on Mackintosh, although not published in English for a long time. My thoughts are refocused by his very last sentence. 'I never knew Mackintosh, but at the same time I have never met anyone – and I have approached many of his friends and contemporaries – who did not speak of him with a light in their eyes.'

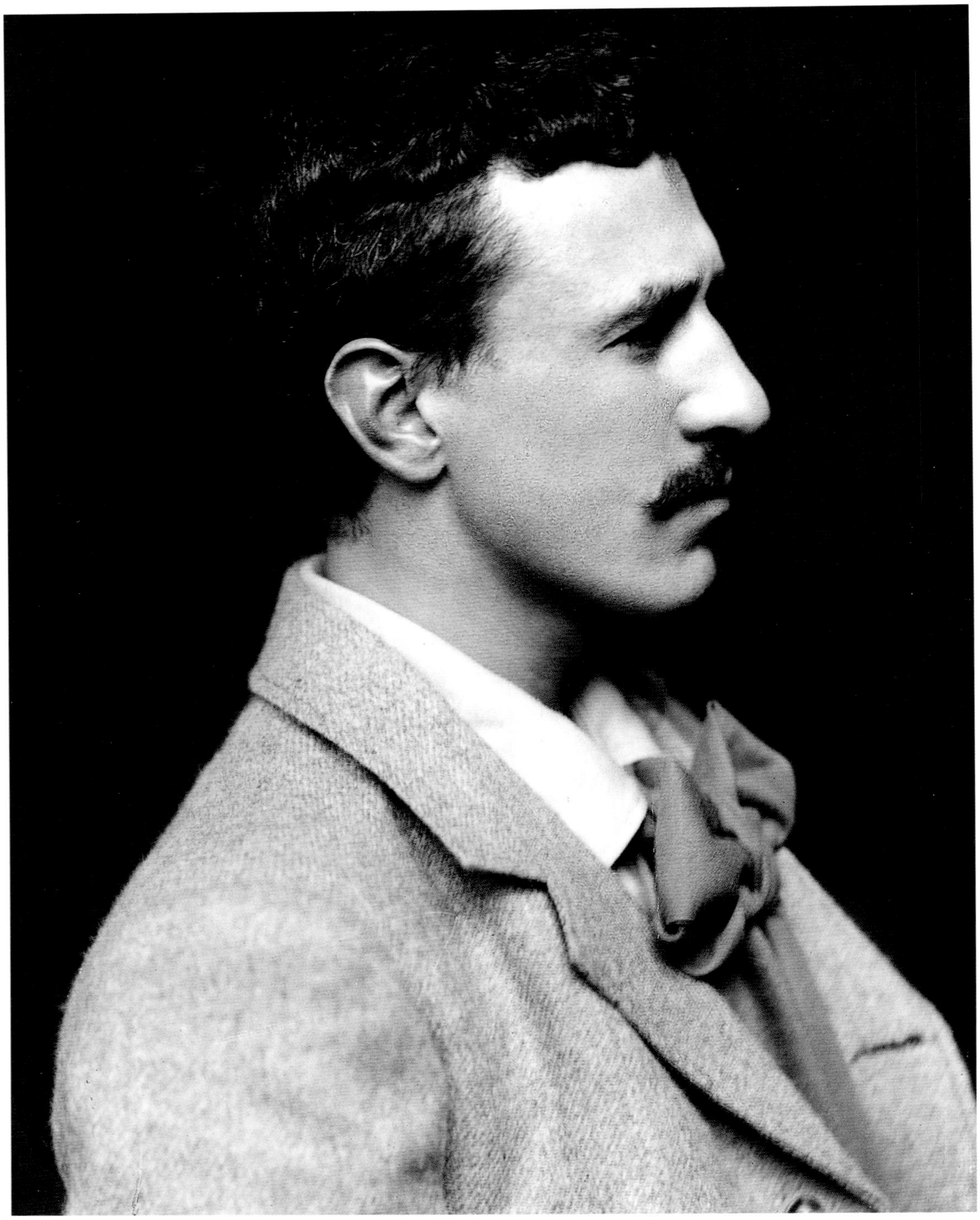

# OVERTURE

Charles Rennie Mackintosh (1868–1928) was a designer and artist. His work ranged from jewellery[1] to graphics, from wall decoration to exhibited paintings, from pottery vases[2] to wood engraving. He designed all kinds of objects of domestic use: tables, chairs, cutlery and napkins; carpets, mirrors, curtain fabric and light fittings; beds, hat stands, wardrobes and clocks. He designed complete buildings – their foundations and structural steel, their sophisticated ventilation systems and their plumbing. He painted landscapes and flowers. But the heart of his achievement was the design of places to be inhabited, rooms and sequences of rooms, their form and light and material.

He was scarcely dead before Pevsner and others began to praise him as a pioneer of Modernism; different critics call him Britain's master of Art Nouveau; to yet others he is the last great Victorian architect. The breadth of his achievement has kept eluding his admirers – but degrees of admiration have also varied widely. 'Much of Mackintosh was rather a fraud,' said a leading English critic dismissively.[3] Half a century later a CD-Rom on his work calls him 'the greatest originator of modern architecture and design.'[4] He seems to encourage exaggeration.

Mackintosh himself talked of one new English architectural star being 'crushed with official recognition and journalistic approval' at a time when he himself was living extremely simply and privately, and his work was virtually unknown. Today he seems far more solidly crushed with popularity than ever was that now forgotten Englishman. What can yet another book on Mackintosh say? What remains so fascinating about him?

There is the range of designs one man can produce, the ever-fascinating variety of his virtuosity. There is how his production varied wildly through his life: a book on his paintings might only look at the 1920s; the standard work on his furniture and interiors has 20 pages a year up to 1912, and just two pages a year, on average, for the rest.[5] There is the legendary quality of his life: his sudden emergence in a provincial city, huge output over very few years, pan-European fame and isolation at home, obscurity and death in poverty. Here the 'enigmatic' personality links with the notion of the heroic failure, a stereotype emblematic in the merging of sot with Scot.

Mackintosh was not a multiple text to be read differently by different approaches and times, he was a real historical person. Not a lone genius, but a man working within real and powerful

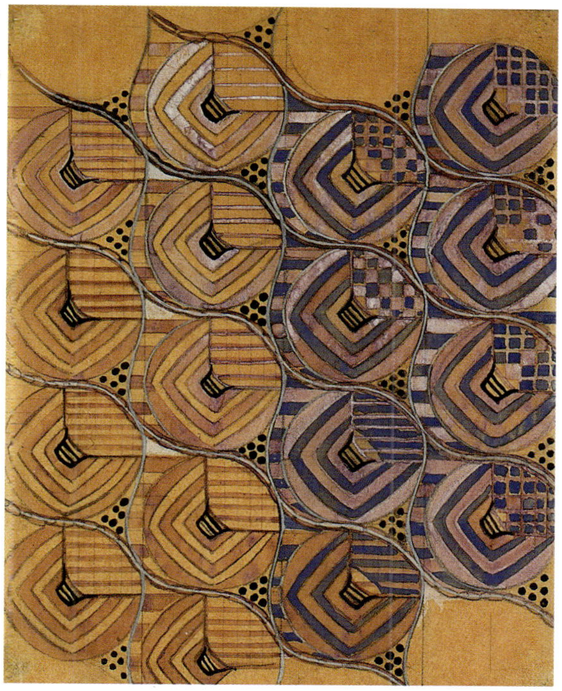

**Abstract Fabric Design in Two Colour Schemes for chiffon voile by Margaret Macdonald Mackintosh. Circles, Lines, Checks and Dots**

This book may seem to marginalise Margaret simply because its subject is her husband. She was an important minor artist and his essential partner – a role we honour in opening with her work. This design is very similar to contemporary CRM work produced in Chelsea around the end of the First World War. As in Glasgow 20 years earlier, the graphic work of wife and husband are once again almost indistinguishable.

**Charles Rennie Mackintosh (opposite)**

Aged 25, photographed by his friend J.Craig Annan not as assistant architect but as artist.

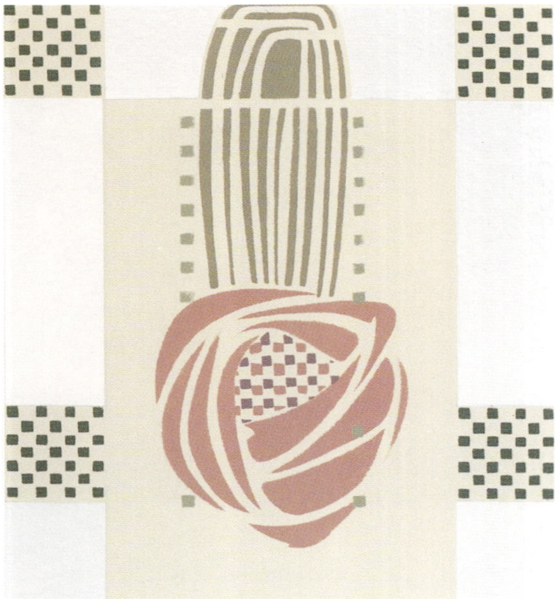

**The Hill House, Drawing Room Wallpaper, 1902**

CRM's varied graphic skills displayed. Above: as interior surface, in the Hill House drawing room walls. Below: on a fabric design from 15 years later, where the swirling grasses appear almost as human figures.

**Stylised Foliage, Green and Purple**

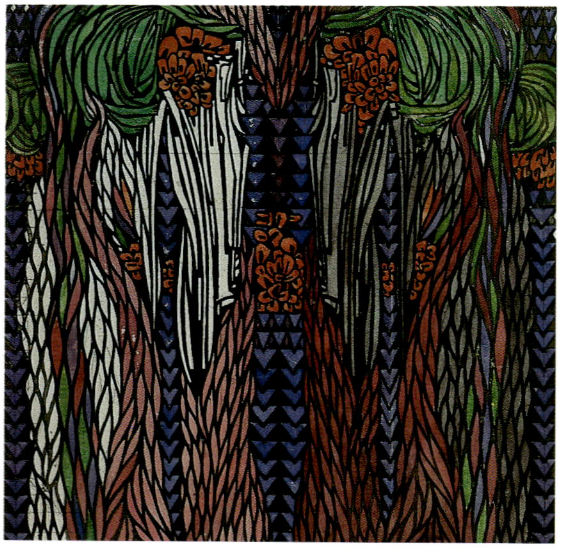

contexts, first amid an active group of colleagues, and then in an intensely private marital couple. And yet there is a Mackintosh for each generation or each critical position; and it is an impossible dream to imagine that under all the layers of Toshie giftwrap and gift tags we can find the 'real' one. We can try to unwrap him but cannot pretend we first met him naked, we cannot forget the context we bring to him, a century later.

Why is there no similar industry for his contemporary Edwin Lutyens, surely as great an architect? What makes Mackintosh so attractive? We see endlessly reproduced graphics; while more serious fans lovingly create his unbuilt projects as 1:12 scale 'doll's houses', their interiors beautifully imagined from the Mackintoshes' designs.[6] Something pulls them to Mackintosh.

Critics who resent the commercialisation or laugh at the addicts risk tarring the works themselves. It is more interesting than that. Why am I writing this, and you reading it? This unusual question is raised by the mechanical reproduction of Mackintosh, from facsimile objects to the lettering at the top of this page to the tea mug I sip from as I type this. It forces us to work harder, really to see.

One central theme running through his life is looking: looking with analytical precision, but with creative eyes. Looking with an empathetic gaze, a loving gaze. We must similarly use all our facilities of discernment – careful enjoyment – to see what he did or didn't actually design. Then we will also see, as David Brett has noted, how 'they [Mackintosh and his wife] attract affection because of the quality of attention that runs through all the buildings and designs; nothing is ignored. Attention like this is a form of love, and one responds to it...'.[7] Here is a clue to their genuine attraction: the intensity of the highly charged interiors.

His skill as interior architect is very difficult to define. It's much more than a stylish makeover of rooms – although that may be part of it. It's to do with the creation of interior places which are wonderful to inhabit. A dynamic experience which he orchestrates: how we move between rooms, enter dark spaces which open out before us, how light is controlled and changed, how we are attracted close to some points and others we take in subliminally as we pass; how some places are calm and static, others dynamic and exciting. It's a skill as varied as the dressing of a beautiful woman: designing and making an outfit which responds both to the structure of the body and to her personality, which hangs well, wraps and reveals in a way that shows her at her best; this choreography includes designing the shoes which enhance the dynamic walk as well as the static look, organising the hair, the makeup, the perfume.

This doesn't turn the body into a simple hanger for fashion. However, with the most stylised and elaborate Mackintosh design it may seem as far from ordinary life as the outfit on the catwalk; there may be a sense of precious totality, which we can only join if in set roles. It is difficult to imagine a trades union committee meeting in the Mackintoshes' own living room – or even a couple of lively children. It is partly this, of course, which attracts us to a fantasy so far from our everyday. But usually, the interior architecture is less all-embracing, and it certainly is far from stifling. The School of Art has stood up to a century of hard use as a public building full of assertive students, but ever offering experiences of great charm.

Mackintosh's career was not that of a successful architect. It was more than that, and it was certainly less than that. In a talk to architects, the young Mackintosh proclaimed: 'The artist cannot attain to mastery in his art unless he is endowed in the highest degree with the faculty of invention.'[8] This, finally, was his endowment; and why he is honoured today.

The aim of this text is neither to describe the pictures nor be a verbal guide to works. There are fine catalogues to paintings, interiors, furniture, textile designs (and a pocket guide to the architecture by the authors). This study is of a singular lifestyle. In this picture-and-text book, it is images which centrally tell of the style and words of the life.

Harry Jefferson Barnes, who worked for nearly 40 years in the Glasgow School of Art, latterly as its director, was the son-in-law of one of Mackintosh's closest friends in England. He mused: 'I shall always be less exercised myself as to the niceties of his architectural theory than by the enigma of his personality'. This text is an attempt at that exercise. And one clue tentatively suggested to this 'enigma' is at least the shadow of the medical condition Asperger's Syndrome, outlined at the end of the book. To picture his life, however, is not easy as there are long periods when we have no idea of his work, his thoughts, or even of his whereabouts. And those who knew him when they were children, in their lively and sunnily coloured reminiscences of later years, are often unaware of the tricks memory plays with us all.

By chance, twice in Mackintosh's life, we have moments of surprisingly vivid insight. The first when he is 25: a scrapbook chances to survive, filled with work by him and his closest collaborators at the Art School – paintings, poems, photographs

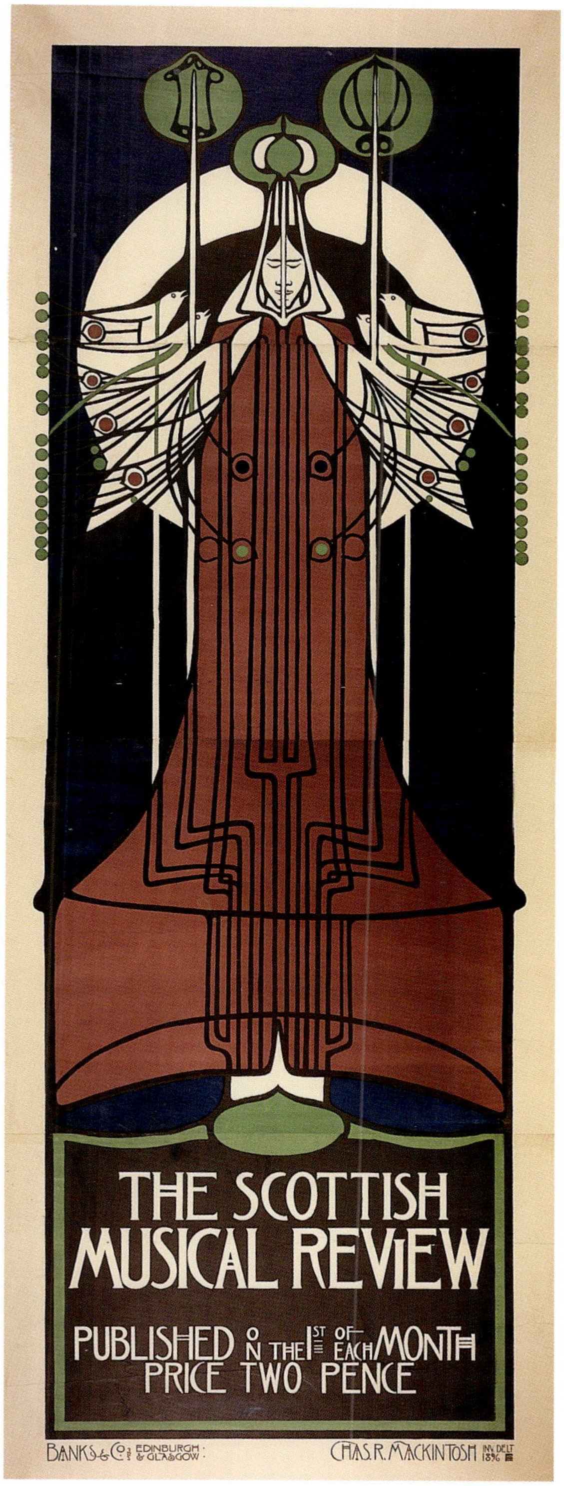


**Poster for the Scottish Musical Review**

CRM's watercolour 'Autumn' is transformed into a vast lithographic poster with his idiosyncratic lettering. He had no training in lithographic printing, and only produced around four posters, all in the mid 1890s.

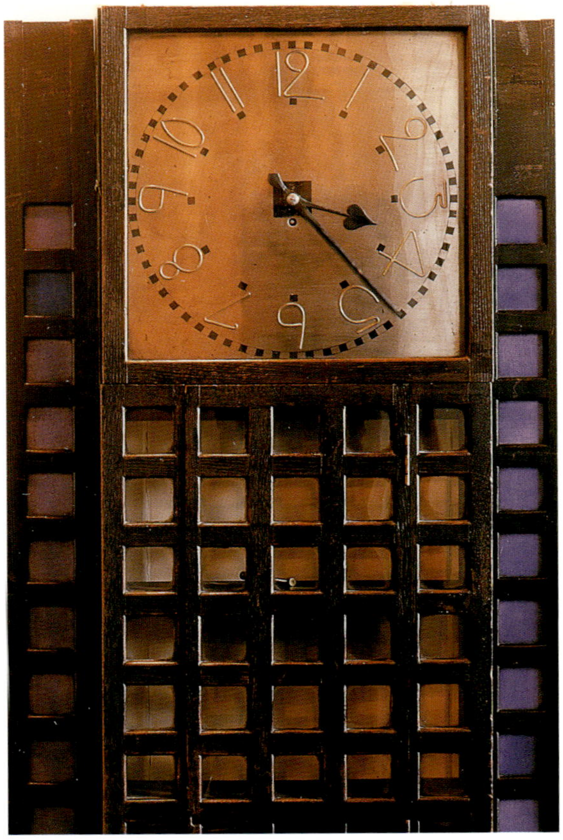

Clock for the Willow Tea Rooms, 1903

This beautifully severe clock case with its elegant numerals shows Mackintosh's Viennese face. Its story also typifies how CRM works seem often to disappear and reappear, vanish and duplicate themselves. It was designed for The Willow Tea Rooms, but for one of the upper rooms (Billiards or Smoking), omitted from the late 20th-century restoration of the very different first floor. Two years later CRM copied it for a dining room in Berlin, but at a slightly larger scale. This one now appears at home in the Director's Room of the Glasgow School of Art.

Charles Rennie Mackintosh (opposite)

In his early fifties, in London in 1920 photographed by his friend E.O. Hoppé.

and handwritten commentaries.[9] The second is when he is nearly 60: a pile of letters survives, a stream of consciousness written often daily to his wife from whom he was unusually separated as she needed medical treatment.[10]

Born on 7 June 1868, near Glasgow's ancient cathedral, in a poky top-floor flat, Charlie was the fourth of 11 children. When he was six they moved half a mile east to the opposite side of the cathedral's Necropolis, and into five rooms in the streets newly built on Alexander Dennistoun's estate. His father obtained permission from the agent to cultivate a garden there, which the children called 'the garden of Eden.' At home Charlie was solitary, developing a strong affection for cats, walking alone. At school, he seems to have been academically poor, never getting the hang of spelling and appearing only interested in drawing, for which he clearly had unusual skill. He was more able to see solutions to problems than to verbalise them.[11]

His father was exceptionally fit, active socially and physically, a keen shot, and organiser of the Glasgow police force's annual soirée. The son was not a strong child, which was very visible in his limping leg and drooping eyelid. He had a winning charm, but was given to inexplicable fits of violent rage. He was teased at school, was oversensitive to criticism. He dreamt of escape from the great mercantile city, a dream of nature and of art. Having never come across an architect, he persuaded his father to allow him to start an apprenticeship.

We can picture a child, yet about large parts of his adult life we know remarkably little. For an eminent and popular figure of the early twentieth century, this is extraordinary. There are years when there is not even one surviving recorded sighting or comment from a visitor, far less projects coming out of a design studio where others work, projects which he built, or even published. But even his famous interiors are astonishingly unrecorded: there is hardly a single photograph of his largest and most costly interior project, which was destroyed in the 1930s. There is not one photograph of the Mackintoshes' famous house taken during his lifetime (though there is a set of their earlier flat). There seem to be no family snaps, no memorabilia, virtually no surviving family recollections. Despite being one of 11 brothers and sisters, almost nothing can be dredged up about his relations with his family since he was a child. At his wife's death, not long after his, her sister's son Sylvan was treated as his only surviving relative and residuary legatee. He, who had absolutely no interest in Mackintosh or his work, died long ago and in a far country. There are powerful silences in this story.

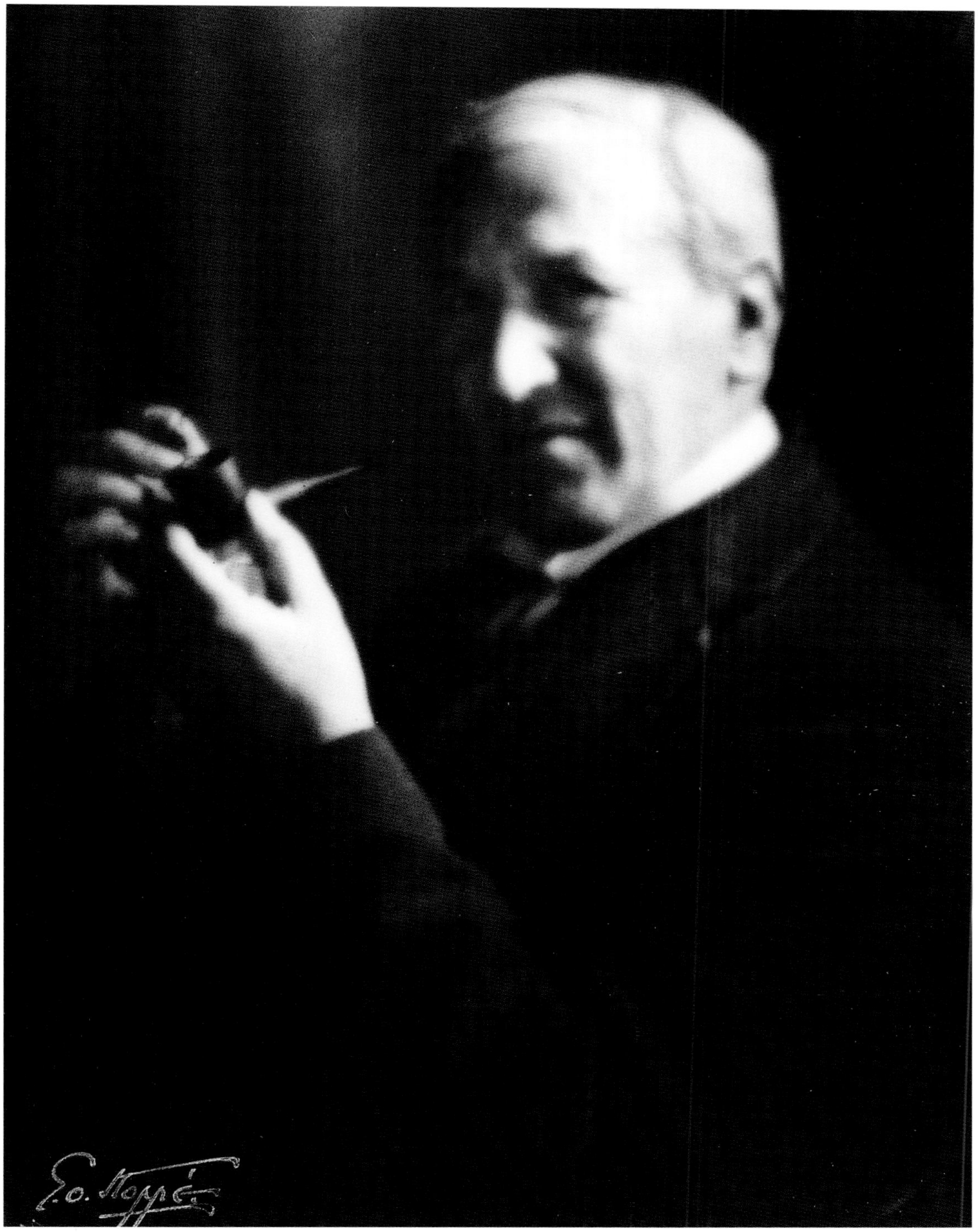

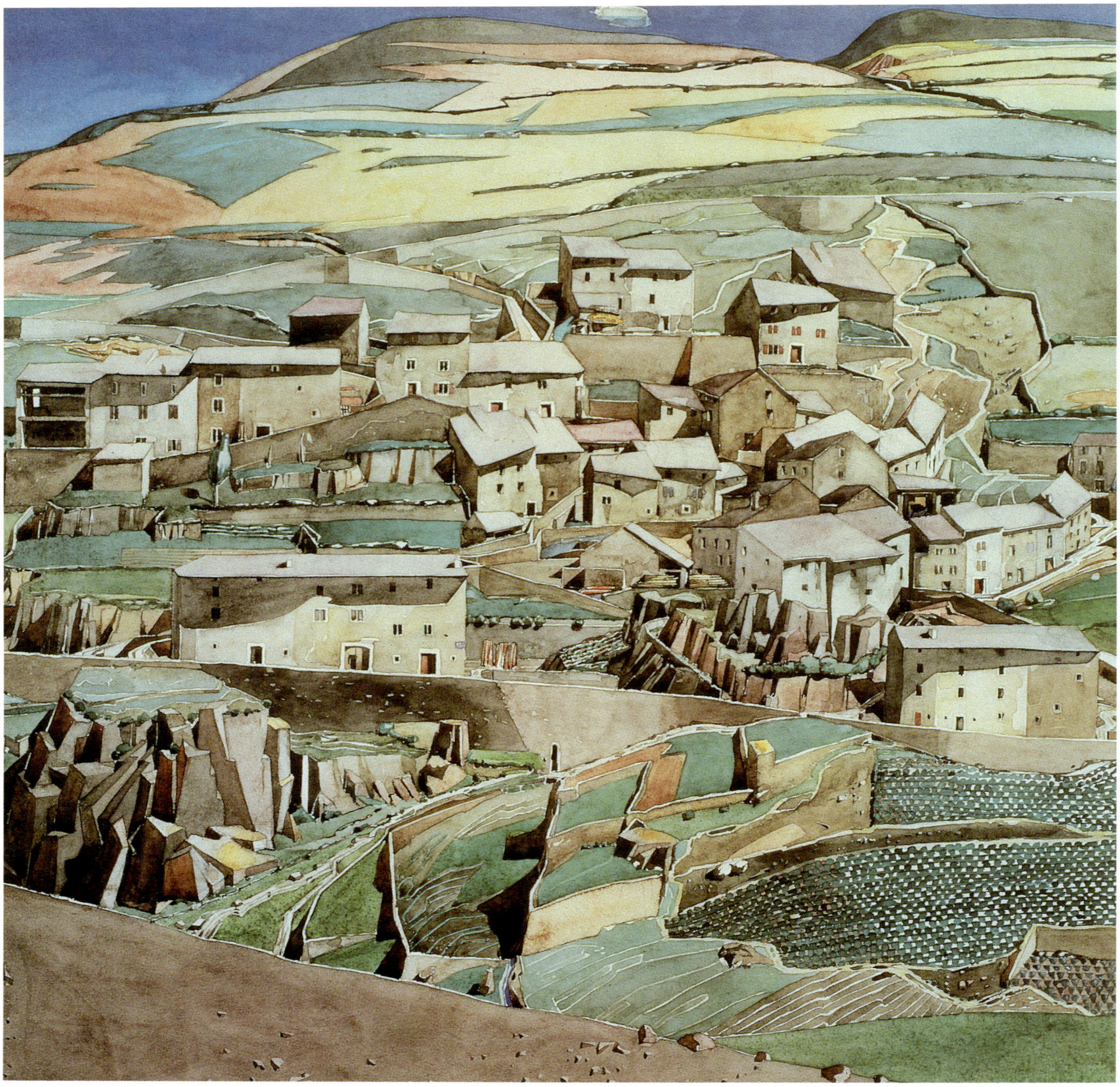

**Fetges c.1926**

When he painted this, he felt it was his best painting to date, and it remains one of his outstanding works. Walter Blackie, although he never met Mackintosh after he quit Glasgow in 1914, remained his stalwart patron. Believing he should be represented in the British national collection, Blackie bought this painting and presented it to the Tate Gallery.

# THE FRENCH PAINTER

In the mid 1920s, an unknown foreign painter is working quietly out of doors, on the Mediterranean coast, where Spain meets France. On summer mornings, he rises early and, with his minimal painter's tools, walks out from the little hotel by the harbourside to a favourite spot. A large man in his fifties, slowed by the limp which makes him seem older than his years, he walks upright, his back straight. His eyes look far away, but seem focused as if looking inwards. The face, under his silvery grey, slightly wavy hair, appears contented. But it gives away little expression as he approaches his Happy Valley.

Like children, he and his wife have their own names for landscape corners around their small town. Another morning in the bright early sunshine and clear blue sky, he walks up to his Apple Tree (he sees it in capital letters), in what they call The Enchanted Valley. Here he sits and reads some papers, and looks.

When he has finished, his wife, appearing to him the size of Alice, comes bounding over the hill with a chamois-stride, to take him home. Though she is into her sixties, her auburn hair, which 25 years earlier had created a sensation in Europe, is as striking as ever. His only desire in the world, he says, is for them to be together and to live their simple, healthy life.

He speaks little. It is only partly because his French is poor; when without his wife and forced to converse in French, he says the effort exhausts him. If he appears taciturn it is more that he is moving imperceptibly inwards, away from the solid skin. Only rarely does an old pugnacious spirit spill its venom; 'the bulk of humanity are a heartless, brainless crew,' he suddenly tells his wife. No one knows that he is an architect. The box of colours, the pencil and his watercolour paper pinned to cardboard, are his tools in this calmest period of his life.

He looks and looks; and draws and paints. His subject matter is what he sees: the extraordinary shapes and forms of his landscape, the conjunction of geometries natural and man-made. He follows no rules, has no master in this unusual art. Of course he knows of Modernism, and these villages have attracted painters for a generation. His favourite bar in the next tiny town, Collioure, still accepts paintings for payment from the penniless. There is a Picasso line-drawing on the wall. But the painter from Scotland, however little loose cash he has, will pay for his own drinks.

Landscape painters across Europe are now struggling with a

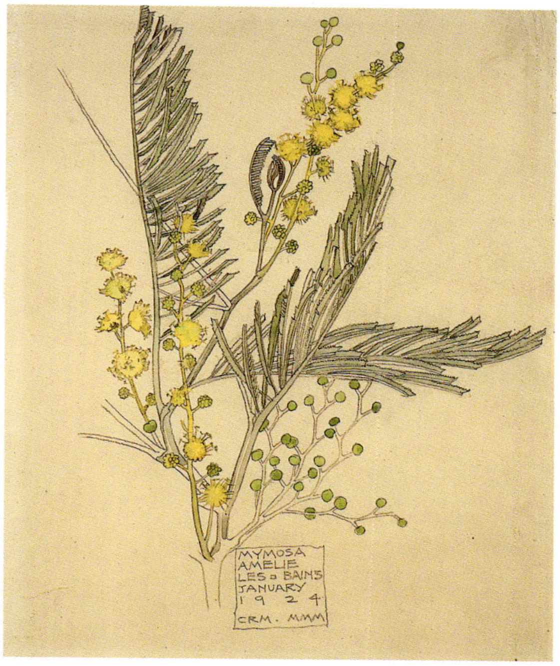


**'Mymosa', 1924**

With 'Mymosa' (sic) he still remembers the English artist who a decade earlier produced a portfolio of plant studies. His new work (like 'Mont Alba') shows a different sensibility, the sweep of the landscape exaggerated into dramatic formal patterns leaving ambiguity of spatial depth and perspective.

**Mont Alba**

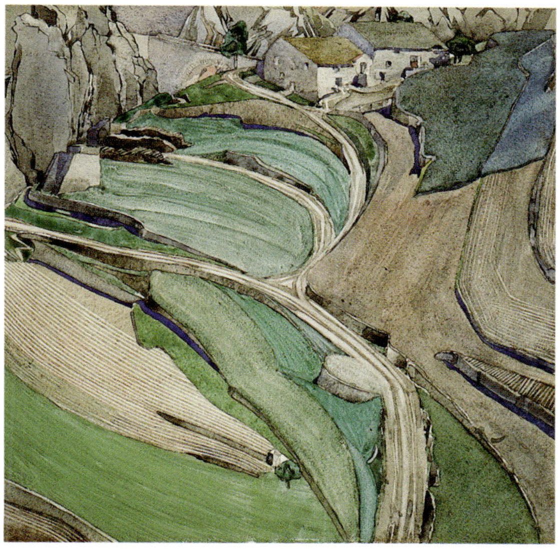

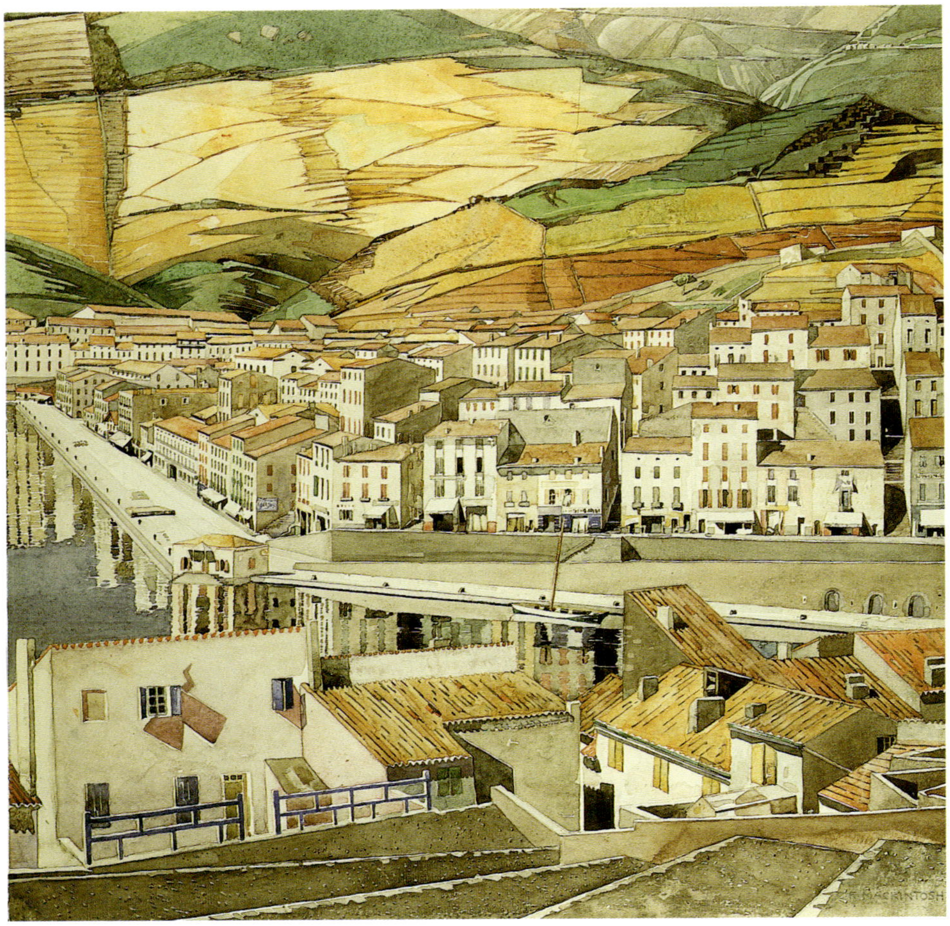


new expression, moving beyond the impressionist – the fleeting light of a Monet – and the expressionist – the brilliant mood of a Derain or Matisse, the wild Fauves who were habitués of Collioure 20 years earlier. But, apart from the solid Provençal landscape geometries of Cézanne, he is uncaring of them. He has his own path. 'My work is not like these others,' he notes,[1] 'I am trying for something else. But even so it must take its place and hold its own in any company.'

He walks and looks, searching for viewpoints. And looks more intensely. For days he is followed around the village hinterland by a crow. He thinks he has found a view of the fort at Port-Vendres. 'I must know all about it before I begin, and I think that will be very soon now,' he writes.

Slowly, he is chiselling out the space of a life, a career. Just standing takes courage, just keeping going. And then looking: staring depression in the face, daring it to overwhelm him. All his expressive powers are now focused in the precision of this new medium. These hard-won 'landscapes' – the two dozen which he produces between 1925 and 1927 – are a million miles from topographical sketches. Not just in his manipulation of landscape elements but in his goals: they are deliberate and precise arrangements, powerful compositions of almost architectonic forms, solid and line, block and surface.

Of course there are no people in these works. When did he last draw people? Was it the little girls and their skipping ropes, when he was still young, hopeful and unmarried? Dancing on the pavement outside his first building; for they were enjoying his school, dressed in clothes he designed for them. He adored children. He never had children of his own. But he works on painting.

Take his two paintings of Fetges, a village they visit just across the Spanish border from Mont Louis. The smaller view, despite interestingly dynamic dry brushstrokes, is still in the soft technique of his last English paintings, the sensibility of the topographical watercolourist (p.21). In other words it is

### Port-Vendres, La Ville

Having stayed in Collioure, the painter moved to the adjoining small but bustling port of Port-Vendres, taking a room at the Hôtel du Commerce on the waterfront. The hotel's large low blind is clearly visible to the left in this view painted around 1924-6. The relation between natural and built landscape, and the clear, formal compositions which they imply seem to fascinate him. These painstaking and slow works are always painted in front of the subject and never either from sketches or from memory.

ordinary. But the second, probably painted in summer 1926, is something else. This was drawn on a spot very close to the earlier one, but the resulting work, about 20in (50cm) square, is electrically different (p.12). A brilliant essay in vibrant colour and shape, its taut atmosphere is generated by the design. Exaggerated asymmetry of the roofs creates jagged and angular forms made even more dynamic by the precisely cut shadows.

He feels that it is his best work to date. His self-assessment, as ever, is acute. 'I find I have a great lot to learn – or unlearn. I seem to know far too much and this knowledge obscures the really significant facts,' he writes to Francis Newbery;[2] 'but I am getting on.' The name of his former headmaster, patron and then lifelong friend, raises a distant echo across 35 years: 'But hang it, Newbery, this man ought to be an artist!' Sir James Guthrie (along with the well-known painters John Lavery, Alexander Roche and E.A. Walton, members of 'The Glasgow Boys') was judging the Glasgow School of Art's 1890 annual exhibition, with the headmaster at his side. Newbery had just explained that the work they admired was by a 22-year-old architectural draughtsman.

It is even harder work now. The compositions, of course, no longer mimic the places he visits. He might double a village's size or render a sea of orange tiled roofs as deep grey.[3] His vision is transforming. It produces a unique portfolio of work which when diminished to book illustration can seem simply picturesque. The actual works, seen at arm's length, reveal why this set can be described as the most powerfully original British watercolours of their time.

However, as Paul Valéry, the French poet, says, we should apologise for daring to speak about painting. Let us atone for such presumption by looking at the work more intently.

By the beach outside town, the painter finds a formation of rocks, 'My ROCK' he says in upper case, as he persists in not drawing or painting it. As always, there is much looking before

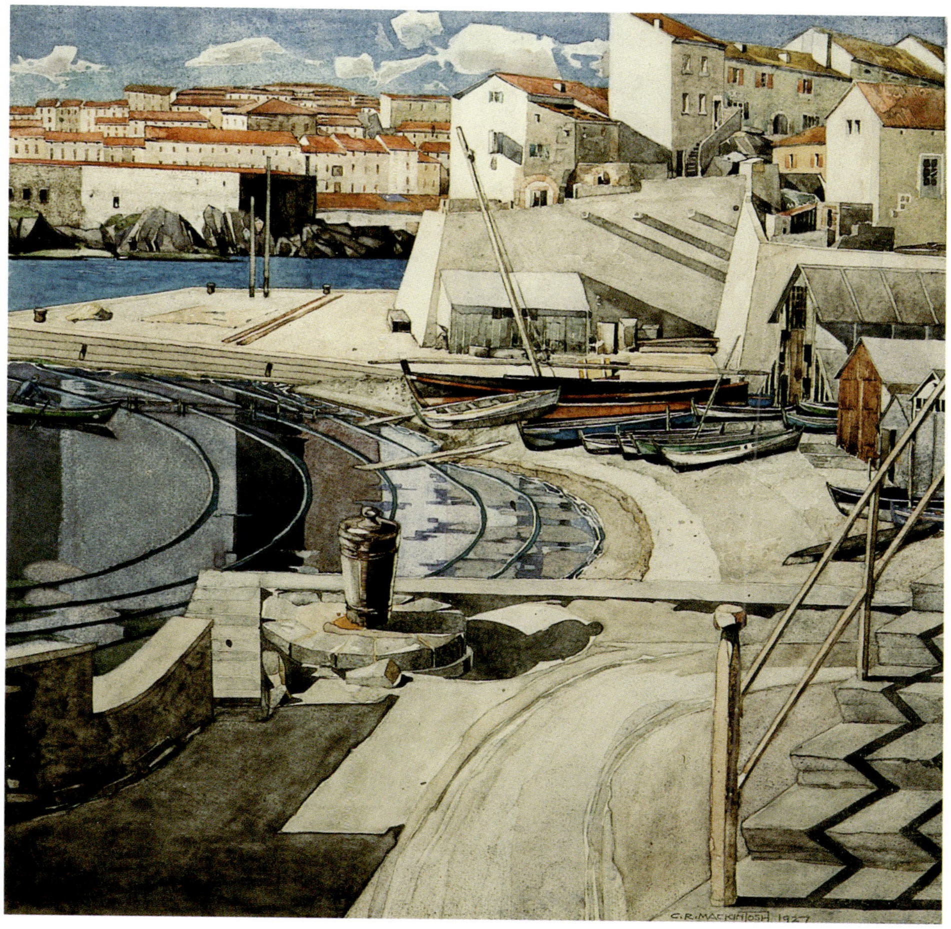


**The Little Bay, Port-Vendres, 1927**

This beautiful, crisp, clear and unpeopled image, signed and dated by the gravely ill painter in 1928 for his friend Desmond Chapman-Huston, is an essay in geometric patterns, created by the built forms, cast shadows and gently rippling water which the painting freezes. Developing his work with colour and light, the painter here shows the fruit of his hard work to clarify and brighten his palette.

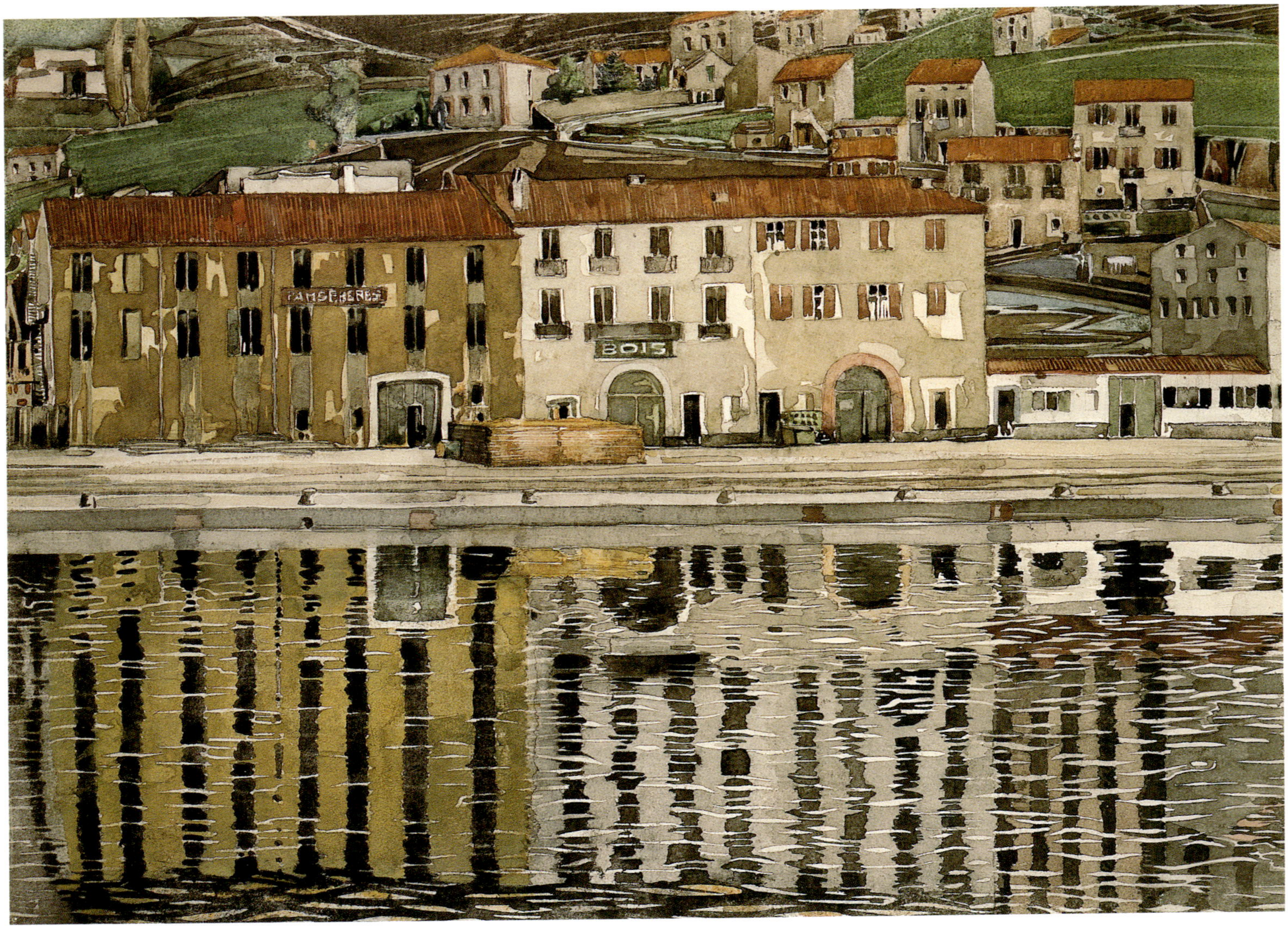


**Port-Vendres**

Nearly half of the artist's 38 surviving French landscapes show the harbour and environs of Port-Vendres, all entirely devoid of human occupation. This rather depressed example is clearly painted in the Hôtel du Commerce, looking across the harbour from his room window.

he commits pencil to paper; close observation and analysis. He looks. He doesn't sketch. His visual memory is extraordinary. 'This is the most valuable gift I possess,' he tells his friend J.D. Fergusson. (He had seen Fergusson's paintings in Chelsea before they left London. 'I still have such a vivid mental picture of them that I can review them one by one, a sort of sub-conscious "peep show", and see them quite clearly just as you showed them to us.'[4])

Yet he doesn't draw from memory. He is out there confronting what he sees and transforming it in his head. And he resists putting it to paper. 'If I could just decide to start a new drawing of my ROCK, I'm sure it might be worth the effort not to be indolent and lazy.' But he is not lazy; the block in front of him is huge. 'So you must say "Here's strength to you, Toshie!" ' he exhorts his wife, 'and perhaps it will be done.'[5] If only it were that easy to decide!

This particular painting finally starts, and he records the

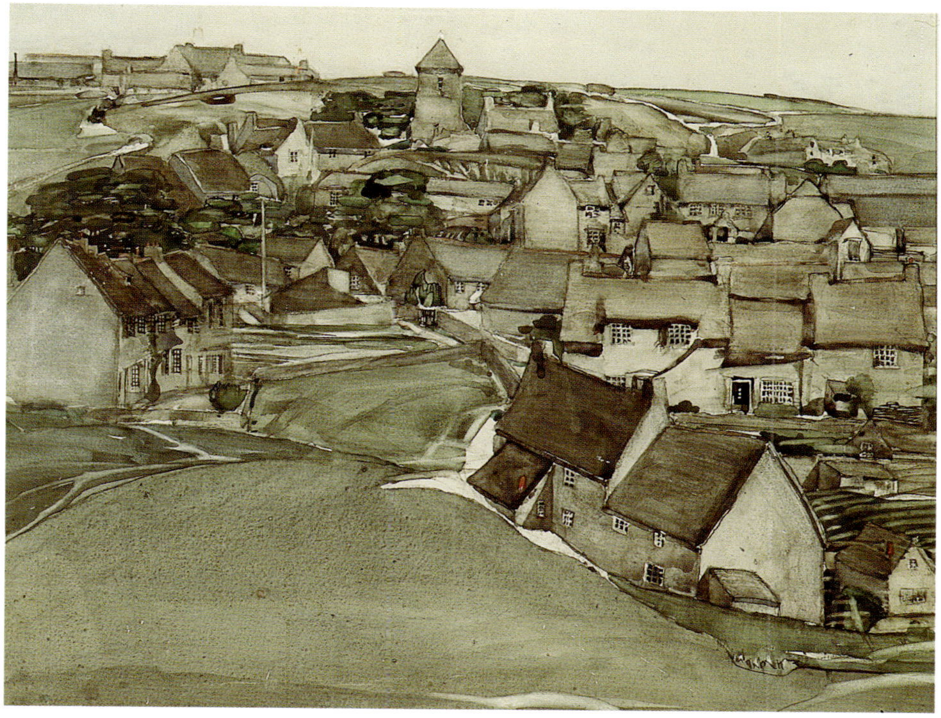

The Village,
Worth Matravers, 1920

In the English winters, when they lived in London the painter and his wife would stay with his old mentor, painter Francis Newbery, who had retired to Corfe Castle in Dorset; in summer 1920 they invited the family of painter Randolph Schwabe also to join them there. Here, in two watercolour views of Worth Matravers, were his first landscapes. His concerns were those of designer and two-dimensional pattern-maker, but he was now drawing as an artist, no longer observing as architect.

struggle as it takes him a month. 'I go very slow, because I still have so many problems to solve and the days of hit and miss or any such methods are past, for me.'[6] There is no modelling, no atmosphere, no people: but solids and solid colour also. A composition of mass, texture, pattern. He needs completely still days in which to paint the water: even his reflections in the harbour are frozen. The stillness is extraordinary; it is far beyond calm or contentment.

He is trying to build paintings in form and light. At exactly this moment, a French painter-architect proclaims, from his painting retreat further along the coast: 'L'architecture est le jeu savant, correct et magnifique des formes sous la lumière.' For the Scotsman in the Midi, 'even in the brightest sunshine, my pictures are still very sombre. I want to get more and more light.' This was once the enthusiastic young man urging Glaswegian architects that 'all will be sweetness, simplicity, freedom, confidence and light.'[7] He is finally coming close.

Critics talk about architecture, he muses, in the same breath as sculpture and painting; he once said himself that they must be judged by the same criteria. But he knows that getting a building built is less like painting a picture than winning an election. Completing even a modest public building like an art school demands steering a process of immense complexity, involving many personalities – some with ideological goals which might be quite different from the designer's, others just focused on a wage packet on Friday; one feeling he defends the public good, another that he defends the client's purse – even from the architect. In what sense, then, could the Glasgow School of Art have been *his* building? And yet he knows, of course, that it is.

'The Architect must become an art worker,' he said at that time, 'and be content to forgo the questionable distinction and pleasure of...a large and successful business.'[8] The art worker architect battles to refine on site, trying to keep close to craftsmen, modifying detail as they progress, and accepting the costs. He wants to allow change in the making process, to draw

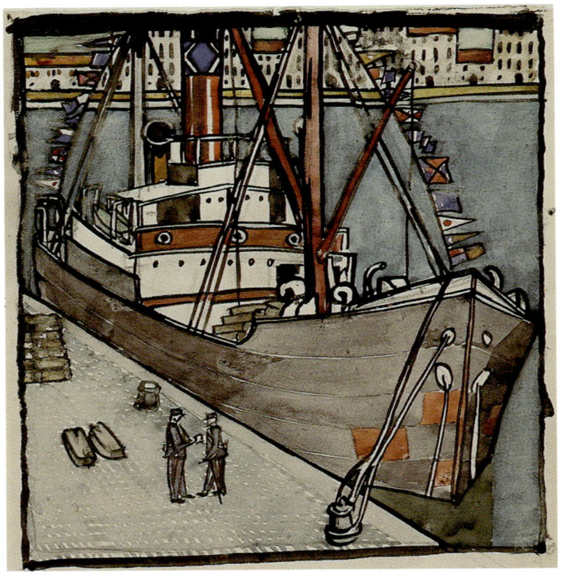

### Steamer Moored at the Quayside, with two Gendarmes Standing on the Quay

Unique among the painter's French output are four lively sketches of the quayside, including this one. Drawn from his Port-Vendres hotel room, its dynamic graphic composition results from superimposing a view to the left onto that directly opposite (seen on p.16).

### Boultènere

Almost all of the painter's French work consists of highly finished studies, like this one.

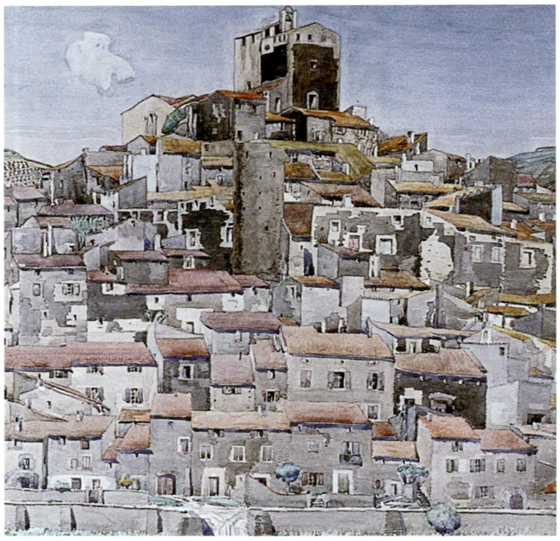

on site, base a contract on trust and few drawings, to keep a building process dynamic and alive.

The businessman architect runs an ever-more-powerful office and erects ever-more-impressive structures, which are ever-more-inhumane and cold. He knows that every party to the building enterprise is constrained by increasing documentation, and that efficiency and control are the future. The art worker in the end must compromise or forgo more than simply the fame and fortune of the large successful business.

But the artist is his own worker. There is no intermediary, and there is calm for the mind in the work of the hand. 'I know by experience, that the making of design after design without executing them is a great strain upon the mind.' He reflects on these words of William Morris which he had read as a student.[9] And the lifelong motto of his now venerable friend, the great eccentric Professor Patrick Geddes, whom they visit in Montpelier, remains a deep theme: 'By creating, we think.' By painting, I see; I affirm my existence.

Struggling out of his dark private forest, the deep depressions which all his life have returned to overwhelm him, never disappear in the clear light. One day, sitting looking at his rock, 'eating my heart out with depression,' an unhappy friend approaches. 'After a while he said: By Jove, you are a marvel; you're always cheerful and happy. And I told him it was health. But I didn't tell him I was much more depressed than he was when he arrived. Nor that his deepest depression was something equivalent to my not being well. I keep my deepest depressions to myself.'

He glories in the outdoors. Up and out at 6 am one morning, he finds the wind too strong, taking him hours to find a sheltered spot. He is clumsy and cannot hold his cardboard steady enough to draw properly. He likes to apply the watercolours *en plein air* – a difficult enough task even in a slight wind. He only paints in the sun. Forced indoors by poor weather, he doesn't work on the drawings. Very rarely, he paints from the hotel window.

He works slowly, seeming able to concentrate best after a week or two of relaxation. 'No wind, the sea absolutely flat and bright blue. I only got as far as the Tamarisk tree, where I sat on my three-legged stool and tried to do three things: to read, to look about me, and to think.' They walk together in the countryside. They travel light; taking rooms in hostelries in the neighbouring ports of Collioure and Port-Vendres for much of the year, but in high summer moving up in the Pyrenees to Mont

Louis or Ille-sur-Têt, away from coast and crowds. They hunt out and are enthralled by all the tiny ancient Romanesque churches along the border hills. They occasionally travel further, even going to Florence. But the painter is not an architect, not voracious for details to acquire for his use or his enlightenment; his pencil is now used elsewhere.

They have worked so hard in transforming their lives together. They live very simply, in humble circumstances in which they are not humiliated. Layer after layer of social convention has been shed to reach this point. Their life is private and calm. They live cheaply, easily and without pressures. They have few external needs, and survive on an extraordinarily small amount of money. In the winter it is cold and quiet; in summer like-minded painters visit from England. It is the most contentedly happy time of his life. 'Nobody here but ourselves, and we are as happy as sandboys.'[10] And any unwelcome intrusion is fought off. 'I don't give a damn what they want, I am not going to be driven out of my charming seclusion!'[11] Matisse, who was a year younger, had earlier loved to escape to Collioure, without censorious pointing fingers, preconceived opinions, and as he said, 'don't forget it's only a village that is not used to regular tourists'.[12]

He is working, but is she? Not a single art work, design or manufacture is known in all these years. 'She didn't do anything at all,' an uncomprehending Glasgow-days friend adds. Another, a noted dressmaker herself, adds: 'When you think of all those days in the hotel, she could have made herself some more clothes.'[13]

He remembers the watercolour she prepared for stained glass called 'The Path of Life'; painted 30 years before, as their lives began to be intertwined and their life goals be clearly felt. Its iconography was clear: on one side a flight of swallows and a rose, signs of enlightenment and love; on the other a flight of

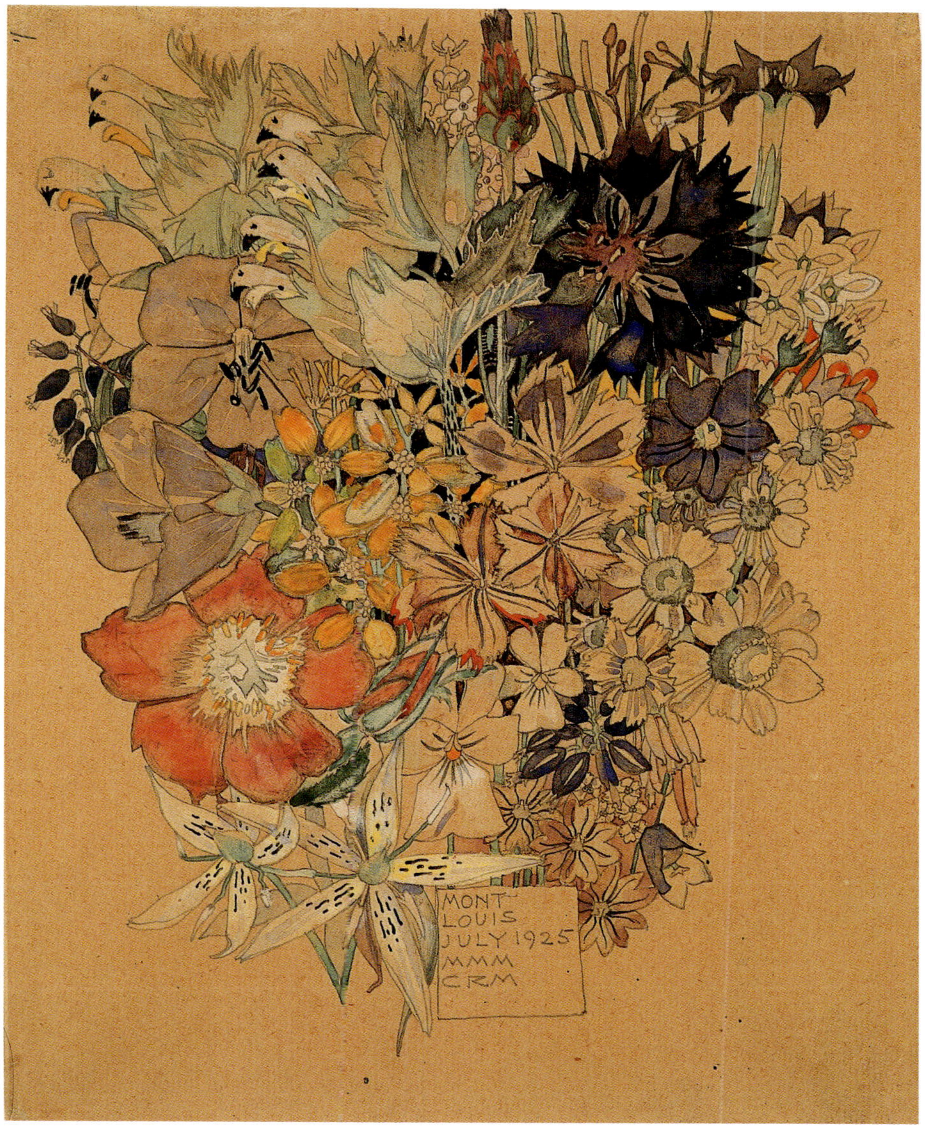


**Mixed Flowers, Mont Louis, 1925**

A few studies of wild Pyrenean flowers survive, notably this 'Mixed Flowers', a bunch of almost 20 recognisable species. The distinctive dark markings on the tips of the Rhinanthus petals, top left, however, stop short of biological precision in humorously morphing into birds' eyes and beaks.

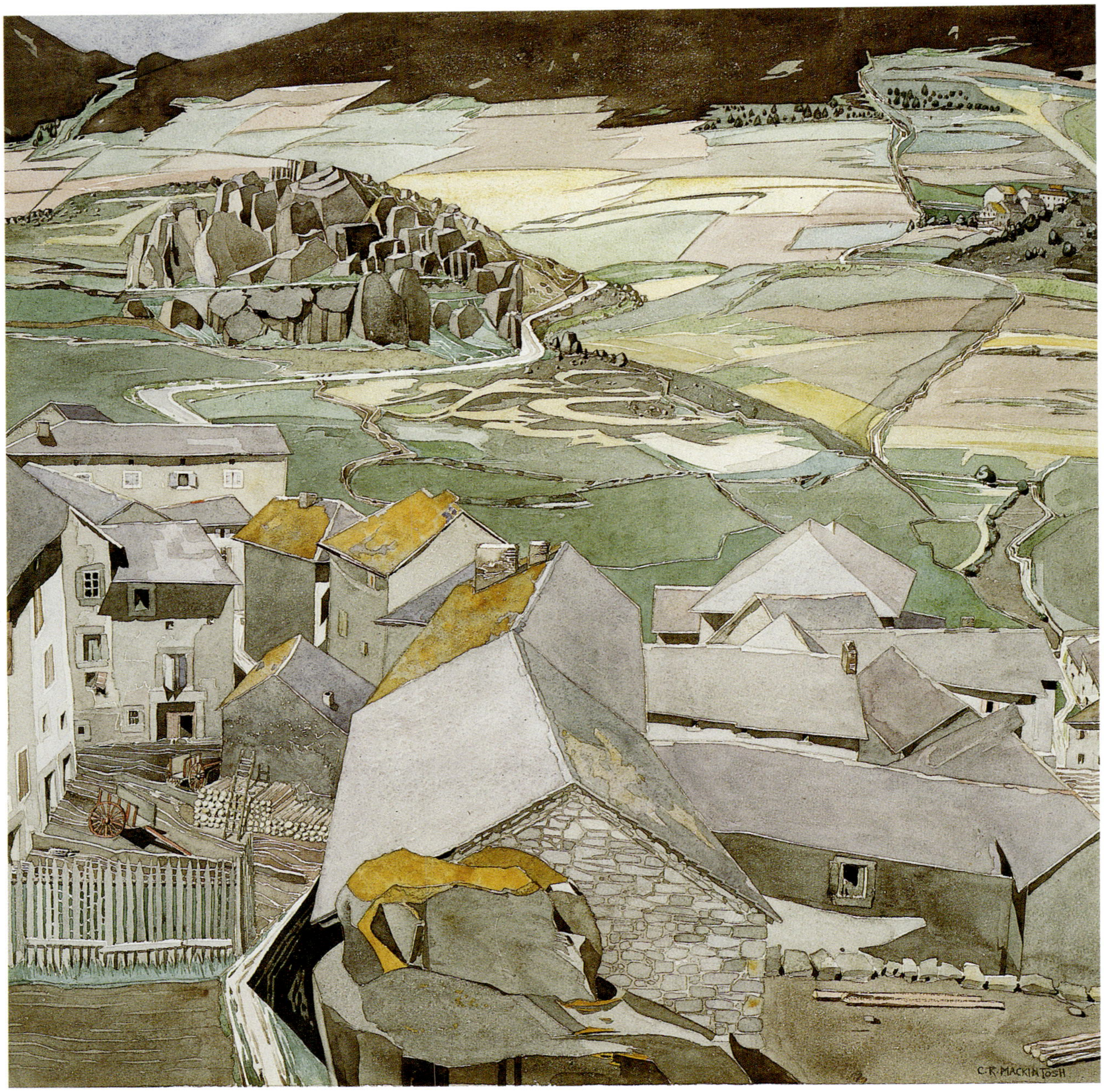
C.R. MACKINTOSH

crows and a thistle, signs of barrenness and materialism; and between, a strangely sexless naked woman, without pubic hair or vagina, stepping out of the picture plane, confronted with this choice of paths.

Looking back to the distant start of the century and such a different life, the artist tells her that she was half if not three quarters of all his architectural efforts. But she seems not attached to his current work. This is an individual path. I have talent, he also says; but she has genius. The genius, as revealed by all these years, is her ability to hold onto him, and them together. To cope with the enigmas of his personality, holding to the chosen path of their mutually devoted life together; her chosen path in life as his essential help. 'Love, when it occurs and persists between two practising artists is a question of each protecting the vulnerability of the other' (says another British artist living in France, much later, about this couple.[14])

What people saw as aloofness in the early years of the century has been quite rubbed away, revealing the mute, determined concentration on his transformational vision. It is a solitary pursuit. But they are not completely hidden. The convivial, quiet café life includes one or two London painters resident locally; others visit and write. Though Whynne Bassett-Lowke can't find him to design him a new house, he is not entirely forgotten. Out of nowhere, Charles Marriott, *The Times* critic, writes in 1924 that 'it is hardly too much to say that the whole modern movement in European architecture derives from him'; as an obituary, of one vanished presumed dead. He is then tracked down by *The Architects' Journal*, and asked to write about current British architecture.

Suddenly, and astonishingly, this rekindles an old fire. 'I cannot write about present day architecture in England because it does not exist!'[15] But he lets the professional magazine ('which supplies the needs of callow youth and flatters the vanity of older architects') know exactly how he feels, and particularly about Charles Reilly. He tells his wife 'you know how much I want to paint well. But I think I have one passion and that is to make Reilly a discredited outsider before I am finished with him.' Reilly is 'a bombastic bounder...crushed with official recognition and journalistic approval'.

The force of Mackintosh's spite is astonishing but not at all inexplicable. Reilly, Professor of Architecture in Liverpool, is seen as the embodiment of the currently fashionable pared-down Classicism. He also submitted an admired entry in the competition for Liverpool's Cathedral[16], for

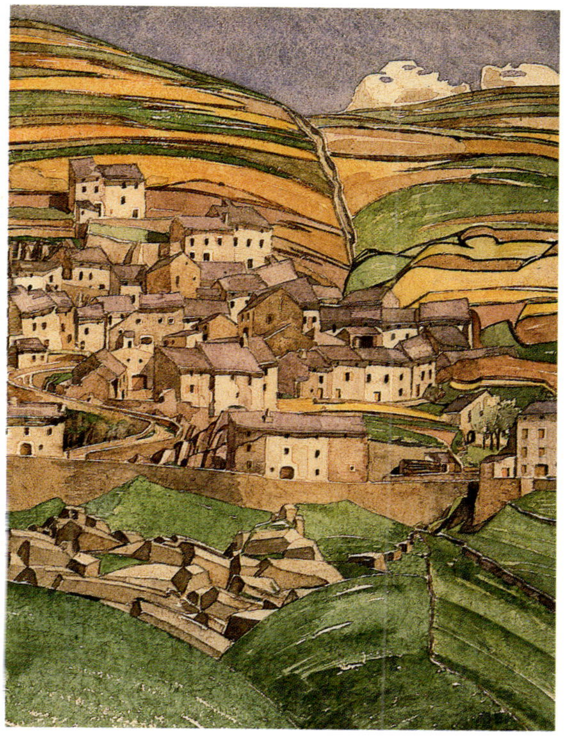

### Slate Roofs

'Slate Roofs' takes almost exactly the same viewpoint as the later 'Fetges', on p.12. While this earlier work is, by comparison, ordinary, it remains a powerful image: dynamic dry brushstrokes in the foreground are broken by crystalline piles of rocks; the outlined, stratified fields rise beyond the village shapes which echo the rocks; there is the painter's typical graphic flatness and clustering of elements.

### The Village of La Lagonne (opposite)

The landscape of La Lagonne, a village near Mont Louis in the Pyrenees,where the painter would spend summer times inland from the heat on the coast. It is observed and designed by him as a powerful two-dimensional composition, with neither colour nor line giving any assistance in the creation of pictorial depth. The perspective, as in many of the best of this series, appears ambiguous.

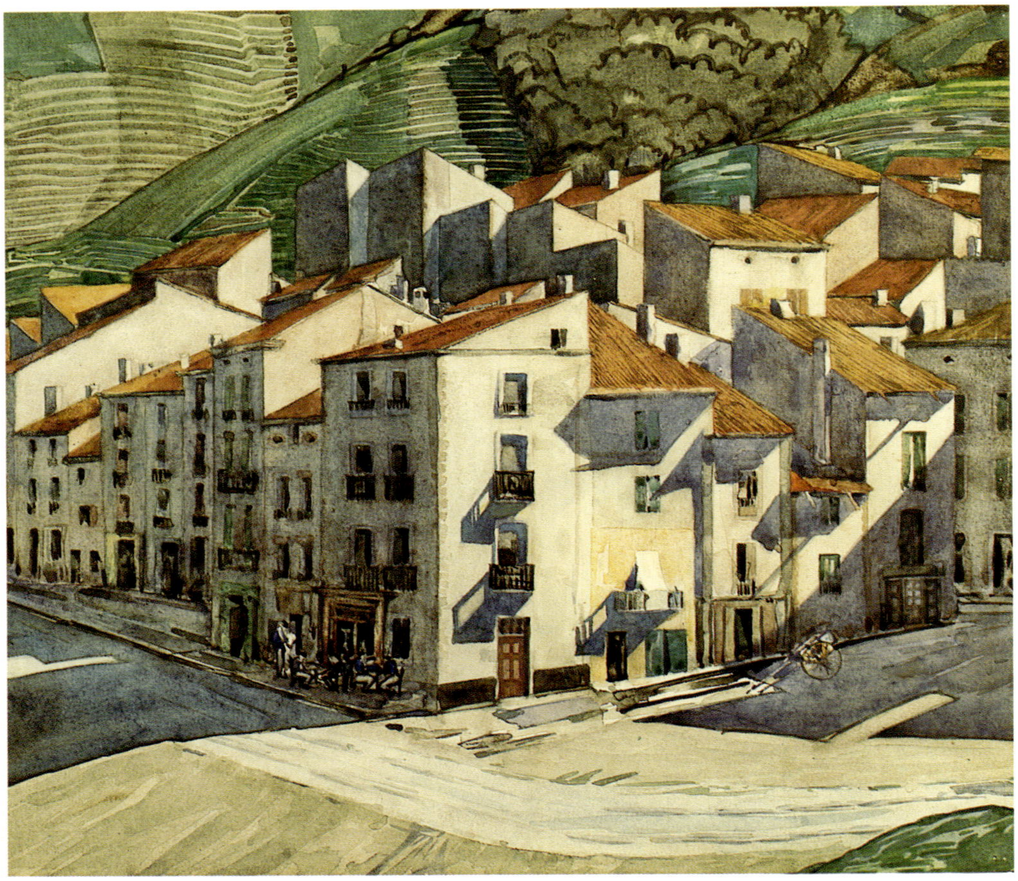

A Southern Town

A powerful, flattened composition of angular geometries, of light and dark, generated by the clustered building forms, their shadows and the encroaching hillsides.

which the artist's rejected scheme carried such high hopes. 'I have waited twenty years, during which I have not said one word about him to any outsider. Now I can get a few more nails in his nasty stinking cheap coffin...When I get him on the run I will drive him like a fiend until he is a raving lunatic!' Reilly comes to embody also transatlantic, efficiency-driven commercial architecture, and the American 'idea to work for the millions and damn the individual. Damn them!' And he attacks authority, bureaucracies and 'American disregard for decency.'

What has been happening to cause such venom to build up over a quarter century? Early in the century the English architectural establishment, calmed from the excesses of late-Victorian eclecticism, was producing tasteful and dry buildings. Canons of proportion and composition were gaining acceptance. Architecture was being formalised as an educational discipline, with university courses, notably in London and Liverpool, soon to be followed by Glasgow. There was growing awareness of the French academic tradition and how easily it linked with American ideas where big business and simple classical formulations went hand in glove. The world of the free spirit, the free style, and the free art worker and craftsman of the painter's youth, was becoming stifled in this airless space. As he looks back over the quarter century, he sees how the work of his kindred spirits from 1900, like Josef Hoffmann in Vienna, has come through a classical simplicity to unrhetorical modernism, though often the interiors are stuffed with 'deco' profusion. In fact Hoffman, unknown to the artist, is about to propose an astonishing, 10-storey rectilinear tower in Vienna clad completely in plate glass. We are in a very different world.

Here the painter's released hatred is all about a past from which he has not yet let go; the image of Reilly contains Glaswegian memories of John Keppie and John James Burnet.

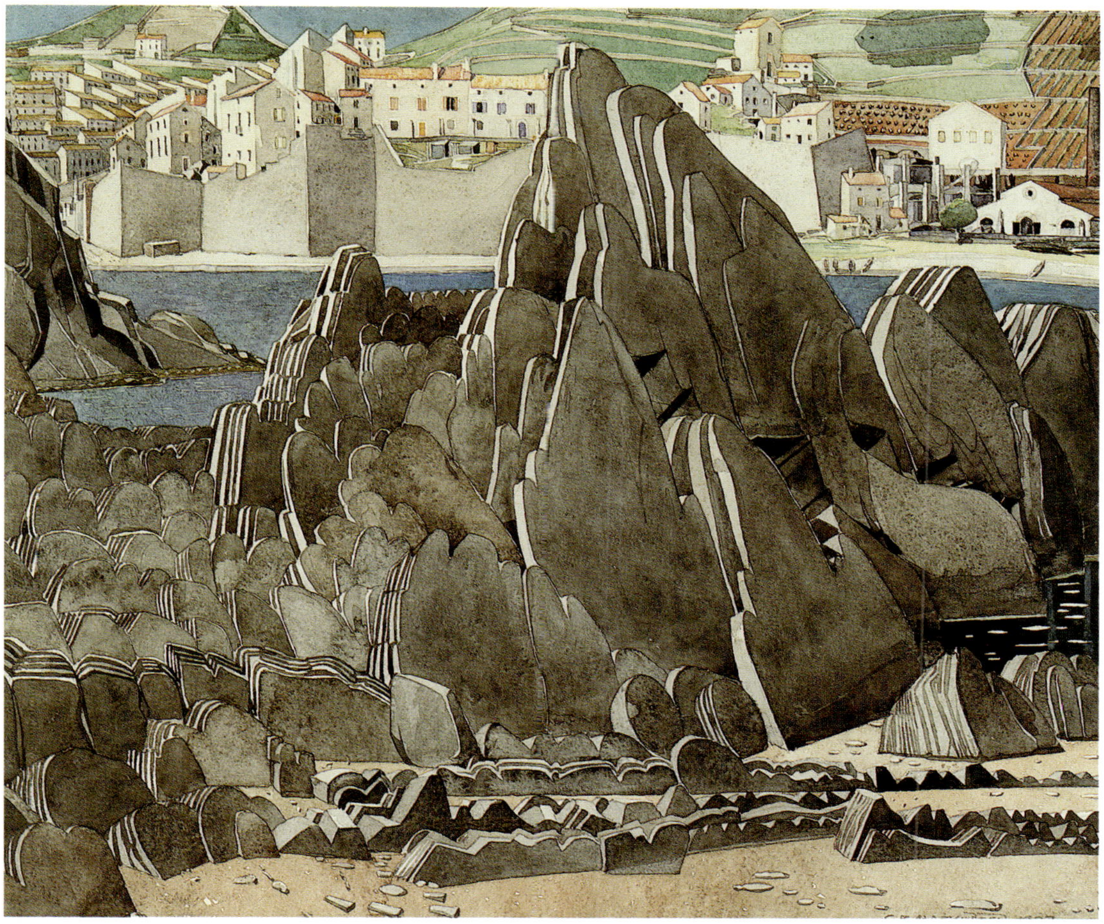

If Reilly thwarted his chance to build the cathedral, Keppie and Burnet, both Paris-trained and with transatlantic glances, in their different ways undermined his credit for the Glasgow School of Art. Nevertheless, here is an inappropriate reaction, shockingly out of proportion to what occasioned it, reminiscent of his inexplicable outbursts of childhood rage.[17] How did it come to this? Once he had been at the centre of avant-garde cultural life, in Glasgow; and, he hoped, in Europe. Skins have been worn away; first, bourgeois pretension, and the role of form-maker to Glasgow's haute bourgeoisie; then the bohemian 'character', the habitué of Chelsea's artistic clique.

You need a change, his friend J.D. Fergusson had encouraged him. Perhaps the possibility of being the painter seeped in when on a Dorset holiday in 1920. It was as an angry reaction at first: if my architecture is thwarted, I'll jack it all in and paint. But in the country, with painter friends Schwabes and Newberys, he too painted a few, muddy grey and depressed landscapes. But the seed was sown. An old skin was beginning to come loose, and over a couple of years London painters encouraged the move. Fergusson went south each summer, a couple of others were moving to Collioure in 1923. The dead skin of architecture was shed in their sublet London studios. Travelling light, with little more than a case of clothes, they were soon in the eastern Pyrenees; spending two months here, four months there, visiting Geddes in Montpellier, and stopping in Port-Vendres before Christmas 1925. Four shillings a day and the food is good and plentiful. They live on his wife's tiny private income. There is now no wish to end what began as a holiday at Fergusson's persuasion.

Slowly the equilibrium returns through a new perception, a

**The Rock, 1927**

This powerful composition is one of the last 1927 paintings, and is formed by moving viewpoint between rocky foreground and Port-Vendres in the background (as he did with the sketch on p.18). This painting of light and form is at the same time highly decorative, with its repeated motifs and crystalline clarity, bringing to mind his decorative schemes of a decade earlier.

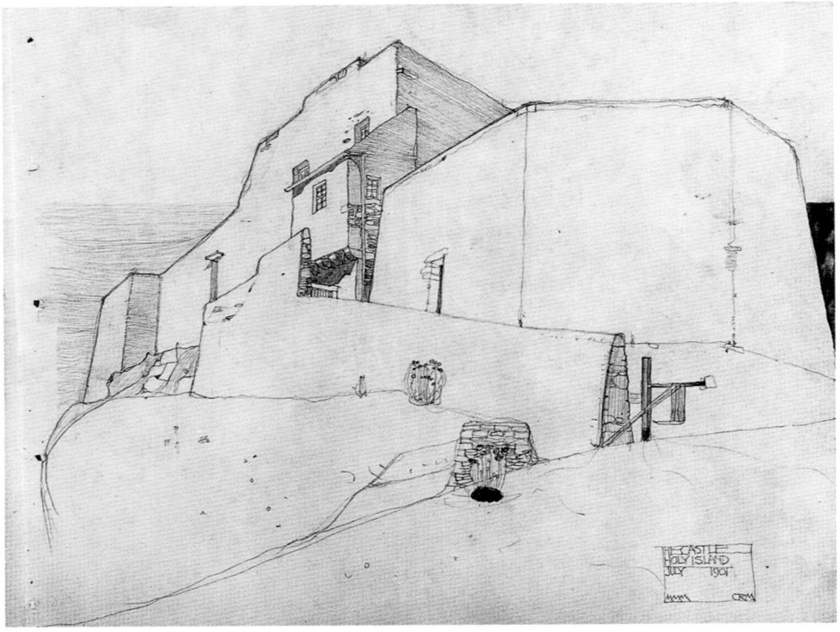


new expression, a new art. 'Life is the leaf,' he remembers himself saying so many years before; but 'art is the flower.' 'You must offer the flowers of the art that is in you – flowers that will often change a colourless, cheerless leaf into an animated, thoughtful thing...How beautiful life often is, but think of the stupendous possibilities of the flower thus offered to art.'

Now, as an almost Zen stillness takes over, his horizons draw closer and closer; his acute vision simply deepens. He fights for understanding, but it is no striving for perfection. He looks at the plate of food the hotelier puts in front of him. The path of his life has followed an extraordinary track, always trusting to his hope in honest error, for there is none in the icy perfection of the mere stylist. He sees 'a great plate of asparagus, all purple tops, no green – far too perfect, not a flaw, not a defect; not much flavour.'

His wife has returned to London for medical treatment, and he hopes the paintings he has sent with her might be exhibited, published, even bought. Fergusson, who is the leading Scottish painter of this generation, is very praising and supportive. But the paintings do not sell.

The 41 surviving paintings done in these three or four years are astonishing. He is convinced of their quality. He is building up a collection, aiming to produce at least 50 paintings for an exhibition at the Leicester Galleries in London.[18] He is excited that friends, including Fergusson and his partner Margaret Morris, will visit. And, when his wife returns, they will all enjoy a recuperative time in Mont Louis. 'Once you get here,' he writes to her, 'the fine air and simple life with a life-long lover should make you feel all right soon again.' He is not yet 60, but their French idyll is almost over.

He sits silently, sipping a glass and puffing on his pipe. He adds: 'my tongue is swollen – burnt and blistered with this infernal tobacco. I have never found the French tobacco warm and burning before. What to do I do not know.' It is June 1927. He will soon have no choice about what to do. Just two years later, a group of Austrian architects try to reach him via the British Council, to invite him to Vienna to celebrate his influence on the art and architecture of their country. The letter does not reach him; for he is dead.

**Castle, Holy Island, 1901**

The architect had spent his honeymoon and several subsequent holidays sketching at Holy Island in Northumberland.

**Le Fort Maillert, Port-Vendres, 1927 (opposite)**

The fort is seen by the painter atop its almost abstract rock composition. In 1901 the architect drew to build; now the painter draws to paint. But the poignant formal resemblance, from opposite ends of his married life, remains.

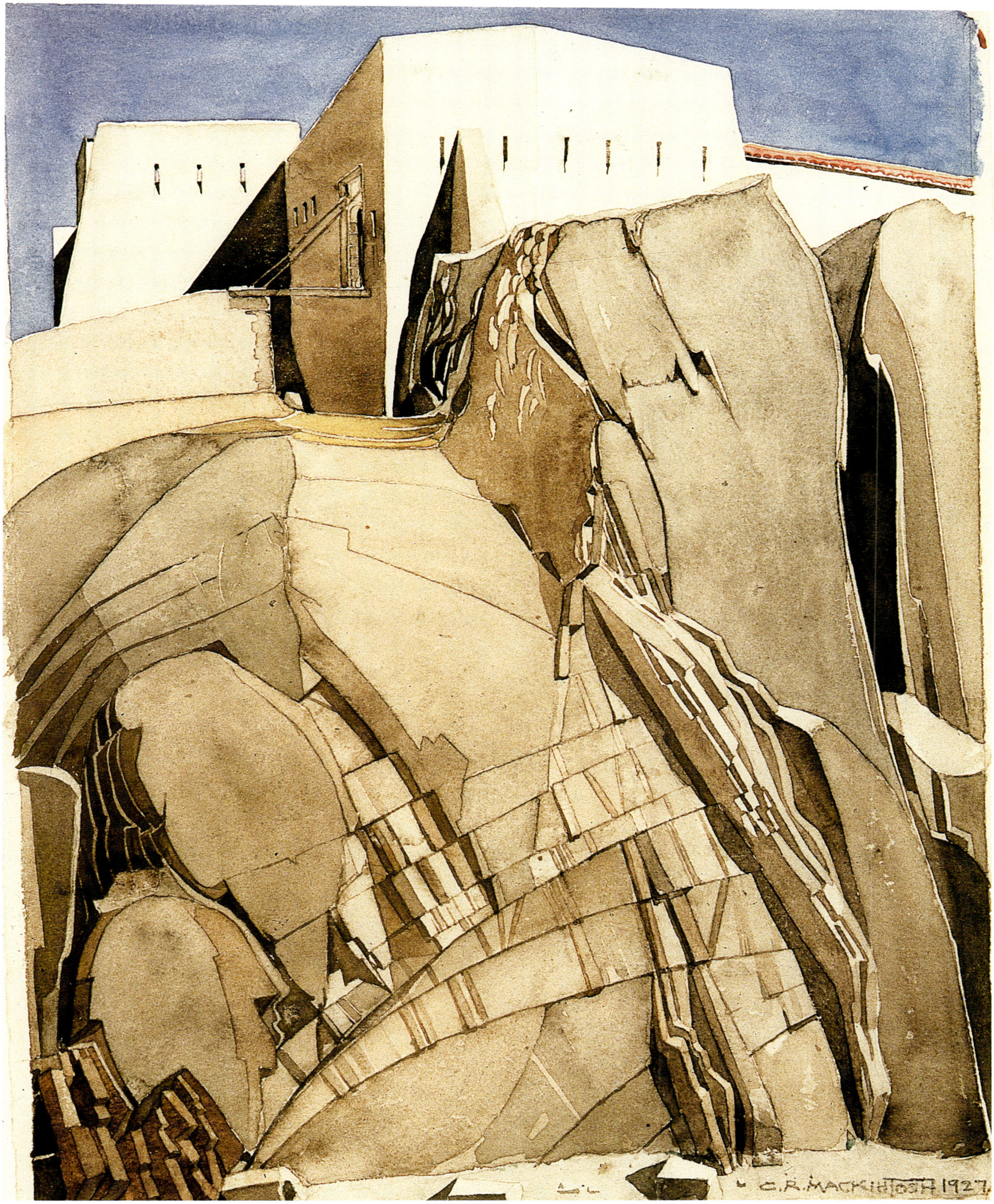
C.R. MACKINTOSH 1927.

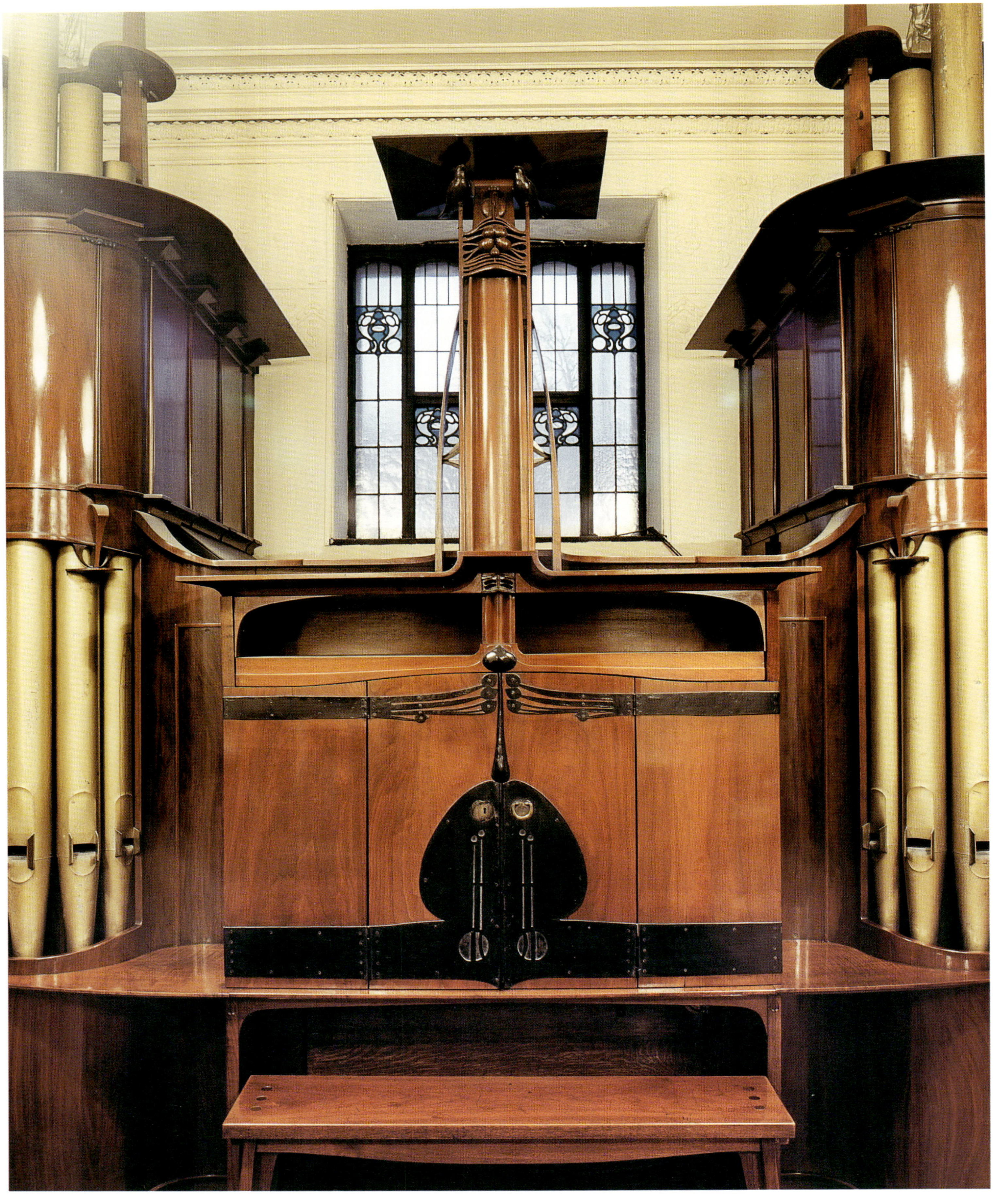

# PROFESSION OR ART, A TUG-O'-WAR

At the Paris International Exhibition, on the Champ de Mars – between the largest span building in the world, Dutert's extraordinary Palais des Machines (where Glaswegian machinery is proudly displayed), and Eiffel's remarkable new 985 ft (300 m) yellow tower – William McIntosh and his tug-o'-war team of Glaswegian policemen become World Champions. It is 1889. They take on all comers and are undefeated. Back home in Glasgow, his 21-year-old son Charlie, looking after the younger sisters, is starting the rather more profound tug-o'-war of his life.

In Paris William McIntosh shows his skill at getting things done by not only captaining the 60-strong Scottish athletics team but, in the absence of competent local organisation, stepping in and taking charge of the whole three-day-event, a display of Scottish field sports. The British and United States' Ambassadors to France are invited and leave impressed. McIntosh, at 53, is as fit as any man 20 years his junior. He is very active, has already toured sporting events with his prize-winning tug-o'-war team, is never off work through illness. Moreover, with his skill at the paperwork and organisation, McIntosh has been promoted this year to superintendent, effectively deputy head, of Glasgow Police.

Charles Rennie McIntosh, still living with his sisters and widowed father, has just completed his architectural apprenticeship. (They have not yet begun to spell their name Mackintosh; that will come with the father's second marriage in 1892). Charlie is lame, having been born with a club foot which increasingly disables him as he grows. He has one droopy eyelid following a childhood illness. Uncoordinated and poor at sport, he is acutely physically self-conscious. In school, he never succeeded, being only interested in drawing and having difficulty with reading and with spelling. All his life this dogs him. While he writes with a fluent immediacy – in letters or lecture notes; for he never writes for publication – it is unstructured, disorganised, more a vibrant flow of consciousness. He has yet to realise that his management skills and financial acumen are haywire.

If, to much of this bundle of behaviours, a century later we might stick a label,[1] it needs no diagnostic skills to see the contrast between the artistic and obviously exceptional, yet clumsy and disorganised son, and the sober, athletic and

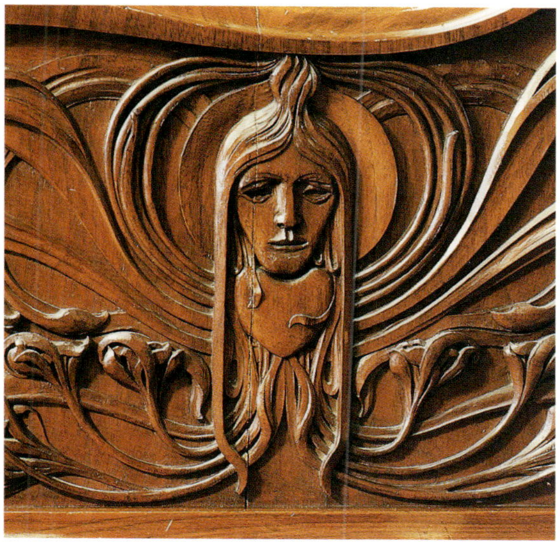

**Craigie Hall Library Seat Detail**

Craigie Hall had been designed by John Honeyman in 1872; twenty years later the practice is called back, at which time new fitments, including the library seat (whose side is shown here), are designed, clearly showing the hand of the young CRM.

**Craigie Hall Organ (opposite)**

Five years later, designing the music room and especially its organ case, CRM has a free hand. His only organ design is an unusual object, including some beautiful and literally naturalistic carving in mahogany of birds, leaves and hearts within a stylised tree under a square cap.

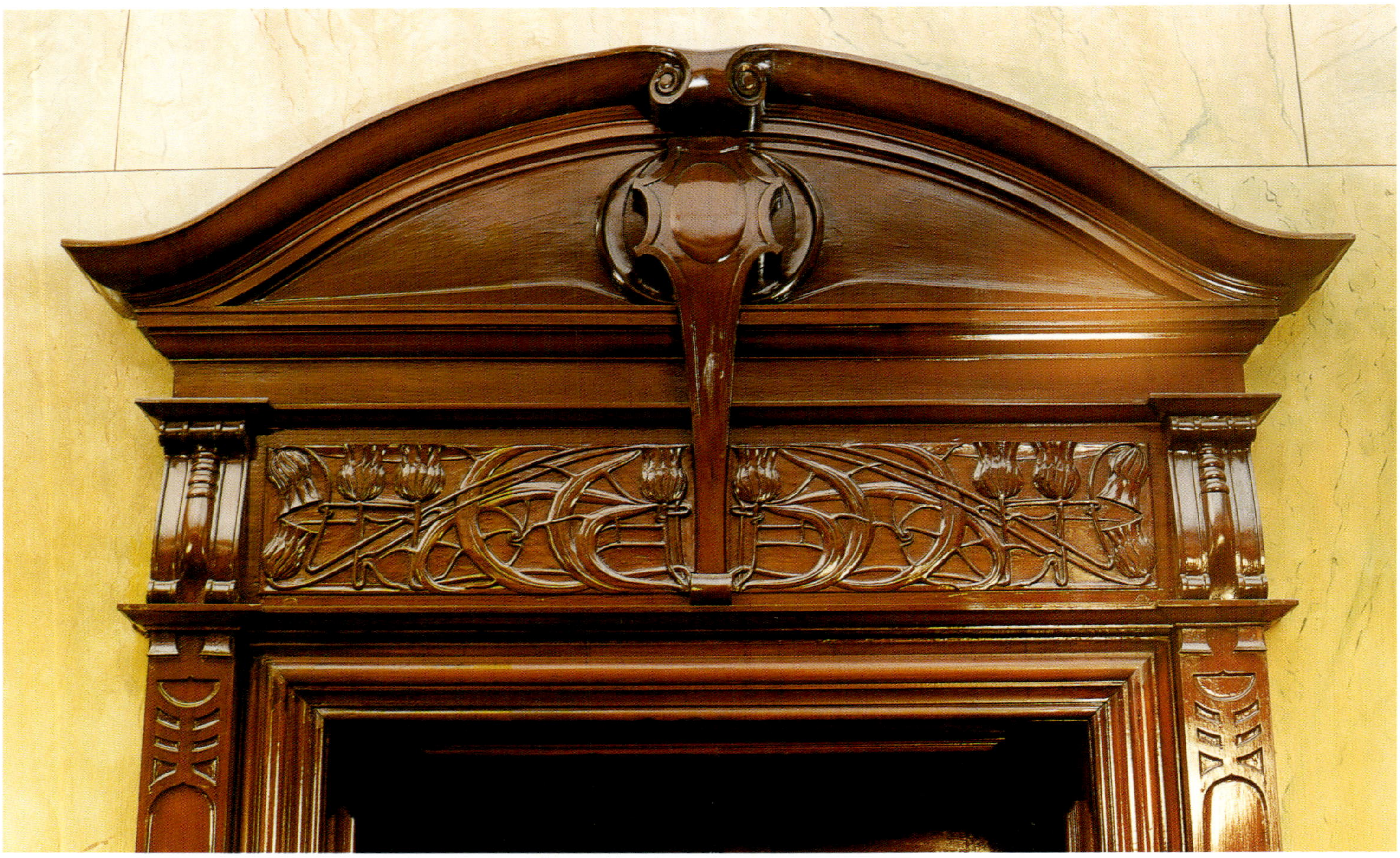

**Craigie Hall Doorcase, 1893–4**

One of a number of doorcases in the hallway at Craigie Hall which suggest the hand of Keppie's assistant, CRM.

organised father. The son's announced wish to become an architect at 16 had been firmly opposed by his father. However, Charlie persevered; his naturally winning charm and dogged demand to get his own way finally persuaded his father to support him for a further five years as an apprentice architect with virtually no income. So now we see him, in 1889, having completed these years, joining the ranks of the employed, as draughtsman for the prominent architect John Honeyman for a first pay of £5 a month. He has been learning building technique in the office by day; he has been learning historical ornament and formal compositional techniques at the Art School in the evenings. But now another prospect beckons, one considerably more outrageous to his strict Presbyterian father than even was the sober profession of architecture: he wants to be an artist.

Through the next decade, this tug-o'-war will develop; architecture and art, in this double world, becoming almost as if dark and light. The practical, masculine and dour world of construction, and the bright, romantic and feminine world of art. He struggles to redefine these worlds, so that they might somehow unite. He reads and talks; he thinks and lectures; he looks, and he never stops drawing, designing.

But, before even thinking of narrowing the chasm between architecture and art, within each of these realms are separate struggles of becoming: becoming creative architect, within a world of conventional, competitive, hierarchical business; becoming artist in a world of conflicting personal and sexual attractions, and artistic beliefs.

Architecture, first, is entered through the door of John Honeyman & Keppie in 1889. From Honeyman, 58, he will learn respect for history and awareness of tradition. Honeyman enjoys working as restorer – including the cathedrals at Iona and Brechin, on both of which McIntosh assists – and he contributes a chapter to the handsome *Book of Glasgow Cathedral*.[2] As keen medievalist and member of the Society for the Protection of Ancient Buildings, since its formation by William Morris in 1877, Honeyman has little time for Georgian architecture. He instils a love of Scotland's medieval and Renaissance buildings in his draughtsman, but this interest is solely in an architecture of monuments rather than whole places; Honeyman shows no concern for the medieval heart of Glasgow destroyed in the 1870s and 1880s (over which S.P.A.B. in England might have campaigned). This sense also rubs off on young McIntosh, who never engages either with the city's built fabric, as did Glasgow's great Victorian architect, Alex Thomson, or with its social fabric, as did the great Patrick Geddes in Edinburgh.

The eminent Honeyman, after 40 years on his own, and his office having suffered a disastrous recent drop in income, has taken on John Keppie as a partner. It is a shrewd move for both. Keppie, though still in his twenties, is the son of a wealthy west-end merchant, a tobacco importer with a country house in Ayrshire. Having briefly studied in Glasgow and at the Ecole des Beaux-Arts in Paris, he had become senior draughtsman for James Sellars, on whose death he moved, bringing contacts and commissions as his side of the bargain, to a partnership with Honeyman.

So John Keppie, at 27, is already an influential member of the city's business community. For many years he will remain the Long Distance Golf-drive Champion of the City of Glasgow. As a designer, however, he is dull, pedantic, ponderous and unoriginal. As a character, he is said to be an authoritarian egoist and bully.[3] He designs the Glasgow School of Art, according to *Who's Who in Glasgow, 1909*; though, years later, more modestly, RIBA records will list among Keppie's principal

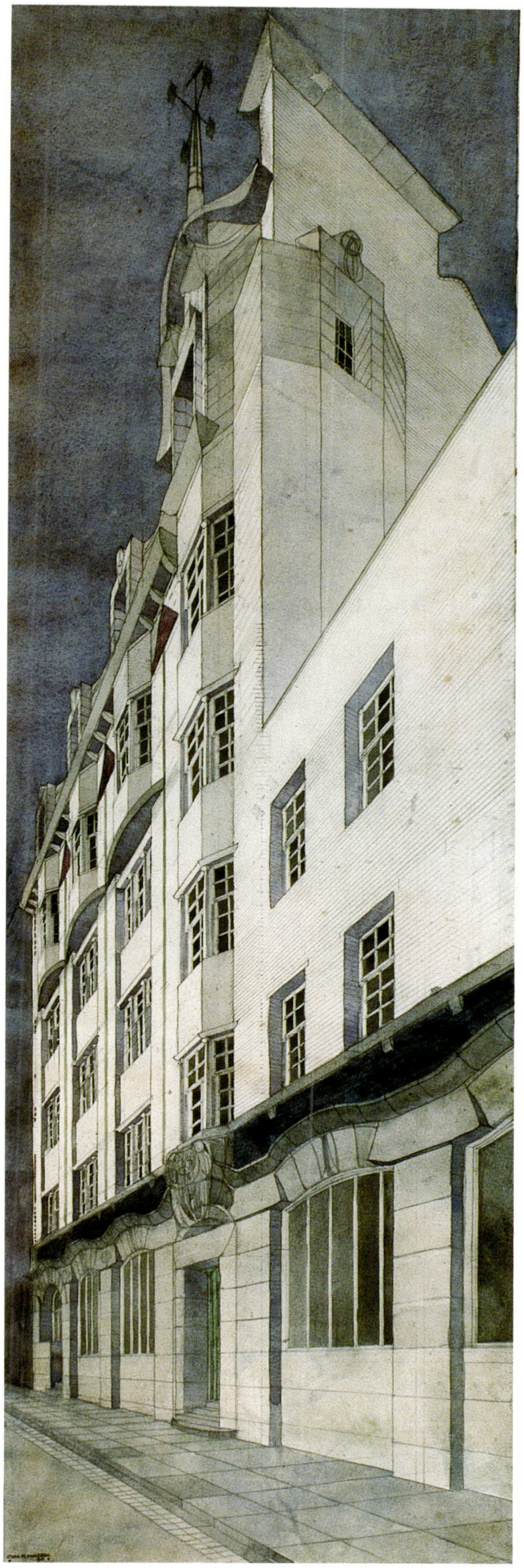

*The Daily Record* Building perspective drawing, 1901

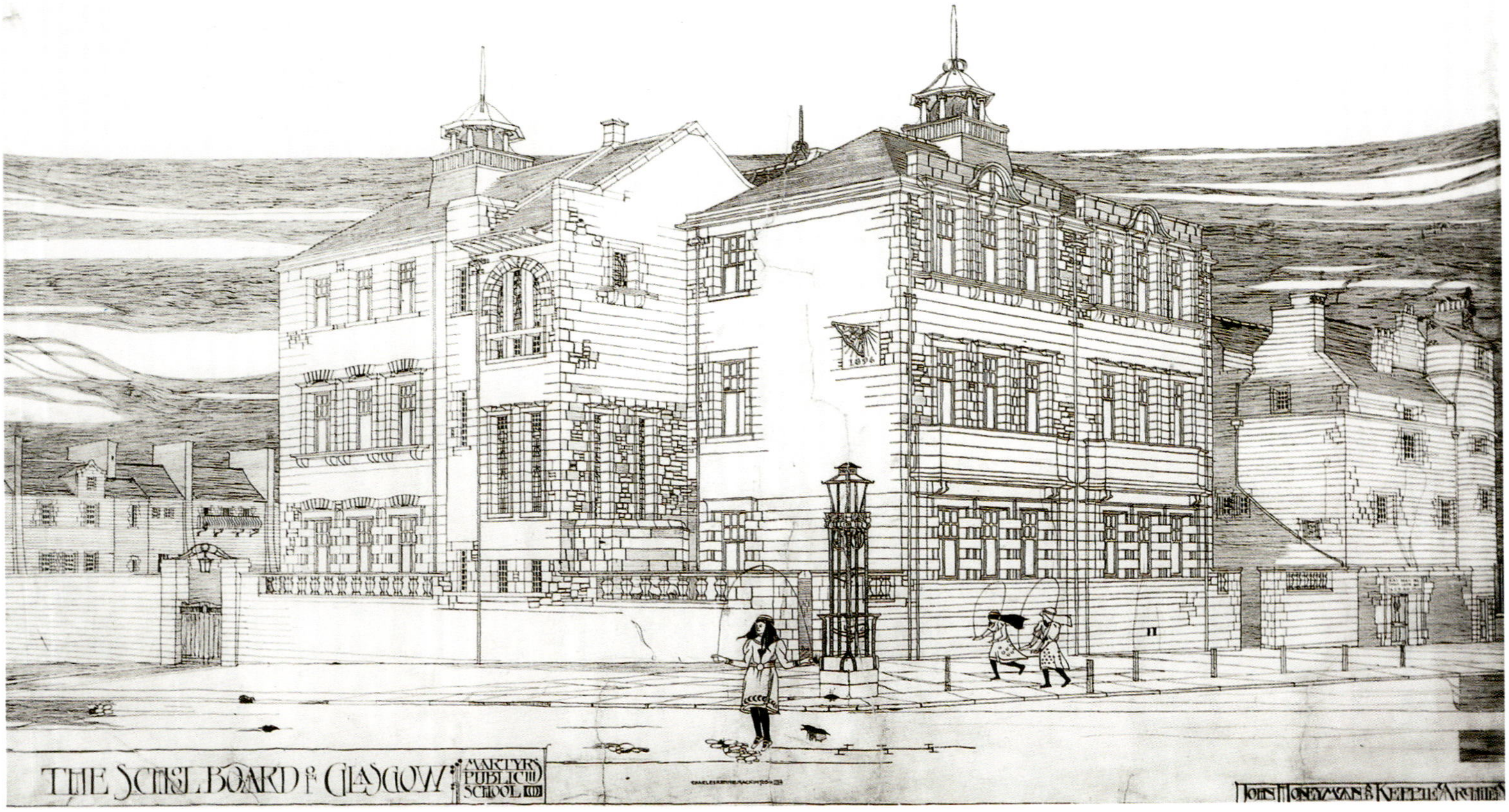


**Martyrs' Public School perspective drawing 1895–6**

CRM's own drawing of his first building. Mackintosh shows skipping girls in clothes of his own design.

**Martyrs' School**

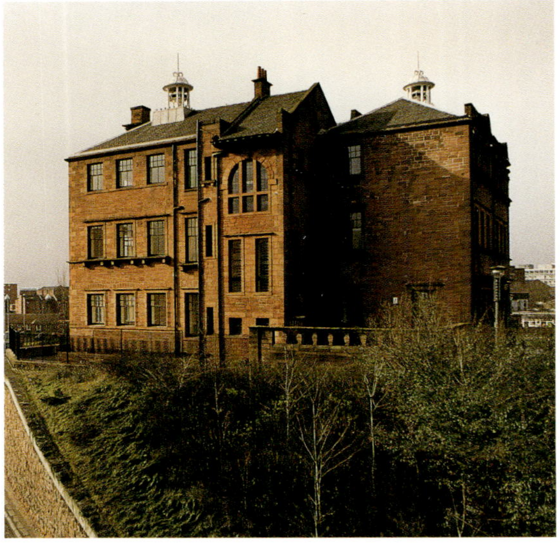

architectural achievements 'Glasgow School of Art, with C.R. Mackintosh.' By 1904 he will join the Board of Governors of that same Art School, and become President of the Glasgow Institute of Architects.

Late in the year in which McIntosh joins, the young woman whom Keppie loves announces her engagement to someone else. A few weeks later his father dies. As the eldest son, he takes a parental care of his youngest sibling, Jessie, who has recently joined the Art School as a day student. He and Jessie remain single, living together until their deaths after the Second World War. At the Mackintosh memorial exhibition in 1933, John and Jessie visit together. She is heard chiding him for having sacked Mackintosh. She buys a watercolour painting.

Back to 1889, if McIntosh is acquiring respect for Scottish architecture from Honeyman, from Keppie all he can learn is office procedure and perhaps construction techniques. Though only a few years separate the draughtsman and his junior boss, they are chalk and cheese. Keppie dresses more like Honeyman, with his short cropped hair, pointed beard, stiff stand-up wing collars, high-buttoned waistcoats. Yet McIntosh and Keppie seem to become close. They retreat to Keppie's country house to

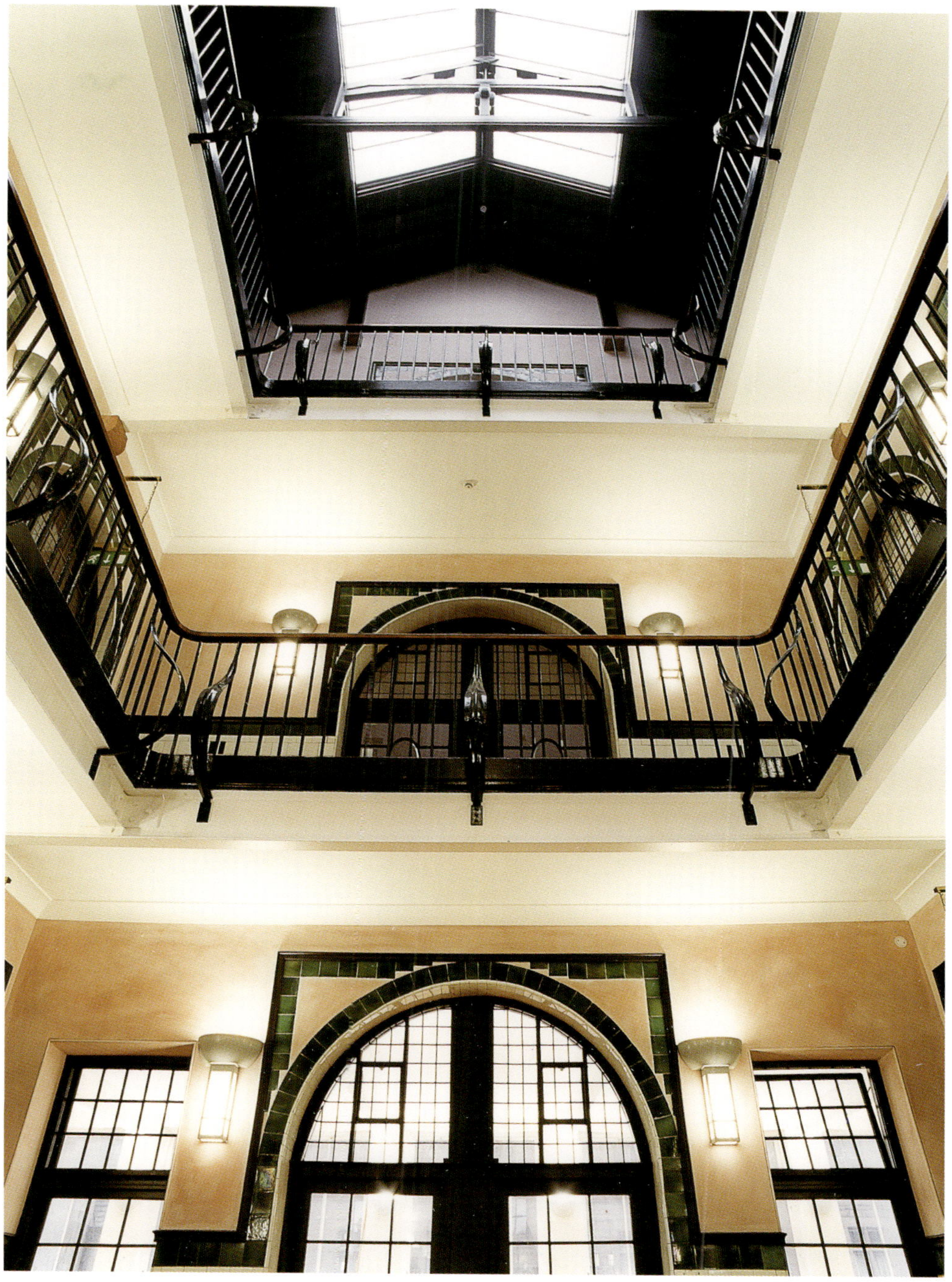

work on competition projects – though from 1890 McIntosh's visits seem more to court his boss's young sister.

And the younger man's views on architecture are no secret; his scorn for the powerful business architect, as much as for the 'imbecility' of the 'advocates of tradition and authority' in architecture, are public in his lectures. It is difficult not to see that he is attacking his boss. They must work closely together, but it is a dangerous marriage. The mediocre but competent business manager and the disorganised but inspired designer know they need each other. At least for the present.

There is, however, a more congenial figure, exactly his own age, whom McIntosh meets on arrival at Honeyman & Keppie: Bertie McNair, a comfortably off, middle-class young man of the world who had become apprenticed to Honeyman in 1888, after a year studying watercolour painting in Rouen, where he had got to know current French symbolist art at first hand.

Bertie and Toshie (as McIntosh is now known away from home, and will be all his life), spend weekends sketching together in the countryside. They are sent far from Glasgow on measuring jobs for the office – they survey a house on the isle of Gigha and travel to Iona Abbey where together they draw the Celtic decoration.

Both young men are constantly drawing and experimenting graphically. McNair talks of how he lays tracing paper over existing furniture designs and improves them. In his art drawings, McNair is always concerned with 'some allegorical meaning'. He introduces McIntosh to his interest in symbolic and hidden meanings. If Toshie easily adopts the obscure

**Martyrs' School Interior**

The stairwell roofs oversail on large beams which, inside, appear as corbels and link delicately with the timber structure. In the hall the roof trusses appear to be linked to form the paired ends of joists continuing from the stairs. But these are simply bracket shapes applied to the wall, they have no structural purpose; expressive of the form of structure, rather than honestly purposeful.

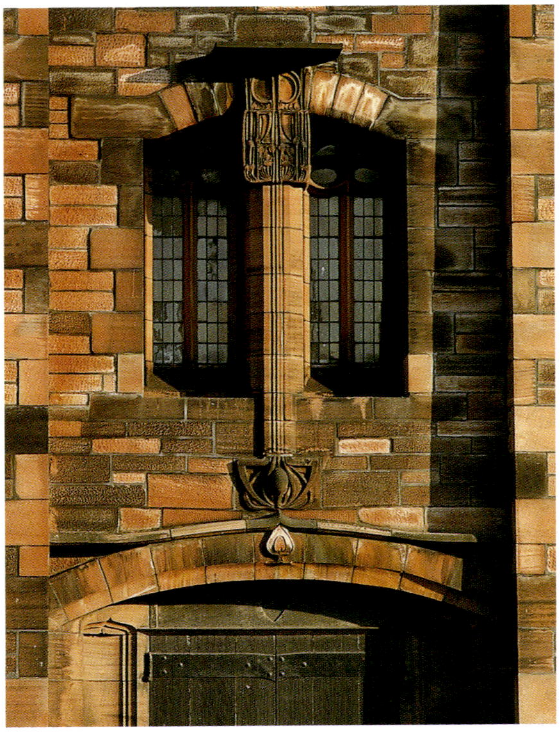

Queen's Cross Church, 1897

Here Mackintosh chooses 'the modern gothic' idiom favoured by his English mentors as a flexible, supple language which also contains the required 'spirituality'. It is also compatible with Art Nouveau tendencies, as will be seen again in the Liverpool Cathedral project.

Queen's Cross Church, Alms Dish Detail

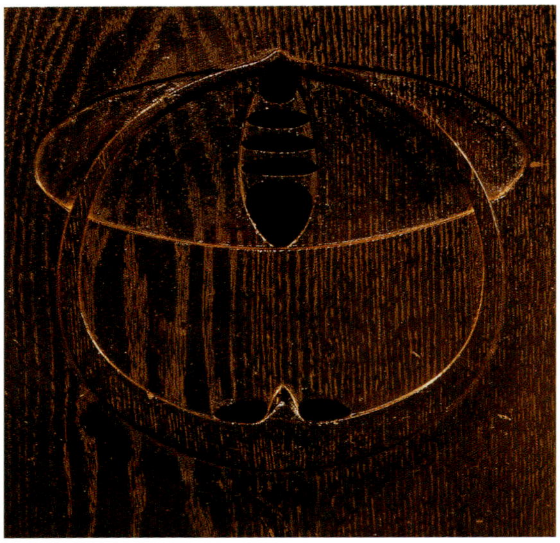

symbolism, Bertie believes in it. In many ways he is the more extreme of the two, both creatively and in his person. But whatever his personal frustrations and tensions in the early 1890s, McNair is not a natural architect. He leaves the office in 1895 to set up his own studio, producing eccentric watercolours and art furniture.

McIntosh had not been long with the office when the social pressures of architectural practice began to grate. In his own head, his architectural position and goals are becoming articulate in the years around 1890. Quite separately, his hopes and aims as an artist are becoming clear by around 1893. He lectures about architectural ideas, he produces symbolic paintings which carry his position forward. But architectural production is different. It takes much longer, depends on complex and competing forces, and is run by an office where his authority is down the pecking order. So, through the 1890s, the young man making a name with fiery talk about contemporary architecture, the young artist creating a stir with poster, mural, symbolic painting or even a piece of furniture, is also the assistant, who through each long work day is detailing buildings whose design he deplores, who fights for his own elements not to be eliminated from a design, and who then finds the final credit taken by his superiors.

There is no wonder if, in the early 1890s, this highly individualistic and naturally courageous designer is recurrently close to despair.[4] The Glasgow Art Club fit-out, a small but prestigious job of 1893, is entirely detailed and drawn by Mackintosh. In July, *The Studio* publishes it, repeating, as they have been told, that 'the architectural alterations, decorations and in fact all the details have been carried out from the designs of John Keppie, and display much artistic taste...'.

Other similar office projects, facades or interiors largely giving form to Keppie schemes, lead to the commission of a new building for *The Glasgow Herald*.[5] By 1895 CRM is chief assistant, entrusted with complete buildings, but obviously helping out and detailing on others.[6] Honeyman has virtually withdrawn from new works, and by now Mackintosh and Keppie projects are separating. Mackintosh's architecture can begin to move on; Keppie's, left to himself, does not.

Following Martyrs' School, his first independent building, Mackintosh is left in 1896 to produce one of the office's competition schemes for the town's new art school. It's not a very prestigious public building, has a tricky brief and a nastily steep back-street site. As soon as that is submitted, he starts

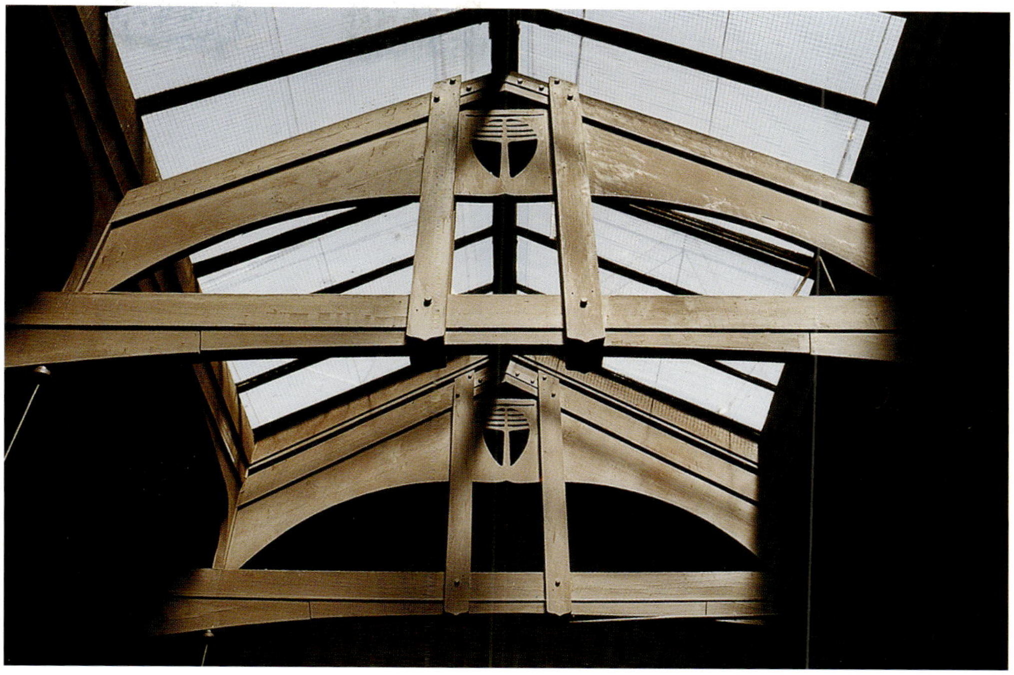

work on St Matthew's Church at Queen's Cross.

At a glance this church seems old-fashioned. But it is more important than has often been recognised, offering rich insight into the young designer. It is a very subtle conjunction of discontinuous elements, of tradition, and unending ingenious designing – where every line has meaning. The more one studies it, the more is revealed beneath that conventionalised first impression. It asks us to look and to think. And in so doing, finally his architecture joins with his art work and his ideas. Here is the work of Mackintosh the architect. 'Modern gothic' is the supple language[7] he uses informally and asymmetrically, carefully building the corner of the two streets, lifting the shape directly from a free-standing English village church, and then collaging a little cluster of vernacular shapes on the other side of the large west window to form the vestry.

Nothing outside, however, prepares one for the interior – a great unity under the barrel vault whose spaciousness is a secret carefully preserved until one enters under the side gallery and it opens out. The galleries cantilever into the main space, the side gallery being particularly powerful and reinforcing the lovely asymmetries which slowly become obvious. Inevitably, it is part seen, part imagined, the artful telling of a never completely explicit story. And the symbolism of the imagery? It has been said that Mackintosh's work generally 'exudes sexuality yet remains spiritually ideal'[8] and this would certainly apply here. The building encourages readings ranging from those which the designer intentionally masks, the biblical and historical meanings of empty niches, of birds, seeds and plants, to those particularly phallic and vaginal forms which he may never have allowed up into his consciousness at all – but which often (and sometimes with embarrassment) spring to the lips of today's visitors.

In 1898, Mackintosh, increasingly bold and independent, competes for the buildings for Glasgow's International Exhibition in 1901. While the winners were elaborately

**Queen's Cross Church Hall Roof**

The trusses are similar to those in the School of Art, here with a central tree motif.

**Queen's Cross Church Chancel Door Detail**

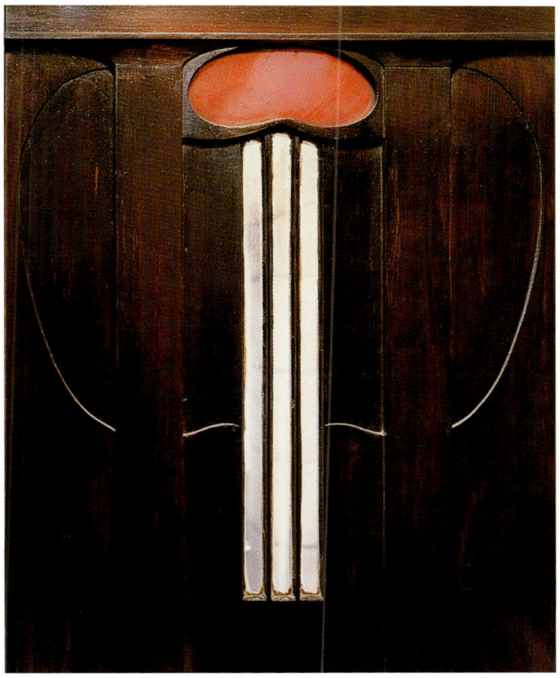

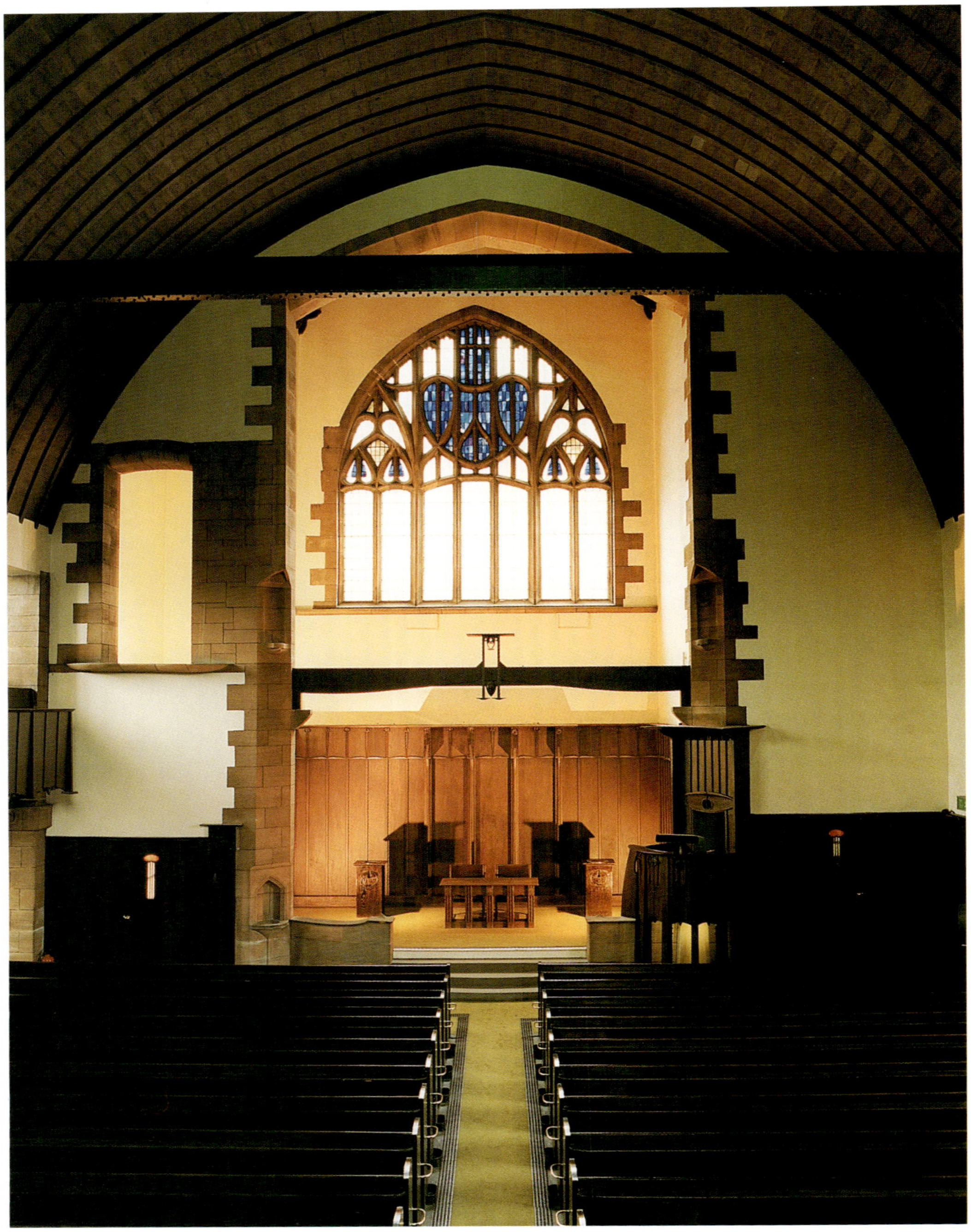

decorated wedding cakes in keeping with the adjacent Art Galleries, Mackintosh has abandoned all that baggage. His beautiful drawings rely on subtle curves and simple forms. There are echoes of Voysey and an extraordinary, coolly shaped shallow-domed concrete concert hall.

Here is the next great work of Mackintosh the architect, but these seeds fall on stony soil; having sprouted only a few glorious drawings they fade into oblivion, producing no progeny.

Now in 1898 Honeyman withdraws further from practice; Mackintosh has brought in the one public building it had long needed, when his design for the Art School won the competition. With him now also bringing in regular if small income, from his tea shop designing, Honeyman realises a partnership could not long be refused. But the young man, not from the social class of Keppie (or McNair), couldn't possibly buy Honeyman out. Honeyman therefore arranges a gradual and largely undisclosed transfer. On the first day of the century, he formally retires and the new partnership with Mackintosh commences.[9] In what is now Honeyman, Keppie & Mackintosh, the financial deal gives half the first three years' profits to Honeyman, a third to Keppie, and a sixth to Mackintosh. For 1904 and 1905, profits will split three-fifths to Keppie and two-fifths to Mackintosh; thereafter, from 1906 onwards, profits will be shared equally. But, by 1906, the world will seem very different.

Architecture, a Profession or an Art?[10] is the big question of the day, and Mackintosh's career keeps this on the boil. In a

**Queen's Cross Church Interior**

Looking from the back gallery, the slight asymmetries are made clear in this axial view: the west window does not align with the lamp over the chancel entrance, the communion table and the not-quite-central aisle. The building's major asymmetry, however, just out of shot to the left, is the side gallery, which juts into the nave from its own space beyond the barrel vault.

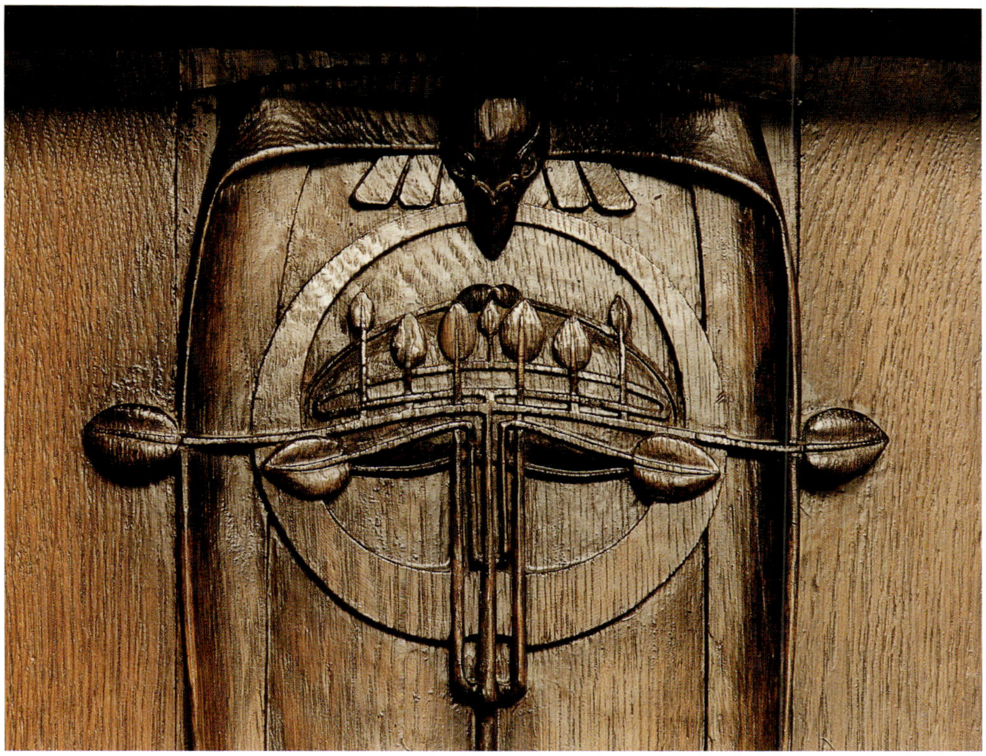

lecture he declares: 'The Architect must become an art worker and be content to forgo the questionable distinction and pleasure of being respected as the head (perhaps the founder) of a large and successful business.'[11]

Does that not imply either going it alone, or accepting the restrictions of the business? Yet he stays, while struggling for personal recognition. When *The Glasgow Herald* warehouse is about to be published (in Germany in 1898), he writes to the critic 'for the time being I am under a cloud, as it were; although the building was designed by me, the Architects are or were Messes Honeyman and Keppie, who employ me as an assistant...You will see that this [i.e. publishing under that name] is very unfortunate for me, but I hope when brighter days come, I shall be able to work for myself entirely and claim my work as mine.'

He may try to be his own man, refusing artistic compromise, yet he must live and has no possibility of setting up individual practice. The blindingly obvious grounding of this truth in the British class structure is seen in the contrasting experience of Edwin Lutyens, his English exact contemporary. Born into the right class (albeit impoverished), social networking skills led him to marry into the nobility and never lack for patrons with the money to build.

As the century starts, Mackintosh is lucky to be partner in a firm with a long-established and good name, Glasgow's fourth-largest practice, even if the new senior partner is a deeply mediocre architect. Yet his attacks on Keppie – like the quotation three paragraphs above – are unveiled. In one of his most mysterious art works, down the right side appear the words: 'the tree of influence, of importance: the sun of cowardice.' It is paired with 'the tree of personal effort, the sun of indifference' wherein are seen plants growing together, strong and independent (illustrated on p.50). Is the latter a self-portrait, and the former his accusation of Keppie once more? It is as if the venom within him holds him obsessed by his so necessary and so unwelcome twin.

**Queen's Cross Church Pulpit Detail**

The symbolism carved into the various elements of the church can be approached but never explained fully. The carving on the pulpit, which is repeated five times round its curved front, seems to show bird's wings embracing and protecting young vegetable shoots; perhaps they are the seed which was sown on fertile ground. Echoes of the parable of the sower (which comes from St Matthew's gospel) abound round this church of St Matthew.

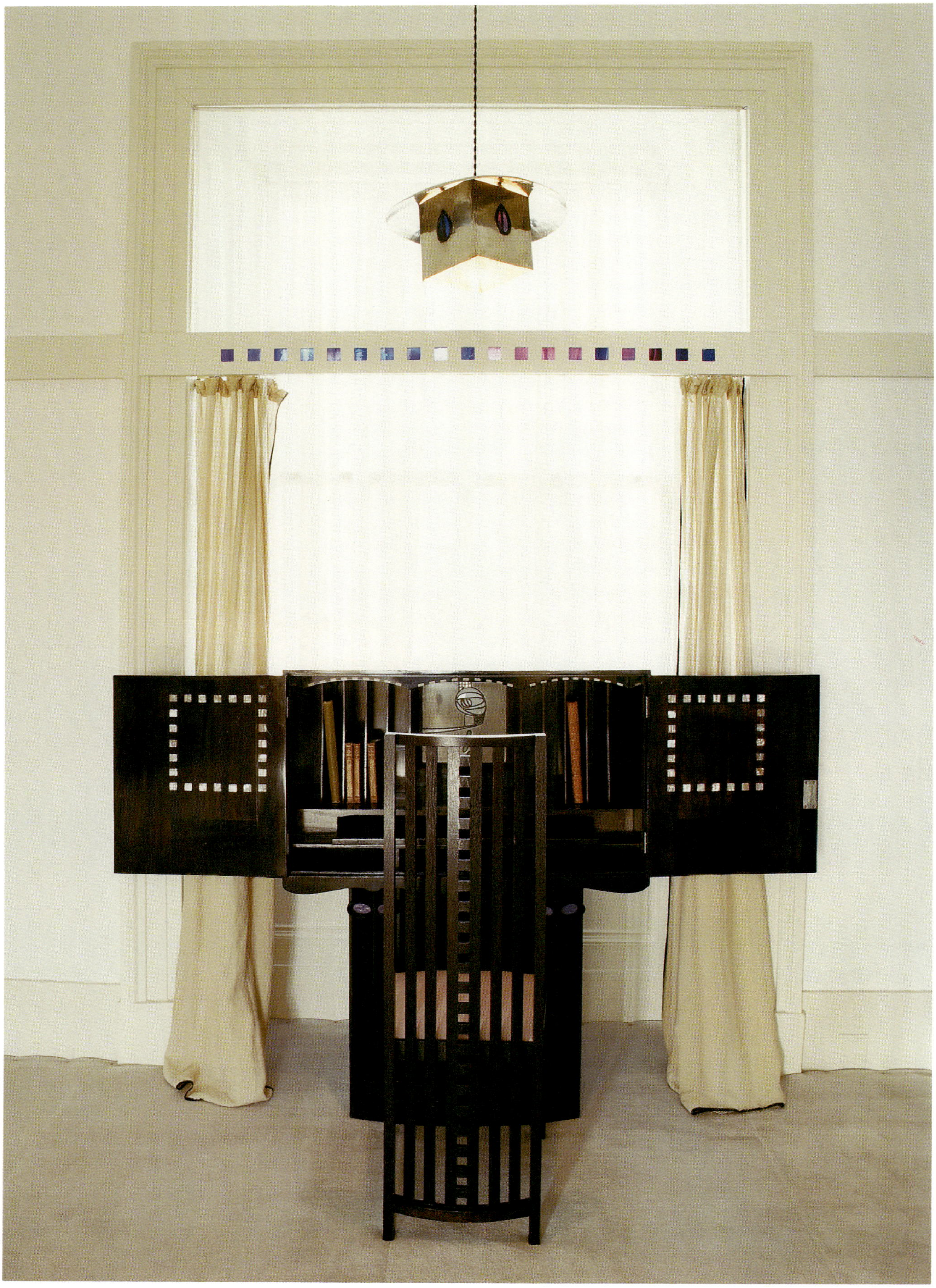

# THE REAL THING

'The whole town is getting covered with imitations of Mackintosh…it is too funny…I wonder how it will end…'. Today, a century after Margaret Macdonald Mackintosh wrote these words, we still might wonder. The dazzling profusion of new Mackintoshish objects, interiors and indeed complete new buildings, confuses and bewilders. In this world of commodity fetishism, all that is solid melts into air. Through the mirage, where little seems to withstand the MacMidas touch, we search for an elusive authenticity. On the streets of Glasgow, in and out of the shops and galleries, we must work. We must use all the faculties of discernment and careful enjoyment, to judge for ourselves: to see what Mackintosh did or didn't actually design, to see through the layers which have been washed away from – and those added to – Mackintosh's works; imagine his places, feel our way into a Mackintosh tea-room interior while staring into a reconstructed space in an exhibition, or while sipping tea either in an actual (partially restored) tea room or in one newly formed with Mackintoshish surfaces and decor. Walking from the recently 'Mackintoshed' hotel in Renfrew Street along from the Art School, we try to distinguish between the hordes of charmless kitsch souvenirs, the careful and accurate reproductions, and the often charming Mackintoshish *objets d'art* on sale everywhere. And that 'everywhere' now includes the profitable shops within two genuine originals, The Glasgow School of Art and Queen's Cross Church.

As we wonder at what another of Glasgow's great architects, Isi Metzstein, called 'Uses and Abuses of the Immortal Memory', we recognise its echoing the cult of Rabbie Burns. We must look really hard to separate the real from the easy copy which is everywhere today, chequer or rose or lettering, it litters Glasgow in 2000, tackily attaching itself to all sorts of inappropriate surfaces and forms.

Take the Mackintosh street lamps. When I first saw these light standards, appearing in the 1990s on pavements around the Glasgow School of Art, Queen's Cross Church, and so on, I smiled at the 'keeping in keeping', the semiology of the streets. I could read the signs: they were spoor indicating the presence of a real Mackintosh. Quite tasteful postmodern designs, by some fashionable young Glasgow practice, I guessed. But no, they have been carefully constructed from recently discovered Mackintosh drawings. Do I now see them differently? One

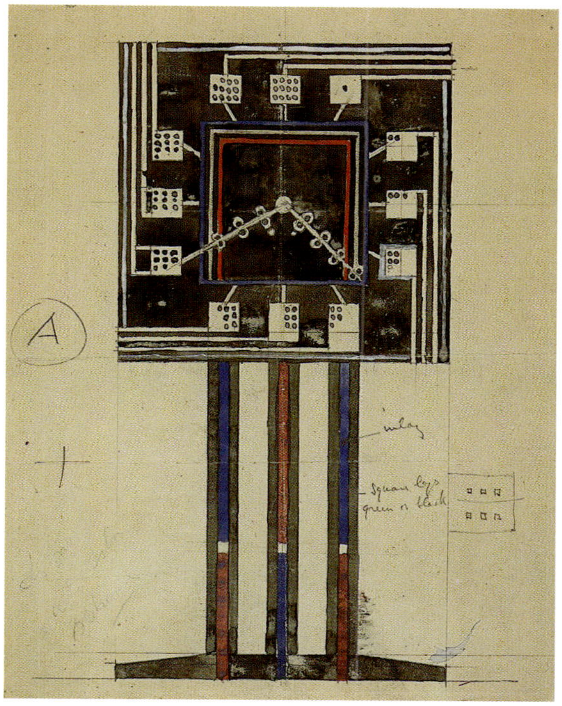

**Design for a Clock for W. Bassett-Lowke**

From the start, copies are made of CRM designs at the request of agents, friends of clients and even for his own use. In 1917, he is designing this clock as he draws it, each side is suggested differently, starting at the top, until the fourth side (8, 9,10,) becomes almost the final choice, for the face is refined yet more in the making. Pleased with it, he has a copy made as a wedding present for Mary Newbery.

**CRM's Writing Desk, The Hill House (opposite)**

The writing desk in ebonised oak and mother-of-pearl, designed in 1904 for the Hill House, so pleases CRM he has a copy made for himself (with this different insert panel).

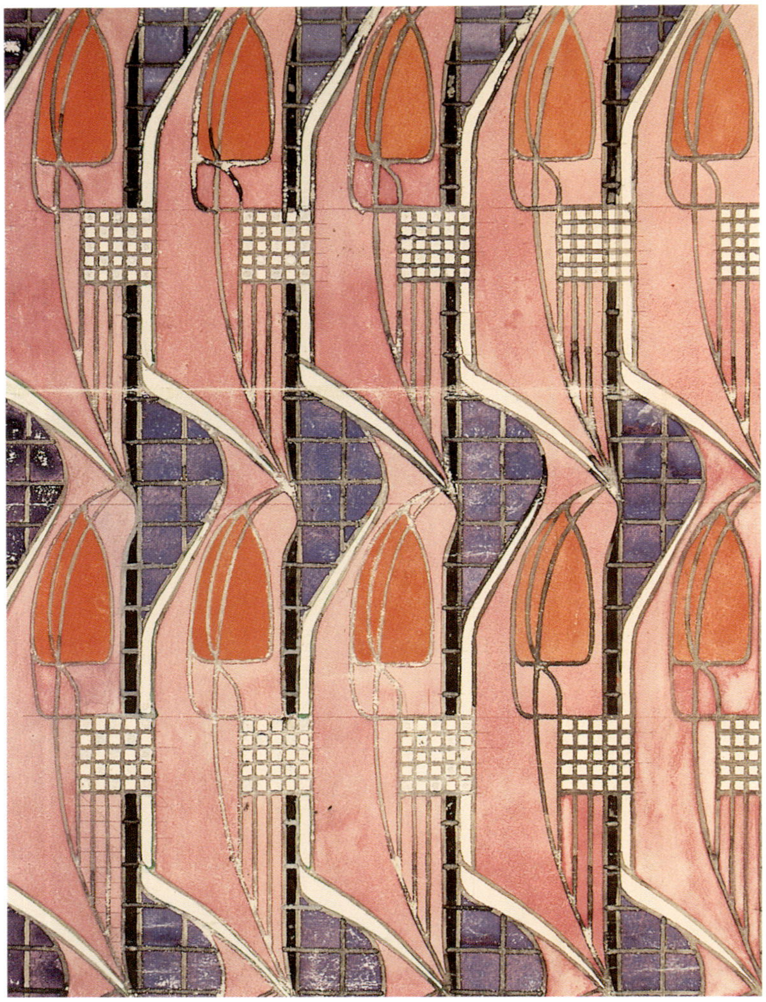

**Tulip and Lattice**

Textile designing in London at the end of the First World War, CRM experiments with 'Tulips and Lattice' motifs, combining the organic and geometric. An experimental sketch (opposite top), and one of the most complete of his design drawings (above), linking echoes of Glasgow (Art Nouveau, stained glass and his five-square thumbprint) in a timeless design which remains fresh today – as seen from the design currently in production (opposite below).

moralising critic calls them 'clumsy', well intended but wrong; 'a non-contextual Mackintosh untrue to his own creative principles.' Continuing as if he were the disciple of a religious leader, he adds: 'Perhaps it should be said that it is not enough to copy or reproduce his work; that is not what he desires us to do. It is to transformation not transference that he directs our attention.'[1]

Well, the Mackintosh House is genuine; at least the interior is. A faithful reconstruction, apart from kitchen and cloakroom, spare room/studio in the attic, and of course bathroom – whose door now opens into a bizarre tall exhibition space. Glasgow University's first rebuilding plan in the 1960s was to recreate a series of linked spaces, all on one floor. But curators pressed successfully for a reconstruction of the three-dimensional spaces of the original house within the Hunterian Museum. A similar argument continues today round the future reconstruction, in some still-unknown site, of the Ingram Street tea rooms, whose story offers a key to Mackintosh's fortunes. It involved him over 12 years, with at least one space being given a second makeover. The whole set of spaces shows his different facets and complex personality, as well as his developing skills. If ever seen again, it would be the greatest breath of fresh air and astonishing inspiration in Mackintosh studies. It would be a sensation, flocked to by a public fascinated by Mackintosh but saturated with the same repeated graphic imagery. It should still happen, but the story so far doesn't encourage optimism.

The tea rooms were very nearly split up and sold in 1949, when Douglas Percy Bliss, Director of the Art School, campaigned to save them.[2] He got Pevsner and J.M. Richards enthused in an attempt to persuade Glasgow Corporation to step in; others, including John Betjeman, joined the campaign and international museums expressed public interest. Finally Glasgow acted, to ensure their preservation, buying the complete tea rooms for £22,000 in March 1950; in pretty good condition and with all fittings and furniture down to the cutlery. As Bliss interestingly argued, 'without the furniture, the fittings would be merely grotesque and a source of derision. Without the fittings, the furniture is merely uncomfortable and dated. The genius of Mackintosh was such that he made a complete unit out of his interiors.'

But, having been unwillingly purchased, they were let out by the city as a careless discount warehouse, suffering various indignities until the interiors were finally dismantled in 1974-5, when the fledgling Mackintosh Society protested 'their condition is appalling and their future is bleak.'[3] Moved between various stores in the 1970s, they were vandalised, soaked and fire-damaged until in 1977 Glasgow Corporation announced plans for 'removal, listing and restoration of [all] the tea-rooms' linked to their proposed Museum of Modern Interior Design in Scotland Street School. Government money supported much study, labelling and recording.[4] 'Moving and reassembling should soon be under way' said a Glasgow Museums spokesman.[5] Yet it would be two decades before the first room was reassembled.

Its great gesso panels, 'Wassail' and 'May Queen', over which green emulsion paint had been slapped while in situ, in the City's ownership in the 1960s, had not been seen for half a century, either in fact or in reproduction, until brilliantly displayed in the mid 1990s. Yet today, the restored Ladies' Luncheon Room which they adorn, shown worldwide in 1996–7, is back again in its 32 crates in a locked warehouse in the wilds of north Maryhill. Around it, lottery grant money allows conservators to labour slowly and lovingly over the other rooms – for which Glasgow, which has recently so benefited from Mackintosh's popularity, still refuses to commit itself to finding space.

Well, at least, the Willow Tea Rooms remain authentically in place in Sauchiehall Street. By the 1920s there was a typical Mackintosh interior next door; it has long since vanished, and no one today knows if it was an earlier, genuine Mackintosh or not; while in the basement to the west, was his utterly different wartime tea room 'the Dugout', so completely erased it is even difficult to know precisely where it had been. After decades as a department store's 'Bridal Suite', the Room de Luxe and gallery have been refurbished and opened again for teas. But, for the weak willed, the whole is undermined by the emporium which must be crossed to reach them – an Aladdin's cave packed with 'The Rennie Mackintosh jewellery collection' and myriad souvenir reproductions, copies, in the style of, loads of glass and mirrors, reflection on reflection.

Now, since 1997, advertised with a Margaret Macdonald menu board and much Mackintosh detail, there has been 'The New Willow Tea Room' at 97 Buchanan Street. Here, upstairs

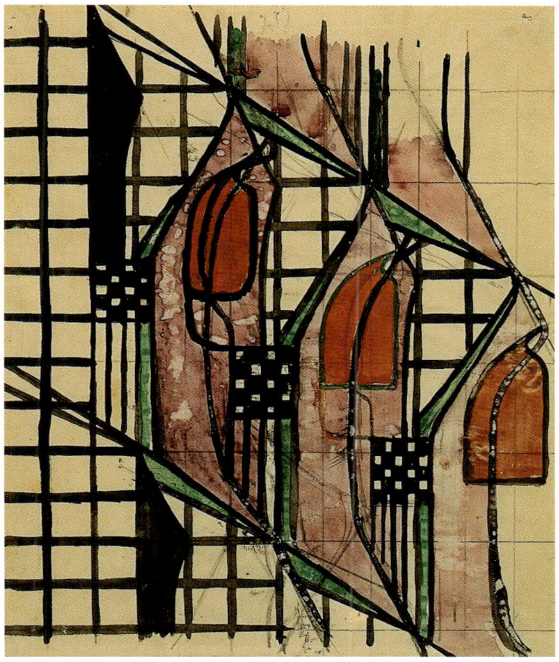

Tulip and Lattice Diagonal

Tulip and Lattice, Textile Sample, 1990s

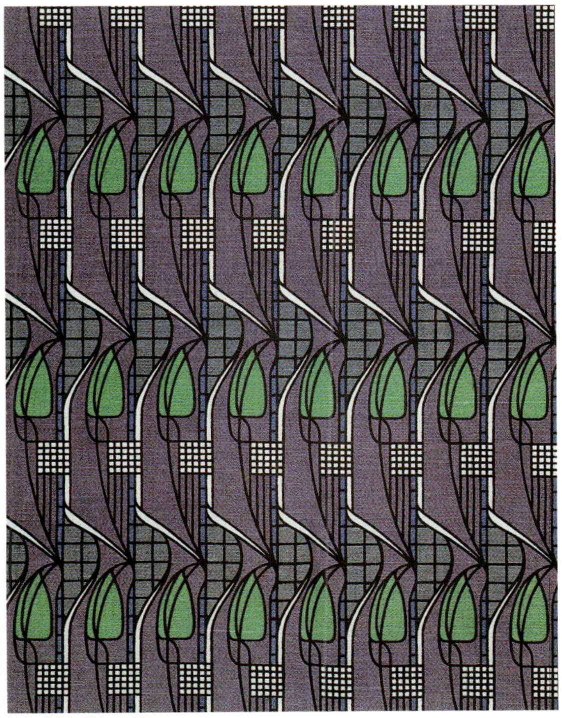

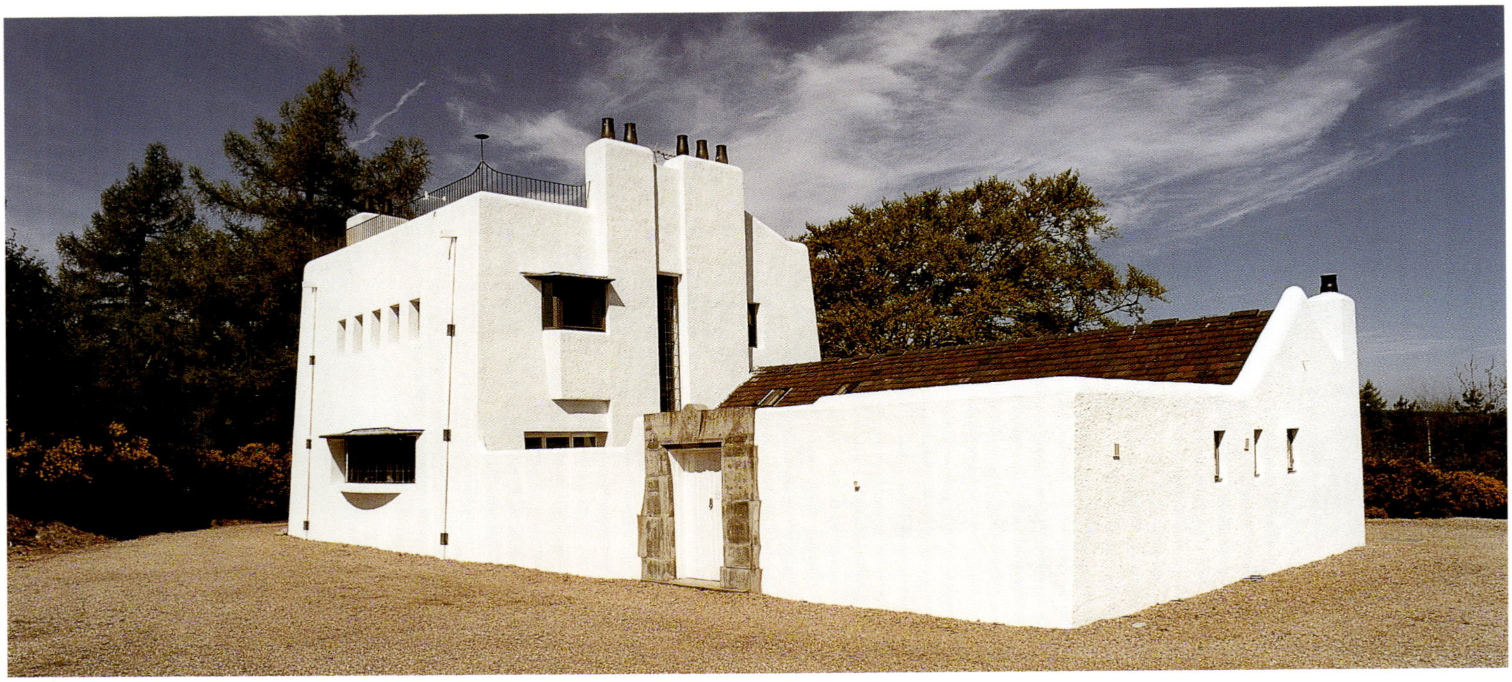

### An Artist's Country Cottage, 1990s

Mackintosh is both out of copyright and treasured as uniquely original. This paradox produces shelves of CRM giftware and memorabilia, but virtually no architecture or interior design influenced by his. The architect Palladio, whose buildings and their images produced Palladian country houses across England and north America, was never precisely copied. In contrast Mackintosh architecture is now reproduced as faithfully as the furniture or graphics. Two schemes which existed a century ago as a few sketches, were built in the 1990s, as attempts to reconstruct a Mackintosh country house for an art lover and this project for an artist.

in The Blue Room there is some very tasteful reconstruction, like the low Chinese Room chairs; alongside which a tall-backed chair appears – but in a display case, as an exhibit. The laden sideboard sells cakes and scones, but more space is taken by Mackintosh-wrapped foods and books about Mackintosh himself. A world of mirages and reflections melts in the mouth.

Cassina in Milan produces 19 different pieces of Mackintosh furniture so perfectly it usually needs some gentle distressing to resemble the originals; Lino Sabattini crafts exquisite editions of 17 pieces of Mackintosh silverware: cutlery, candlesticks, bowl.[6] Mackintosh fabrics also appear, but compared to the designer's original colour sketches these seem dead, like one of the widespread Mac motifs turned into lifeless wrapping-paper.[7] What has happened here? Unlike the objects, there were no surviving textiles to copy, only the watercoloured drawings. They would originally have been roller-printed, of course, and could never reproduce the 'life' of the sketch with its variable effects from his loaded paintbrush. But, aha, a different company also reproduces the same fabric, and this time not following the normal process of translating a sketch to a fabric pattern, but in facsimile of the sketch, with all its colour variation and even its incompleteness. Sitting in the Mackintosh chair thus covered is almost like sitting on an upholstered Van Gogh.

The path to authenticity leads through a fascinating, but pretty dense wood! That all reproductions are inevitably interpretations is clearest in the new Mackintosh architecture.

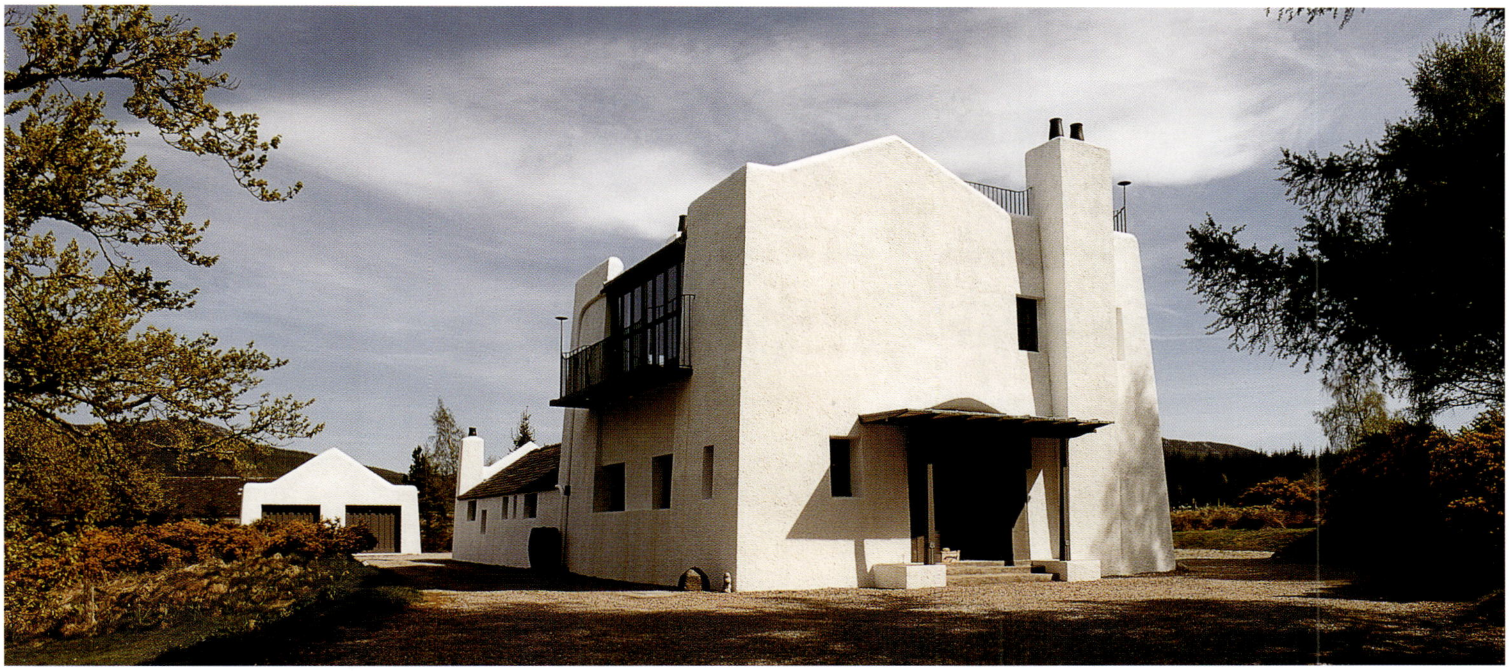

The vast House for an Art Lover was created in a Glasgow park in the 1990s from a small packet of 14 competition entry drawings of nearly a century earlier. Inside the house the scale of elements and details seems slightly disturbing, and obviously was surprising to the loving recreators.[8] Take the nine decorative stone panels on the south front. In Mackintosh's drawing they are the size of a thumbnail. That was now redrawn and enlarged to a scale from which stone carvers could work; but how much less would a craftsman have needed in 1900? And how much less if Mackintosh visited every day, scribbling and chatting and demonstrating? What is the issue of reproduction about: must it be 'mechanical' once it leaves the 'master's' pen? To those who had not made the mental leap to the building industry of a century earlier, and particularly to Mackintosh's Arts & Crafts sense of the creative role of the craftsman, the amount of interpretation, research and design work needed throughout this 1990s project was staggering and unexpected.

The required attention to detail greatly increased the amount of time and money needed to complete the project,[9] as we no longer live in an artisan or craft-based economy of skilled and cheap labour. Not all the interiors are constructed as Mackintosh's plan – it has to be commercially viable, after

### An Artist's Country Cottage

A couple of elegant sketches for *An Artist's Cottage in the Country* were published in 1901; the designer of this charming and carefully Mackintoshed building near Inverness 90 years later, Robert MacIntyre, describes himself modestly as 'fortunate enough to be available to serve as Mackintosh's job architect.'

### An Artist's Country Cottage Dining Room

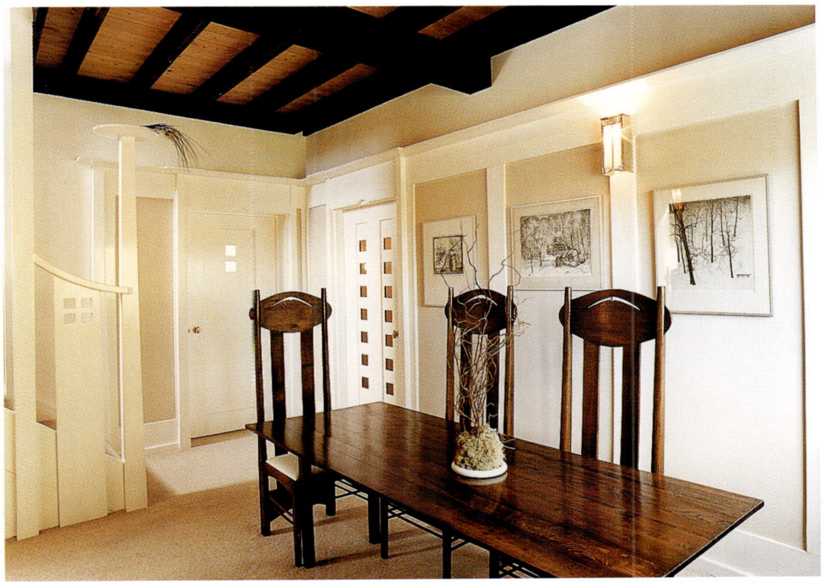

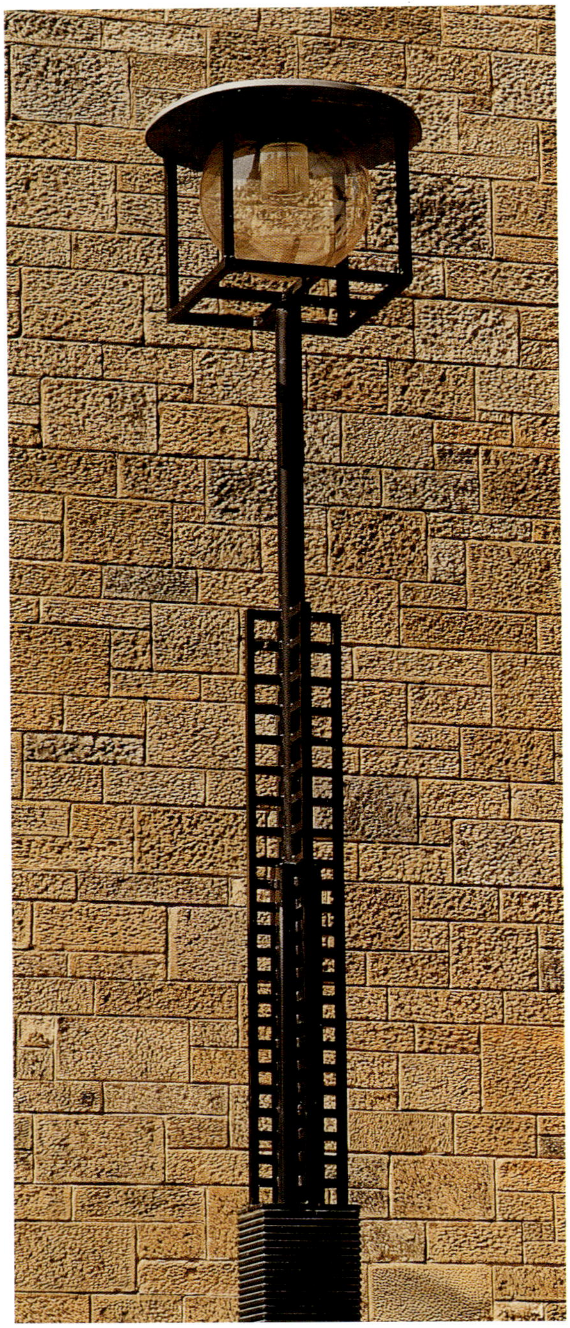

**Glasgow Street Light**

Mackintoshish street lights in Glasgow now tastefully indicate the proximity of a work by Mackintosh himself. They are faithful realisations from a drawing, found by chance in recent years, made by CRM after he left Glasgow and whose purpose no one knows.

all. Even so it took six extra years to complete. It is a 'masterpiece', according to Andy MacMillan, then head of The Mackintosh School of Architecture and the architect in charge of its realisation. What is this 'it' which shimmers in the air in front of us? In a corner, NeedleWorks lovingly recreates embroidered silk panels for the music room; they simultaneously make half-size replicas for sale in the basement shop, as well as smaller memorabilia like 'Mackintosh' napkins and tea cosies.

A much smaller house also completed in the 1990s from Mackintosh sketches of 1900, is an Artist's Cottage in the Country, built in the north of Scotland at Strathnairn, just south of Inverness. It more closely resembles Mackintosh's sketches as its purpose remains similar, though today instead of a coal fire per room, each bedroom has en-suite washing and W.C. The architect describes it neatly: 'This is neither the restoration of an existing building nor the replica of another. The intent of this project is to realize a building design prepared by an architect of genius in 1900...My client wanted Mackintosh as his architect, and I was fortunate enough to be available at the time to serve as the job architect.'[10]

It is a very modern problem to be uncomfortable about completing buildings a century after they were designed. Yet, paradoxically, it helps undermine the cult of the 'artistic genius', that a century later we can build, with contemporary craftsmen responding to the problems in their own ways. Mackintosh would have distinguished between recreations and mechanistic copies which die of sterility in their attempt at authenticity. He would be happy with the Art Lover's House, and the range of creative craft work it incorporates; he would be horrified at the Mackintosh fonts available on CD-Rom, one of which for obvious reasons you see above, for he never designed a typeface – that would have been unbearably mechanical!

A key feature about interior design, as opposed to architecture, is that it inhabits the world of shopfitting, ship fitting, and even theatrical set design. Interiors are ripped out and replaced, they are covered over; they are reproduced elsewhere, they are renovated, changed, amended, developed. At least once Mackintosh completely gutted an earlier tea room and replaced it; another time he designed a complete new makeover for a bedroom with a replacement set of furniture. These are not pristine works of art – is there ever such a thing other than in the hands of curators? Many of Mackintosh's fitments were in fact copied in his lifetime, can be again today,

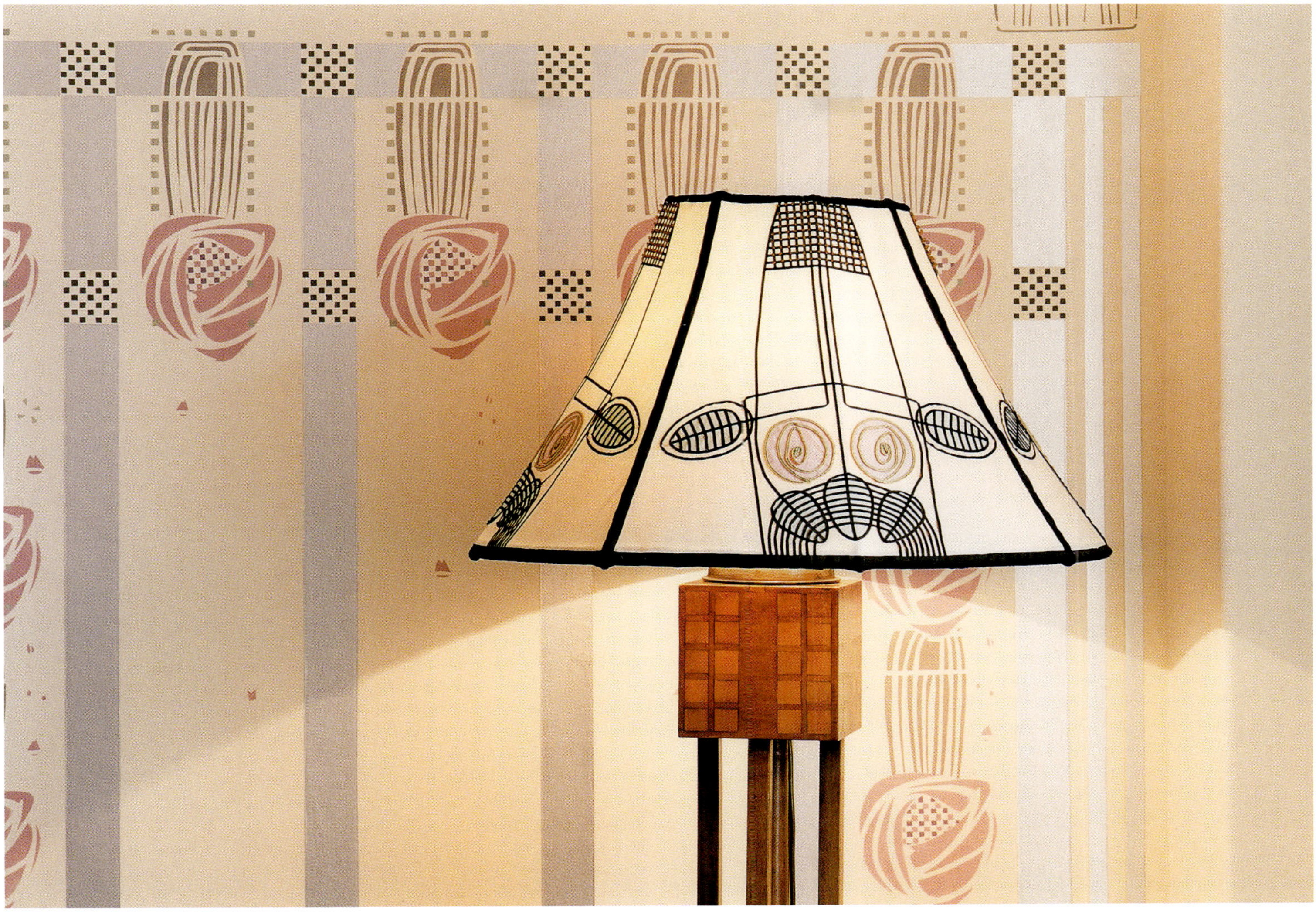

and anyway the originals are easily moved.

The Director's Room at the Art School has recently been completely changed with new light fittings. Metal cube cages with open bottoms, each holding a glowing bulb; very stylish Mackintoshish shades, I think, with a 'square' of nine square holes – a typical Mackintosh thumbprint – cut out around the corners of each cubical cage. Neat. Now I see these are the lights he originally planned in 1900 but which were too expensive.

Mackintosh was obviously pleased with the 'domino' clock he designed for Derngate, so he had another made, and gave it as a wedding present. A copy set of Derngate furniture was made for a friend who'd admired it.[11] Experts talk of 'replicas', – such as the copy sent to Moscow in 1903 of a table Mackintosh designed for Wärndorfer the previous year; replica or not, when found, damaged in a family playroom in Clydebank, it sold for the vast sum of £30,000.

At the Hill House, Mackintosh added bits of furniture over the years (also making the odd copy for himself of the best

**Drawing Room Lamp and Wall Stencils, The Hill House, 1905**

In the Hill House, and dating from the very beginning of domestic electricity, against the subtle silvered and painted wall stencil stands a beautiful, tall, rectilinear lamp standard, in sycamore with mother-of-pearl inserts. It could easily be mistaken for a product of the 1920s. Mediating between them is the lampshade whose design in white silk repeats four times; black beads used to drop from each point where the black curves touch the bottom rim. The original shade wore out and was remade by MMM in the 1920s; the wall stencilling is much more recently, carefully restored. Is the standard lamp the only genuine relic here?

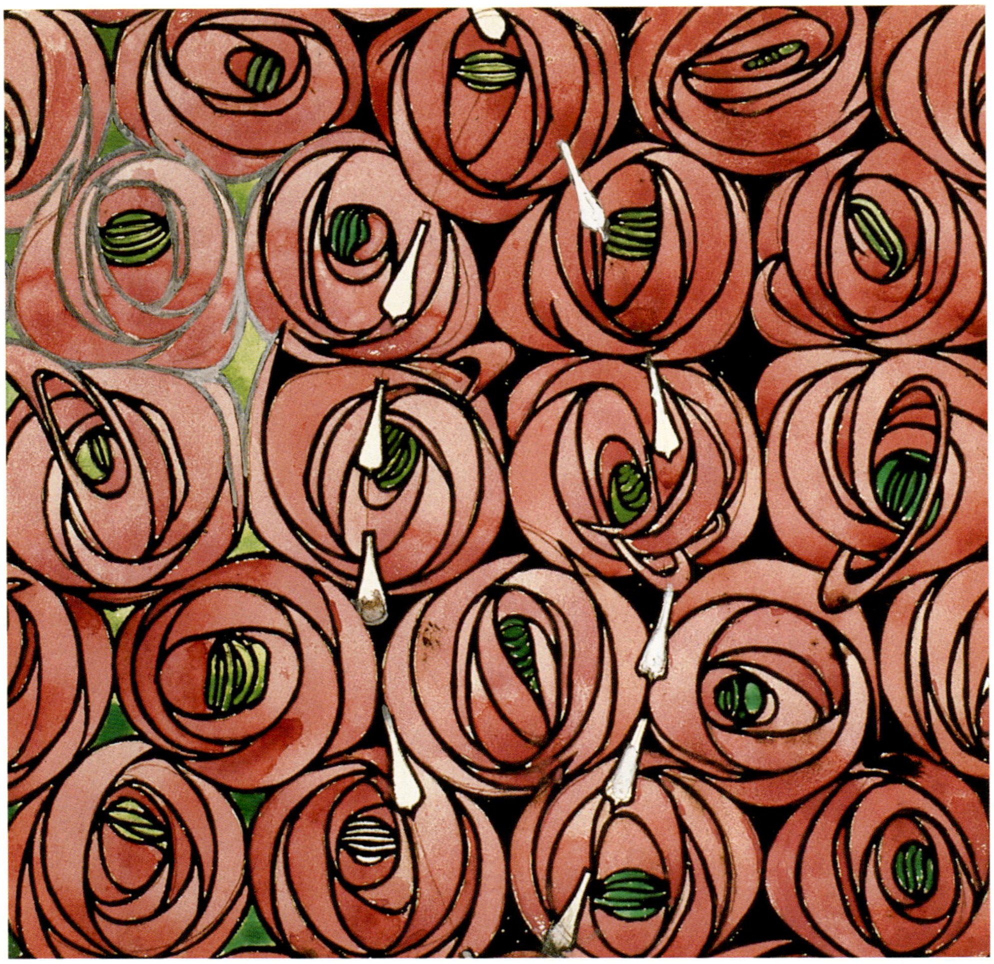

pieces), Margaret remade the needlework lampshade, but most drastically, he completely changed the effect in the drawing room. The current curator suggests that his second scheme – with a very dark ceiling – is 'like listening to a Beethoven Symphony when the horns and flutes are slightly out of tune.'[12] Not at all. It is indeed like a symphony of that period which typically might be scored without horns because the local court orchestra had no brass players, and a couple of years later be rescored for a fuller orchestra. Life goes on, and so did Mackintosh's ideas. Mackintosh, with the chance to revisit a design, would not hesitate to develop his ideas. Today's curator says 'In an ideal world a return to the original, white-ceilinged scheme ought to be the objective. That was how Mackintosh conceived it...the plum ceiling is not the background against which Mac composed.'

**Rose and Teardrop**

Watercolour sketch for a textile design, 'Rose and Teardrop', where every rose in the repeat of 20 is different. If ever made, no CRM fabrics remain; and today different manufacturers roller print this in flat colour similar to that on p.39 and as CRM might have expected in 1920, others produce fabric in photo-realistic facsimile of the sketch.

In fact, the client didn't like the large light fittings which dropped from the ceiling to the picture rail (as others still do in the hall outside). The gas smoke stained the white ceiling, while she also found them too hot close to her head. So they were removed, replaced by wall sconces, and with the ceiling now left too high, Mackintosh suggested it be made a dark, milky black by washing buttermilk over a deep plum.[13] Conservation has currently sluiced it down to the original white.

So what is genuine, and what gives value? If the designer's intention can change, what is sure? There is sale-room fixation with authenticity proven by what they call provenance. The modernist fixation with originality sits uncomfortably with Mackintosh, who happily plundered the store of architectural history as well as reusing his own designs. One of his clocks is a straight copy of an Austrian original.[14] So does value reside in the work itself and its uniqueness, or rather is it in our relation to the work, not just personally but also in our wider culture? These values flow with the spirit of the times and, in late twentieth-century Britain, to focus on the price of everything and value of nothing was a watchword. We can each try to judge for ourselves a chair in a sale room, an interior carefully conserved or a glossy reproduction; we can inform our value by a sympathetic and critical evaluation of Mackintosh's intentions.

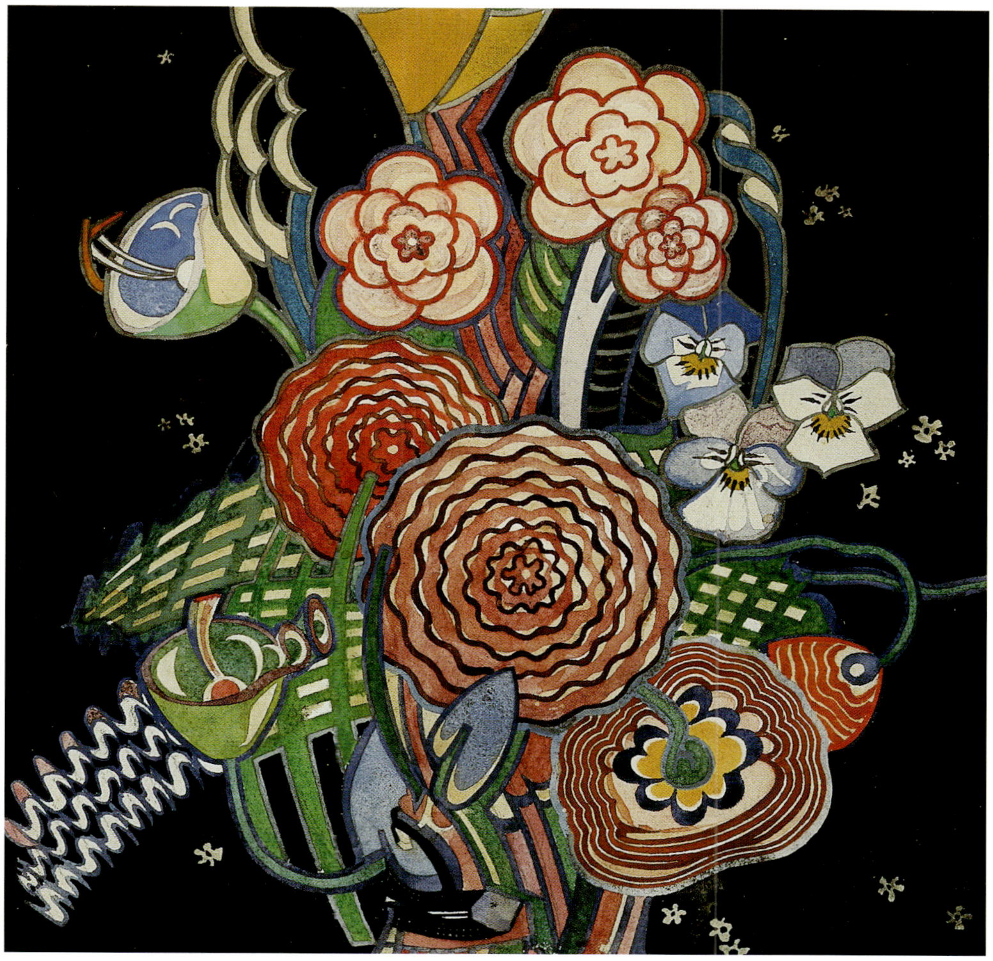

Basket of Flowers

One of a number of similar bouquets of stylised flowers, reminiscent of Ballet Russe peasant colours and vibrancy, painted by CRM in London and offered for sale at between £8 and £10.

Taking the categories of 'use value', 'age value' and 'historical value' (which art historian Alois Riegl suggested a century ago), we can see the Art School surviving in the first of these three. Repaired and renewed as required for its ongoing use, despite the growing temptations of MacMidas merchandising, this still holds at bay its imprisonment as a museum. Here the authentic experience continues in use. But once that is lost, as with all the tea rooms, once the physical items – screens and chairs, lights and mirrors – are separated from the activity they assist, then they float away from the quayside of use. They become ruins or mummies.

Age value, that is where the lines of ageing are written on its face, is the sensibility of William Morris and surely of Mackintosh. (Honeyman, as a leading Scottish member of Morris's Society for the Preservation of Ancient Buildings, deplored restoration.) This romantic (and modernist) notion enjoys the melancholic nostalgia of decay, the pleasure of ruins. Mackintosh's work never reached this architectural permanence, being ever tied to usefulness and ease of replacement – his teaspoons and clocks were so easily upgraded, his tea rooms and bedrooms so easily madeover.

The third category, historical value, refers to objects which have become symbolic and thus represent shared social values. The campanile of San Marco in Venice collapsed a few years after Mackintosh's student visit. It was rebuilt as the precise copy which stands today. This view refers not just to the intrinsic design merits of the work, but acknowledges that it has become a legitimate shared symbol. Here we see Glasgow in its relation

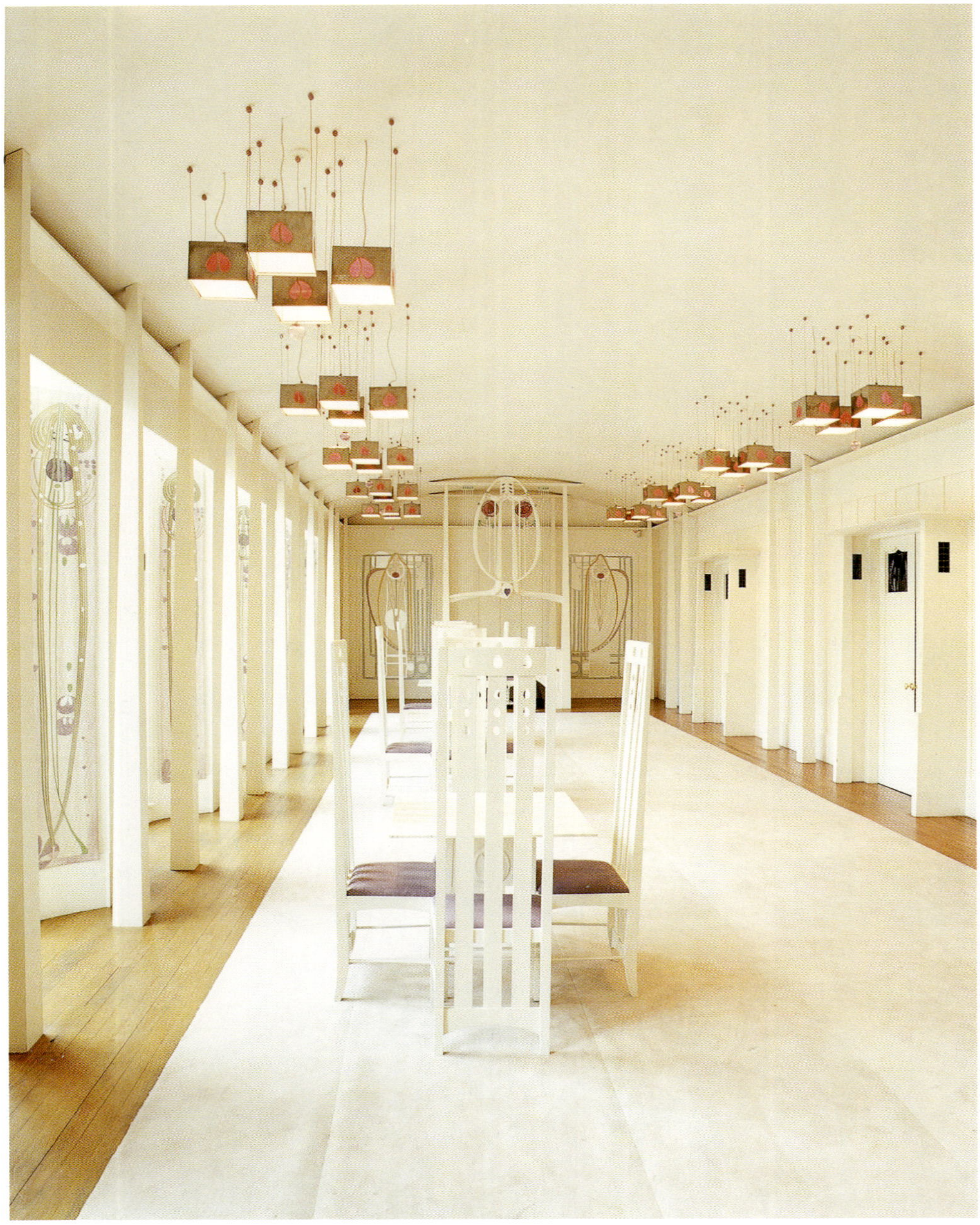

**Music Room in the House for an Art Lover, 1990s**

The salon and music room of the House for an Art Lover consisted of a subtly coloured perspective view and three wall elevations, which CRM drew for an ideas competition run by a German interior design magazine in 1901.

to Mackintosh trying to live with these shifts in values. The Mackintoshes' own house interiors were restored (not just elements exhibited). The Ingram Street tea rooms are being repaired and rebuilt; but Glasgow is not yet committed to restoration, in the sense[15] which means reinstatement in a new condition of completeness which never actually existed historically before. The Dutch Kitchen could be restored in the original location today even though none of the fabric remains; and of course, once it is seen as of historical value, it would be economically viable. With the Ingram Street tea rooms, even without selling tea and cakes, there would be adequate traces of the real experience preserved within these restored remains; it would not be new, nor old, but layered, with the real sandwiched within its layers of memory. For today, Mackintosh's work is indeed symbolic of Glasgow. It has attained the historical value status.

The notion that Mackintosh spins money today percolates into all available pores. When fitments and furniture were made for the House for an Art Lover in Glasgow, another set was commissioned for The House for an Art Lover even more recently built in Japan. (The destiny of the work of architecture in this age of mechanical reproduction is, that if you can make one here, you can as easily make one there.) But while Mackintosh himself is out of copyright, as is obvious from the streets of Glasgow, those craftsmen who interpret his designs today so that they can be recreated, raise the question of the copyright of their interpretations. Mackintosh himself never considered registering his designs through the Patent Office; it was rare in the cabinet trade although it was a routine process in some industries in his day. His work was all small batch

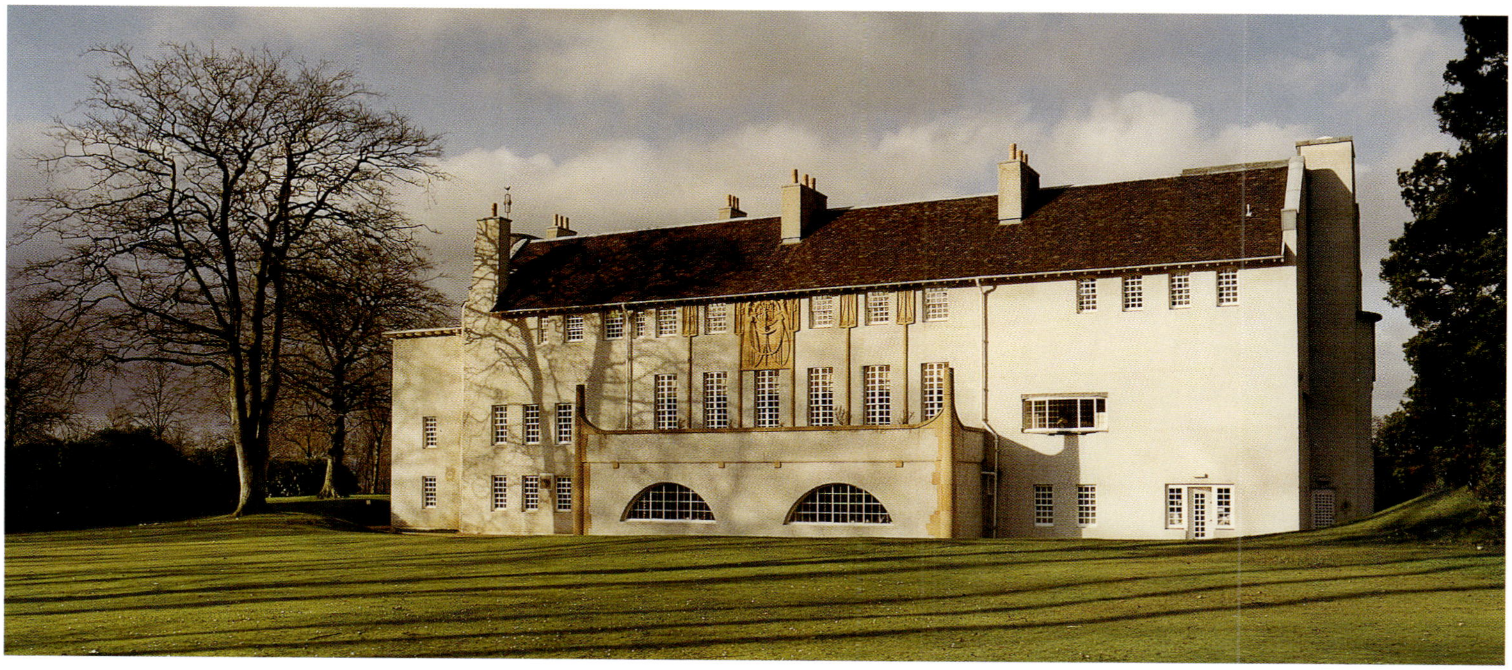

production for specific patrons or places.[16] He was copied even then, but if imitation is the sincerest flattery, what are we so suspicious of? Why do we see it as theft? Is it from the antiques trade and the sale-room prices based entirely on uniqueness?

When Margaret took some of Toshie's paintings to a London gallery, it was pointed out that they weren't signed. 'I'm sorry there are no signatures,' he responded to her urgent query, and he asks her to sign them for him. 'I always forget about that; it seems so unimportant'. The gallery understood better. Attribution makes a huge difference in the market: today Mackintosh attracts a much higher price than Macdonald, and at those moments where their work is almost indistinguishable, much money hangs on professional judgments. There are London textile designs in bold geometric colours which I would expect to be his and find are actually hers.

The beautiful little watercolours, on which the two vast gesso panels in the 1900 Ladies' Dining Room were based, were sold in 1993. As works of art there is very little to choose between the 'May Queen' and 'Wassail', carefully twinned pieces painted and fabricated by the couple in close parallel. The cartoon by Mackintosh fetched £72,000; Macdonald's less than half that. Such is Toshie's and Margaret's relative market value today.

Pity that the white reliefs from the Willow Tea Room are not yet on sale. I hope soon to buy one smothered with roses, as in his original drawing, which obscured the 'Kandinsky' that Pevsner foresaw when it was washed clean of their sweet smells and sharp thorns.

### The House for an Art Lover

A delightful and grandiose confection first built in Bellahouston Park, Glasgow in the 1990s (and then cloned in Japan). It is self-styled as 'inspired by Charles Rennie Mackintosh, a key attraction and one of the city's most popular venues.' Developed from CRM's published competition drawings, initially by architects John Kane and Graeme Robertson under Andy MacMillan, it has involved a host of skilled craftspeople in its loving recreation. The amount of interpretation, research and design work called on through this project was staggering and unexpected, while the imposing scale of the house and its fittings was consistently surprising to those close to the project.

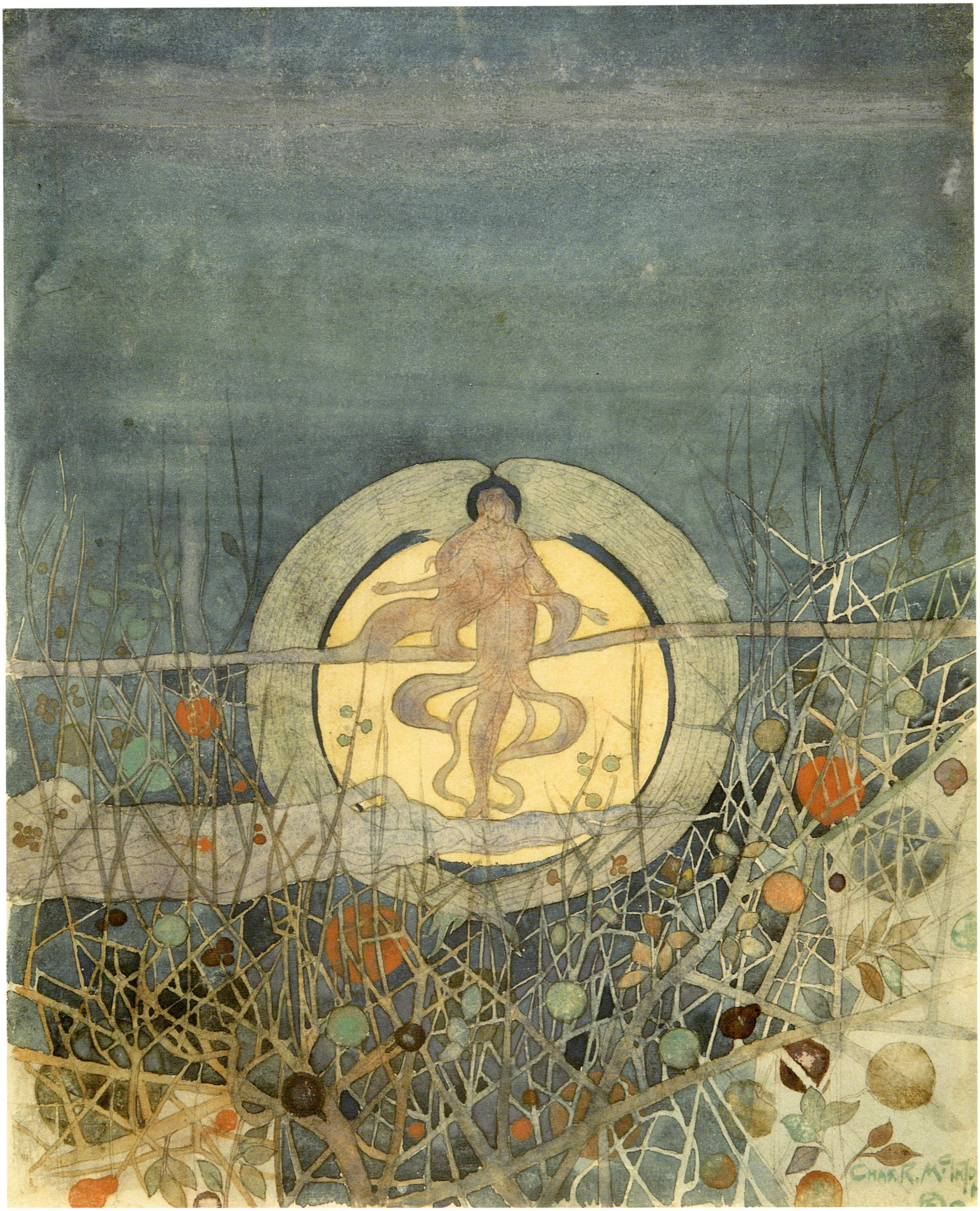

# ART OF LIFE, A TUG-O'-WAR

The other tug-o'-war is entered through the door of the Glasgow School of Art on Sauchiehall Street. Here, in 1889 the evening student McIntosh wins first prize in Architectural Design and a Free Scholarship. He collects a prize for a church design, a bronze medal, certificates, and prizes from the Glasgow Institute of Architects. He is an assiduous student, with a flair for draughtsmanship, who has been coming to evening classes for five years already, since starting his apprenticeship. (Apprenticeship is the complete architectural training for most; few bother to take unnecessary evening classes as well. But McIntosh is ambitious.)

In 1891 he wins a National Silver Medal. His project is criticised in the professional press as a stick with which to beat the system, but it gets him publicity. The same year he wins the most coveted architectural award in Glasgow, the Alexander Thomson Travelling Scholarship, and then – just before he sets off on the travels it allows – he gives his first public lecture, choosing to enthuse, to the few who turn up, on Scotch Baronial Architecture. In a welcome break from Keppie's, the wide-eyed young architect travels north through Italy from Palermo and Naples for three months. His travel sketches are exhibited on his return, and this brings him for the first time to the attention of Francis Newbery, head of the Glasgow School of Art, and whose protégé he quickly becomes. In 1893 he gives a fiery talk on 'Architecture', arguing vehemently 'how absurd to see modern [buildings] made in imitation of Greek temples! We must clothe modern ideas in modern dress.'

What might 'modern' mean to him? For it is certainly not the stripped down, ornament-free, 'functionalist' image which hijacked that word two decades later. Perhaps Mackintosh's sense of 'modern' becomes clearer in the church he designs a few years later. That building certainly is adorned with a symbolic language much more resonant than its first-glance historicism suggests. This same lecture goes on to hint at what we might expect: 'Why a piece of architecture should be passed with only a passing glance...is beyond my comprehension; the more so when you consider that the fairy tale which it embodies

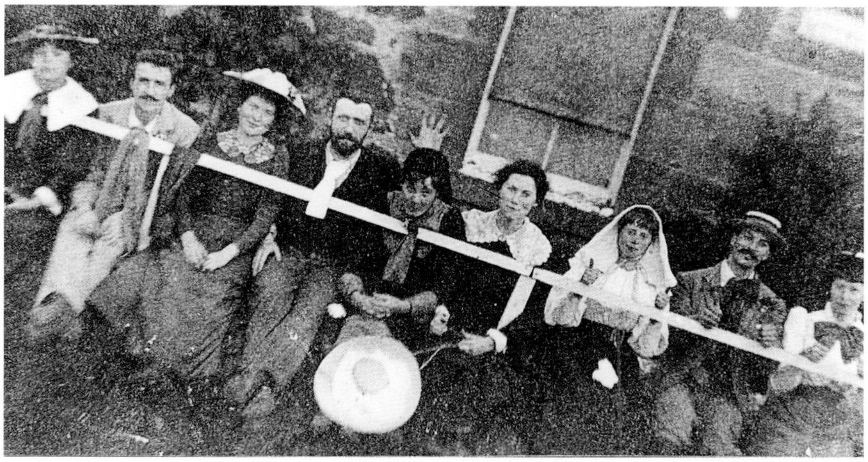

### 'The Immortals'

CRM and his friends lark about; but their positions and gestures repay attention. From left, Katherine Cameron, CRM, Janet Aitken, John Keppie, Agnes Raeburn, Jessie Keppie, Frances Macdonald, Bertie McNair, Margaret Macdonald.

### Harvest Moon (opposite)

As CRM breaks with Jessie around 1894, moving closer to Margaret, he exhibits 'A Panel – The Harvest Moon' (marked 'not for sale'). It is his first known mystical work; if its horizontal imagery is ambiguous, the bodies melting into each other are clearly sexually charged. But then, within an ornate drawn frame, he inscribes 'To John Keppie October 1894, Chas R.Mackintosh'. (The painting itself is signed McIntosh, 1892.) Next he makes Jessie a beaten brass casket, decorated with budding but not flowering roses. What is the meaning of these gifts to those whom he rejects? Once jilted, Jessie lives all her life with her brother, while CRM's 'Harvest Moon' remains always in John Keppie's office, unseen by his broken-hearted sister.

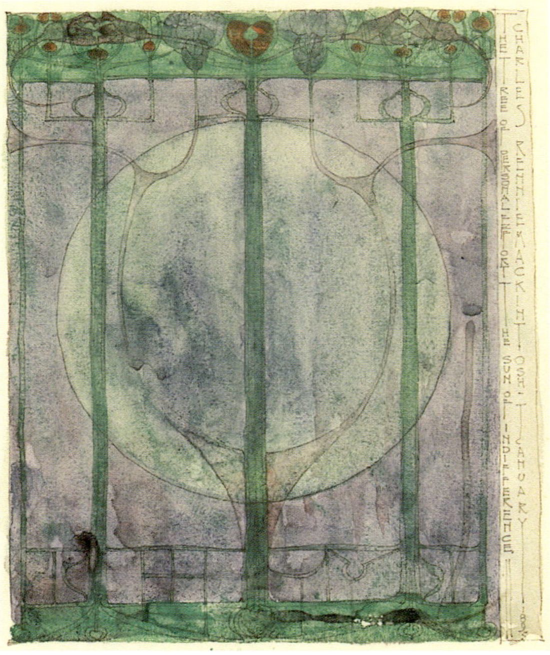

**Two Watercolours, 1895**

In January 1895, CRM paints two extraordinary statements of position; they are almost abstract sketches with powerful, if veiled, symbolism. His own credo: (above) The Tree of Personal Effort – The Sun of Indifference; and his antagonist (below): The Tree of Influence – The Tree of Importance – The Sun of Cowardice.

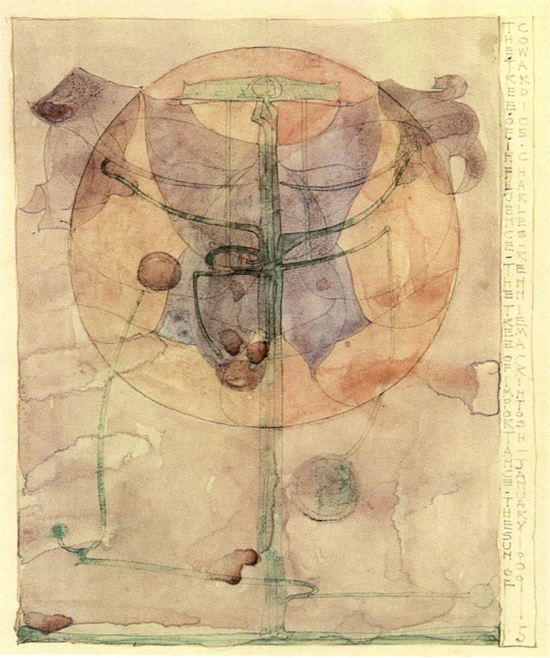

is told in an even more obscure and indirect manner than in painting...'.

Painting is the new means of expression in which, in 1891, McIntosh is encouraged by Bertie McNair to produce his first symbolist work, a watercolour. At that time, said McNair later, 'not a line was drawn without purpose and rarely was a single motif employed that had not some allegorical meaning.'[1] It will be nearly the end of the century before the symbolic world which they have been starting to express in paint, might be possible in architecture. Back in 1889, Jessie Keppie, after her father's death, becomes a day student at the Art School, where she too (perhaps with fraternal assistance) soon wins prizes. In the 1889–90 Design Ornament class, Chas R. McIntosh gains first and Jessie Keppie second prize. By 1892 they are formally, if not publicly, engaged. Now he can see a future secure within a wealthy and respected family, and one intimately bound to a future in his office. Through her, he now meets other day students, while, at the same time Newbery, sensing similarities in their work, suggests McNair and McIntosh exhibit their work with two of that group of affluent, middle-class day students, the Macdonald sisters, Frances and Margaret.

At the 1893 Fine Arts Institute show Frances and Margaret, Jessie and McIntosh all exhibit. Now these four, with a few other women and Herbert McNair, form a close group of friends, exploring a new artistic expression, but also new relations between themselves and their notions of art. It is a pivotal year; and the birth of what becomes known as the Glasgow Style. A new English magazine *The Studio* is founded, suddenly validating new worlds of visual and symbolic possibility. In April it publishes Aubrey Beardsley's illustrations to Wilde's 'Salomé', and the architecture of C.F.A.Voysey; within a few months Carlos Schwabe's illustrations to Zola's 'La Rêve' and paintings by the Dutch artist Toorop.

Art Nouveau, a force set in motion by the Arts & Crafts movement, now sweeps through the world of art and design, allowing painters to design interiors, freeing architects to paint and design objects, letting designers paint and produce buildings. The graphic designer Talwin Morris, for example, began as architectural draughtsman (like his great namesake William a generation before), and in 1893, aged 28, he arrives in Glasgow as chief designer to the Glaswegian publisher Blackie. He also designs curtains, buckles and door handles; his friend McIntosh does wood engravings and jewellery, posters and furniture, and later he will also do book covers for Blackie.

The Macdonald sisters excel at embroidery and metalwork. McNair is an accomplished graphic artist and radical furniture designer. It is a wonderful moment to be young and believe you could do anything.

When architects Keppie, McIntosh and McNair work on competition drawings at the Keppie's Ayrshire home during the week, relief comes at the weekend with the arrival from Glasgow of a group of Art School friends. Jessie, modest and homely, is there as family; there are the Raeburn sisters, Catherine (sister of the more famous D.Y.) Cameron and Janet Aitken; and there are the Macdonald sisters, Margaret tall, stately, with commanding charm – and majestic auburn hair which she washes in distilled water; Frances, seven years younger, petite, vivacious and pretty. McIntosh is handsome, popular, energetic, kind, generous, talkative; he is also stubborn to the point of arrogance; proud and at times cut off; he is prone to tantrums and violent outbursts of rage. The visitors stay near the Keppies in two houses at Dunure, north of Culzean. They call it 'the Roaring Camp'. They call themselves 'The Immortals', perhaps in mocking irony at the power of such a fleeting moment.

Their competing models of the artist are, on the one hand, one whose only duty is to personal individuality – coming from the Aesthetic Movement, Japan, Whistler; and, on the other hand, one with a social role coming from the Arts & Crafts, the Pre-Raphaelites.

While his friends remain in the world of imagery, McIntosh, through the essentially social art of architecture, effects a reconciliation of these opposite forces.

In 1893 Chas R. McIntosh reinvents himself. Now he can really be an artist. Aged 25, as Charles Rennie Mackintosh he emerges from the Sauchiehall Street studio of his friend, Craig Annan. He has sat for his portrait. He had put on a pale tweed jacket and a loose-collared white shirt. A wonderfully long, green Liberty scarf is loosely knotted in a large bow – in what's known as *style libre* – as a tie round his neck. That day, Annan and Mackintosh produce a series of portraits of The Young Man as an Artist. He looks out of the picture into the future, moustache perfectly curled, slightly droopy left eye, and tiny kiss-curl on his forehead. To his friends Charlie, the architectural draughtsman has become Toshie, the art worker.

Now, as their synergy spins the four Macs upwards, the art work of those around them – like the Raeburns or Jessie Keppie – are forced centrifugally to the periphery and to banality. As

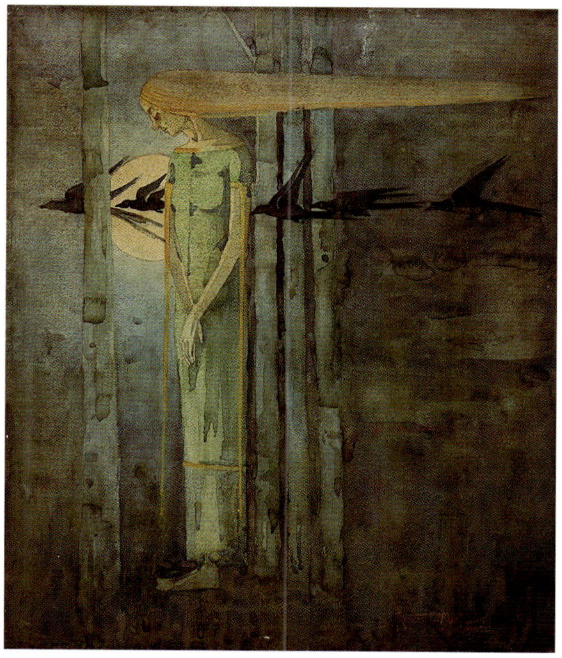

**Ill Omen or Girl in the East Wind with Ravens Passing the Moon, Frances Macdonald, 1893**

Frances' watercolour was painted up to two years before CRM's choice of the lonely and valiant personal effort against that of influential importance and spiritual death, the art worker against the businessman architect (in the images opposite). Frances' image of the unhappy woman suffering the chill winds of misfortune is virtually without precedent. It may allude to CRM's other tug-o'-war, and it has been suggested that the three trees behind the girl represent McNair and the Macdonald sisters, signalling to the fourth, beyond the girl, to join them.

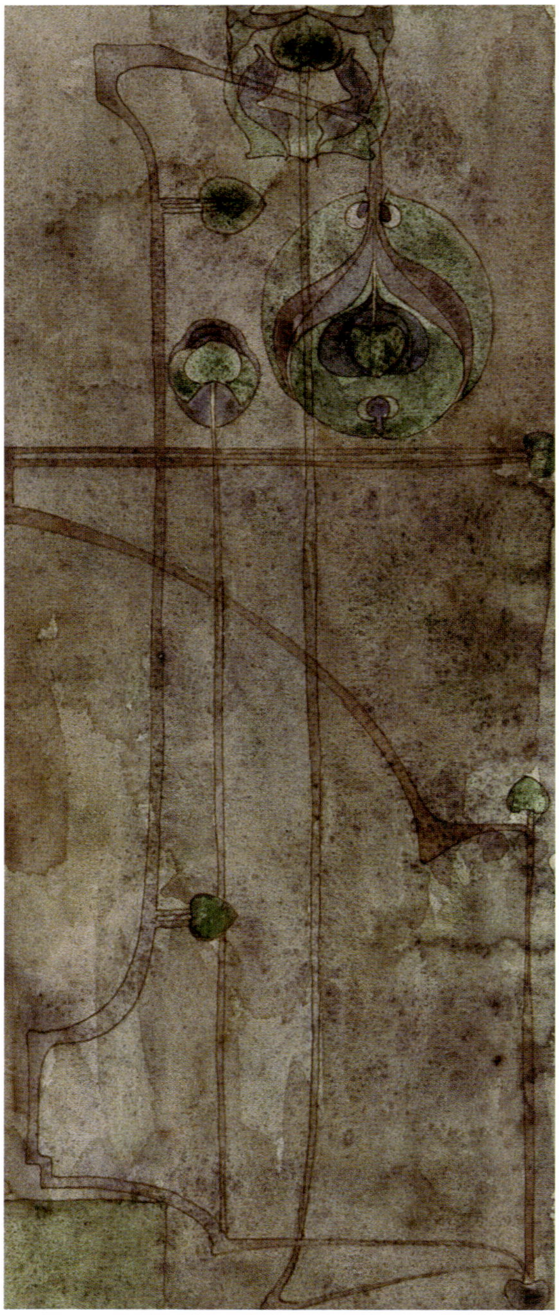

**Stylised Plant Form**

One of CRM's most abstracted plant sketches, and therefore closest to Art Nouveau in form, if not in the colour and atmosphere which increase its sense of mystery. This is circulated among his friends in the November 1894 issue of *The Magazine*.

1893 becomes 1894, Mackintosh increasingly realises that he is torn between Jessie and Margaret. He will have to make choices; and he cannot bear to do so.[2] This primal struggle for his soul could have been occurring even without these women; it is between safe respectability, and abandonment to art. But it is Margaret, strong-willed and three years his senior, who is forcing him to choose. Her much younger sister Frances may be more inspired, more imaginative an artist, but Margaret is the more assured, with the driving commitment to her art. And to her destiny with Toshie. Will he join her, become truly himself alongside her, and master of his own destiny? Or will he remain victim of circumstance? He must commit to the ideal of love, to the genuinely new art.

The force is difficult to resist. Also, it is almost impossible to hear this theme sounding less triumphalist, even played in a more minor key, allowing other resonances to be heard. Is she not goading him to take a path which inevitably, in the end, will cut him off from the real world where architectural practice demands down-to-earth compromise and realism? Will it not, in fact, throw him even more surely, in the end, on the mercy of circumstance? Margaret's rejection of the materialist for the timeless values of art, is almost a religious vocation. And a high ground from which Keppie's commercial office must always be under attack, and from whose values those of Mackintosh must be valiantly defended.

The world of The Immortals is preserved in a few snaps taken at Dunure, and in a series of scrapbooks kept by Agnes Raeburn. She presents herself as editor of their hand-made Magazine, and it appears four times between 1894 and 1896. It contains an extraordinary mixture of extreme naiveté and fascinating comment; of genuinely important and utterly trivial imagery. And its mix of contributors is as wide, from naive student to the photographer J. Craig Annan and Irish painter Jack Yates. With a jolt we realise these are not teenage students, this scrapbook is the work of graduates, with their own studios; Margaret is 30. But to the young architect McIntosh who, after a decade in dour practice, is trying his hand elsewhere, it offers a different platform. 'You must not be content to be cabbages!' suggests his painting of them in an orchard, artfully random with its gently ironic explanation. This is the only forum for his symbolic work for, unlike his colleagues, he never publishes such paintings. He might even be taken aback to know that, over a century later, we look at them; as a lens through which to see him, and even for themselves.

Meanwhile, to the call of a higher vocation in Art, which seems to bound from Margaret's lips, Mackintosh is sold. It is no small thing to break with the boss's sister and all that this might entail for his career. But the engagement to Jessie is, with pain and difficulty, abandoned. As she is left behind, the Glasgow Style, born in 1893, now focuses on The Four who, by the mid 1890s, are independent of the Art School. McNair has left Keppie's (and architecture) to open his own design studio. The Macdonald sisters have theirs, and Mackintosh too opens a studio, near Honeyman & Keppie's office, where he retreats to design furniture or graphics, where his friends meet to talk and argue and drink. Though reserved with strangers, Toshie is immensely popular with young architects and students, talking avidly and with great confidence. And his work output is phenomenal. In 1898–9, he is beating metal, designing posters, painting, starting work on tea room and other domestic interiors, decoration and furnishings – as well as, at Keppie's, designing fitments and furniture for the School of Art which will open at the end of '99. Almost none of this work is done with The Four.

Now his independent practice begins to appear. Designing furniture and domestic interiors,[3] including a dining room for the publisher of *Dekorative Kunst*, where it is illustrated. The art of The Four, meanwhile, outrages. It is full of explicit sexuality, even (unusually) including that of Mackintosh, whose 'Spring' (1895) shows naked women languorously lying on their backs being awoken by the sun.

These are times of extraordinary, widespread experiment in ideas and images; the years of *The Yellow Book* and of Patrick Geddes's *Evergreen*, each of which in their rather different ways raises sexuality as a topic. These years see a reshuffling of the self[4] across a Europe-wide group; a collective Oedipal revolt and narcissistic search for the new self, a new life orientation in visual form. This critical assault on historicism (clearly seen on the street once the Art School is opened at the end of '99), may indeed try 'to show modern man his true face', as the Viennese architect Otto Wagner put it. But, in Glasgow, their art is also an escape from the grim reality of the industrial centre of the greatest empire of the world, a surrogate religion offering refuge from modern life.

By 1895, John Lane, publisher of the avant-garde *Yellow Book*, has Frances and Margaret's set of Christmas illustrations. They appear with McNair's in 1896, in which year The Four respond to the Arts & Crafts Exhibition Society's request for

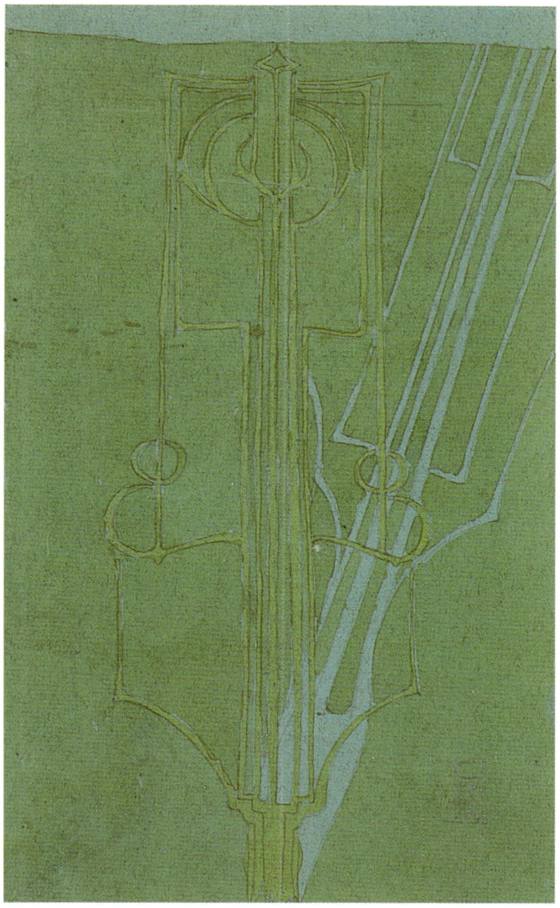

**The Shadow**

Another highly stylised organic shape, with its ghostly, mysterious colourings, not least of the 'negative' shadow whose form doesn't exactly match the right shape. This is stuck in the Spring 1896 final issue of *The Magazine*, a scrap book kept by 'The Immortals' during these few years, produced in four issues, and perhaps in direct echo of the Pre-Raphaelite Brotherhood, whom they greatly admired. 'The Brotherhood' had produced four issues of their own magazine which they had called *The Journal*.

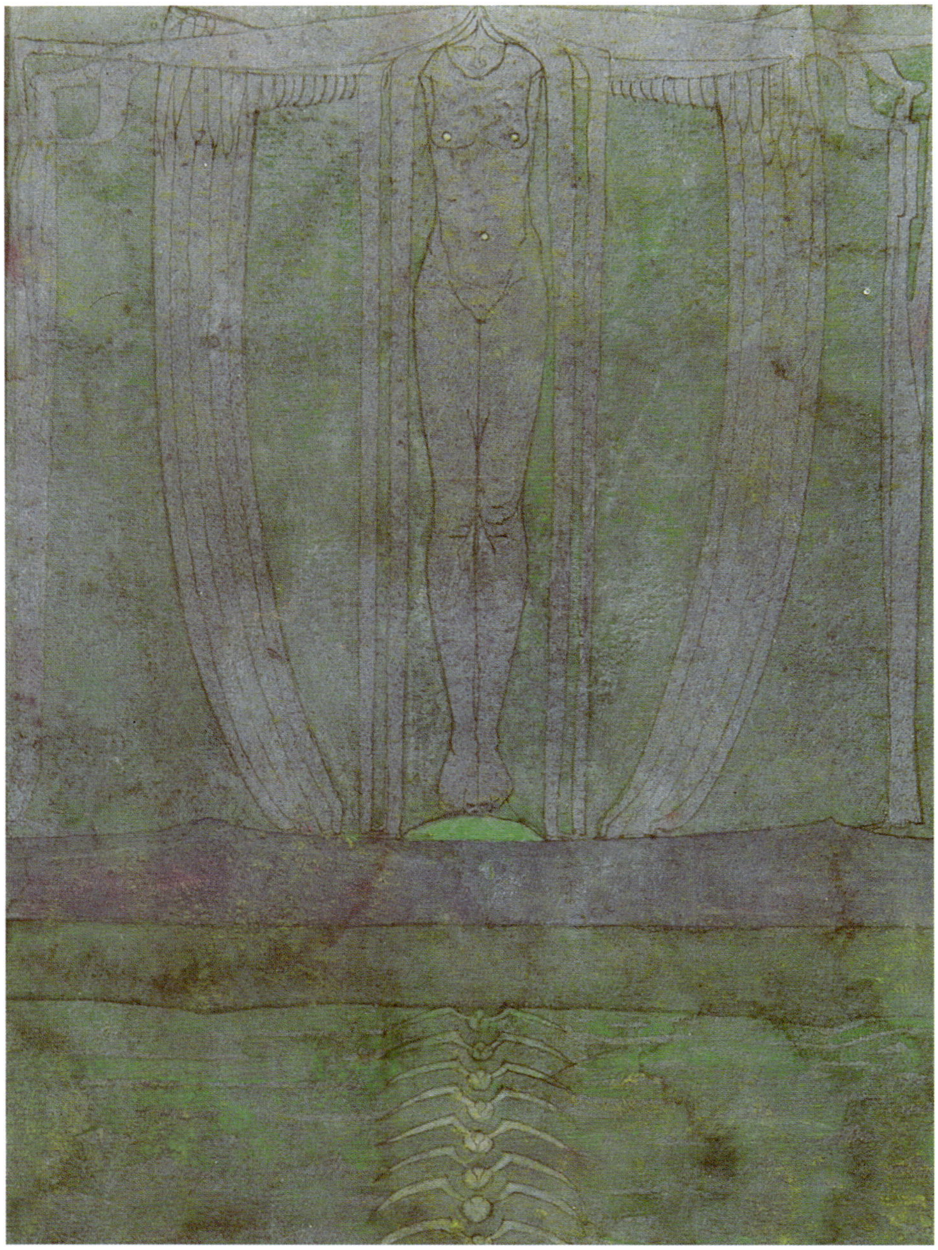

**The Descent of Night**

This small, remarkable and evocative watercolour stuck in *The Magazine* in 1894 suggests CRM's personal tug-o'-war between Jessie and Margaret at this time. Timothy Neat sees it as an image of despair at the moment of its transformation by hope, to lead towards resolution and redemption.

works to exhibit 'in the modern style', with McNair posters, a silver clock case and beaten metal panels by the sisters, and a Mackintosh hall settle and the watercolour 'Part Seen Imagined Part'. The little attention they receive is negative: 'Juvenile enthusiasm,' says *The Magazine of Art*;[5] 'originality-at-any-price is willing to sacrifice all claim to beauty and revel in absolute ugliness if novelty can by that means be attained.' Tragically, it alienated Mackintosh from those English progressives who could have been his best British allies.

The editor of *The Studio*, however, is attracted enough to visit them in Glasgow. It is the start of their brief period of English publicity. They have been derided in Glasgow, particularly for their posters (very few of which remain, to let us see what was so attacked). *The Studio* now defends Mackintoh's strange posters: when a man has something to say and knows how to say it, the conversion of others is usually but a question of time.' The Macdonald sisters have been dismissed as 'the spook school', and their men understandably tarred with the same brush. 'In spite of this nickname,' *The Studio* now says, 'there is a distinct effort to decorate objects with certain harmonious lines and colour which may evolve a style of its own, owing scarce anything to precedent.' But they will not be drawn on the meaning of their imagery. They 'disdain any attempt to set precedences...we have no basis...nor do they advance any theory...'[6]

Foliage, butterflies, birds, sun, bulbs, moon, water – are emblems of the Glasgow designers; then absurdly slender naked women and, centrally, the rose. Some carry particular charges for The Four. Sadness and tears dominate the sisters, with women's tresses, entangling and enveloping everything – a theme linked with Toorop (who exhibits alongside them in

Vienna in 1900) and one which influences Gustav Klimt in Vienna in the few years after that.

They are captivated by the disquieting dream world typified by the Belgian poet Maeterlinck. Maurice Maeterlinck sweeps across Europe – his *Pelléas et Mélisande*, a tale of a long-haired beautiful waif encountered in a forest by Golaud who falls madly for her, marries her, only to find her fall for his brother Pelléas whom he then murders, is an archetypal Macdonald sisters' image. It is set to music immediately by Fauré, Schoenberg, Debussy and, in 1905, Sibelius. The Macs are entranced by the Celtic twilight movement, and ancient myths – which lay bare the instinctual life repressed in the bourgeois city; by the powerful erotic and exotic mix of symbol and imagery. Their magic and mysticism reminds us that Frazer's *The Golden Bough* had just been published; the ambiguous sexual imagery (first clear in Mackintosh's 'Harvest Moon') reminds us that Freud's 1902 *The Interpretation of Dreams* was still just a few years off.

The Glasgow work begins to be seen abroad in 1895 when Newbery arranges an exhibition of work in Belgium, followed by a prominent show at the 1899 Venice Biennale.[7] By then, however, within three years all has changed. After the Oscar Wilde scandal, Beardsley was sacked and *The Yellow Book* abandoned.[8] In Glasgow, *The Magazine* is past. Bertie gets a teaching post in Liverpool, returning north in 1899 only to marry Frances and take her to England. At last, in 1898, Margaret begins to work with Toshie;[9] but real collaboration has to wait for their marriage.

These two young artists setting out in life together in the years up to 1900 make an extraordinary contrast with Edwin Lutyens, the only English architect of similar age and talent. Lutyens' betrothal at that moment to Emily Lytton, involves disclosure of Lutyens' financial statements to elderly agents for his intended's family, and all the old English dynastic manoeuverings. Ned Lutyens has already been offered, by Gertrude Jekyll, a key to social networking, but this alliance offered a fundamentally different career base to the young Englishman from that of Mackintosh with Macdonald.

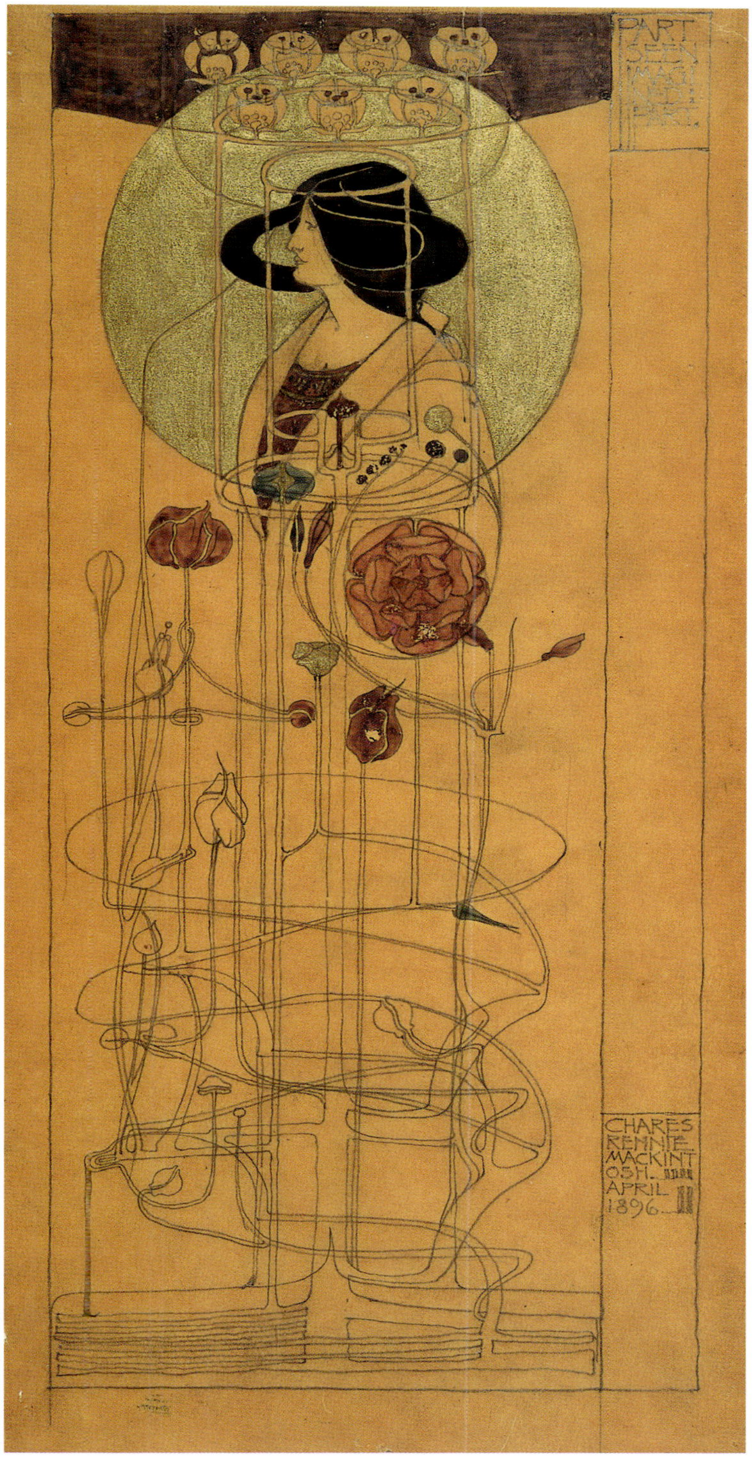


**Part Seen, Imagined Part, 1896**

CRM presents this token to Margaret as a key statement of his commitment to her, seen and imagined, four years before their marriage. It contains more layers than meet the eye, with the plant's femininity only revealed within in the light of the masculine sun. She treasures this gift all her life.

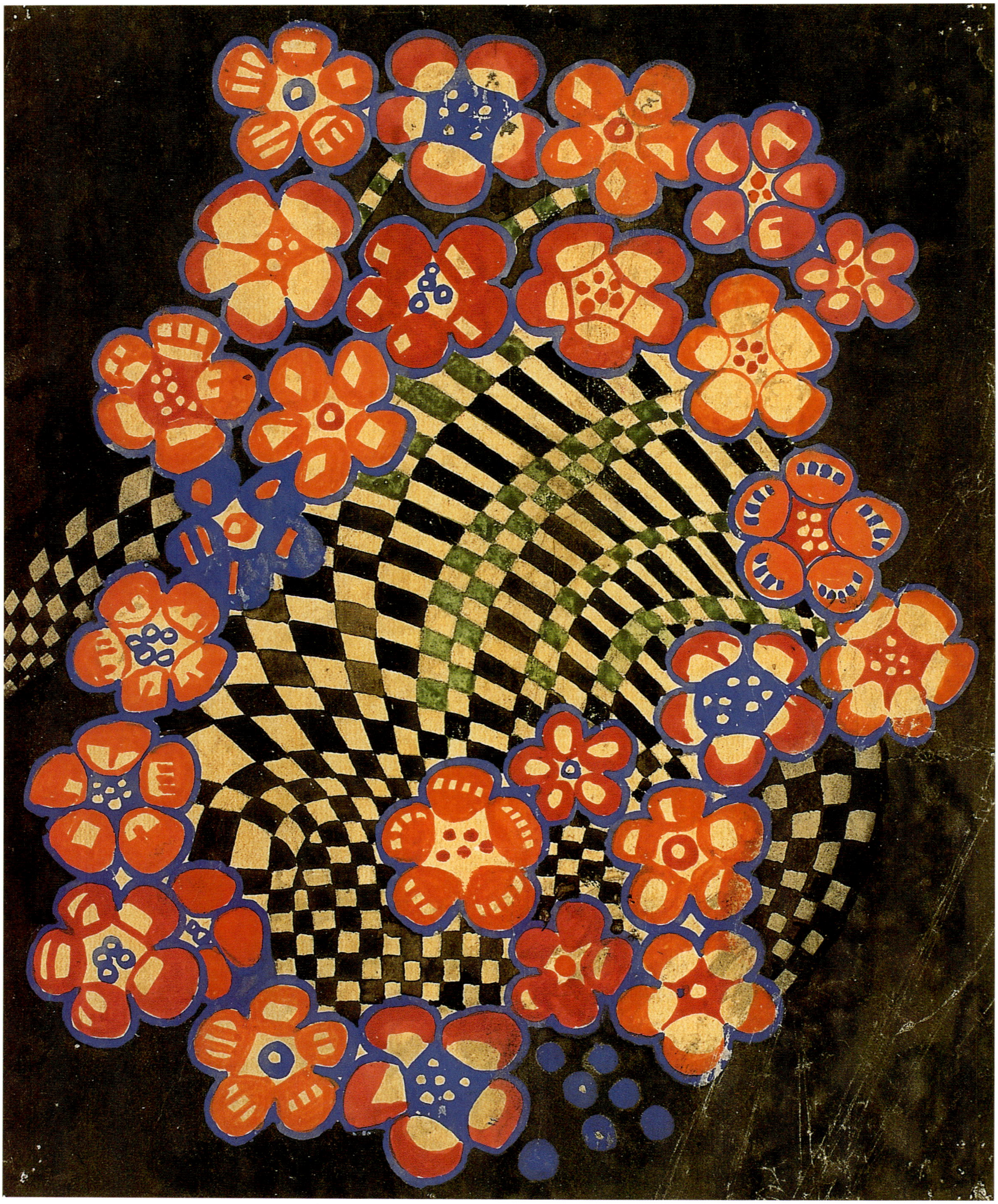

# THE DESIGNER AT WORK

Who can say how the architect designs? 'The architect ...depends very greatly for his success upon a kind of instinct, a synthesis, or integration of myriads of details and circumstances of which he cannot be directly very conscious: but the appreciation of which makes the master in every profession.'[1] It is easier perhaps, Mackintosh adds, to say what the architect should be conscious *not* to do: not rely on rules of proportion or on mimicking the past. 'You cannot learn to walk without tumbles and knocks and bruises, but you will never learn to walk so long as there are props. The props of art are: on the one hand, the slavish imitation of old work (no matter what date or from what country); and, on the other hand, the absurd and false idea that there can be any living emotion expressed in work scientifically proportioned according to ancient principles.'

So copying existing architecture is derided by the architect who clearly lifts complete elements from other buildings in the most shameless and playful manner. And proportioning systems are derided by the architect whose subtle geometries attracted an abstruse 1990s research paper purporting to decipher them.[2] There is no doubt he is fascinated by composition, by visual balance and dynamic symmetries. Naturally, like all architects, he has learned rule-of-thumb compositional methods – using squares and rectangles based on their diagonals, and golden section[3], which biologists like Patrick Geddes and D'Arcy Thomson on the east coast, are relating to growth and form in nature. It is easy to read too much into his two-dimensional pattern-making; but it is as easy to read too little. The stencil in the porch at the Hill House is a clear sign as we enter: a chequerboard of 13 by 13 squares, it is divided 5:8 by the ghostly negative shape of a budding, tulip-like plant. (5:8:13 are in the Fibonacci series which tends towards golden section.)

His classical education, being in the structure of his language, is never a conscious influence, yet it remains. The pairs of caryatids, statuesque women stencilled on the Buchanan Street tea room walls, reveal their sexiness through being lightly clothed rather than nude – which is exactly how the ancient Greeks felt about the female body, part seen part imagined. In the frieze round the Hill House hall, the swirling forms of the highly expressive 'metopes' break out of their square frame, as did the ancient Greek originals in three

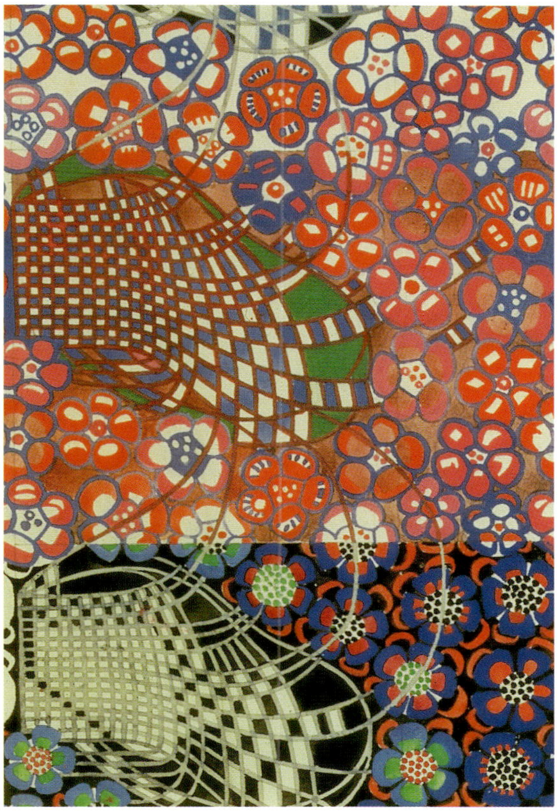

**Blue and Pink Tobacco Flowers**

These related studies (opposite and above) show the endless ability of the fertile design mind to borrow, transform and develop.CRM never stops inventing, drawings for textile design (as above) can change colourways and indeed the design itself develop as his hand works its way across the paper, and then later become a painting (opposite). That design above itself develops from a drawing which he traced (and reversed) directly from the hair of the major figure in MMM's painting on p.61; which itself derives from her earlier version on p.60.

**Tobacco Flower (opposite)**

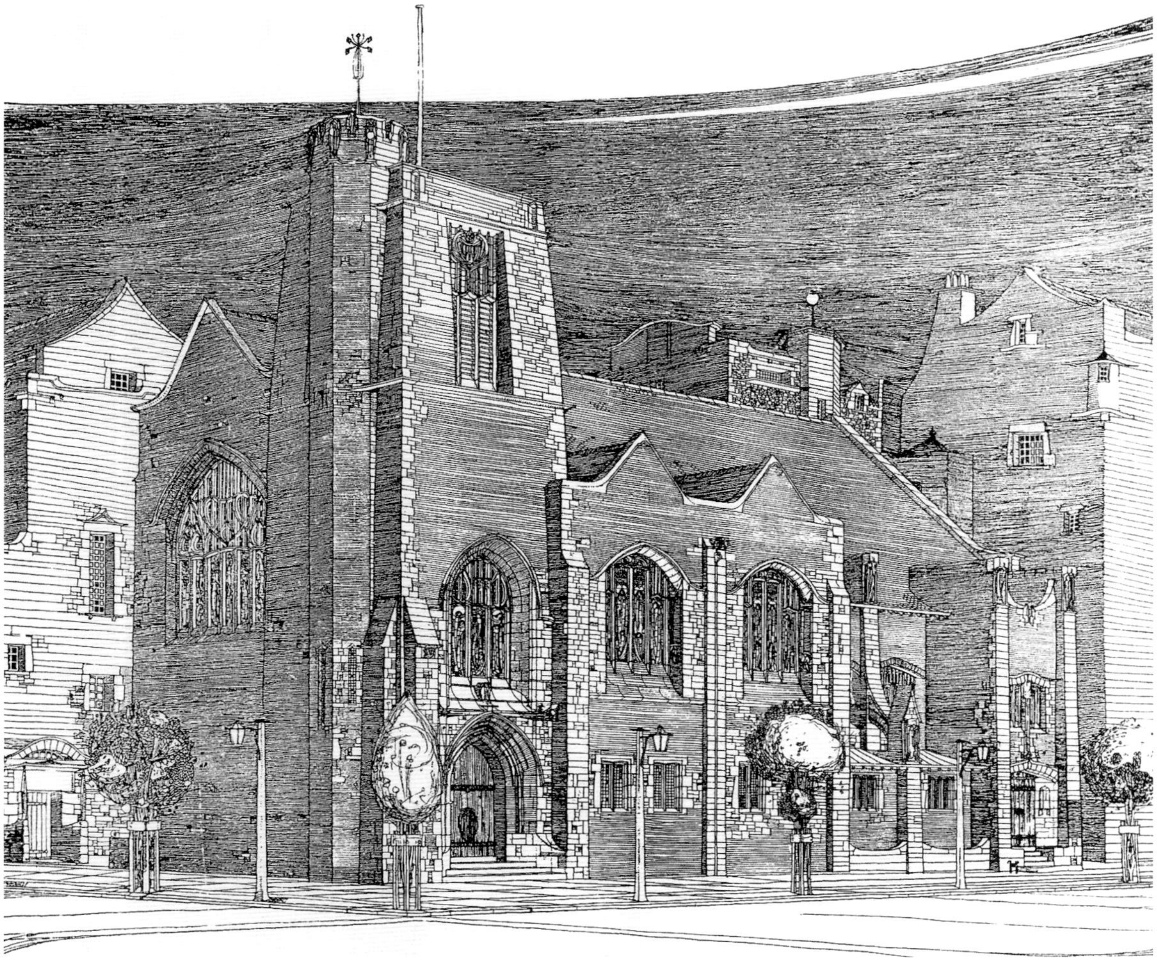

dimensions, separated by their trisected 'triglyphs'.

He uses squares and cubes continually as compositional devices, from the smallest decoration to the precise forming of an interior space, and to the massing of large-scale architectural elements. A repeated motif is of nine squares in a square, or that built out into a cube – as at the Hill House in the stair light or the occasional table in the drawing-room bay, or, quite differently, in its garden layout. He enjoys playing with asymmetry where one might expect symmetry. The church, for example, is an extraordinary essay in not-quite symmetries (although its plan is precisely double square, from one end gable to the other, excluding the wonderfully ambiguous side ambulatory); quite apart from the one great southern side gallery, there are the off-central aisle and the northern side windows, one being a four-arch opening, the other a three. Externally, asymmetries always build into very tightly controlled compositions – as a walk around the Hill House shows most clearly.

But this dynamic balance is seen at its most subtle in his urban facade, the north front of the Art School. Here four- and five-bay windows are juxtaposed in a situation where that is not immediately obvious – for it is impossible to get a straight-on view. Even careful observers miss it: Sandy MacGibbon, perspectivist for Honeyman & Keppie, who later became professor of architecture in this actual building, shows in a published drawing all the studio windows equally sized and spaced.[4] An oft-quoted thesis describes it like this: 'at first sight it appears perfectly symmetrical, then the asymmetry of the

**Perspective drawing of Queen's Cross Church, Glasgow**

In his designs of a century ago, CRM plays with images of forms. For example, at the Hill House he inverts the form of Crathes Castle and here he inverts the church tower he drew in Somerset. He repeatedly works with a few key devices – the rose, the bird, the tree – and he abstracts them, developing forms further and further: we see the iron knots on the Art School window supports, the cut discs sticking up from the bunched railings, while the vestigial 'willow' image in the tea room's semicircular order desk has become virtually abstract.

entrance block becomes evident, and after that one realises that the entrance itself is not exactly central, this game continues...'[5] In fact (as seen on p. 139), there is a block of 3, five-bay, widely spaced windows and a block of 4 more closely spaced ones – 2 of them five-bay and 2 four-bay. These elements are separated by the central block of the facade. The railings on the street edge, in a regular beat against that syncopated one, lay yet another grid across the image. Within the central element itself, bay windows are to the left and doors to the right; with the tower, little studio window and chimney each offset higher up, and only a first-floor balcony symmetrically binding the block together. Yet the main entrance, offset in that central composition is in fact central to the complete building: the symbolic timber column between the two little doors is at the exact centre of the facade.

This is highly significant, but wonderfully veiled; never explicit. To the inattentive glance, this facade simply follows the 'modern' (i.e. from Pugin and Morris, and thence via Pevsner to mainstream twentieth-century ideas) principle of functional appropriateness: simple large north-facing studio windows. As ever, Mackintosh comforts the inattentive first glance, but offers much more to those who see what they are looking at.

The architect, like a composer scoring a long symphony for a large orchestra, must hold both a clear sense of the overall structure and shape and have the ability to mould it lightly and gently with myriad detail sounds, all building together to the overall effect. In between these scales – the overall geometry and plan and the articulation of decorative details – Mackintosh uses compositional elements with wonderful freedom. Forms flitting through his memory are recalled, plucked from his notebooks, collaged. He understands exactly 'how to crib'.[6] The immature artist imitates, the mature artist steals.

The two very distinguishing characters of vital imitation are its frankness and its audacity: its frankness is especially singular; there is never any effort to conceal the degree of the sources of its borrowing. There is a sense of power capable of transforming and renewing whatever it adopts; and too conscious, too exalted, to fear the accusation of plagiarism – too certain that it can prove, and has proved, its independence. These sentences are Ruskin's, Mackintosh surely knew them, and they are most apposite.[7]

As he copies and adjusts, it is easy to show some sources, though others are less obvious. In 'Harvest Moon' (p.48) he

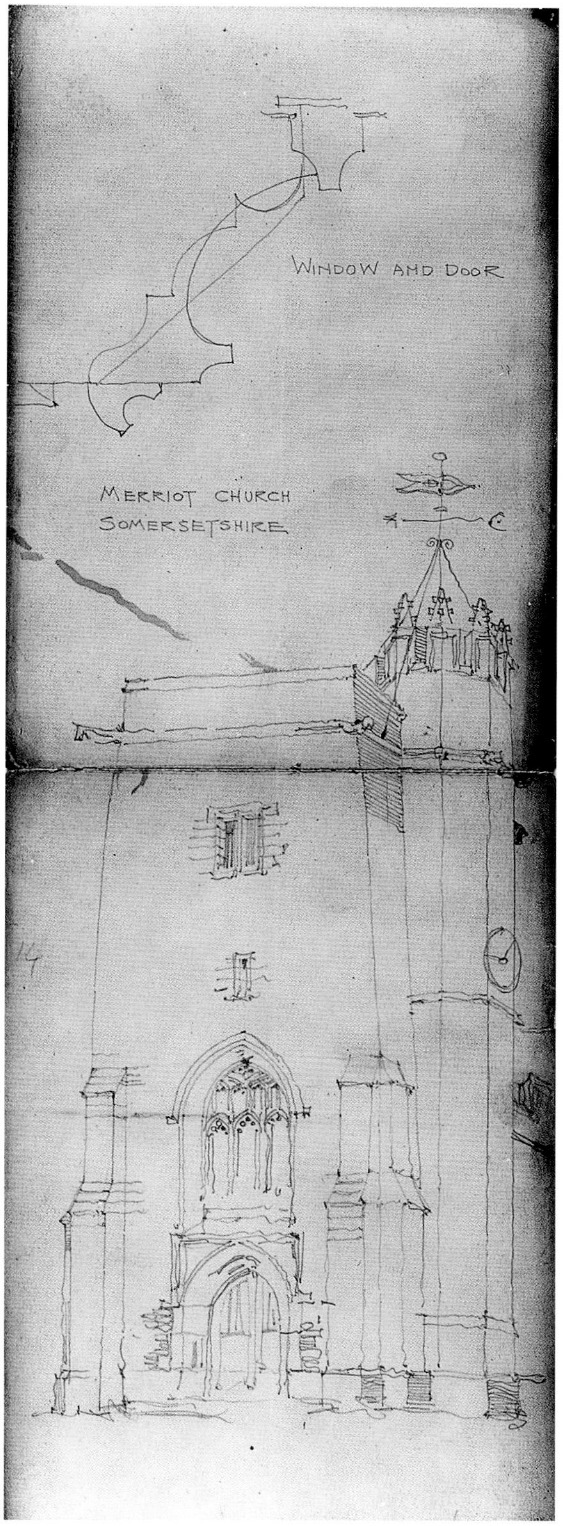


**Merriot Church, Somerset**

He mimics, lifts and changes. It is easy to show some sources like this one in his sketchbook.

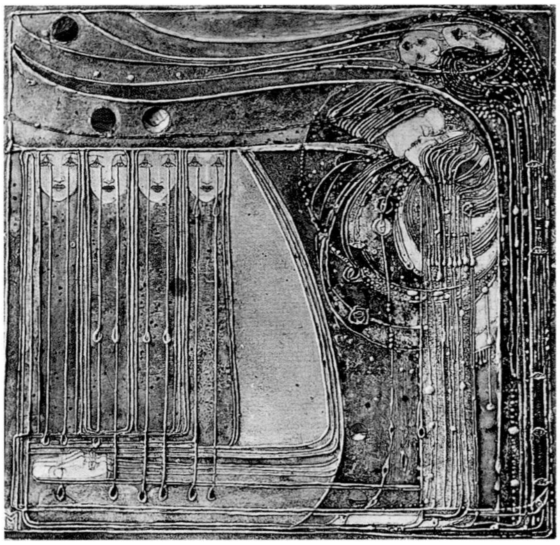

**The Opera of the Sea, MMM, 1901-3**

These small square gesso panels by Margaret Macdonald Mackintosh are from 1901-3; based on Maeterlinck, inserted in the piano CRM designed for Wärndorfer's music room in Vienna and obviously influential on Gustav Klimt's 'Watersnakes II'. Opposite, its development by MMM 15 years later into a large panel in oil, tempera and paper colle intended for The Dugout tea room in Sauchiehall Street.

**The Opera of the Winds, MMM, 1901-3**

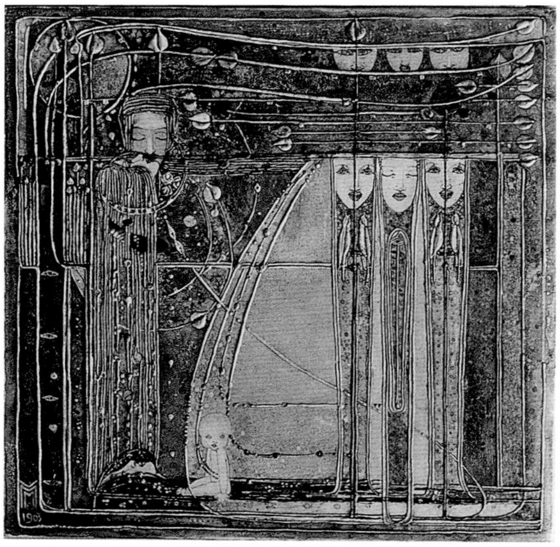

lifts a nude from Alexandre Cabanel's well-known 'Birth of Venus' (1863), letting it float over much more ambiguous sexual imagery below. But does he consciously refer to The Palace of Huntly in his facades for the newspaper buildings? Does he consciously remember the old Suruga Inn in Japan in the galleries at the church?

Certainly as architect he is not interested in novelty in plan, any more than in claiming his architectural ideas as his own. The plans are always conventional, and the houses derived almost as directly from Lethaby as are his lecture notes.[8] Watching how he creatively adjusts images suggests that this ability to play with a range of free associations, untied by logic and order, is perhaps a creative attribute also linked with dyslexia. What we see is his transformational sensibility, all part of his journey of discovery, which in the Glasgow years can be clearly traced. Thereafter, as his world closes in around, it seems largely to vanish.

His own best designs are often worked on further: look at two beautiful music-room tables. The ten-legged one he designs for Wärndorfer[9] and the eight-legged one for Hous'hill;[10] and another pair, the Hill House table which Billcliffe sees as less elegant or subtle than the white version[11] in his own house which seems to me very different and flat. Looking at Mackintosh's clock with domino dots from 1917 we see the thought process in action within one drawing (p.37). As his hand draws its way round the face, he is also developing the design. Each side is suggested differently, starting at the top, until the fourth side becomes the final choice, and almost what is constructed, for the face refines yet more and the hands are redesigned. Here his compulsive thrust towards individuality links with the Arts & Crafts respect for the handicraft skill itself. If an element has to be crafted more than once, to repeat it identically turns the carver into a slave.

He uses stencilling on walls as it is economic and relies on good design rather than costly materials, but also it allows for variation as it proceeds. In Buchanan Street Tea Rooms 'these same trees...are not absolute replicas. Some half dozen varieties lend interest to the detail and yet conform to the symmetry which a repeated pattern demands.'[12] With their sophisticated mix of hand paint and stencil, Guthrie & Wells, the fit-out contractors, must be decorating these walls with the designer very close by. What information passed between him and craftsmen is inevitably largely transitory. He is always there, on the site, straddling the difficult line between using the

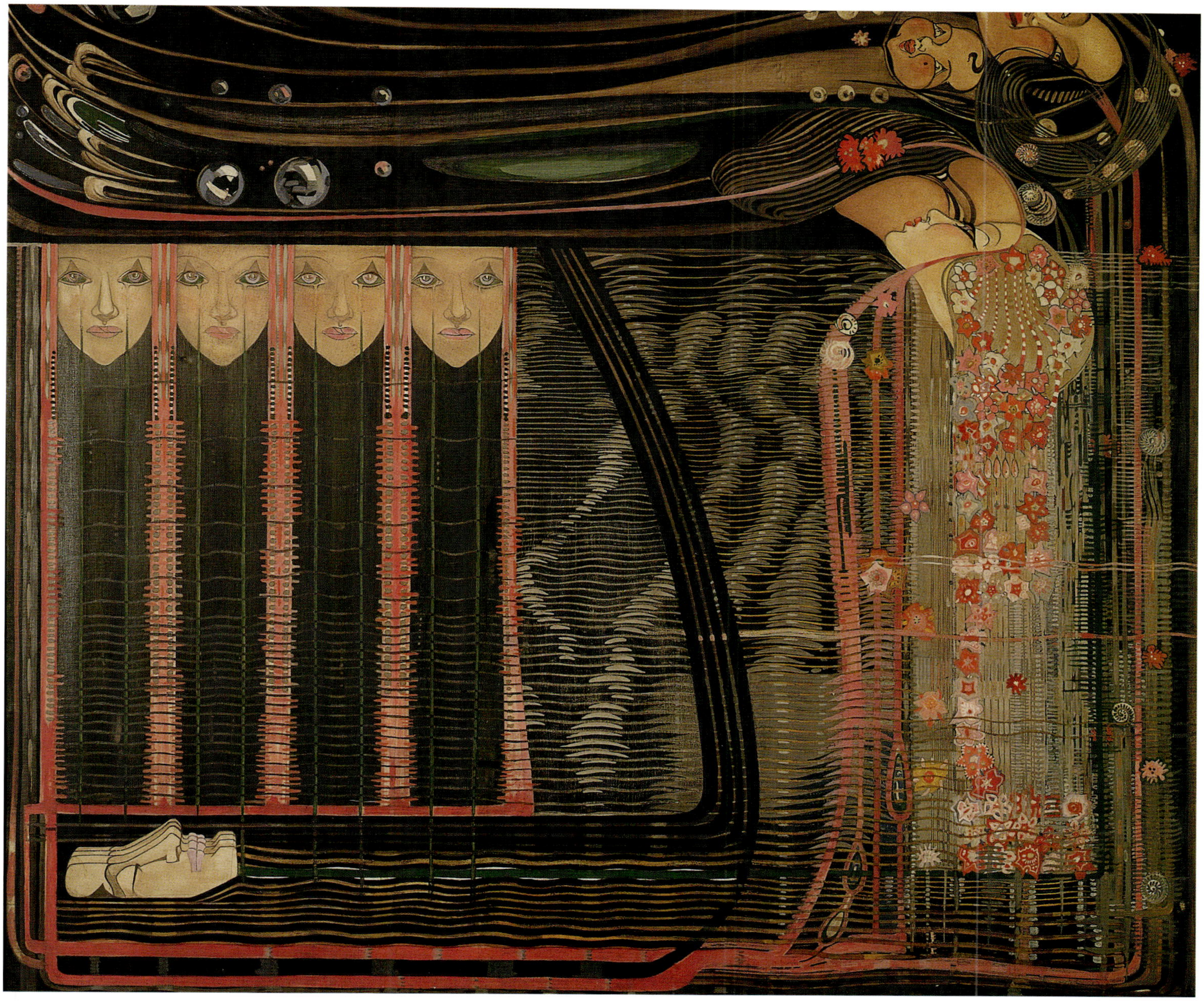

craftsman as his hands, and letting the craftsman work with his own mind. There are no full-size working drawings of chairs or fitments, like those drawings over a metre square which his French contemporary Hector Guimard produces. Mackintosh in his early years becomes skilled in various crafts, and clearly he makes: the full-size plaster maquette for the doorhead sculpture at the Art School he formed in the office. Everything can be seen as a prototype, something which can be played with more, developed further.

Seeing these design processes, and their joyous abundance of invention, engages us. It reminds us of all our own inherent creative imaginations, how we bring them to bear on the present, and our imaginative projections into the future.

**The Opera of The Sea, MMM, 1916-17**

In his constantly developing ideas, CRM traces the hair of this central figure, using it reversed, in his own watercolour 'Pink Tobacco Flower'. This inventiveness was not just to choose the 'best'. In the fabric design 'Rose Teardrops' each of the 20 roses is intentionally different. He loved to do this – in the later work at the Art School, the 'ionic' capitals in the Board Room are each different, as are the pendant panels round the library gallery.

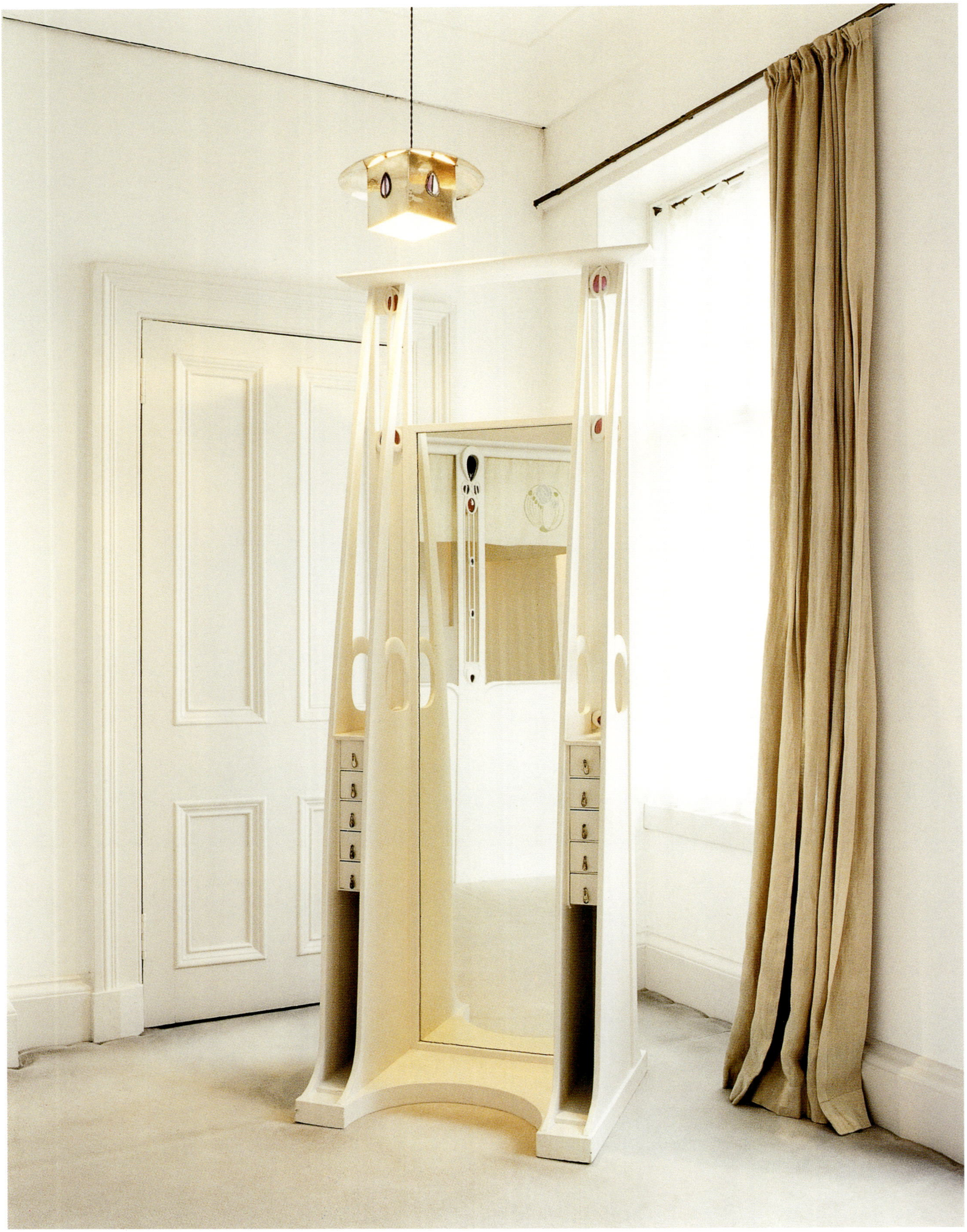

# ONLY DREAMS ARE TRUE

1900. New century, and the tug-o'-war between the worlds of art and architecture finally resolves. Architecture had won its clear path: with the School of Art (well, half of it) completed and in use just before the year began. Art also had its clear path: joined with Margaret Macdonald and the world of the spirit. A few years ago, the architect and artist in Mackintosh, polarised as black and white, seemed almost like two parallel lives within a split personality. Finally, they no longer occupy separated worlds; no longer parallel opposites of day and night, of darkness and brightness, masculinity and femininity. Now, as the integrated personality is reflected in the flat which makes their own marriage concrete, so Mackintosh integrates his different talents into his great works in the years after the turn of the century. Now the two have come together, as two overlapping circles, forming this traditional symbol of marriage. A cadence; but sounding more like the haunting final cadence of Debussy than an upbeat Mozartian finale.

The Art School's strength was in its architectonic qualities: its form, space and structure; it is tough, hard and rugged; much of it is dark. But its lines of development fade in these years when Mackintosh's architectonics and spatial skills contract, come indoors, and are used within the more intimate soft and lighter domestic world the two now openly share. To enter their own drawing room, Desmond Chapman-Huston says, 'is to realize very vividly that only dreams are true.'[1]

After years as a spiritual couple, Margaret Macdonald and Charles Rennie Mackintosh are quietly married on 22 August 1900; she is nearly 36, he is 32. Now they create half-a-dozen interiors quite unlike anything else in the world. Early in the year they work together on the white Ladies' Dining Room for the Ingram Street tea rooms, and on their own flat. After their wedding they prepare work for the Vienna Secessionist exhibition. The following year they enter the Art Lover's House competition and in 1902 design a music room in Vienna. There is then The Hill House and in 1903 the final and supreme tea rooms, The Willow. As they exhibit fragments around Europe, apart from the shells of Hill House and (the already designed) Windyhill, all their work is in carving out interior spaces and layering them with surfaces and objects.

With the attention to detail which this approach demands (and there were other projects too, which I've not mentioned),

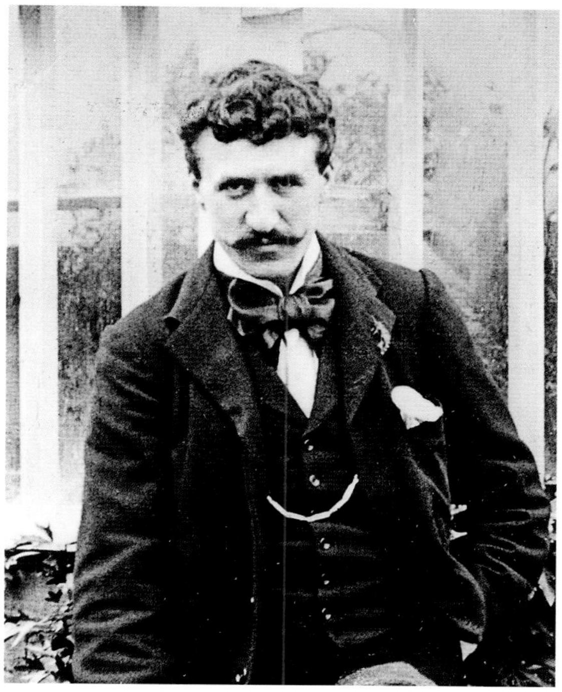

CRM (above) and MMM (below) 1900

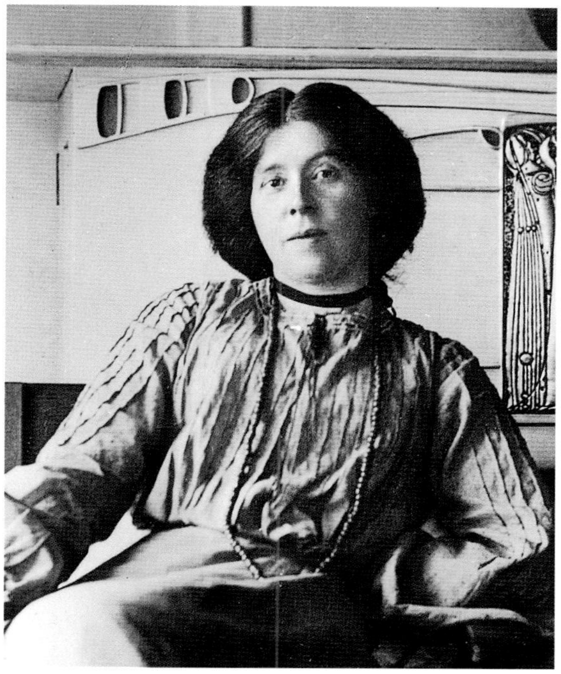

Mirror, The Mackintosh House (opposite)

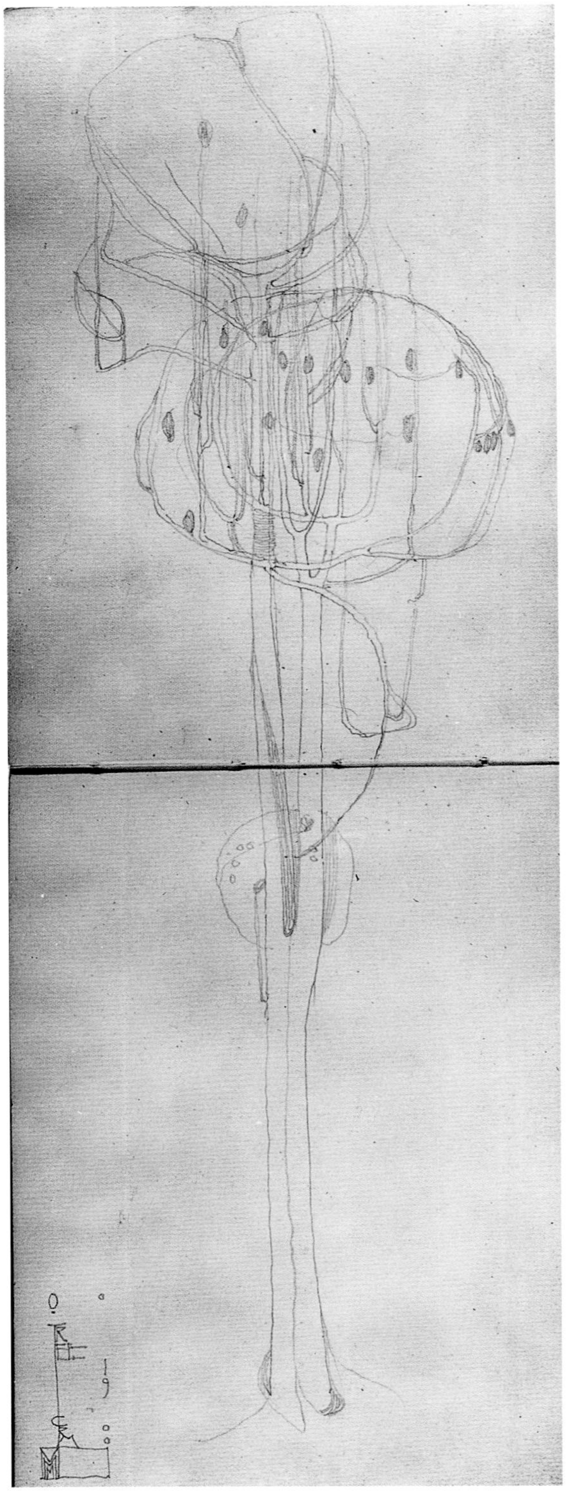

**O Tree, Holy Island, 1900**

The only known drawing from their honeymoon and the first to be signed with both their initials, as becomes his practice. Affirming their union, a stylised rowan sapling, with double trunk, rises to a great vitality of overlapping swirls.

it is a punishing schedule. When Mackintosh takes a brief break, sailing to Orkney in May 1903, Margaret tells a friend of her hope that he will get 'the thorough rest...he really needs.'[2]

Now the artistic interior is developed as the supreme work of spatial art. Mackintosh abandons painting entirely in 1900: his symbolist art is now entirely seen in three-dimensional enclosures and their contained objects, in the completely unified spatial work of art – the *gesamtkunstwerk*, which, according to Muthesius, he alone in Britain is able fully to realise. 'The beginning and end of Art is...to make dreamers, and to stimulate our life of dreams,' (Chapman-Huston). Certainly the rarefied atmosphere is recognised by visitors to their own flat. With its pristine qualities, pure shapes and pale surfaces it appears almost as a shrine.[3] Like minimalists of the 1990s, the flower arrangement had to be just so, the pile of magazines to align with the table edge.

The uncluttered simplicity of these interior spaces is not utterly novel. There was the heightened artistic refinement of Godwin's white interior for Oscar Wilde, there was William Morris's call for 'honest whitewash'. Both aesthetic nudity and the Arts & Crafts virtuousness were equally shocking to the Victorians for whom white was disturbingly naked, and kept for utilities, privies, service rooms and cow sheds.

In 1899 the Viennese called for 'walls white and gleaming, holy and chaste'.[4] No wonder they took to the Mackintoshes when they arrived. For they did it.

Their own collaboration, which really develops on their marriage, is simply that he used her skill as detail decorative artist within his larger designs for items of furniture or ensembles of interior surfaces and spaces.

Only at Ingram Street, in the days just before their wedding, working on the first and largest gesso panels together, are they actually playing a duet. 'Just now, we are working on two large panels for the frieze...Miss Margaret Macdonald is doing one and I am doing the other. We are working on them together and that makes the work very pleasant.'[5] In Vienna in the autumn, where these panels are part of their exhibit, the applause for their duet offers a second honeymoon. Other than with panels for the Viennese music room, they never repeat it. Margaret's work is seen as occasional crafted touches of colour adding sparkle to his ensemble, or else, more frequently, it is an artwork within the Mackintosh frame. Always very carefully considered, as a particular accent or focus. Her input is always limited in quantity and in size – making it all the more

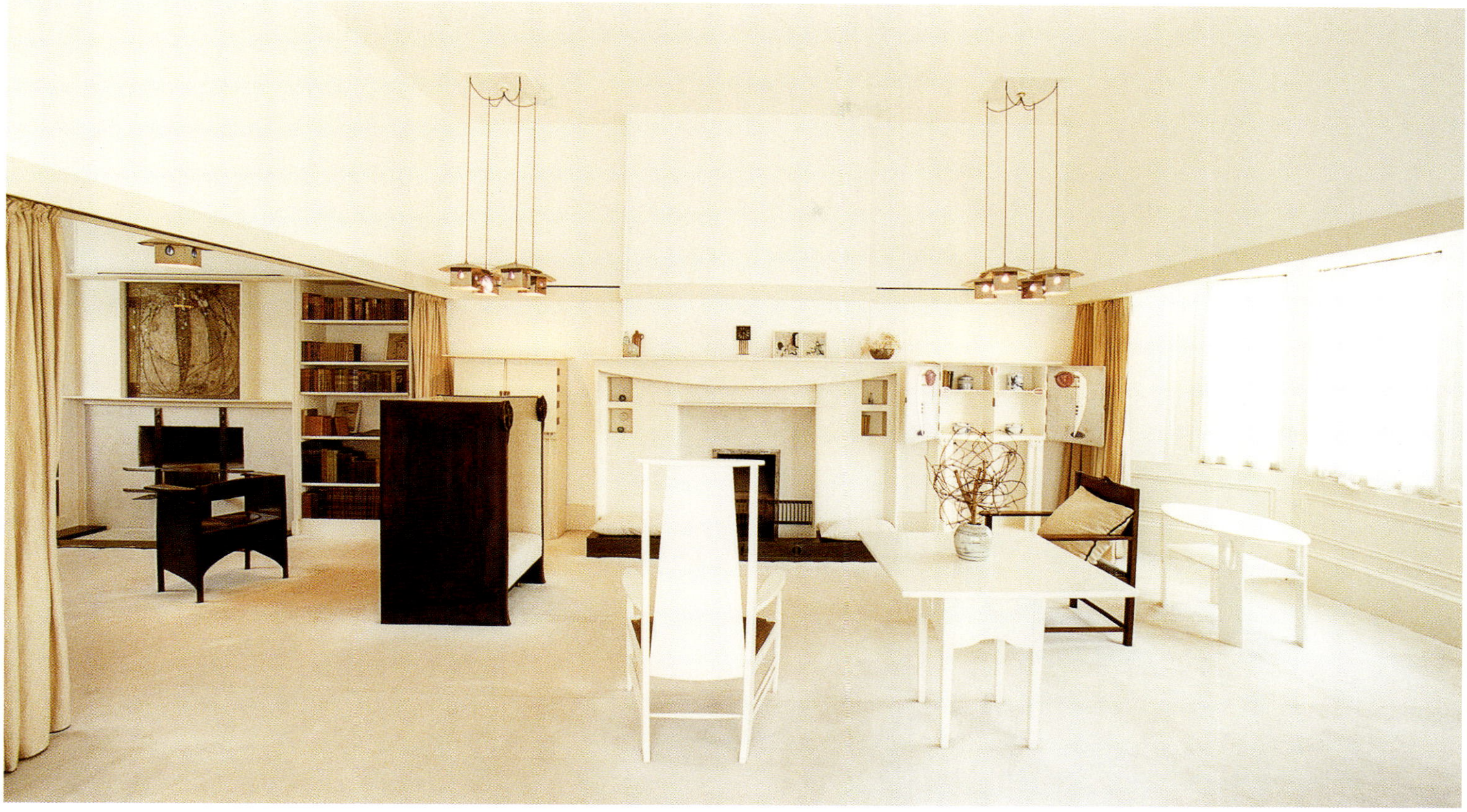

telling; a decorative gesso panel inlaid in a piano-case or a beaten metal panel on a wardrobe; a stencilled soft furnishing or a fabric addition like the wonderful bright anti-macassars for the Hill House chair backs. It is very much in the Glasgow Style aesthetic (not just that of the Macs) to find simple large-scale forms offset by a key detail: the desk of flat planes with tiny silvered brass drop handles, the rectilinear bookcase with one gently curving line of grey and pink leaded glass. At the Hill House Margaret is remembered making the gesso above the drawing room fireplace on site. 'She used a piping bag, like you were icing a cake,' says Agnes Blackie, a little girl watching, 'and then stuck things onto the plaster. It was very beautiful.'

This, of course, tends to reinforce the stereotype of 'male equals architecture': severe order and rectilinearity, overall form, the big picture, the object; yes, the phallus. And that of 'female equals interior': enclosure, the containing surfaces, softer, flowing, concealing and elaborating, ornamenting; yes, the womb. Seen in the traditional frame (Victorian as much as modern) where architecture is for the boys, decoration for the girls, it is almost impossible simply to appreciate the richly designed, beautifully layered, and highly structured Mackintosh interiors.

The male modernist critics accepted that simple polarity – and

**Drawing Room,
The Mackintosh House,
Reconstructed in the Hunterian Art Gallery, University of Glasgow**

'It is far away in that mist encircled grim city of the north which is filled with echoes of the terrible screech of the utilitarian, and haunted by the hideous eyes of thousands who make their God of gold. Vulgar ideals, and the triumph of the obvious, are characteristic of the lives of the greater proportion of its population; and yet, in the midst of so much that is incongruous and debasing, we find a little white home, full of quaint and beautiful things, with a big white studio empty of everything but the Artist's jesso panels, all prepared and made beautiful for her by her artist husband, in order that her genius may have a fitting home, and her exquisite, quiet art congenial and fitting surroundings.'
Desmond Chapman-Huston, 1910

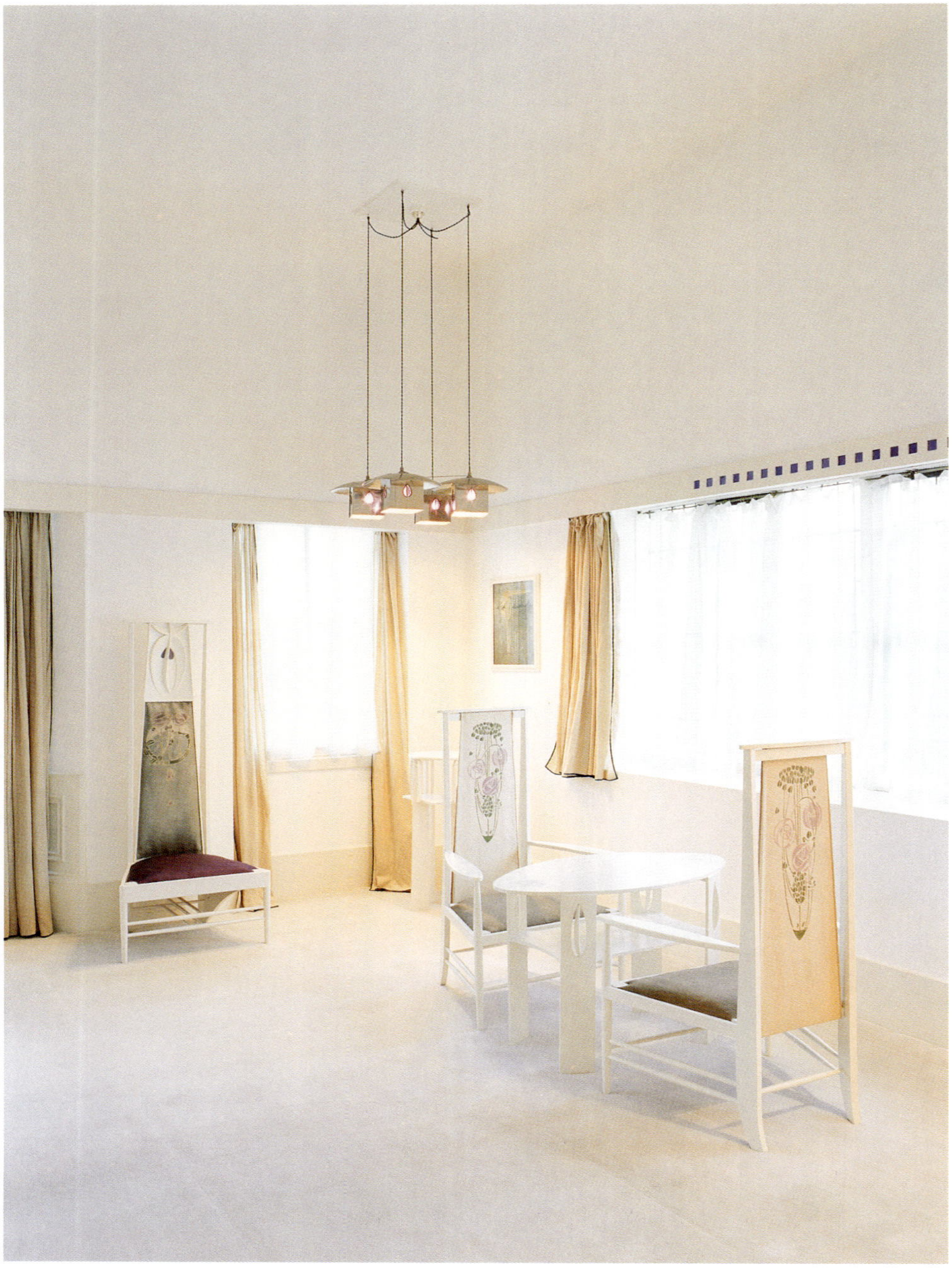

also that only men had the 'male' attributes, women the 'female' ones. So Toshie couldn't really have been into decoration; it was inferior to the rigorous architecture, indeed undermined it; and it was the result of Margaret's malign influence over him, and her 'wholly inferior talents'.[6] Today's politically corrected art historian commandos restore balance with heavy artillery; their colleagues, with equally lengthy words and weighty theory, urge us not, on the other hand, to overemphasise Margaret's role: 'Feminists intervene with a masculinist historicity that, while theorizing textuality and denying a modernist language of superlatives, explicates its directions by privileging female artists who most represent male artistic hegemony.'[7] Yes; well, I think it might be easier just to look at the works.

It is a traditional notion that architecture consists of a 'mould of form' which is clothed in a 'glass of fashion'. And that the form is deeper and more important. Mackintosh, crucially supported by his wife, valiantly stands against that 'Modernist' hierarchy. He understands that, for the complete experience, the surfaces which attract the eye and the hand are at least of equal importance to the armature beneath; he shapes and frames spaces with a formal rigour, and then embellishes and details them with a loving care.

The drawing room of their own flat certainly is one of the most original and important interiors in modern design history. They empty the tall, early nineteenth-century space, running a rail round at doorhead height (decorated at intervals with richly designed square insets of coloured gesso), from which fine muslin curtains obscure the windows, filtering the light. There are large panels of light-grey canvas on the walls, with the

**Drawing Room, The Mackintosh House**

Edward Morse, in *The Japanese House and its Surroundings*, 1885 (which CRM knew) describes the typical British interior as 'a labyrinth of varnished furniture with dusty carpets and suffocating wallpapers hot with some frantic design.' The white, spacious and calm clarity of CRM's own drawing room is the antithesis of such clutter, a delicate atmosphere conjured with minimum elements.

frieze, cornice and ceiling white. Furniture, some white some dark, is carefully placed: objects precisely balanced in the pale 3-D space. Gas piping from the central ceiling rose runs four ways across the ceiling to drop elegantly to clusters of lamps.

In the dining room, the rail at doorhead is black. Coarse wrapping paper on the walls, with a rough, dark grey-brown surface, encloses the sparse and simple furniture. Pine, oak and black-stained fireplace; designed napery and cutlery, fenders and fire irons. This dark sanctuary for almost ritualistic meals is lit only by candles, one room without the hiss of gas jets. The bedroom is white, tight and stuffed with the most remarkable white objects: four-poster with silk hangings, tall free-standing mirror, wardrobe.

It had not appeared from thin air. Indeed it develops specific forms already used – like the great simple timber fireplace (covering an existing marble one) as done for Margaret's parents; or reusing white furniture first designed for Jessie Newbery's parents. This sense of elements able to float between clients and locations, to appear alone or come together collaged in new ways, to form new spaces, repeats in these years. For the Vienna display they borrow elements from their own house, from tea rooms and from private clients, fashioning new room settings. For Turin they repeat this, also designing new elements some of which come back to their own home – a home which they completely reconstruct once more, when they move in 1906. In these few years of flux, an aesthetic is developed and honed. Extraordinarily, it then stops. For eight more years in their new house, the Mackintoshes live amidst the forms created at the start of the century.

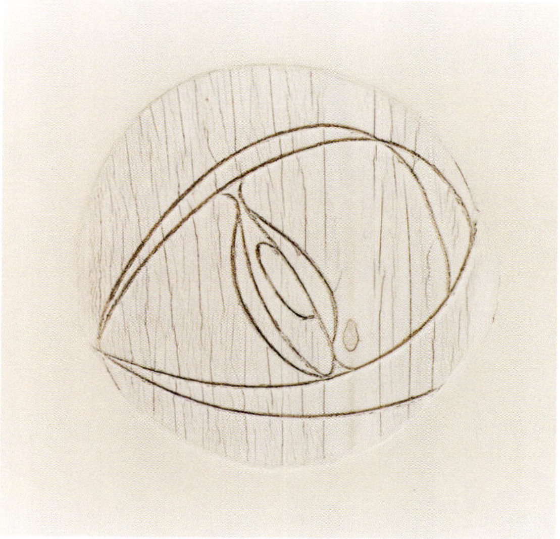

**Oval Table Detail, The Mackintosh House, 1902**

Two details in the drawing room of their home which is reconstituted in the 1906 house. These can be seen in The Mackintosh House, which has been reconstructed in the Hunterian Art Gallery, University of Glasgow.

**Leaded Glass Roundels, The Mackintosh House, MMM, 1900**

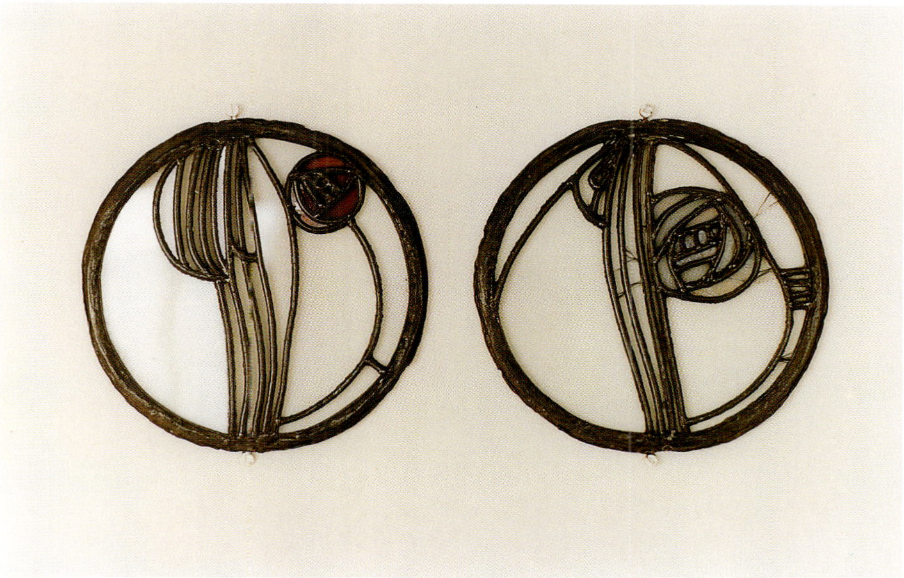

Muthesius writes of Mackintosh rooms as being 'refined to a degree which would tolerate no admixture of the ordinariness which fills our lives', and 'refined to a degree which the lives of even the artistically educated are still a long way from matching...They are milestones placed by a genius far ahead of us to mark the way to excellence for mankind in the future.' Just before his wedding, Mackintosh writes to Muthesius: 'We have a very nice trip in prospect for October. We are to get a room to ourselves at the Vienna Secession and are to go and arrange our

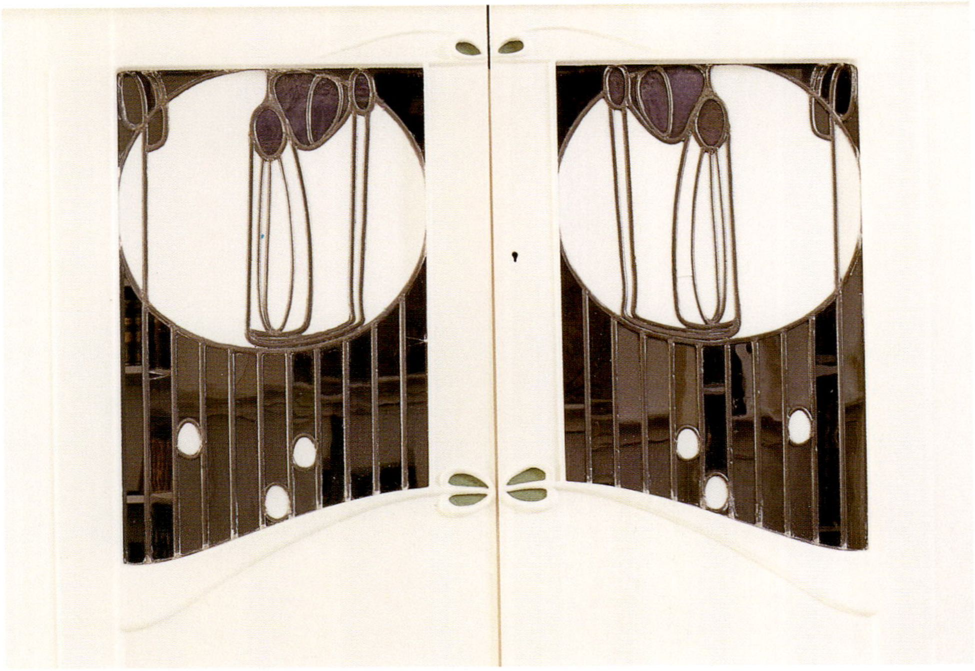

own exhibition. All the expenses are being paid. We are going to make a great effort as it is a chance one seldom gets.'[8] He understands its potential. Fritz Wärndorfer had come to Glasgow to set it up. The Vienna Secession is the key to Modernism in 1900. Olbrich's building, dripping gilding over its rigorously geometric form, is new.

The Secessionists already had links with Glasgow painters, who had exhibited twice (including E.A.Walton in '98). But the Mackintoshes are astonished by their reception.[9] They are held in high esteem, drawn by an admiring crowd of students in a flower-decked cart through the Vienna streets with flowers thrown at their feet. Mackintosh, regarded as one of the founders of modern art, talks long into the nights, receiving unstinting praise and ungrudging acclaim. It is a six-week extended honeymoon which creates an 'unbreakable bond between Vienna and Glasgow,'.[10] In these six weeks of November and December 1900, the exhibition has an astonishing 24,000 visitors, with over 240 works sold. 'Mackintosh is said to consider his Viennese journey the high point of his life,' said Eduard Wimmer later to Josef Hoffmann.[11]

In December 1902, Hoffmann comes to see them in Glasgow for a few days, writing later that 'the development of the art of the Scot Mackintosh into a wholly new, original style is amazing. His rooms in pale grey wood and violet struts and embroidery adorned with rose-red flowers, his original lighting and glass, his heating apparatus, indeed every detail, were remarkable and full of promise'.[9]

The first issue of *Dekorative Kunst* (in October 1897) had already said that they 'gave in a very short time a new face to Glasgow – they exerted a fresh influence, able to give new blood to the sluggish veins of London.' But now they are public property in German-speaking Europe; a whole issue of *Ver Sacrum* ('Sacred Spring', the Secessionist journal), with colour reproductions, is dedicated to Toshie, Margaret and Frances. Margaret designs a cover for *Deutsche Kunst und Dekoration* in 1902. Toshie is made a corresponding member of the Secession, joining Whistler, Van de Velde and Rodin.

**Bookcase,**
**The Mackintosh House, 1900**

The beautiful Art Nouveau furniture for their 1900 flat which comes to their 1906 house.

**Lug Chair,**
**The Mackintosh House, 1900**

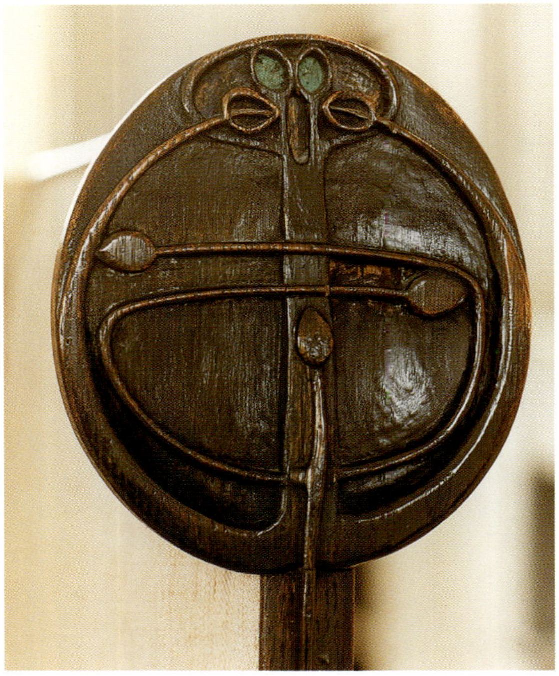

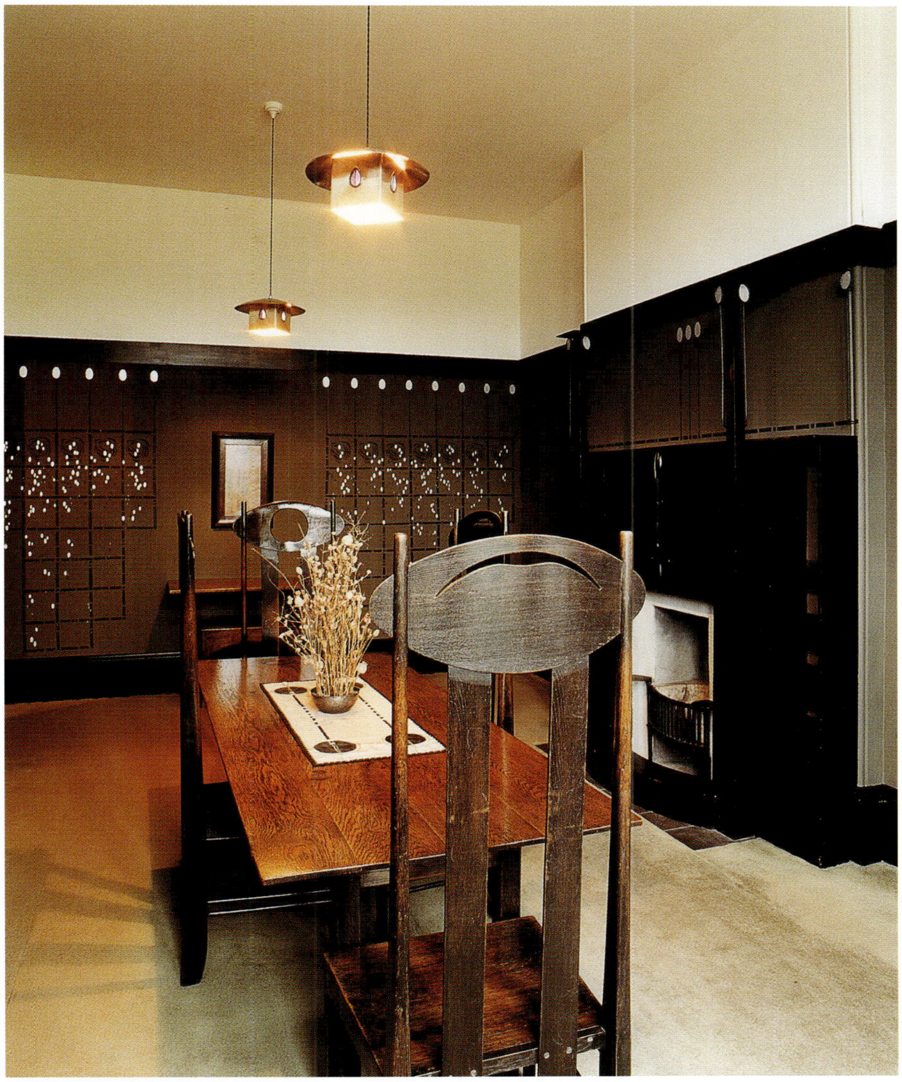

After the exhibition, Fritz Wärndorfer commissions a music room from the Mackintoshes (and a dining room from Hoffmann). These are built by 1902, with the wall panels by Margaret and Toshie completed on site some years later while they are staying with the Wärndorfers. The music room becomes the meeting place for the avant garde of central Europe. It is the most talked-about room of the time; its influence on design in Austria and Germany through the next decade is profound. Most immediately, the decorative panels have a far-reaching effect on the direction of Gustav Klimt's work.

Margaret's small square gesso panels for the piano, 'The Opera of the Winds' and 'The Opera of the Sea' (1903 p.60), with mother-of-pearl encrustations and virtually no added colour, really appear as if magically left by a receding tide. Their powerful shapes and geometry encourages critics to believe she is elaborating a design by Toshie. Of the 12 decorative wall panels, based on a Maeterlinck poem, six are from each partner.

The white room, with its lavender- and rose-coloured accents is in the same language as their flat, and a revelation to the Viennese. To one, it is a place of pilgrimage for lovers of art, a delight for the connoisseur, and for strangers visiting the city it is perhaps their greatest work; to another 'an artistic curiosity of the first order'; and another notes how its surfaces are 'not only to be viewed but must be touched in order not to miss any details'.[12] This last word in Viennese modernity, 'the well-known masterpiece of the Maeterlinck interior', becomes in Europe the visual complement to Debussy's Maeterlinck opera.

But, beyond *The Studio*, it is barely noticed in Britain at all. None of The Four is even invited to exhibit at Glasgow's International Exhibition in 1901.[13] However, Fedor Shektel, designer of the Russian work there, stays in Glasgow for several months and can't miss the Mackintoshes. He organises a Moscow exhibition in 1902, including Mackintosh's white furniture from Jessie Newbery's parents and Wärndorfer's oval

**Dining Room,
The Mackintosh House**

Rebuilt in their new house in 1906, the dining room from their previous flat includes the fireplace, and incorporates a set of CRM's first high-back chairs designed in 1897, with vestigial birds flying through the oval headpiece. Under the rail which runs round at doorhead height, the room builds a subtle palette of earth colours, with the dark trellis set off by tears of silver.

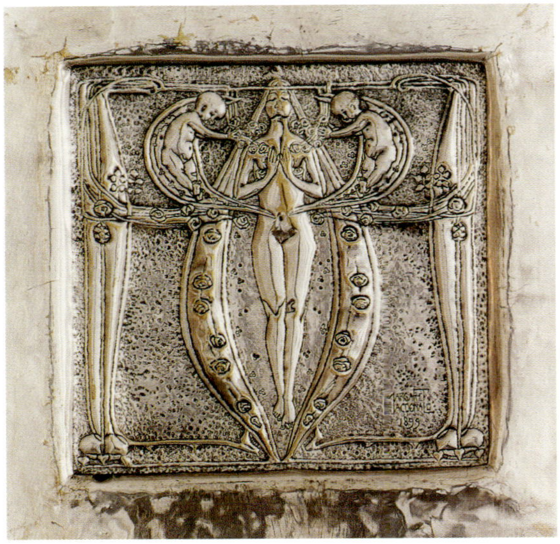

Metal Panel in Bedroom, The Mackintosh House, MMM, 1899

Bedroom Wardrobe Doors, The Mackintosh House, 1900

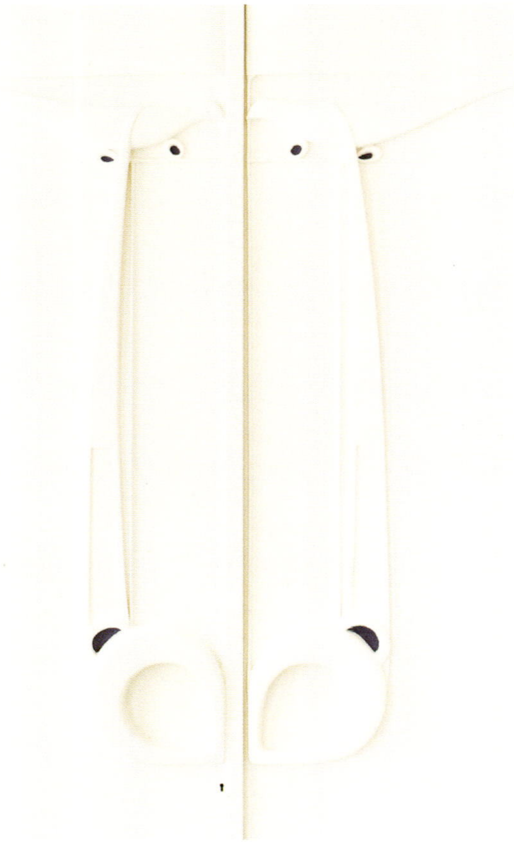

table. For an exhibition in Turin in 1902, Newbery invites the Mackintoshes to design the Scottish section. They form three settings separated by banners, each treated like Vienna in white wood and canvas. One bay shows a mix of Glaswegian work, including E.A. Taylor furniture and Jessie King book illustration, the smaller objects displayed in elegant and simple Mackintosh cubical showcases. The middle bay, in two halves, has a McNair interior opposite embroidery by Jessie Newbery and her students. The third is also in two halves: one being a Mackintosh space, the 'Rose Boudoir', the other a gallery of Toshie drawings focused on Alexander Koch's plates of the Art Lover's House scheme.

Koch, publisher of *Deutsche Kunst und Dekoration* who has his own Peter Behrens-designed room nearby, devotes a complete issue of his magazine to the Glaswegian work in Turin. These international shows are a major meeting point for design and designers across Europe; a wonderful opportunity for Mackintosh, whose fame is quickly magnified. In April, Wärndorfer meets him and Hoffmann at the Turin exhibition. Soon Mackintosh work is being sent to exhibitions in Munich, Budapest, Dresden, Milan, and Moscow again. Another Secession exhibition is planned for 1904, to which Mackintosh was going to send Turin panels and other pieces, but the Secession splits and it aborts.[14]

At Turin the power is in the settings and not just objects; there is a new expression of feeling through form and space. The exhibits become the enrichment of the rooms themselves, an enrichment which Mackintosh handles fastidiously, down to the collecting and arranging of dried flowers. For *The Studio* the Mackintoshes are 'co-partners in the same scheme, and to whom the "House Beautiful" is one built and adorned by one handiwork... Standing as an expression of thought in art...'[15]

By 1906, however, the round of European displays and meetings quickly fades from the Mackintoshes' lives, and brings no work. Perhaps with such loud but paper-thin prestige, his European friends presume he is too busy to take on more. In fact, the main work of 1906 is moving house. Even by 1903 they wanted to move, away from the smog of the city centre. Margaret's having to work at her intricate designs in gaslight all day in the winter was straining her eyes and her temper. Finally they move, rebuilding their interior world within a Victorian house on Gilmorehill. The ground floor, the zone of earth, is in earth colours for cooking and eating. A dark, narrow stair leads up (over black-and-white chequered sail-cloth steps) to the brilliant and surprising, L-shaped white room which is the complete first floor. Here, in the back part, Margaret paints, over a white carpet wearing her white kid gloves. On the second floor are bathroom and a slightly more spacious white bedroom, while Toshie has a studio in the attic.

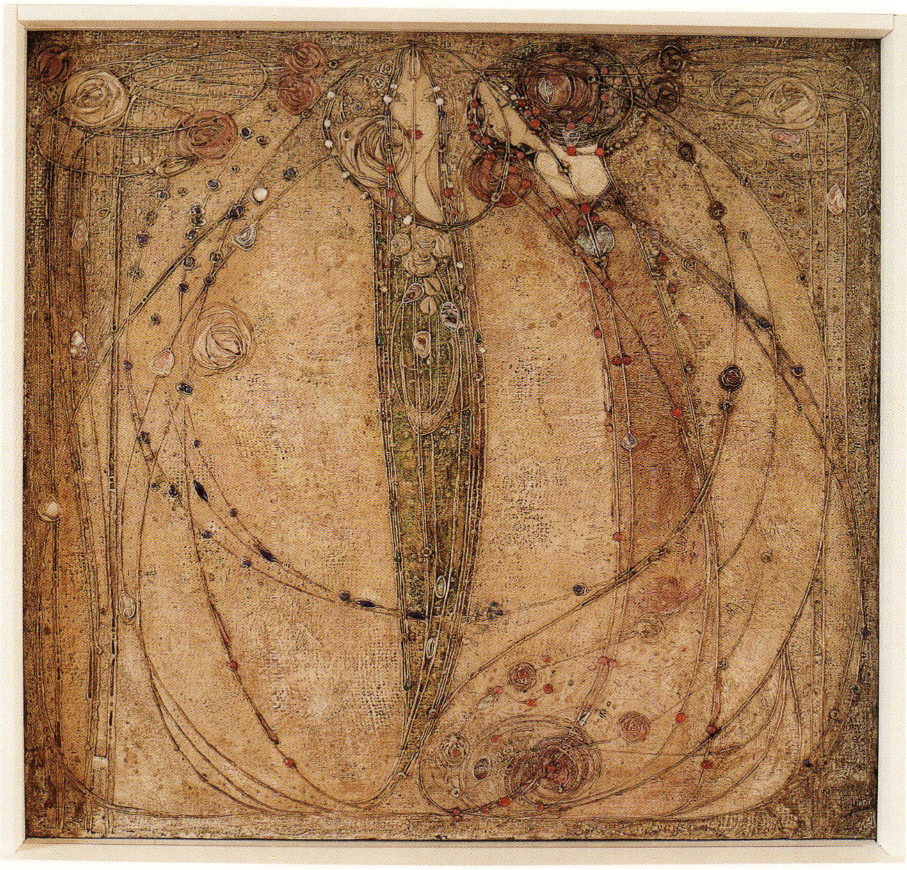

The interiors, while adding new brilliant effects, attempt to recreate the qualities of that earlier flat: its colour schemes and furnishings, even the fireplaces come with them, and the grey corduroy cushions either side of it, for their Persian cats. The influence of Margaret, waning by 1903, is last seen again in this work. 'The room as work of art, as united, organic whole,' as their enthusiastic friend Muthesius puts it.[16]

However, as Muthesius also notes, this art interior demands a fastidiousness of behaviour. Does Mackintosh have an obsession with tidiness? In this world of soot and gas flames, how can they keep it clean? Toshie must knock out his pipe with exceptional care. The white furniture has six coats of eggshell enamel, and Margaret sponges off dirty marks (recalls Mary Newbery[17]) with slightly warm olive oil. 'Amazingly white and clean looking. Walls, ceiling and furniture all have the virginal beauty of white satin,' says another visitor.[18] How much energy, and whose energy, goes into holding onto this oasis of purity in the sooty city. What a job for the maid!

With its light, spacious calm, it approaches a Japanese ethos; but these spaces can only be Mackintosh. If they read about Japanese flower arrangement in *The Studio*, their own personal arrangements do not follow Japanese rules. While fashionably 'Japanophile' rooms are cluttered with screens, parasols, bamboo furniture, potted plants, fans and Noh mask imagery, the Mackintosh flat only contains Mackintosh designs. On the mantelpiece are just two little Japanese prints which had been a present from Muthesius. 'Joyously attractive and fresh...awfully nice...a red hot fire...Sunday parties, peppermint creams... actors and artists, all the Art School people...' muses Mary Newbery. But after 1906, she adds, they live there very quietly.

**The White Rose and The Red Rose, MMM, 1902**

The Mackintoshes' first gesso panels were the vast twinned works, one by each of them, which faced each other over the Ladies' Luncheon Room in Ingram Street in 1900. It is extraordinary that such bold and accomplished works should be their first – and indeed CRM's last – essays in this little-known medium. MMM completed 15 panels, keeping this one, painted for the Rose Boudoir in 1902, for themselves. No photograph does justice to the medium's delicate richness which we see as the central face, beads or scrim catch the light. Gesso (glue, whitening and plaster) is laid on canvas (which can show through), the pattern is drawn over, lines plastered with an icing bag and glass cabochons and mother-of-pearl shells inset, before it is sealed, painted in oils and lacquered.

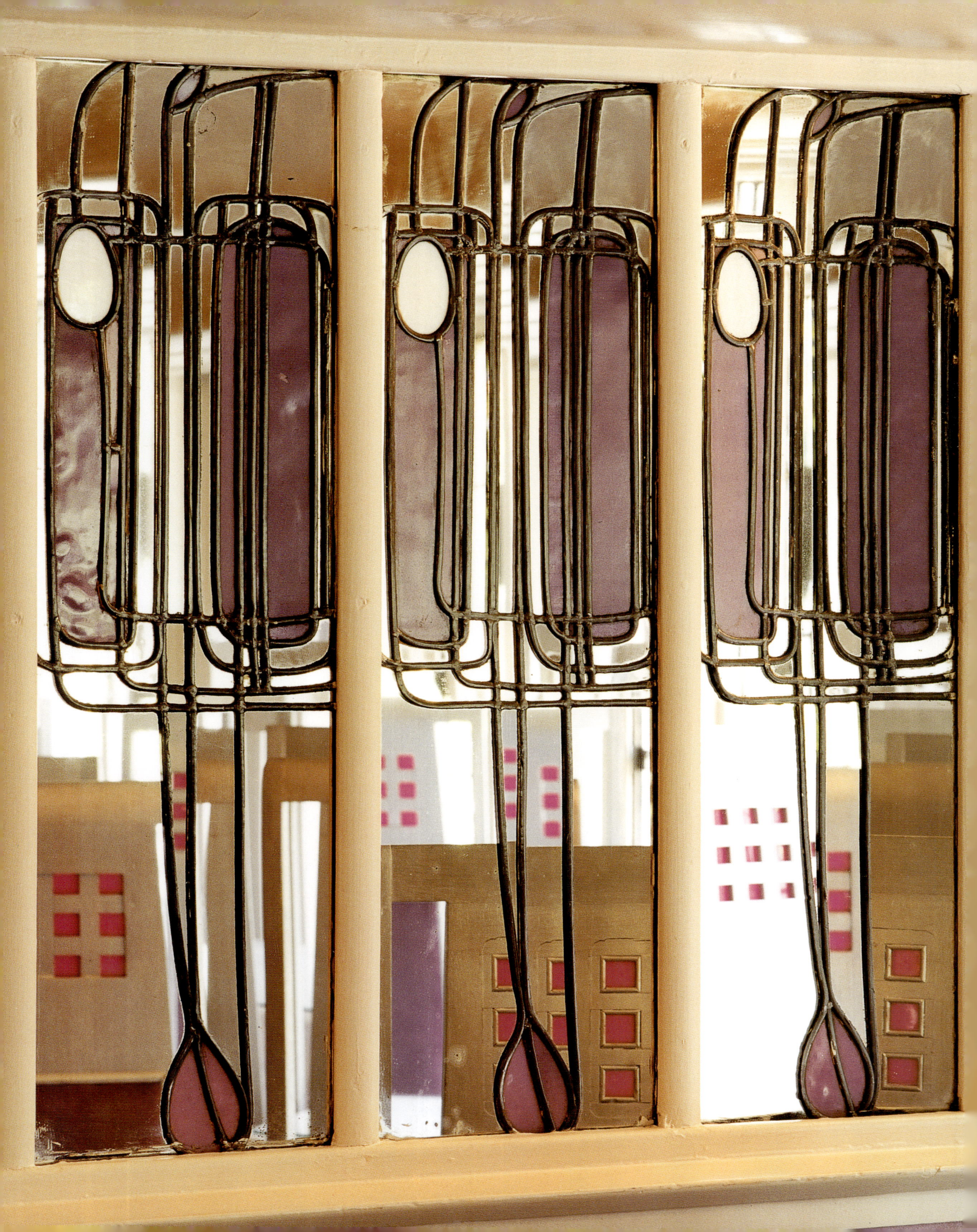

# THE GLASGOW TEA CEREMONY

Catherine Cranston more or less invented the Glasgow tea room phenomenon. She filled the need for a miniature social centre which served many purposes: to be a safe meeting place for bourgeois men in a city famed for the evils wrought by drink; but more, it uniquely offered 'ladies' rooms' where respectable women could go out and meet, at a time when women without men in the urban scene were usually taken for servants or prostitutes. These were not cafes, but offered a range of privacies in the public world; rooms for lunch or private dining, rooms to read and write, to play billiards or smoke. They were almost clubs without bedrooms; and, centrally of course, without alcohol. 'Tea shop as moral agent' runs one cross-head in a book on Glasgow in 1901.[1]

For 21 years from 1897, Mackintosh was Cranston's designer. An independently minded woman of avant-garde taste old enough to be his mother, she became his most stalwart patron. As Ned Lutyens had found his Gertrude Jekyll, Toshie now found his Kate Cranston. At Buchanan Street he designed murals around George Walton furniture, then at Argyle Street it was his loose furniture and light fittings within Walton's interior scheme. His first complete room was at Ingram Street where, from 1900, he remodelled interiors over 12 years. Finally, at Sauchiehall Street he did the complete interiors and front facade in 1903-4 of a building she had bought in 1901.[2]

To Mackintosh, the tea rooms offer the most complete public spaces of his career. Here he is not just privately engaged in life as art, but in giving form to an art of public life. In his words, 'to clothe in grace and beauty new forms and conditions that modern development of life insists upon.' And here he has a trusting and supportive client who seems to accept his every decision. In contrast to the Art School building committee, his other long-term client, where he felt every day was a battle, 'Miss Cranston is delighted with everything I have suggested,' he says in 1903.[3]

The Glasgow tea room is unique. Other remarkable women establish 'artistic' tea rooms in Glasgow – in stores like Copeland & Lye, Pettigrew & Stephens, or the Les Magasins du Tuileries at Tréron et Cie which, in 1904, has a tea room in white and gold. But none matches Miss Cranston's where the mundane business of having to eat in town is raised to an art. She offers a complete environment of escape; the place we

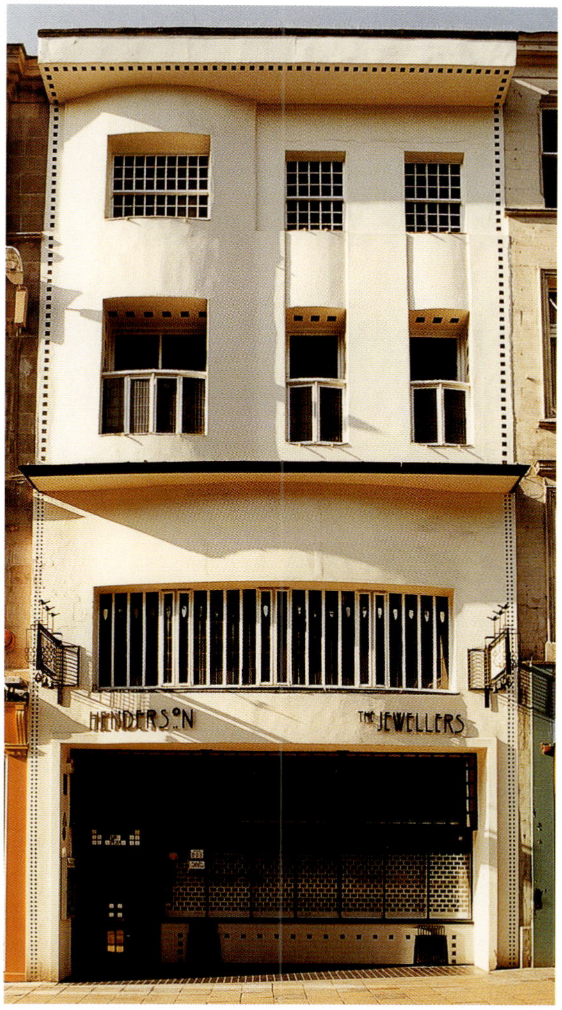


**Willow Tea Rooms facade**

On the higher floor, behind windows whose section above the encircling doorhead rail is deeply recessed, are found the dark stained and panelled 'Billiards' and 'Smoking' Rooms, with motifs of applied squares.

**The Willow's Room de Luxe (opposite)**

The low cornice at doorhead on which the vaulted ceiling rests, is a rail which runs all round, holding together walls of mirrored panes separated by thin white vertical bands, below which walls are upholstered in pale grey silk, stitched with beads.

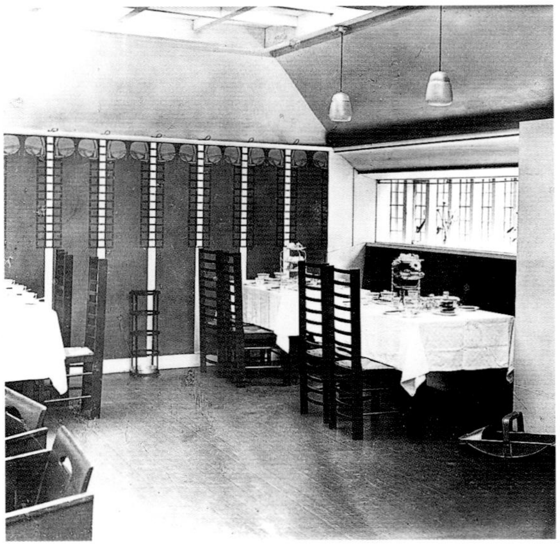

**Willow Tea Rooms, The Gallery, 1903**

The Mackintoshes' first flat (1900) is well-known from black and white photographs where we must guess at the colours, yet their later house seems never photographed. Similarly, it is poignant that his first complete room, the Ladies' Luncheon Room, (below right) is well-known, while later rooms at Ingram Street are virtually unrecorded (though the bits still exist).

**Argyle Street Tea Rooms, The Dutch Kitchen, 1906**

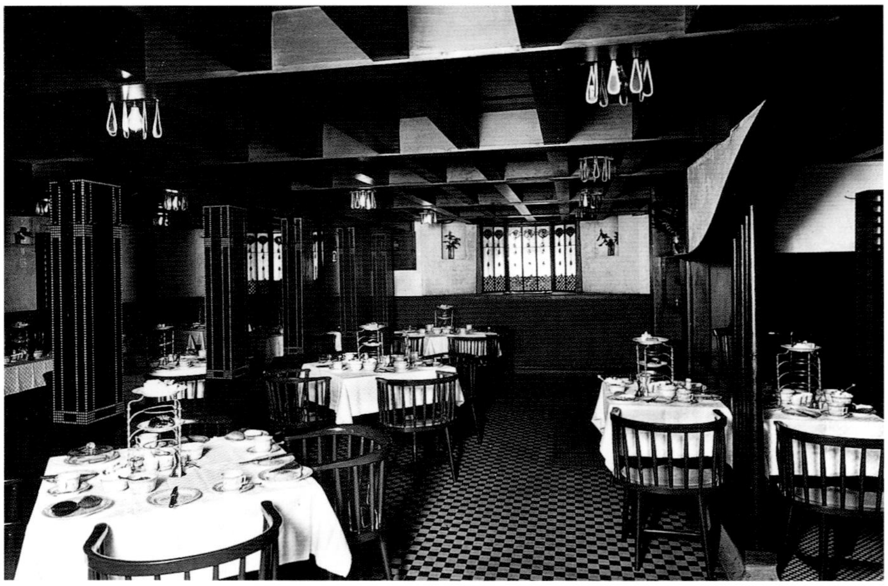

couldn't live in but where we thrill to play-act for a while: colour, furniture, cutlery, carpets, curtains, metalwork, seating surfaces and flower vases, all are part of the *mise-en-scène*; the wall covering and integrated art works, the use of mirror and stained glass, the light fittings and windows; the alcoves and room spaces; the promenade between and spectacle from one to another. Mackintosh completely understands how the whole might picture an attractive fantasy. In April 1900, the 32-year-old designer is out in Ingram Street at 6 am every morning for a week, decorating the barricades which intimate this magic to come. After one tea room is opened, Mackintosh even arranges the flowers every few days for the first weeks.

The complete fantasy experience includes sexual fantasies otherwise kept well hidden. On the walls, the vaguely veiled eroticism of Mackintosh's imagery, hitherto confined to small private watercolours, is now splashed over Buchanan Street murals, and in the great gesso panels at Ingram Street; Margaret's 'May Queen' centring on a camouflaged vagina, and opposite Toshie's 'Wassail', its two maidens flanking a central phallus. On the floor are the lovely, carefully selected young waitresses, especially at Sauchiehall Street where they are dressed in pale costumes with bow ties and chokers of large pink beads designed by Mackintosh. 'To the young man from the country, she may be a little tender. For it is not impossible that, his landlady apart, she is the only petticoated being with whom he can converse without shame' – is how they charmingly worded the attraction a century ago.[4] Mackintosh, says the design critic more directly, 'has indicated the design and colour of the gowns to be worn, so that no disturbing element might mar the unity of the conception'.[5] Miss Cranston has taken the intimate Glasgow Style for her public fantasy, and the ordinary people love it. Edwin Lutyens, writing from his Glasgow visit to his fiancée Lady Emily Lytton, jokes with precision: 'gorgeous and a wee bit vulgar...all a little outré.'

Following the Buchanan Street murals, Mackintosh was involved with Argyle Street. Here the entire first floor was one luncheon room, decorated by Walton with a dark-green stained oak wainscot 5 ft (1.5 m) high and narrow panels of stencil decoration in the same colours as the stencilled frieze above. For this huge room, divided by Walton into more intimate spaces with screens matching the wainscot, Mackintosh designed his first recognisable tall chairs with an oval halo behind the sitter's head.

Then, in 1900, started his involvement with the most complex series of tea room spaces, those at Ingram Street, involving galleries and views from one space to another, as he developed and added new interiors over the years. In the silver-walled entrance corridor, a low screen in which are set glazed panels separates it from the Ladies' Luncheon Room, Mackintosh's first complete tea room. Here, high over the entrance lobby but seen from The Luncheon Room, hangs his great curvaceous gesso panel 'The Wassail'. It is 15 ft (4.5 m long) and paralleled, on the opposite side wall, by its partner, Macdonald's 'May Queen'.

At the room's other sides were a back gallery and the window wall, which was handled as a space of its own. Double depths of column at the street, with a high-level rail binding the inner columns, marked individual window bays as individual places, each with its own banquette seat and black, tall-backed chairs facing it. Restrained decoration on the screen to the corridor doesn't fight with the richness of the extraordinary artworks: above are the vast panels, their first productions in gesso on hessian and scrim, the bejewelled and beflowered ladies formed with twine, glass beads, thread, mother-of-pearl and tin leaf; below are alternating leaded glass panels, of pure, abstract vegetable designs, simply in translucent pale pea, black and white.

North-west of this commercial centre, Sauchiehall Street was now the centre of department stores and the arts, attracting a more feminine and artistic custom. Here, for the most remarkable and last of the Cranston tea rooms Mackintosh remodelled the facade of No 217, opposite the old Art School and city galleries, amending the structure as well as carving out and linking the interiors. With the theme from Sauchiehall, 'avenue of the willow', the interior design was built around lines of D.G. Rossetti:

'Oh ye, all ye that walk in Willowwood
that walk with hollow faces burning bright...'

Macdonald's gesso panel is the more literal representation, but the willow is behind all Mackintosh's imagery, often abstracted to an extreme, as seen in two ground-floor elements:

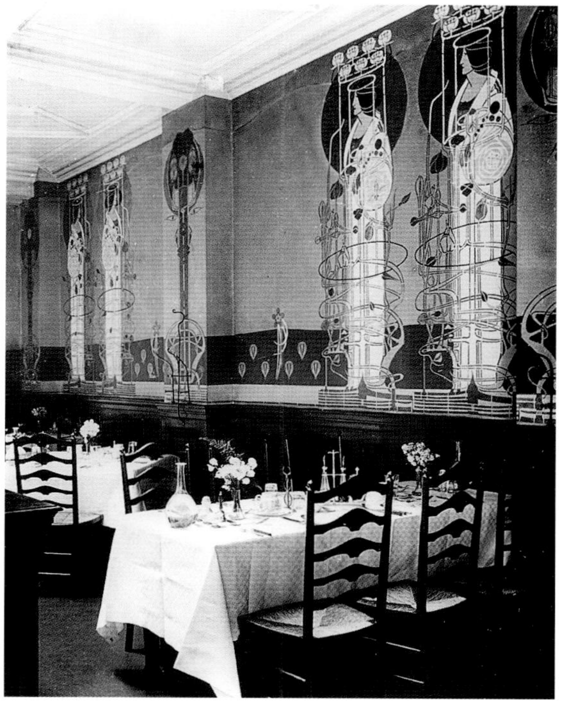

Buchanan Street Tea Rooms, The Ladies' Room, 1896

Ingram Street Tea Rooms, The Ladies' Luncheon Room, 1900

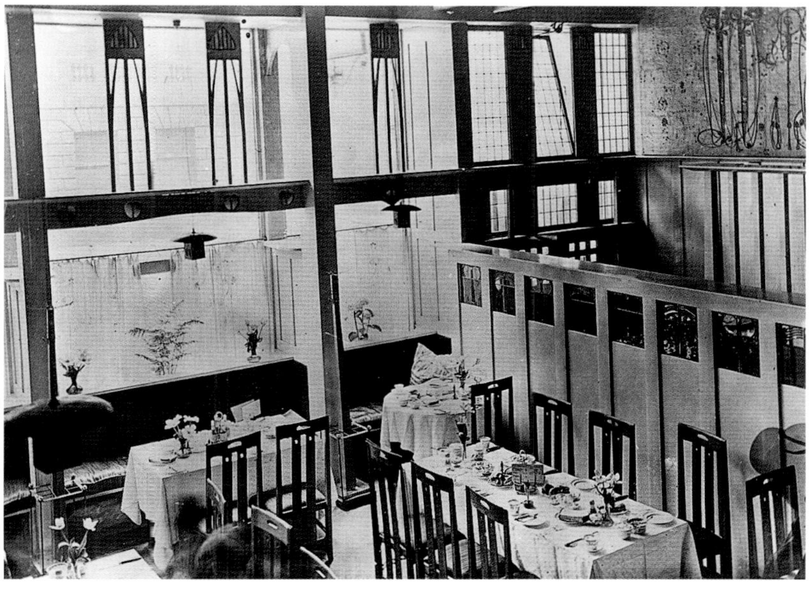

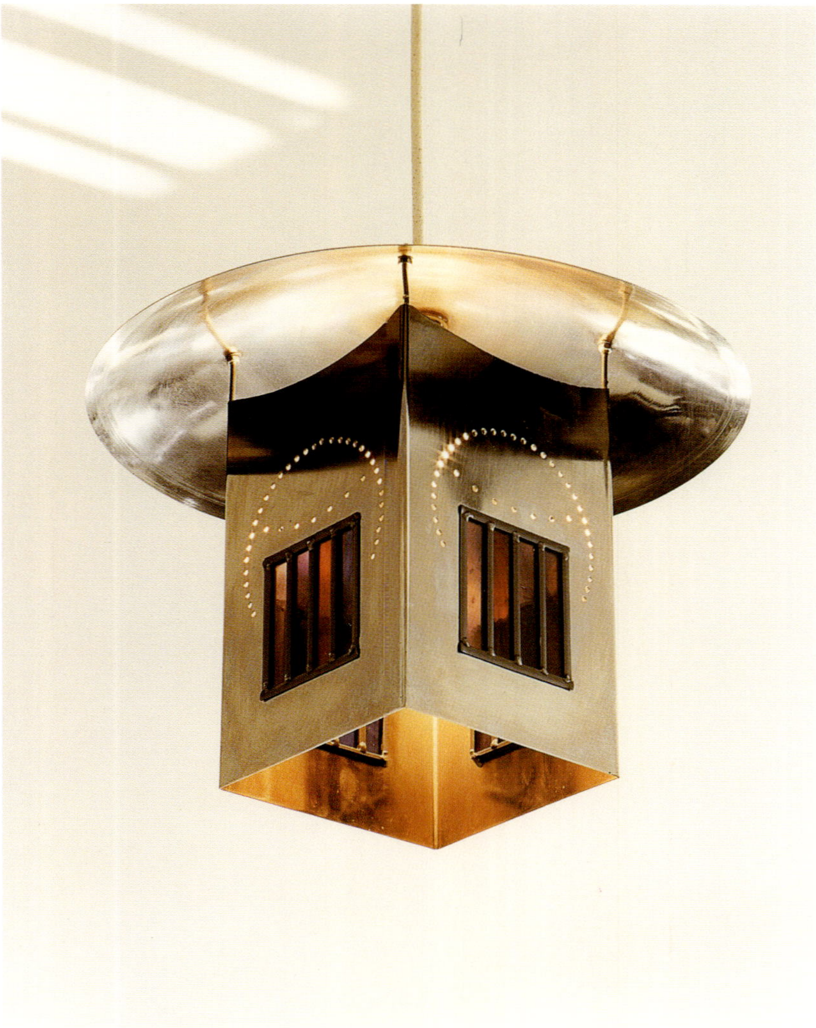

**Light Fitting, 1990s, in a new Tea Room**

At the Ingram Street Ladies' Luncheon Room, little drop lights, similar to so many of his others, are so simple and yet so beautiful: their golden down-glow, reflected in the saucer above, and the fireworks on the sides, four little vertical strips surmourted by a sparkling halo. Here, a charming modern version in the 1990s Mackintoshish tea rooms in Buchanan Street.

first, the lattice back of the curved settle which, separating front and back diners, was the order-desk chair; and second, the extraordinary plaster panelled frieze round the wall.

The ground floor front and back salons, and the top-lit mezzanine gallery at the back, form three interrelated but distinct places differentiated by their decor. The street front, in silver, white and rose, is the 'Ladies' Tea Room' with its ladderback chairs; deeper, beyond the manageress' great chequered throne, is the dark 'Luncheon Room' for men and women, with its boxy armchairs; the 'Tea Gallery' above is a rose-bower in pink, white and grey. Then, on the first floor, overlooking Sauchiehall Street, is the Ladies' Room, a silvery willow grove, the exquisite 'Salon de Luxe'. This is entered through glazed double doors, the most simple and straightforward in form, but among the most remarkably decorated doors in the world.

The Room de Luxe trod a narrow and risky path – weighted down by all its baubles and drips of pink glass, this line could go no further: in some quarters it was quickly a subject of mirth. The original central chandelier, made up of myriad rose-coloured glass balls on strings surrounding a large bulb, has long since vanished. That's a pity, for seeing it, and other details from this interior – like the strings of glass balls in the balcony edging – would make us wonder how close we are sailing here to the tawdry. It was not mentioned in the U.K. press, not even by *The Studio* – though *Dekorative Kunst*, in April 1905, gave it practically the whole issue. One 10-year-old found it 'a world of magic...it released something in me, giving me joy and the urge to draw and dance myself.'

Impervious as ever to fashion, Kate Cranston – still wearing her great dresses and hats which had been fashionable half a century earlier – continues to commission Mackintosh after all other work has left him. In 1906 he creates a semi-basement room at Argyle Street, 'The Dutch Kitchen', with black ceiling, black-and-white chequered floor, mother-of-pearl squares on the columns, and bright emerald-green rather traditionally shaped Windsor chairs. The following year at Ingram Street he produces a galleried 'Oak Room' reminiscent of the Art School library which is probably on his drawing board at the same moment, and next he squeezes in an 'Oval Room'. Two more rooms are redesigned here in 1911.

First 'The Chinese Room' for men, under whose black ceiling were blue lattice screens with exotic touches of red and of mirror. Up till now, Mackintosh has used colour very sparingly. The scallops of the Art School library balustrading hint at something already far from those Art Nouveau refinements in pinks, purples and silver and cream. Now, suddenly, we have bright blues and reds on black; it is dark and exotic. Second, his last room at Ingram Street, the altered Cloister Room of 1912, is quite different again. This low barrel vault (which hid his earlier decorative scheme), had layered wall panels of shiny, waxed wood, decorated with delicate vertical strips of harlequin lozenges painted red, green and blue, and with much mirror glass round its low vault. Panels covered in thin strips of leaded mirror are under an extraordinary, melting doorhead. Was this a totally new, restless space developing from the recently completed Art School library?

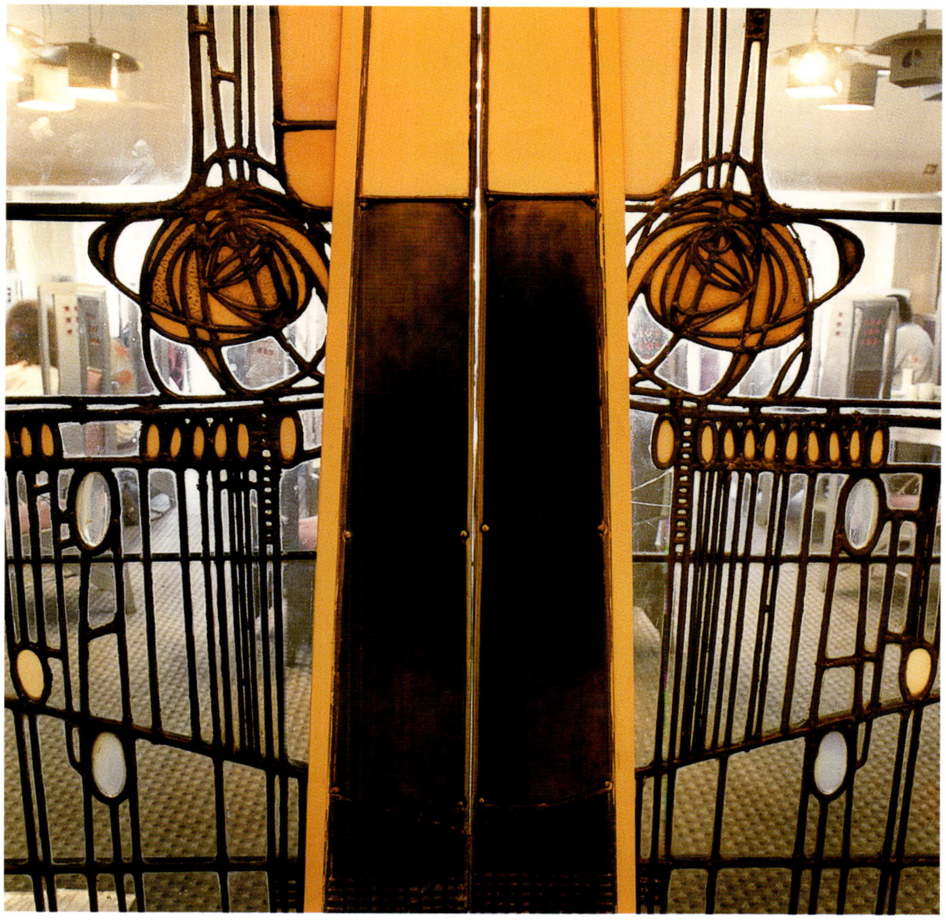

Finally, in 1916 he designs a room in the basement next to The Willow, the new stair down to it destroying his own ground-floor fireplace. This is known from one deep and brightly coloured drawing, and one glorious yellow settee with purple satin upholstery. Somewhere on the walls, Toshie and Margaret hung their somewhat embarrassingly unattractive twin canvasses entitled 'The Little Hills'. In this space completely without natural light Mackintosh demands a glossy black ceiling; a plaque states it was opened 'during the Great European War'; with a stunning ability of fantasy to save us from the effort of imagination, it is called The Dugout. There is no record of what emotions it aroused.

Cranston's husband dies in 1917; it devastates her, and she immediately loses interest and begins to pack up, finally quitting by 1919. Mackintosh's patronage is over.

**Room de Luxe Doors**

On its opening, late in 1903, the Willow's Room de Luxe was an immediate *cause célèbre*. It is strange to imagine this fairy place of pearls and roses as purveyor of teas and mutton pies to everyday folk. An amusing tale by my aunt's father, Neil Munro (written for the *Glasgow Evening News*), encapsulates an ordinary pair's first experience of this 'Room de Looks'. Duffy 'thocht his teaspoon was a' bashed oot o' its richt shape till I tellt him that was whit made it Art.' Needing more solid food, they go down to the luncheon room; (Erchie explains to his friend that 'a pie's no becomin' enough for the Room de Looks'). However, in the end, 'when the pie cam' up, it was jist the shape o' an ordinary pie, wi' nae beads nor anything Art aboot it, and Duffy cheered up at that, and said he enjoyed his tea.'

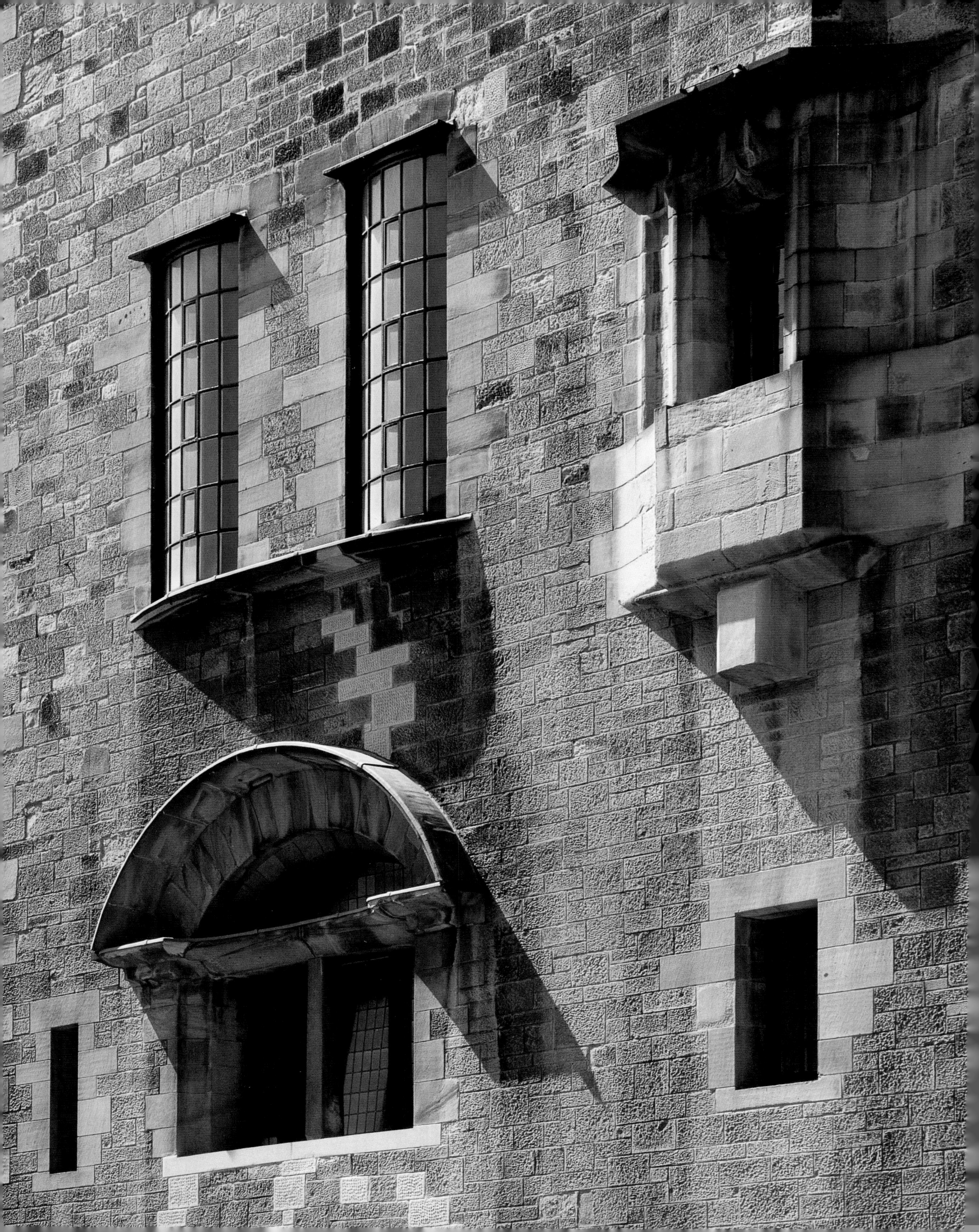

# A WALK IN GLASGOW

The work of Mackintosh, embedded in the fabric of central Glasgow which he knew, can be seen in a pleasant half-hour's walk from Charing Cross to The Lighthouse. The streets still take the gridded form first built before his birth; but much in Mackintosh's time was being replaced with second-generation building. That booming development at the end of the nineteenth century means that – apart from the generally ugly and out-of-scale insertions of the 1960s to 1980s – these streets are lined with buildings of his generation.

We start at what used to be the central bustle of Charing Cross, and now is marked on its south side by the ugliest building in Glasgow (by popular vote) where the din and fumes of the outrageous 1960s M8 motorway slice across it in a cutting. Passing the finely ornamented corner flats, carved with their name, Charing Cross Mansions (designed in 1891 by J.J. Burnet, later a key client figure at the Art School), we walk into town along Sauchiehall Street, distantly recalling in its name a boggy valley of willows between the ridges which today are Renfrew Street and Bath Street. By 1901, this was 'the brightest and gayest street in Glasgow, the only street of pleasure.'[1] Immediately on the left was the shop of T. & R. Annan and Sons, Glasgow art dealers and pioneering photographers (J. Craig Annan exhibited photographs alongside his friend Mackintosh in Turin in 1902, winning a medal.) Here Honeyman & Keppie's interior work (*c.*1903) includes a fantastic metal lift shaft, with cranked steel structure and cast-iron filigree snaking up to the rooflight. But it is Keppie and surely not from the hand of Mackintosh. A few minutes further, as we pass the Grecian Buildings (1865) by Glasgow's greatest architect, Alexander Thomson, the most picturesque view of the School of Art comes into view, towering over it, up Scott Street to the left.

Continue east along Sauchiehall Street, and just over its brow, the block beyond his Art School houses the rooms where Mackintosh studied, as well as the McLellan Gallery, where his memorial exhibition was held. Opposite are the Willow Tea Rooms where the facade, so unlike any urban front in Glasgow, has been almost completely restored. Through the jewellery and trinket shop, we climb Mackintosh's stairs to the top-lit back gallery. A half flight further, until very recently its magnificent glazed doors opened to the Room de Luxe, the shapes and colours of their leaded lights endlessly entrancing the eye;

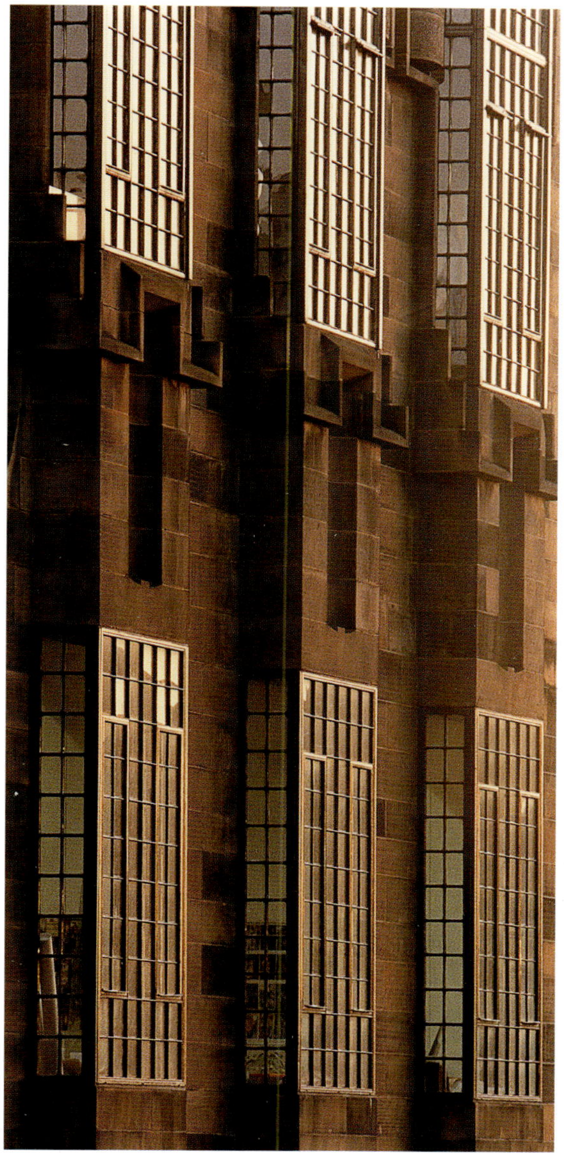

**The Glasgow School of Art**

The western face of the Art School, 1907 (above), designed and built a decade after the eastern face (opposite.)

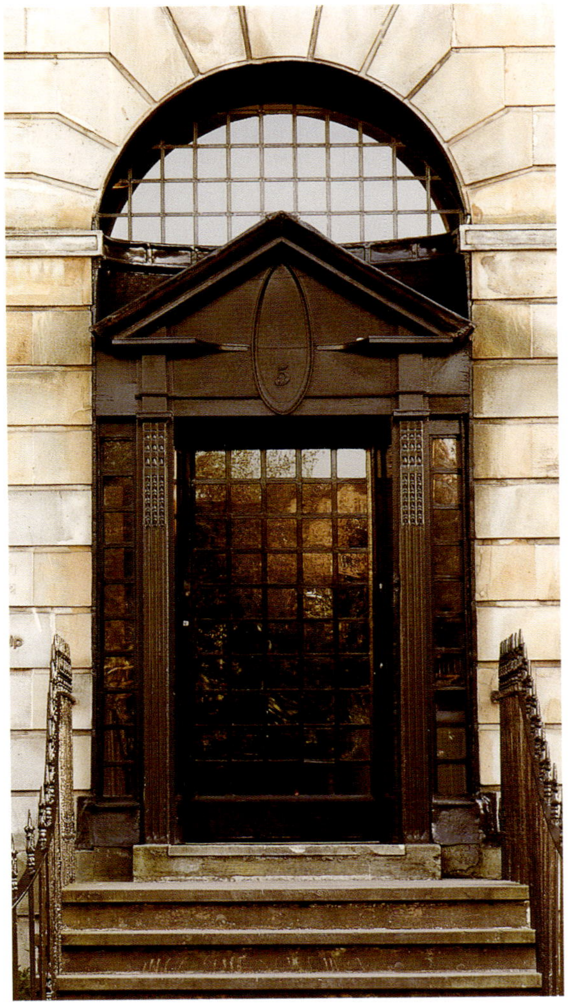

**The Lady Artists' Club, 1908**

A few doors along from their old flat, CRM designed this beautifully proportioned doorcase. Perhaps the panelled entrance hall beyond is his, but the club's committee didn't agree on his appointment and his work quickly stopped.

watching them swing as waitresses bring through the tea-trays, seeing how different they look from different sides and in different lights! These doors were removed to travel with the 1996 exhibition, were promised to be back in place, in their original and everyday – their extraordinary and exotic and magical – use by now. But their fragility and great insurance value has made that hope unrealistic; they are, as I write, likely to be exhibited somewhere within the Willow building, perhaps on the second floor, rather than be reinstated. They remain Mackintosh's most elaborate essay in stained and leaded glass.

After tea, if we now turn up Blythswood Street, we pass the left-hand corner of Blythswood Square, where the Mackintoshes had their flat in 1900 (when this was called Mains Street). Turning into the square to the right, we see the classical portico which Mackintosh stuck into the round-headed arch of what was the Lady Artists' Club, 1908. (Backing onto this club, entered from Bath Street, is still the men's domain, the Art Club whose interior fitments remain one of Mackintosh's best prentice works.)

But we continue, across the square, past the Royal Scottish Automobile Club down to St Vincent Street. Look right at the crossing, to the picturesque massing of Alexander Thomson's great church (1858); but turn left, to continue down to the commercial centre. A couple of blocks on, on the left, we pass No. 144, by one of the finest of Mackintosh's contemporaries. On the footprint of one narrow, steeply sloping plot, his good friend James Salmon raised 10 floors of offices behind a facade of articulated glass and sandstone (1899-1902). From its audacious grandness down to its tiny jewel-like oriel, this block known as 'The Hatrack' – which also incorporated a tea room early last century – is perhaps Glasgow's best example of Art Nouveau.

A moment later, at the crossing, looking to our left up the hill of Hope Street, we see the towering Lion Chambers (a reinforced-concrete pioneer, also by Salmon and his partner Gaff Gillespie, 1904-7). However, we turn right down Hope Street and then quickly left into Renfield Lane. Here, behind a Salmon & Gillespie block of 1894, is Mackintosh's warehouse and print works for *The Daily Record*, 1900-1. The site shape and layout is conventional, his effort being concentrated on the surface to this narrow lane. It is clad in white glazed bricks. If this is presumably to increase reflected illumination, that will help only the opposite neighbours. For Mackintosh it is a play on image, as ever; here the image is that of the enclosed light-well of Edwardian blocks (which never appear on an outside!).

The ground floor, however, is a grey sandstone arcade; the undulating heads very minimally formed and exquisitely precise, the shapes of capital, keystone, arch, implied most economically – apart from the doorway whose mannerism is a brilliant play of forms, thrown away down this narrow lane. Looking upwards, the bays of the surface are articulated simply; the dotted green bricks topped with red triangles, as stylised trees, carry the eye up to the sky, where we glimpse a great cap of stone waves and a baronial turret! (illustrated on p.29).

Out into Renfield Street, we glance right to Ca'd'Oro (designed in 1872 by Mackintosh's future boss, John Honeyman) and beyond it, down Union Street, to the fantastic Egyptian Halls (Alexander Thomson 1871-3). But, not diverted, we carry on east to West Nile Street and then turn right. There, ahead, is Mackintosh's *Glasgow Herald* building (1893-5) now, since 1999, The Lighthouse, in Mitchell Street, opposite the awful car park.

With the notion for a corner tower, Mackintosh returned as always to the storehouse of his architectural sketchbooks. Then, actually drawing on blank sheets in his Italian sketchbook of 1891, he made the first sketch designs for the *Herald* tower. As we see, he put the tower at the most visible corner, 150 ft (46 m) in the air. In the narrow context it looks nearly as picturesque today as in Mackintosh's dramatic drawing. The stonework on the facade is well worth a close look – the restless, lively detail, the windows bowed and canted back to reveal the thickness of the wall, the playful mouldings and strap work. Identical floorplates are faced with quite different windows as you progress higher, windows and mouldings begin to melt in the Art Nouveau sun, the corner tower almost bellies out at the top to display its role in holding back the 8000 gallons (36,300 l) of fire-fighting water which makes the tower necessary. And inside, straightforward progressive concrete floors and a large capacity hydro-pneumatic lift.

We leave The Lighthouse through Mitchell Lane (past its new entrance beckoning us into Page & Park's gloriously revitalised building), coming finally into Buchanan Street. Mackintosh's was the back door, the trade entrance; here we see *The Herald*'s public face, an extraordinary pomposity by Sellars, Keppie's master. Turning left, we are almost at the door of the 'new' Willow Tea Room (1997, a confection based on various Mackintosh designs, particularly the Ladies' Luncheon Room from Ingram Street) for another well-deserved cup of tea and Glaswegian scone.

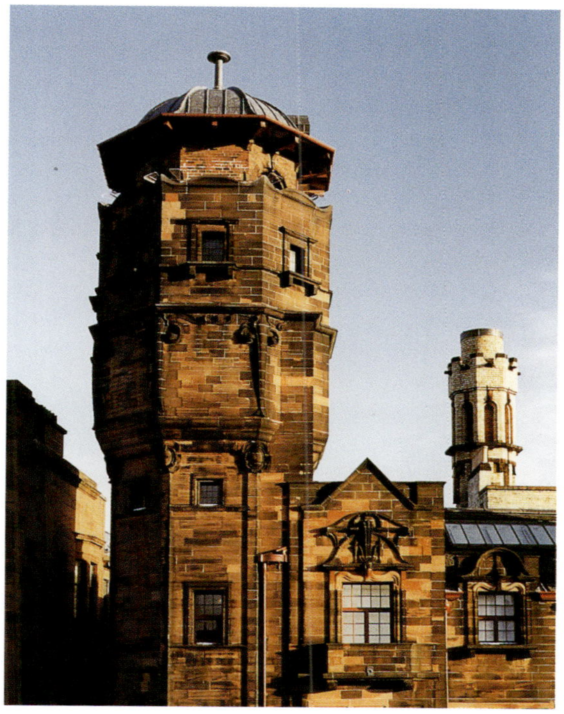

**_The Glasgow Herald_ Warehouse 1894**

*The Glasgow Herald* was CRM's first big architectural job; a simple newspaper distribution warehouse. The only particular requirements were a water tower (above), and a clear route through the building at ground level for dispatch vans.

**Willow Tea Rooms**

Detail seen in Sauchiehall Street, the 'avenue of the willows'.

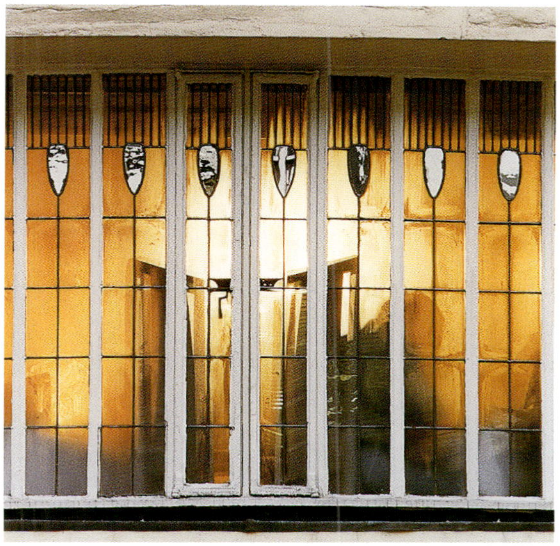

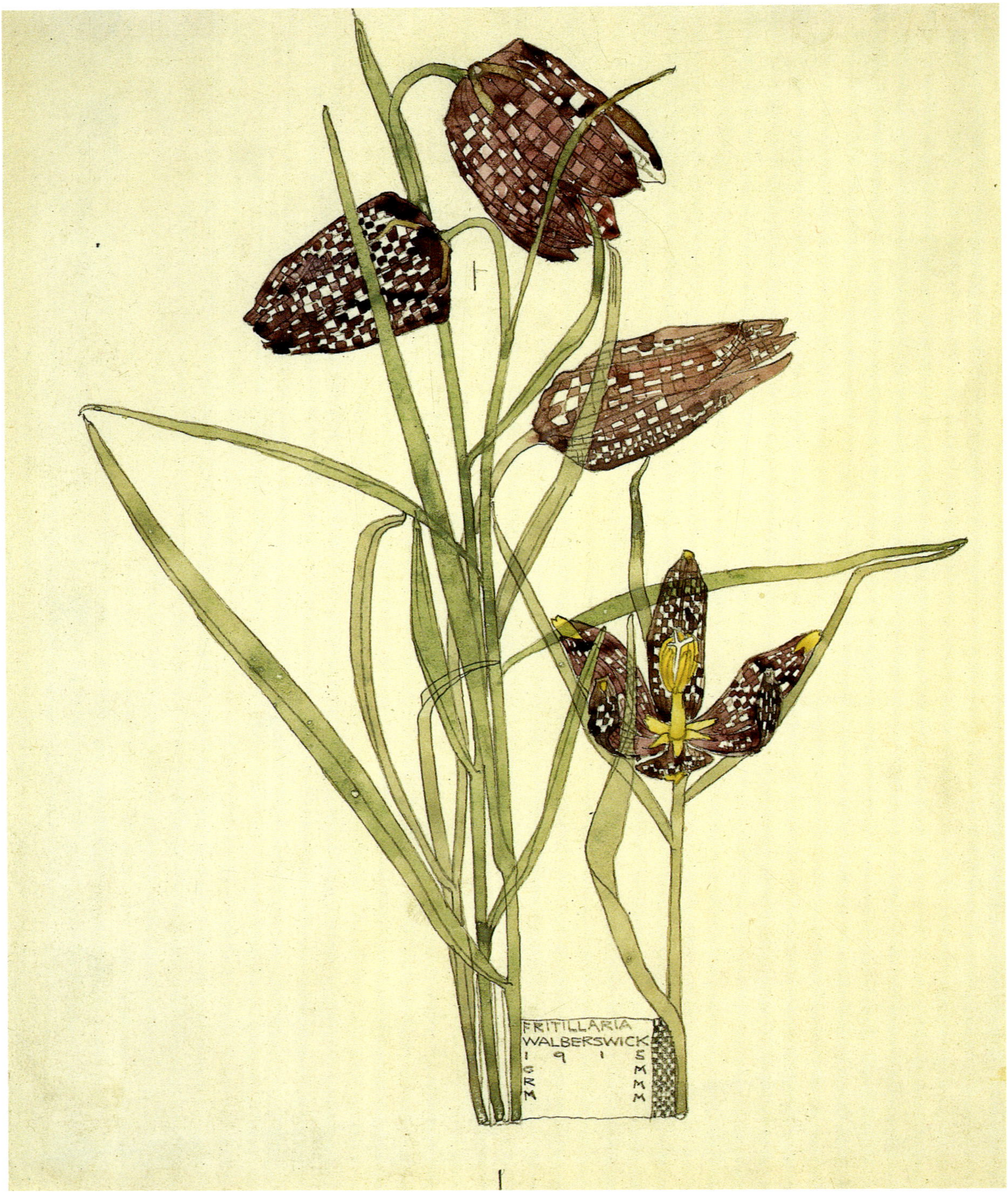
FRITILLARIA
WALBERSWICK
1 9 1 5
CRM MMM

# AN ENGLISH ARTIST

Spring 1915. Elsewhere, the European war is raging with its spluttering, red-faced propaganda. Its vile slaughter is not yet glimpsed in the eyes and the limbless crutches of the few who will be returning to these English village lanes. The Suffolk coast remains quiet, local, isolated; although there are occasional scares of a German invasion from the sea.

The painter sits quietly in the enclosed garden at Westwood, the house where he and his wife lodge, in the little village of Walberswick. Slowly he has been rebuilding his sense of concentration. Once rested and primed, he chooses a garden plant, and begins to observe it, with an extraordinary precision. And then, once he knows it, he draws it. Picasso, once he had looked, was known to dismiss his model before starting to paint; that was an exercise our painter doesn't bother with. With no preliminary sketch, without hesitation, his firm pencil line forms and often overlays stem, petal and leaf. He reveals its essence. The structure and shape are clear – indeed some of his drawings may eventually find their way into the Botany Department of Glasgow University and be recognised as among the finest of botanical drawings. Much more than technical precision, he reveals nature: the appearance of the natural life, rather than what the botanist knows it to be. There are echoes here from his endless student days spent in structured copying, and of that fresh Ruskinian wave, stressing the perceived form of nature, which dominated the Art School by the century's end.

Ruskin talks of 'the function of our architecture being, as far as it may be, to replace [fields], to tell us about nature.'[1] What an extraordinary and wonderful dream. The painter sits and winds backwards. Ruskin sees architecture as 'full of delicate imagery of the flowers we can no longer gather.' These flower studies today are full of the qualities of the architecture he can no longer conjure.

In July last year, they had arrived, as they had done often enough before, to lodge with Mrs King at Millbank, next door to the cottage of their friends the Newberys. At the end of summer, Fra Newbery was steeling himself, a bit unwillingly, to return for the next academic year as director of the Glasgow School of Art; their art-student daughter Mary stayed on a further month. Then she too departed north, leaving the artist and his wife alone. 'Whatever they really felt,' Mary says, 'they didn't show it. Dignified,' she adds. They are travelling light, having arrived

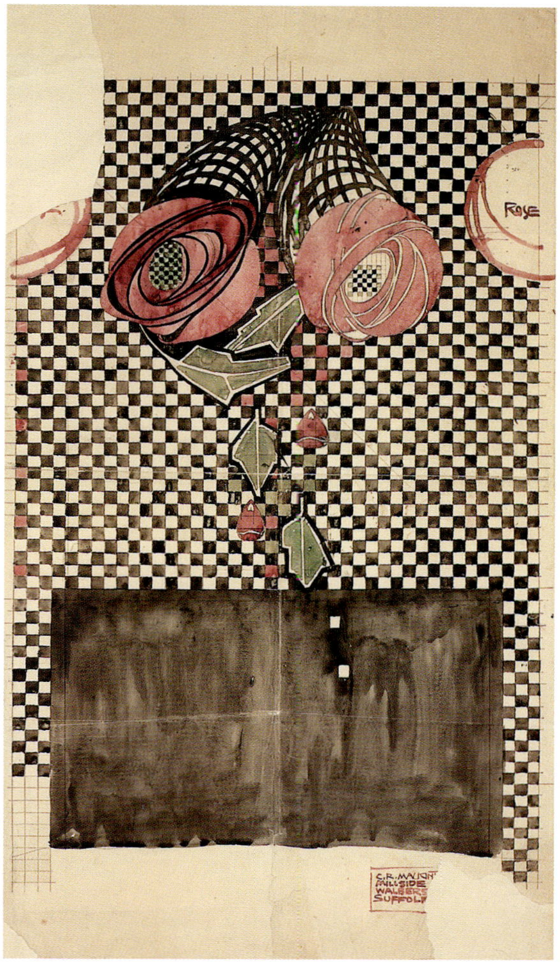

**Roses on a Chequered Ground, 1915**

Almost the only exception to flower studies during the year in Suffolk, is his graphic design for 'Roses on a Chequered Ground', which hints at future work. What must he be thinking as he laboriously fills in these squares?

**Fritillaria, 1915 (opposite)**

The artist draws flowers all his life, but in Walberswick, from 1914 to 1915, this activity becomes central to his existence. This English marsh-meadow plant's chequered petals are actually precisely observed, though it might appear (as nature following art) to be created as his stylisation.

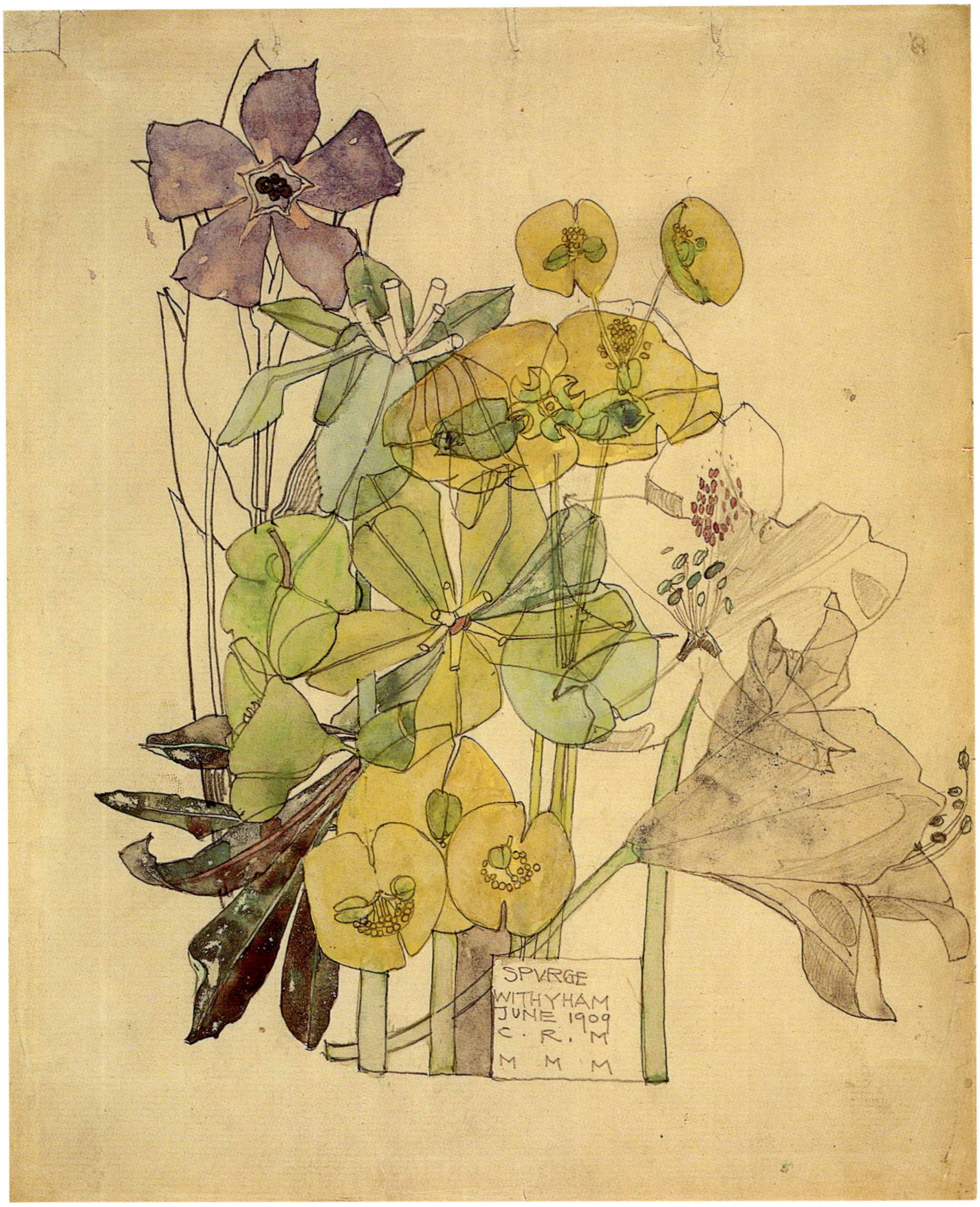


**Spurge, June 1909**

This beautiful compositior of layered forms, overlapping and clarified by the colour washes, was done during a visit to East Sussex in June 19C9. Labelled 'Spurge', it also has a blue periwinkle at the top and two rhododendron flowers to the right.

on summer holiday with just their clothes. Then, before he could recover strength to face the next decision – would they move on to Vienna, or... – the War broke out, blocking any future in Europe. He could not face returning to Glasgow. Where can they go? His wife persuades him to stay, returning herself to let the Glasgow house and then going back to him in Suffolk. He has badly needed a real rest cure for at least two years, she tells a friend.[2]

Their friends gone, they had to move on from the room at Millbank cottage. For a while, as winter drew in, they found space in the Anchor Inn, and now they have a room at Westwood. 'What is there to do in a village from six to ten? Nothing, is there. You have a drink, and if you're a habitual drinker, you have one all night, don't you?' Ginger Winyard, son of the landlord of the Anchor talks, thinking of the artist.[3] Now the virtual hibernation of winter is over and spring in the garden is indeed a rebirth.

Just like their French destination a decade later, this English retreat has been a hidden, fashionable artist's haunt for a generation. 'A picturesque and paintable little place,' said *The Artist* in November 1891, 'as absolutely primitive as anything could be.' Little has altered since then; the cataclysmic changes beyond are scarcely felt. So the artist can retreat into the quietest quiet, and there start to recuperate, to refresh his creative being, to begin looking again. No one knows he is an architect. This shuffling of the self, this slow and private redefinition, leaves behind both the professional city life and the bourgeois life of Glasgow's west end. Renewed out of those dead skins, he retains his sanity through using his eyes; using them to study forms; not words nor ideas, but the formal qualities of nature in its most intimate beauty. He draws life-size with a wonderful concentration, producing images of great elegance.

And the European network withers away. Wärndorfer, whom he remembers taking to Helensburgh in 1902, leaves Vienna embittered for the U.S., (later to regain contact with Hoffmann, but never with the artist). Muthesius, so influential in Germany, fades from view here; his son Ekhart never meets his godfather.[4]

Once more the artist must feel the purifying effect of nature on character. In this Walberswick garden he touches again his father's 'Garden of Eden,' the beautiful and glorious horticultural obsession of the policeman. 'The needed neo-technic re-civilisation has its literal seeds in the literal garden,' Patrick Geddes said.[5] And, as his friend the artist well knows, Geddes places direct observation above all other tools of the mind. Through these months, he recuperates, through the work of looking, in the garden. To a child who knows him in the village, 'he has really piercing eyes.' As his wife writes to Geddes's wife, 'already Toshie is quite different.' Within a year, she continues, she expects him to be fit again.

It is too crude to see this as art therapy. But it certainly helps restore his whole person. The sense is reminiscent of William Morris's memory of the art-worker in a world of undivided labour, a world which 'allows the hand to rest the mind, as well as the mind the hand...the kind of work which the world has lost.'[6]

Now their momentous private break spills into a time of

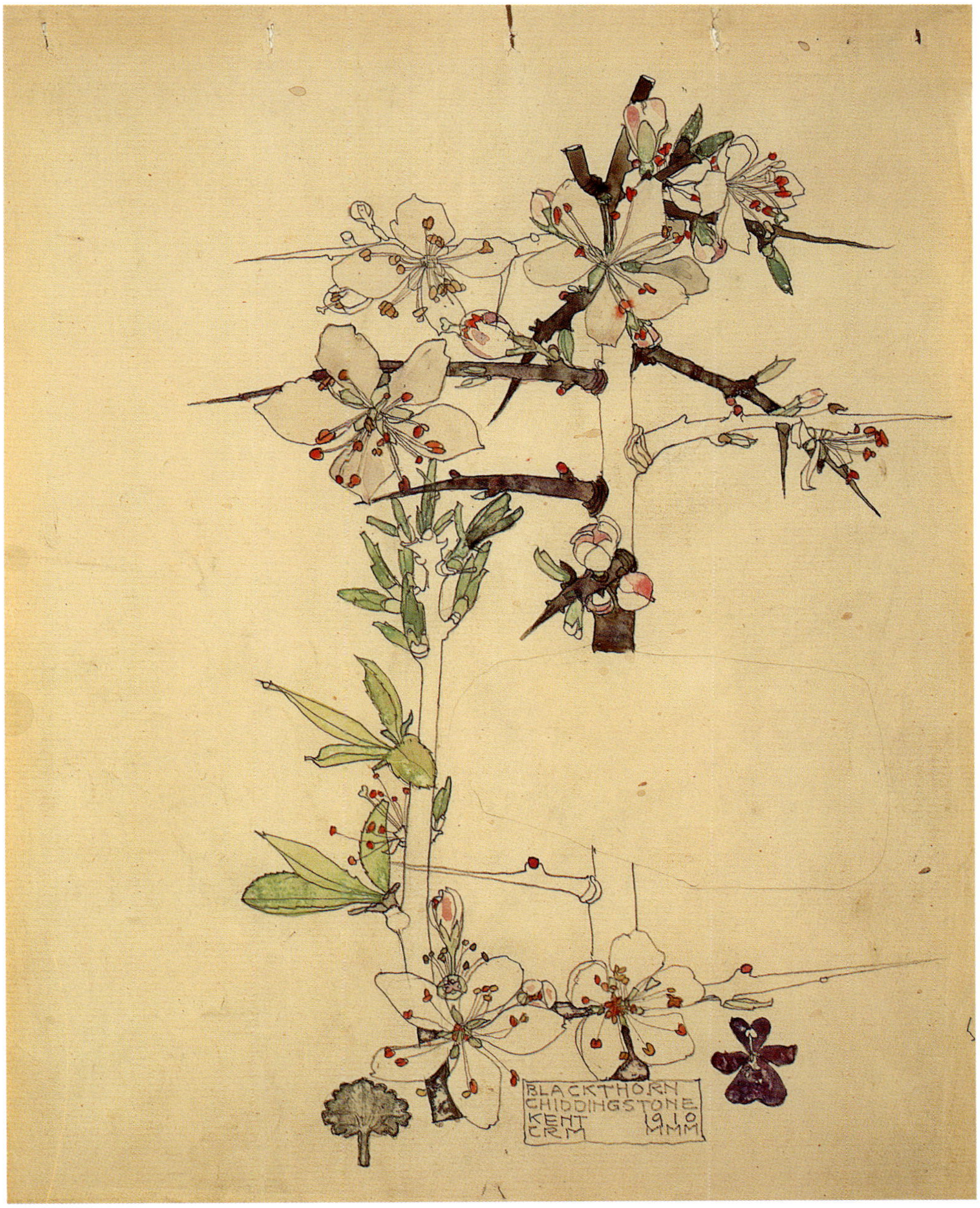


**Blackthorn, 1910**

In Spring 1910, the artist visited Chiddingstone, Kent, both sketching its architecture and calming and refreshing himself by concentrating on its profusion of flowers, which he recorded with great concentration and beauty. It seems that with the Blackthorn, most unusually, part of the drawing did not work and had to be eliminated.

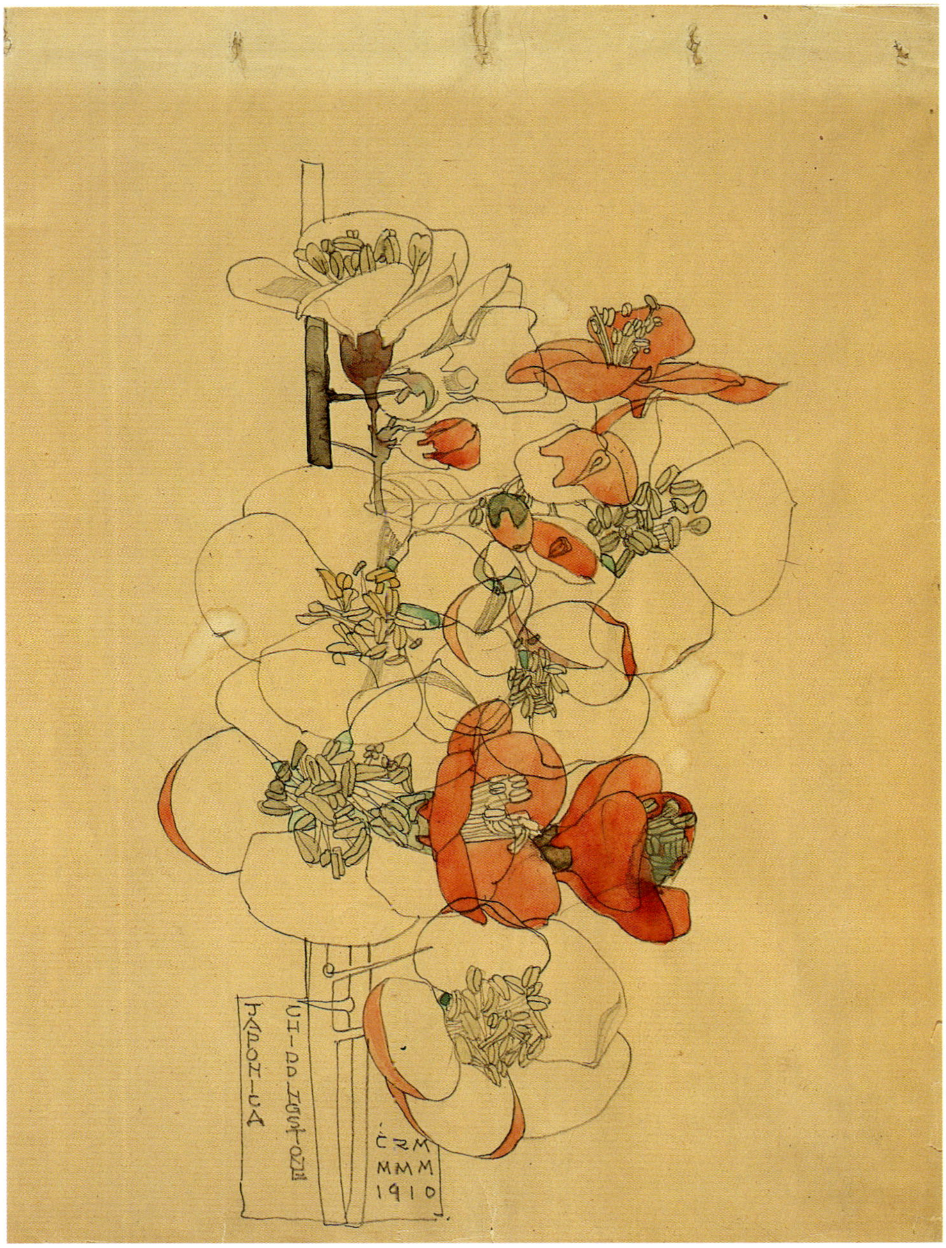


**Japonica, 1910**

Like the Blackthorn (p.85), the Japonica drawn at Chiddingstone has a Japanese echo in its design. Again like Blackthorn, the colour is used sparingly and with great care, in this case to highlight the scarlet flowers.

public ending and deeper changes. The shock to this artist's system, widens to all around. His professional career crisis becomes one shared by many contemporaries; it is a watershed. 'The lamps are going out all over Europe,' said Viscount Grey as the Great War began, 'we shall not see them lit again in our lifetime.' It has a very personal resonance. The architecture he deplores – cold, academic, technocratic – is French and United States influenced. The designers with whom he feels close bonds, whose aesthetics and ethics he shares, are German and Austrian. In this war, far from home, his friends have become the enemy; his opponents the allies. His isolation is profound.

As the days lengthen and warm, the garden at Westwood once more reveals its charms. It is an ancient, enclosed village garden planted with a rare range of cultivated plants. He is drawing them again: he chooses and cuts specimens with care; and he transforms them.

In the village, a 'studio' was organised for him by Jessie Newbery next to her husband's one; in reality it is a fisherman's hut on the riverbank towards the sea. It is somewhere to walk to, a few minutes from the bedroom at their lodgings. It is their own, and here they can even invite visitors for a little party. Sometimes he picks wild flowers by the way, but almost all the drawings are of commonly found garden ones.

And so a project builds. Perhaps he can make a collection of these drawings. He had previously sent watercolours across the channel, exhibiting in Liège, Ghent and Paris; before the war halted that. Perhaps Koch or one of his German contacts would have published the portfolio as a book. But for the war. By mid summer, he has over 40 completed watercoloured drawings. It is his only work for nearly 12 months; obsessive, a ritual work of recovery; an average of one drawing a week, until his welcome in East Anglia suddenly ends. It is a major body of work. Each drawing is carefully named and finished. (The naming sometimes displays his difficulty with spelling, but hardly ever is a misattribution). His knowledge of plants a silent tribute to his father.

He sits on the step of his fisherman's hut, drawing sticks and flowers, colouring them with the kind of box of paints which children use. Watercolour is added with great deliberation. Areas are left uncoloured, in the tradition of botanical illustration – but also of architectural drawing. Colour doesn't always eliminate the overlaying of elements. It is added to the picture, not to the plant.

Painting indoors by day, the artist walks out at dusk in his great black cape, deerstalker and pipe, a large limping 45-year-old. A little boy, imagining him to be Sherlock Holmes, follows in the shadows, hoping to pass unnoticed. Down beyond the dunes, he walks towards the beach. On, right to the edge of the sea, where he stands looking to the horizon. For a long time he remains, unaware of the water lapping at his boots. The boy scurries back home. Slowly the painter turns and returns to the village. Just before entering The Bell Tavern he spots the boy playing and quietly asks if he's enjoyed his walk.

Sitting with his drink beside him, he puffs on his pipe. After a while, leaving the drink standing on his shady table, he is off again to The Anchor Inn and another drink, in the corner, himself to himself. And then back to The Bell, and an evening floating between the village's two pubs. 'A very restless man,' whispers a young native.[7] Unusual, reclusive behaviour, and not at all that of a classic alcoholic.

How can he let go of the past? In the middle of winter, he had received a letter sent on the last day of 1914 from Glasgow. It is written on the new headed paper of what a few months before had been his own partnership, the mainstay of his professional life, the statement of his architectural achievement, of his social achievement in the bourgeois city: Honeyman, Keppie & Mackintosh. A decade after Honeyman was last seen, his name still stands there; but as soon as the artist leaves, the word Mackintosh is removed. His mediocre former assistant Graham Henderson moves into his place and within two years John Keppie & Henderson will replace what in 1900 was John Honeyman & Keppie; the 15 years which added a third name – and added the only reason for the practice's memorability – is submerged. The conventional, parochial practice, transformed by one extraordinarily talented

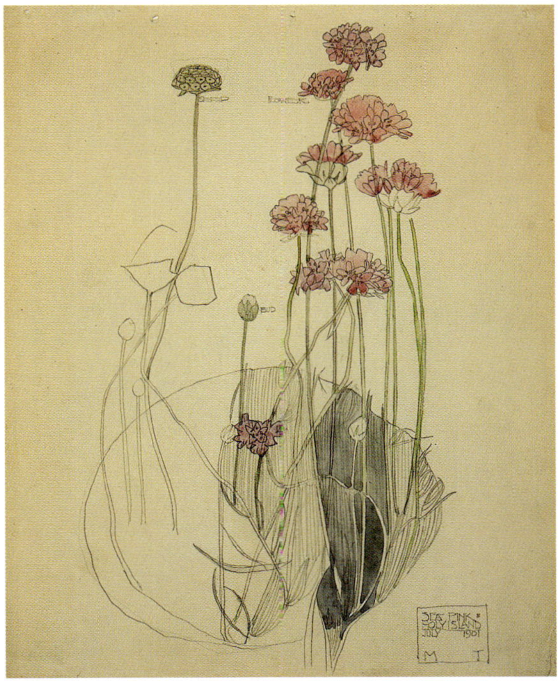

**Sea Pink, 1901**

From his first, tentative formalising and colouring of flower studies (above), the artist now produces around 30 powerful, major images at Walberswick in 1915. 'Burberis' (below) is in fact not berberis but mahonia, one of his rare misidentifications.

**Burberis, 1915**

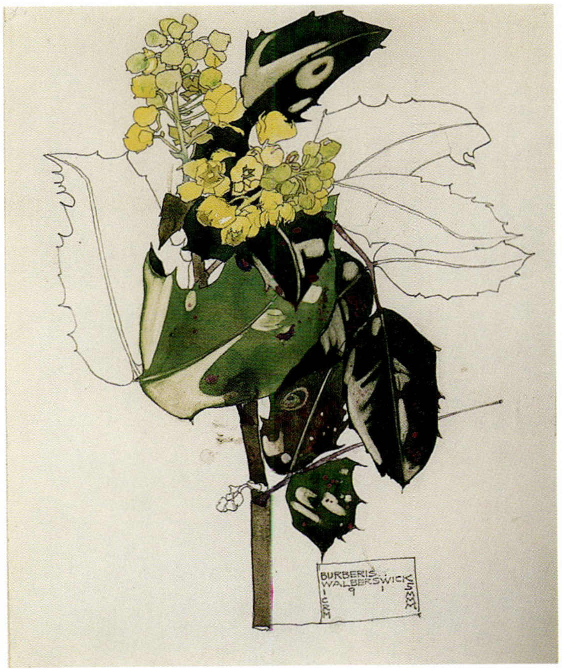

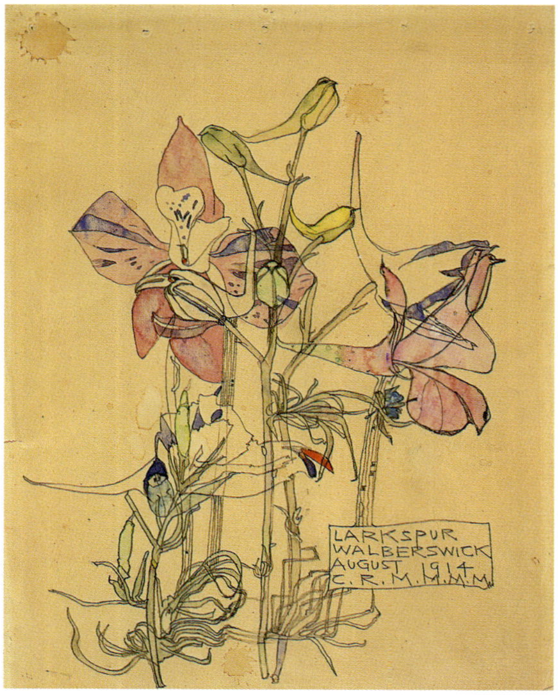


Larkspur, August 1914

member, has reverted to an even more forgettable condition.

On New Year's Eve, John Keppie is formally solicitous: 'I heard from Newbery you were in Suffolk. I had almost given up hope of hearing from you...'. He only writes because the artist still has some financial debt to the old practice. He stiffly passes his regards to Mrs Mackintosh and adds, without emotion, Newbery 'has been very unwell with nerves and is not likely to be back at the school for some time yet.'[8] The painter keeps his feelings to himself. And keeps hold of this letter till he dies.

As summer approaches, both his equanimity and creative force are reconstructed. Other artists are returning for the summer, including E.A.Walton, the 'Glasgow Boy' (and older brother of George, the artist's early collaborator for Miss Cranston) who has a place nearby. The flower drawings are shown to Walton and other artist friends, whose response is encouraging. In June the painter writes to his staunchest Glasgow friend, describing his flower studies as 'straightforward, frank work... much thought of by the artist men who have seen them here.'[9]

Despite the company of these artists, this is a very private couple who together are working through a profound life change. He seems taciturn and uncommunicative. His glances pierce. His Glasgow accent is very foreign. There is no sense, at least visible in the village now, that they might ever move on. What of his wife? For she is an artist too. Where is she, as he walks alone on the shore, sits alone in the corner of the pub? Someone says they saw him shining a lantern from the top floor of Westwood; signalling out to sea.

He is oblivious to the local whispering, until one night they come back from a walk to find a soldier standing with fixed bayonet outside the house. Others, upstairs, are going through their personal papers. They are holding a bundle of his letters clearly from the enemy, letters from Austria and Germany. The painter is outraged. He is a patriot! They are humiliated by this invasion and search, but the papers are confiscated and he must appear before a tribunal. His wife becomes ill with worry. Only with difficulty is he able to establish his bona fides. He tries to contact Patrick Geddes, who is in India but sends his daughter,

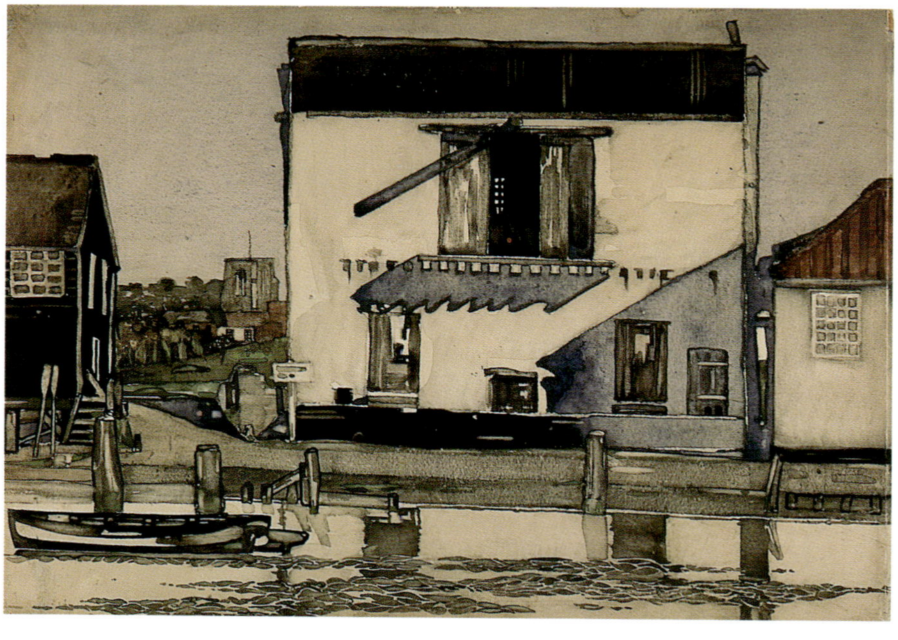

Venetian Palace, Blackshore-on-the-Blyth, 1914

One of very few paintings at Walberswick which is not a flower study, this has a nicely wry title. This is the last known work exhibited by the artist before he leaves England, being shown at the Royal Academy in 1923.

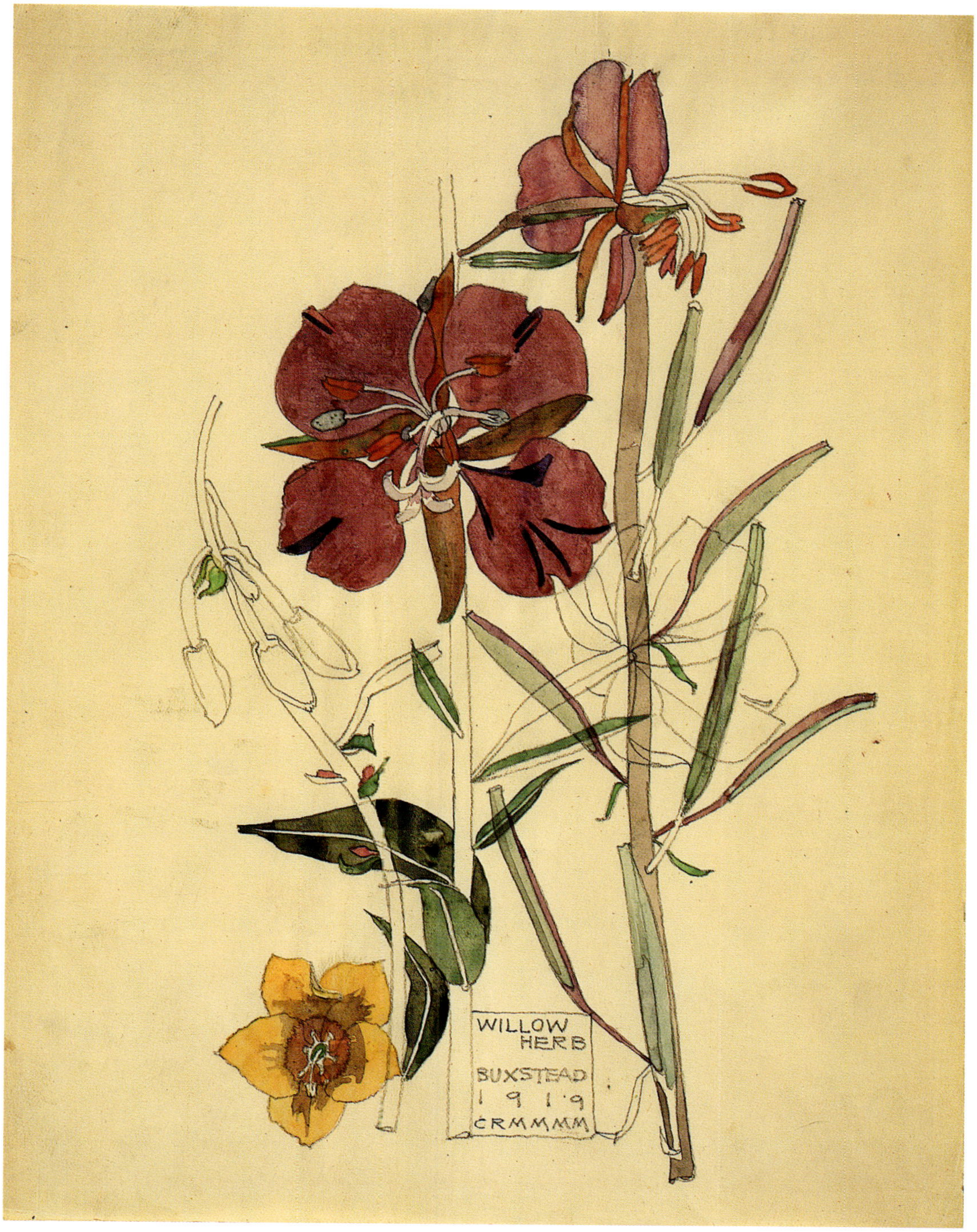


Lady Mears, to the War Office in London to speak on the painter's behalf. His name is cleared, but he is affronted and can hardly be restrained from taking it to a higher court, to The House of Lords if necessary.

There are now widespread rumours about a German invasion and non-residents are being kept away from these coastal areas. Clearly, the painter's welcome is overstayed. He is ordered to leave East Anglia.

Has he brought it on himself; wearing funny clothes and making no attempt to integrate locally? Village folk wouldn't respond this way to a lovable eccentric artist. But surely he doesn't mean to appear gruff; his socially inept behaviour is unintended. Of his possibly causing offence, or his extravagant over-reaction, he is quite unaware.[10]

It is all a misunderstanding, of course. And it touches the deeper misunderstanding, which is why his reaction is so extreme. The letters they found – from Muthesius moving towards the Deutsche Werkbund in Germany, from the Secessionists who asked advice on setting up the Wiener Werkstätte in Vienna – give away a direction in which the architect Mackintosh could have been heading. Secret thoughts of the cultural spy, for there had been no one in Britain, certainly no like-minded group in provincial Glasgow, with whom he could share it. And so now, inevitably, these ideas are arrested, and expelled.

**Willow Herb, 1919**

Very few wildflower studies were done after the move from Suffolk, including this, drawn when he had a little other work nearby. The paired initials at the bottom are a record of the visit and imply his wife's presence; a habit begun on holiday at the start of the century, more informally (as with 'Sea Pink', p.87) calling themselves T(oshie) and M(argaret).

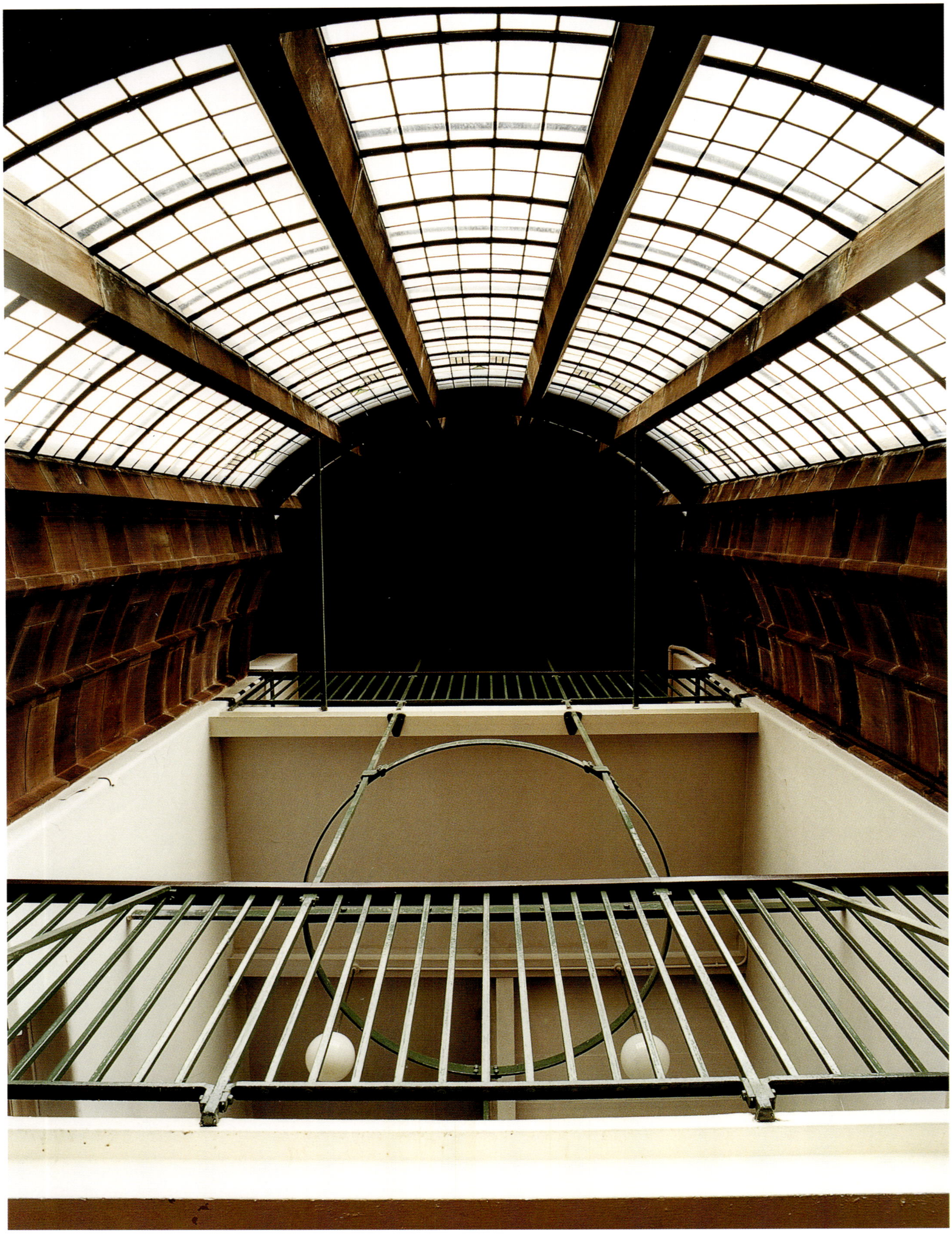

# DYING PRACTICE

In the first few years of the century, Mackintosh had a variety of other work, beyond tea rooms and houses, to keep him busy. From mid decade, other than the Art School, he had very little. After the Art School, virtually nothing until he finally quit in 1914.

The *Daily Record* building, begun in 1900 and not completed till 1904, is a printing works on a narrow lane in the business centre. Its arrangement is conventional, as with *The Glasgow Herald* a few years earlier; Mackintosh's only space to shine is in the facade. Between the arcaded ground floor and the top-heavy cap, in the same red sandstone, it is faced with white glazed bricks decorated sparsely with tree motifs.

From the end of 1901, he worked on a competition scheme for Liverpool Cathedral. In London, Bentley's Catholic Westminster Cathedral in a 'byzantine' style, was recently opened; Liverpool wanted a 'gothic' cathedral and most of the 102 entrants, including Mackintosh, obliged. He developed details from Sedding and his pupil Henry Wilson, but nothing at this stage[1] gives any sense of an exceptional building. The assessors were Norman Shaw and Bodley, whom also Mackintosh had praised in his earlier lecture. But his scheme does not reach the second, detailed competition stage. No critic since has suggested that this was not a fair judgment.

Mackintosh thought otherwise, and didn't like what he saw of the system. The winner was a 21-year-old unknown, except that his father was a well-known architect and his grandfather England's most famous Victorian architect. Bodley, the assessor, was then appointed to help the young winner, Giles Gilbert Scott. Charles Reilly was working in Bodley's office at the time, had helped run the competition and been close to its decision-making; he had recently been appointed to head architectural education at Liverpool University.

Mackintosh's second school, Scotland Street, was designed in 1903 and completed in mid 1906. Like the first, a prentice work built very close to his birthplace in Townhead, this was a standard School Board layout, with a symmetrical central division running through both building and playground; the boys' entrance and stair tower, cloakrooms and lavatories, being echoed by the girls'. He wanted it built in white rather than red stone; with the interiors covered in black tiles rather than School Board standard colours; with small pane windows (as in

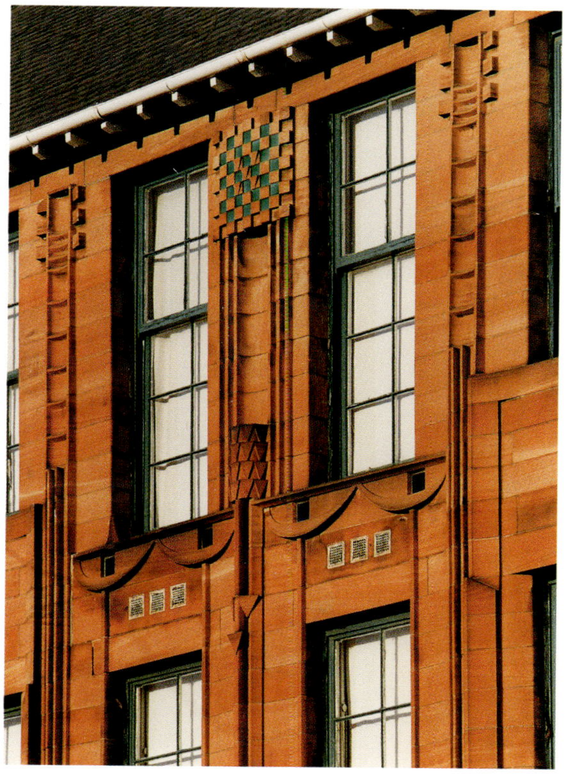

**Scotland Street School**

Interior of east stair tower, looking up (opposite); centre of south facade (above); tile detail inside stairwell (below).

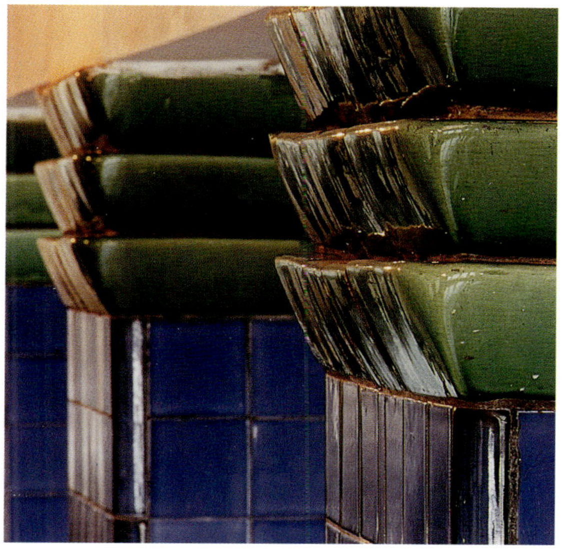

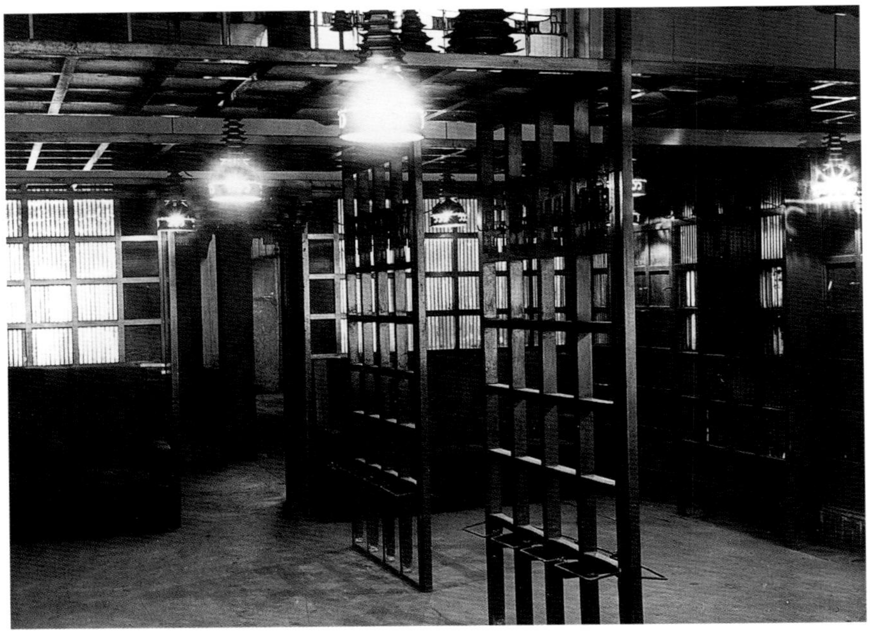

**Ingram Street Tea Rooms, The Chinese Room**

In the summer of 1911, Cranston once again pulled CRM out of his depressed torpor (for he had hardly designed anything for years, and had not a single new commission in 1910), with the commission for two final rooms at Ingram Street, the Cloister Room and the Chinese Room (seen here when empty and finally abandoned in 1950). This room had been the first she opened, in 1886, ornately decorated and with some chinoiserie around the entrance. CRM strips it back, paints the tall ceiling black, covers the walls with coarse hessian painted blue and then adds a lattice against walls, as a low ceiling and as freestanding screens, all painted strong blue, and some infilled with leaded glass, mirror and red plastic. It is a powerful, exotic, complex space constructed from few, simple elements.

his drawing) rather than standard large ones. In none of this did he get his way. At one point when they overruled him, a coldly furious letter reached the office: 'I am directed to state that the board have no desire for controversy, but the attitude taken by Mr Mackintosh in his interview with our committee and his letter, left them no alternative but to state their position in clear terms…'.[2]

It took an inordinate time to start building, and things were not going his way. In 1905, apart from designing a room setting for a Berlin exhibition, and a few more bits of Hill House furniture, there was no work. However he was commissioned for a new house in 1906. He sent images of Windyhill and the Hill House only to be told this was not what was wanted: these were not proper Tudor country houses! Despite all his earlier pronouncements attacking the use of historical styles, despite his badge of 'Individuality', and his having delivered Hill House with the ringing words: 'Here is the house: it is not an Italian villa, an English mansion house, a Swiss chalet, or a Scotch castle. It is a dwelling house.', despite all that, he now grovels to the new client: 'if you want a house in the Tudor or any other phase of English architecture, I can promise you my best services.'[3] It was then designed by Mackintosh, as an anonymous English-style house, but he couldn't keep up the alienation it implied.

Luckily, before the end of 1906, the Art School decided to go ahead and build, and though they couldn't just use the earlier project – requirements of both the client and safety regulations had changed – they returned to the original architects. Mackintosh constantly fell behind the deadlines set for its progress, but by late 1907 it was building, and completed two years later.

Back in 1901, Honeyman & Keppie were appointed as architects by a rich mining engineer, H.B. Collins, who had bought the house and land of Auchterbothie on the south side of the Clyde, near Kilmacolm. Mackintosh designed a lodge gate in 1901 and a 'plowman's cottage' in the grounds in 1906.[4] It seems an appropriate, small, square house in local rough whin walling, 2 ft 6 in (760 mm) thick. It is robust, with a romantic nationalist spirit perhaps, but Mackintosh's

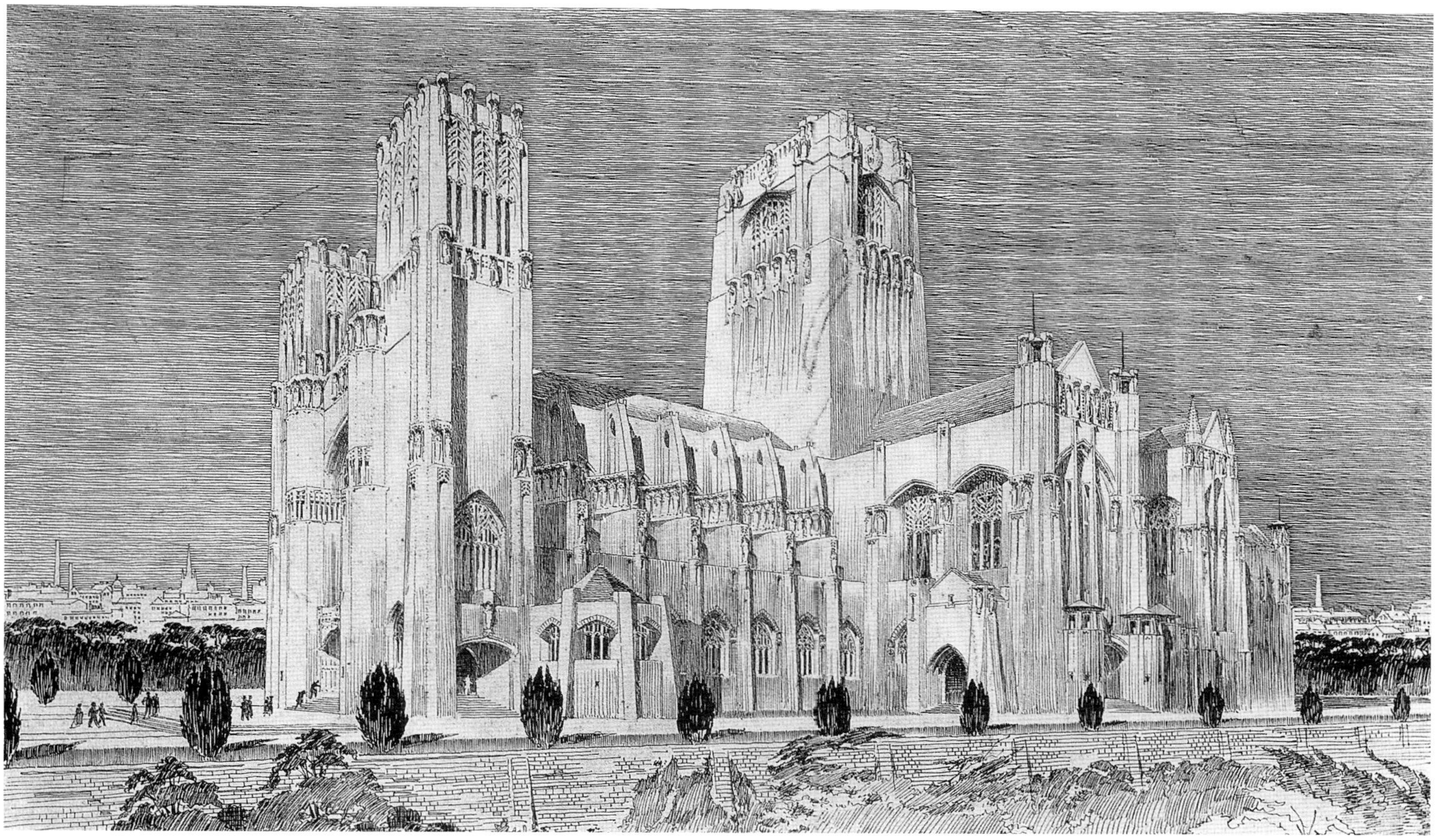

personality is invisible. When Collins needed to expand this building in 1908, Mackintosh proposed to cloak it with a new two-storey wing, making a considerably larger L-shaped whole with a winding stair in its angle, in the old Scottish tradition.[5] In 1912, asked to expand it yet further, he proposed a single three-storey tower. (This was not built and the accepted solution, more clumsy and ordinary, and not drawn in Mackintosh's hand, was built in 1913.)

Not only is Mackintosh's work of little interest in these years, there was little enough of it. In 1910, the office only undertook half as much as the previous year; in 1911 the figure was halved again, and it kept getting worse to the end of the partnership. Unlike Keppie, Mackintosh responded with depression and drink. In 1911, perhaps fearing bankruptcy, he transferred their house into Margaret's name. Former colleagues tell that by then his lunch hour often lasted from 1 pm to 4.45 pm.

Early in 1913, the practice took on two competitions. Mackintosh failed to produce his scheme for Jordanhill teacher training college; Graham Henderson completed an entry, which, though banal, won the commission for the firm. Henderson soon became a partner on the strength of it. Mackintosh by that time had agreed that *his* partnership should end.

**Liverpool Cathedral Competition, Perspective Drawing**

CRM having become his partner in 1901, Keppie kept his commissions to himself and his assistants, leaving CRM to find his own work through competitions. None was successful and almost all are long lost and forgotten. However all seven of his drawings for the Anglican Cathedral, Liverpool, remain. CRM's project (one of at least two which the office submitted) was published in March 1903 and highly commended, but not chosen as one of the final schemes to be further developed. It was an important design of which CRM was proud. He always resented its failure to get any further in the competition.

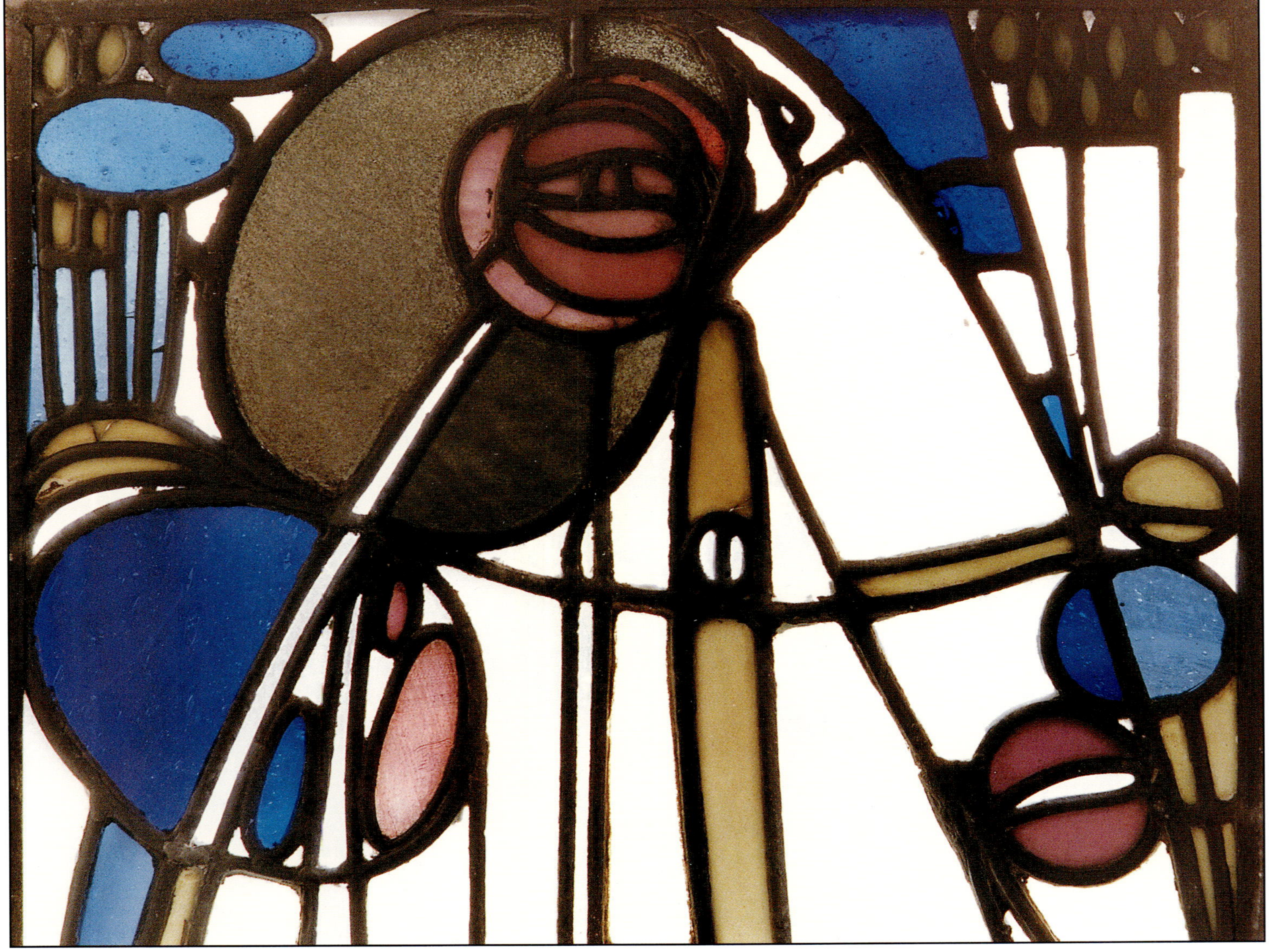

**Stained Glass Detail from the Rose Boudoir, 1902**

Fra Newbery, asked to curate the Scottish section of the International Exhibition of Modern Decorative Art in Turin in 1902, invited a range of Glasgow Style designers to submit work, and CRM to design their settings in three linked rooms. One of these three was devoted to the Mackintoshes, incorporating a room setting, 'the Rose Boudoir' which included this stained glass. Its highly stylised linear pattern, which could be executed in various materials, is typical of the Glasgow Style rather than of CRM at his most original. In Turin, various critics confused the work of various exhibitors (one called CRM 'Mr Macdonald'). Though the exhibition was a general success, it was also the beginning of the end of the Glasgow Style.

# AUTHENTIC GLASGOW STYLE

A century ago, the 'Glasgow Rose' was the universally recognised symbol of what was known as the Glasgow Style. It is a signature in many of Mackintosh's interiors around 1900; stencilled on walls, inlaid in glass or metal. His 'Ver Sacrum rose' displays its most sophisticated, archetypal graphic. But this hallmark image by no means indicates his presence.

Mackintosh was a tirelessly inventive designer but no solitary genius. Much of his work was closely linked with his lifelong and devoted partner Margaret. They, along with her sister Frances and Herbert McNair, were for a very brief time, a century ago, the avant-garde Glasgow gang known as The Four. This quartet was embedded in the wider group of innovative and lively designers and artists of the Glasgow Style. This wider style was closely influenced by nationalist and Celtic revivalist ideas in Scotland, by the Arts & Crafts and the Aesthetic Movement in England, and not least by the great centres of European contemporary design of the moment, most obviously fin-de-siècle Vienna.

Perhaps the rose's first use was in a textile design by Jessie Newbery (and again, perhaps it wasn't), but very soon it was everywhere in Glasgow, an easily copied image, used by all from the finest designers to the humblest house-builders. It is on metal or gesso, embroidered and enamelled, in illustration and painting, on furniture and graphics, on elegant candle sconces for the rich dining table and on the decorative tiles and stained glass of the middle class 'wally closes' of the city's tenements. With this universal application in front of us, where influential images spread like wildfire, we, the viewers, cannot avoid the work of judging quality for ourselves, of separating the Mac and the mock, the charming, the banal and the profound. The fascination of the Glasgow Style is its sudden starburst quality, its seeming to come from nowhere and then disappear almost as fast; in its offering an unusual spotlight to minor figures; and yes, in how seductively easy is the mechanical mimicry of all that imagery today.

What was more difficult at the time, was identifying authorship. How could this be? First, there was that 'Arts & Crafts' legacy which advocated group craft working, with not just a work ethic but the physical craft production itself often shared. In Glasgow, the band of happy craftsmen (William Morris' dream) was particularly close-knit. Almost all were linked to the School of Art, and hence to the pivotal figure of Francis Newbery. Newbery's educational programme

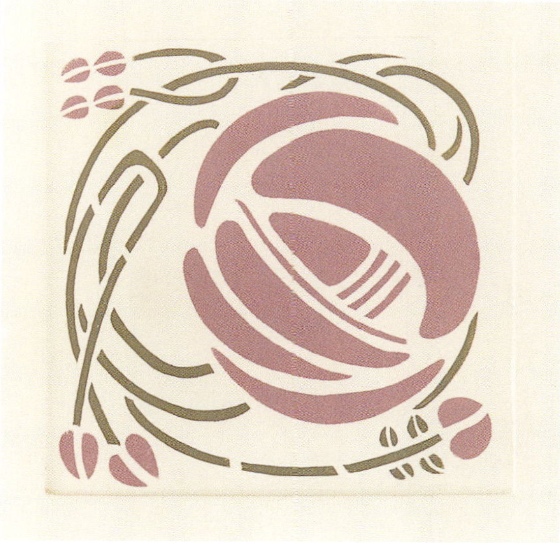

**Rose Stencil, Windyhill, 1900**

The rose, the universal Glasgow Style thumbprint, was stencilled by CRM on the bedroom wall at Windyhill.

**Photograph of The Rose Boudoir, Turin International Exhibition, 1902**

At Turin, designers employed by shopfitters Wylie & Lochhead (E.A. Taylor, and John Ednie) had their only exhibition alongside The Four within a CRM setting and next to the Mackintoshes' Rose Boudoir.

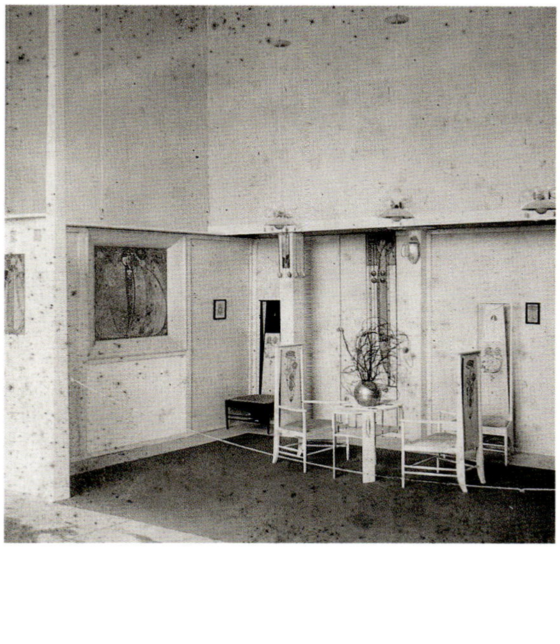

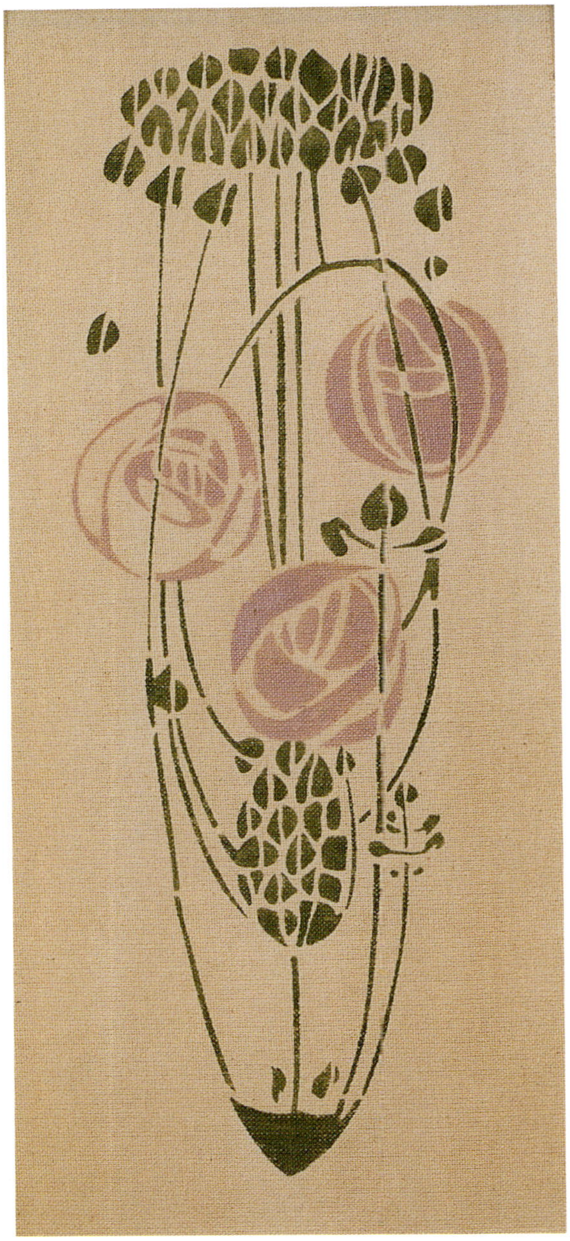

**Stencilled Chair Back, The Mackintosh House**

The floral motif of the Rose Boudoir is stencilled, probably by Margaret, on the canvas back of a delicate and feminine upholstered armchair, first seen in the Rose Boudoir in Turin in 1902 (see p.95), two copies of which then remained in the Mackintoshes' own home. Instead of a timber upholstered chair back, CRM uses simply a roll of canvas between the top and bottom rails, which flex uncomfortably when leaned on while sitting in the chair.

emphasised the crafts and applied arts and he provided new workshops for their production.

Mackintosh's own legacy from these Arts & Crafts beliefs is clear when he was asked by Viennese friends to advise on the setting up of their craft centre, the Wiener Werkstätte. He wrote enthusiastically, that it would 'achieve the greatest accomplishment: namely the production of all objects for everyday use in beautiful form and at a price that is within reach of the poorest, and in such quantities that the ordinary man on the street is forced to buy them because there is nothing else available and because soon he will not want to buy anything else.'[1]

For Mackintosh, as he uniquely put it in this statement of belief, written to Josef Hoffmann, it was no issue of style. The seeds of the Wiener Werkstätte and, parallel, Muthesius' Deutsche Werkbund flourished. But in Glasgow there was no such fertile soil, and Mackintosh's position was little recognised; in architecture perhaps the only one who understood what inspired him was his friend James Salmon. 'Nowhere has the modern movement in art been entered upon more seriously than at Glasgow,' wrote *The Studio* in 1907. 'The church, the school, the house, the restaurant, the shop, the poster, the book, with its printing, illustration and binding, have all come under the spell of the new influence.' But by then its bright radiance was dissipating very quickly, and, in the eyes of commentators, Mackintosh's real originality was never able to escape its after-image.

Newbery's own work (which was painting) never seemed influenced by this Glasgow Style, which indeed was a small and fleeting episode in his long tenure at the School of Art. Even in the key decade up to 1900, Glasgow Style designers are barely mentioned among the nearly 600 major prizewinners at the school.[2] Others were not part of the school club: Talwin Morris, for example, came north to design books; George Walton, though born into a local artistic family, came into design by a quite different route and always worked quite differently; John Ednie, George Logan, or E.A. Taylor, had been the designers for shopfitters and cabinet-makers. Glasgow, it has been said, was ripe for an avant-garde[3] and it certainly, if briefly, got it, with many young designers cashing in.

And with all these different forces released, ascribing to Mackintosh – or to anyone – becomes confusing. There is a brooch by Peter Wylie Davidson often assumed to be by Margaret Macdonald, and very similar to another by her – until his initials are noticed engraved on it. There is a bookplate for John Keppie signed by Mackintosh and an almost identical one by

Frances Macdonald. As for the Macdonald sisters, today's leading expert Pamela Robertson describes their work as 'often indistinguishable',[4] and *The Studio* editor a century ago felt 'some relief...that the Misses Macdonald are quite willing to have their work jointly attributed; for...it would be difficult if not impossible for an outsider to distinguish the hand of each...'[5]

If Ednie was the local whose work most resembled Mackintosh's, Walton and Mackintosh had worked together on the first tea rooms and Walton's 'Abingwood' chair has sometimes been mistaken for the work of Mackintosh. But the clearest difference is in working method: Mackintosh always was hands-on, working with his craftsmen, delighting in design development and creative dialogue. Walton was dignified and aloof, demanding that his drawings be executed with precision. (In this, of course, it was Walton who was the modern man.)

Mackintosh really understood material. Though not a craftsman himself, he knew how to beat silver, to make wrought-iron. The keystone over the School of Art doorway he modelled himself in plaster, full-size, in the office. Once, at Windyhill, he was seen teaching an old carpenter how to cut wood with an adze. Such links are very different from the general Glasgow collaboration based on imagery, based on similar skills rather than, in Mackintosh's case, on complementary skills.[6]

Working together on the same object, even with graphics or a poster, was a practice The Four took much further than others – though always without Mackintosh. Their lives, as their art, were almost as indistinguishable as the tendrils of intertwined trees and tresses in their graphics. More than two-thirds of Margaret Macdonald's work is collaborative, in the 1890s most of that is with her sister Frances and sometimes also with McNair. (Margaret's working with Mackintosh, really from 1900, is quite different.) There is a central contradiction in a style so based in individuality – a theme Newbery encouraged in the school, and which Mackintosh's lectures always repeat – yet this individuality is so often expressed through collective work. 'If you knew Mackintosh, you'd know he couldn't allow anyone to touch his work. Because that's the most savage Mackintosh that was!' recalls Mary Newbery[7] 'Howarth said to me that he must have had others working on the School of Art. I said you didn't know Mackintosh! If anyone else touched his work, he'd have literally torn them apart,' she continues.

Half a century later, new art critics (the best is Janice Helland) focus their aim on him as partner and collaborator. If politically correct, this psychologically misses the target.

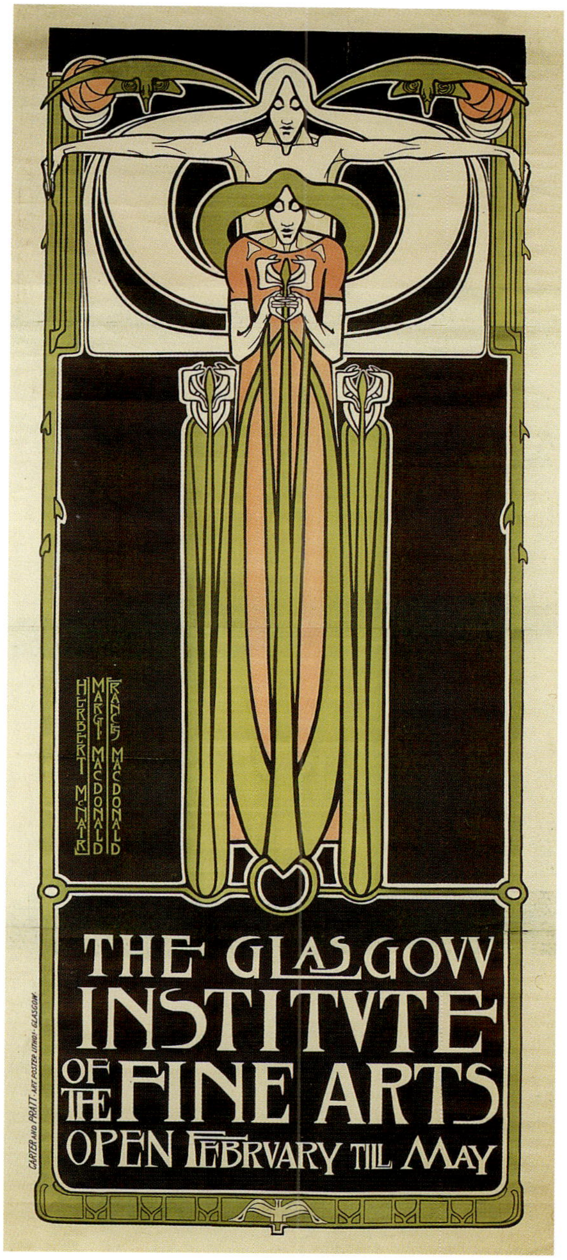


**Poster for the Glasgow Institute of Fine Arts**

It may be difficult to imagine how three individuals can design a poster together, but this 1896 example is signed by MMM, Frances and McNair. CRM's few essays in such work are visually very similar (as on p.9); the crucial difference is that they were always done alone. They were producing a new visual iconography, and recognisable 'Glasgow' calligraphy, exhibited alongside Toulouse-Lautrec and Beardsley in the 1890s.

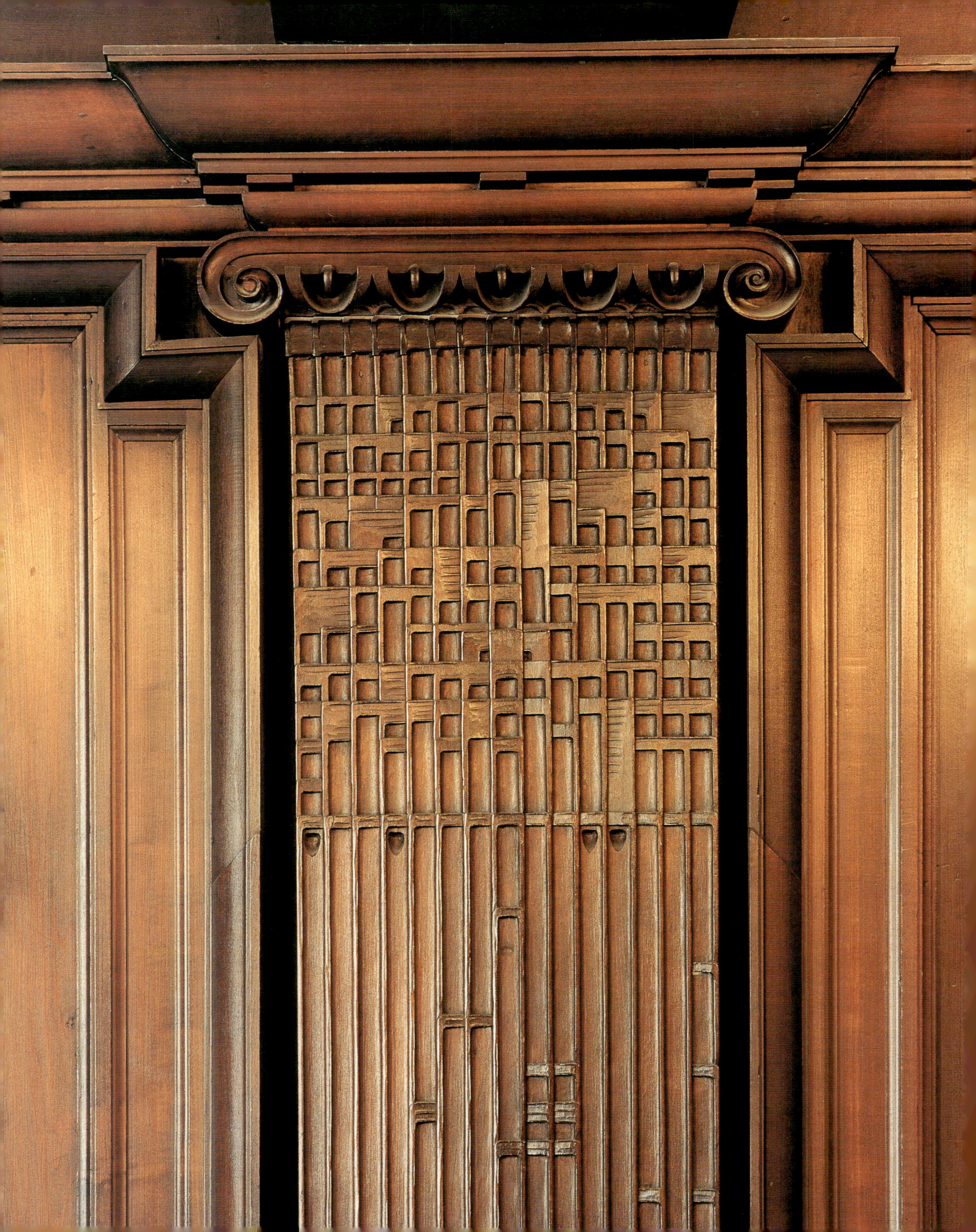

# CRISIS

This is 1908, and his life is in crisis. 'I wonder how it will end...'.[1] Much had been invested in the move, two years before, from the commercial centre to the bourgeois West End, to owning a house, and to denying any decay in their collaborative relationship in the years since the Hill House. Inside, their haven is extraordinarily different from the opulent classicism of Wellington Church across the narrow street or the gothic university spires alongside. Yet somehow it also seems stuck. So much baggage came with them. Along with the chance to start again, come the actual fireplaces from their old flat; to rededicate their partnership, they rebuild their old bedroom, the new room for living is filled with the old cabinets and writing desk, the complete dark dining room is rebuilt. All forms from a moment now passed, these have been recreated here with almost a touch of desperation. The move has not masked the crisis for long. It will only get worse until, after six long years, they cut loose.

For a while after 1900, the magic did seem to work. Within the flat designed to frame it, their marriage also came to show an artistic perfection. It was very different from the family life he had left; and the longer they remained childless, the more different it grew. He would join his father and sisters, with visiting nephews and nieces, for Christmas; yet Margaret is not remembered being there, nor on his trips to his sister's family. When family visit Toshie and Margaret, his children's maze is remembered, with different coloured wools wrapped round the legs of his white furniture to guide each child to their own present. Margaret is remembered by a niece as 'superior, condescending, aloof'.[2]

Christmas presents which used to be carefully lettered in a box – as are his drawings – 'from Uncle Tosh' now say 'from Margaret Macdonald Mackintosh and Charles Rennie Mackintosh'.[3] For Christmas 1902, he is Uncle Tosh also to the Davidson children at Windyhill, for whom he dresses up as Santa Claus. His physical clumsiness here causes a memorable stir when the robe catches fire on a candle. 'It might have been a very bad accident. We were fortunate indeed to get off with a few burns,' he wrote to Muthesius.[4]

But even by 1903 the charmed life was cracking. 'As often occurs', Margaret wrote to a mutual friend, 'antagonisms and undeserved ridicule bring on feelings of despondency and

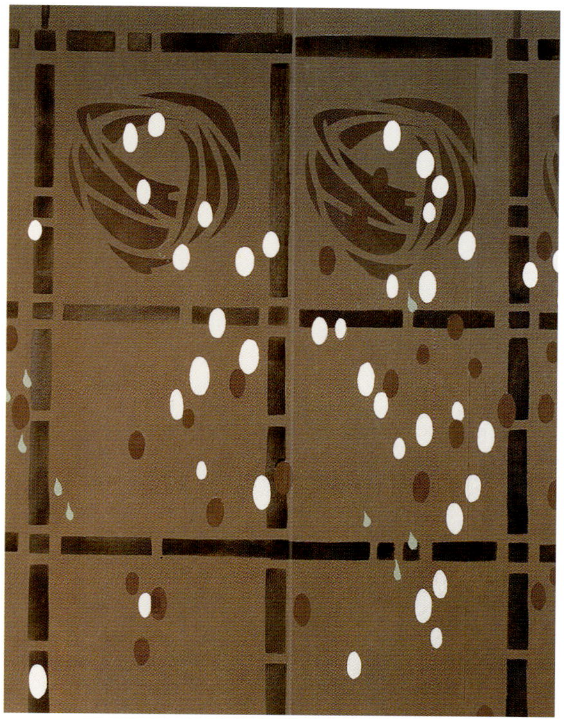

**Dining Room Trellis Stencil, The Mackintosh House**

In 1906-7, CRM is stencilling his own new dining room with silver teardrops against a dark rose on its lattice. He has virtually no work (beyond his own house) all year, until asked to carve a new, smaller, board room out of studio space in the School of Art. By now sober Beaux-Arts classicism covering regular streel frames, the increasingly austere Franco-American inspired fashion, dominates architecture, and its education here. J.J. Burnet, one of its best advocates, is an Art School governor, as is Keppie, by now quite unsympathetic to his partner's architecture. CRM's sardonic comment on the conventional classicism appears in the perverse almost-Ionic columns, each one different, which squeeze into the room between the stuffy oak panelling and under assertively exposed beams and extraordinary light fittings.

**New Board Room, GSA (opposite)**

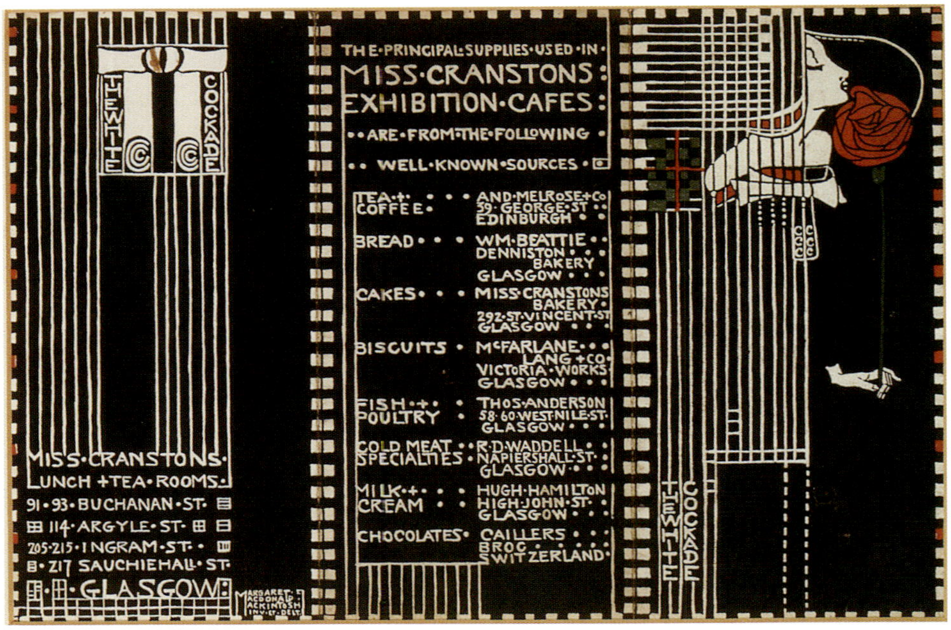


despair'.[5] Later that year: 'we both wish that we could go and live somewhere in the south of England, but the bread and butter being here, we cannot'.[6] Yet Mackintosh seems unable to avoid being caricatured as an Art Nouveau 'spook'. The only English book to describe his work said: 'the aesthetic movement in its maddest moments was never half so mad as this...the Scotto-Continental "new art" threatens in its delirious fantasies to make the movement for novelty a motive for the laughter of the saner seven eighths of mankind.'[7] When, just then, the Wiener Werkstätte invited him to set up a studio in Vienna was he not tempted? Did he, in declining, harbour some hope for a similar mood taking off in Glasgow? He seems stubborn; 'It is indeed a great delight to oppose an all-powerful enemy and this is precisely the reason why Charles Rennie Mackintosh is working in Glasgow,' says *Dekorative Kunst*, in a rather neat attempt in 1906 to comprehend the enigma.

### Menu Card for Miss Cranston's Tea Room, MMM, 1911

The Scottish National Exhibition in Glasgow in 1911 brings a little welcome work to the Mackintoshes, when Cranston commissions interiors for her White Cockade Tea Rooms from CRM. There is not a s ngle memory or record of this work beyond the stylish, and rather Viennese white-on-black, menu card designed by Margaret. (Cranston has two restaurants at the exhibition and for the other, the Red Lion, the menu card is commissioned from Margaret's sister Frances Macdonald.)

But he has virtually no work. By 1903, Newbery had appointed his own Glasgow Style graduates, all of them 1890s students, to teaching posts. A course in interior decoration had started in 1900. Yet neither Toshie nor Margaret teaches. Surely Mackintosh would have been welcomed, had he wanted such a post. Or was the world of architecture changing too quickly under Newbery's feet?

The great change in fashion in the first decade of the twentieth century focuses in Glasgow in the person of the Art School's first Professor of Architecture, the Frenchman Eugène Bourdon. In 1904, J.J. Burnet led a deputation to Paris, where Bourdon was asked to report on the reform of Glaswegian architectural education, and then to become the first professor of architecture at the Glasgow School of Art. (One might wonder what he thought of the truncated new building?) He arrived in 1904 'to battle – to wage war upon the strong cult of eccentricity in architecture which emanated from Austria and Germany, enemies alike of freedom and justice.' Perhaps overstated, being from the obituary of a man killed on the Somme, this is an accurate reflection of the mood as remembered a decade later. Bourdon was specifically brought

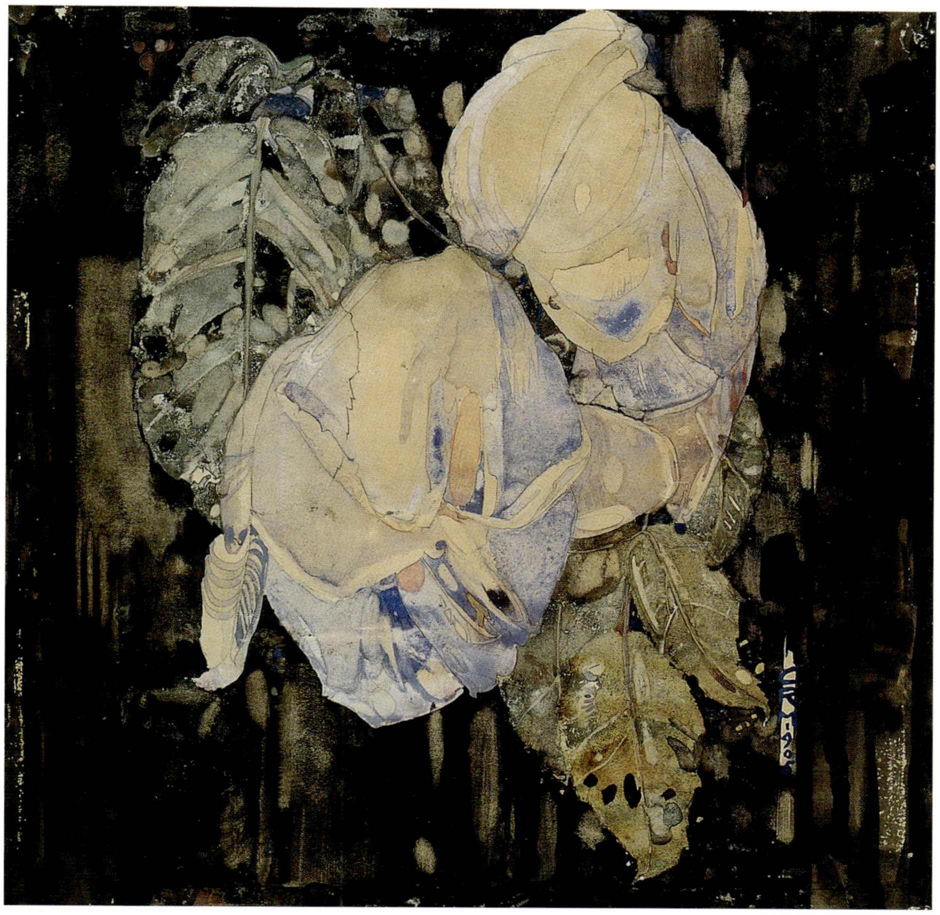

over to counter Mackintosh's presumed 'spooky' individualism, to 'stamp out the Mackintosh influence' as Margaret wrote in a letter, to replace it with an ordered academicism, as had Charles Reilly in Liverpool. This is within a year of the Liverpool Cathedral competition which, though won by a gothic design, was where Mackintosh blamed his not winning on the intervention of Reilly.

In 1904, when Honeyman finally disappeared, the office really became two independent units. But very soon Mackintosh's two essential and devoted assistants, Robert Frame and William Moyes, emigrated one after the other. Keppie's devoted assistant, Graham Henderson, as mediocre a designer as his boss, also follows his ease in compromise; he remains and will eventually surface as President of the RIBA in 1950.[8] An important German book of 1904 quietly noted that 'Honeyman and Keppie has recently taken C. R. Mackintosh into partnership, since when their work has become very uneven'.[9] Once the School of Art is complete, it will no longer be uneven; nothing upsets its mediocrity.

From 1905, Burnet has been building his King Edward VII Galleries at the British Museum (1905–14), and, closer to home, his Elder Library (1901) and Clyde Trust (1905) show a sober Beaux Arts classicism in Glasgow. In contrast to the 'thrusting modernity of the 1890s', Burnet describes the new emphasis as: 'so simple in its conception that it appears a perfect harmony, a simple and beautiful monument to its integrity and purpose...'. This classicist 'order' is now the mainstream into which Glasgow's Art Nouveau and traditionalist architects reintegrate. Toshie's closest spirit, 'Wee Troutie' Salmon (and his partner Gaff Gillespie), converge with this mainstream, their soaring Lion Chambers (1904) being a meeting of the elemental classicism and traditionalism.

In Germany and Vienna, his friends are becoming successful. Muthesius has organised for Behrens and Hans Poelzig to head the Arts & Crafts schools in Düsseldorf and Breslau; Van de

**Faded Roses**

Having designed an astonishing range of fitments, surfaces and objects of all sorts and sizes for Cranston's own house in 1904, CRM has very little work to employ him for most of 1905. Gusty fashions have changed, and he seems to have little inclination to bend with this wind. Though, as Pevsner intriguingly said, 'he could be a witness for the defence and for the prosecution of both Art Nouveau and anti-Art Nouveau,' it was the Art Nouveau brush which tarred him. And in 1905 that is now faded. The depressed, deep melancholy of lost beauty is powerfully conveyed in the 'Faded Roses' he now paints. This, his first larger-scale painting for nearly a decade, uniquely has a botanical precision overlayed with a powerful emotion conveyed in the boldness of the colouring and technique.

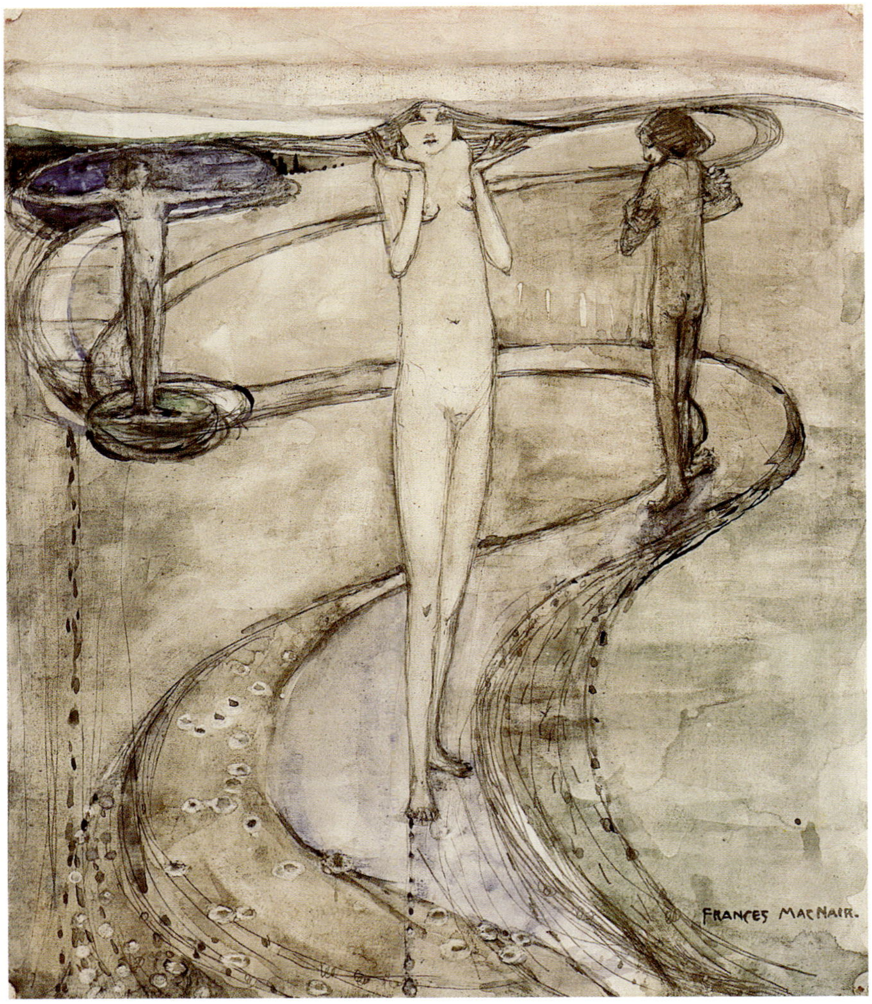


'Tis a Long Path Which Wanders to Desire, Frances McNair, 1909

In 1908, CRM's father dies, the group of Glasgow Style designers fragment, and the Viennese architect Olbrich, who had been devoted to CRM, dies aged 40 in a blaze of fame, their relationship having chilled for unexplained personal reasons. The McNairs return to the childless Mackintoshes, bringing their acute marital problems, his alcohol dependence, and their small son. Once again feelings inexpressible in words are pictured in Frances' key enigmatic images, whose deep theme remains that of the artist's quest, on the long and crooked road strewn with honest error, having rejected the straight but arid path of material success.

Velde and Bruno Paul to head those in Weimar and Berlin. Their new approach, so based on British foundations, consolidates in Europe: while in Glasgow Newbery fails in his attempt this year, 1908, to persuade Voysey to take the chair of design at the Art School, his architect governors (William Leiper, David Barclay, Burnet and Keppie) solidly opposing change.

The Viennese work itself was losing its sharp edge, and his friends have slipped into a classicism typified by Hoffmann's Kunstchau Pavilion (1908) in which Klimt's new paintings have also faded from terror to decorum. Why can't Mackintosh bend with the wind? He knows his name is stronger in Europe than in his native island off its north-west coast. But it is a fame not as architect as much as for interior and furniture designs, still daubed by that fleeting brush named Art Nouveau.

Mackintosh unfortunately has a different reputation at home. Exultant and proud one minute, he is bitter, resentful the next. He becomes intractable, taking any suggestion as slighting criticism. And he drinks. Previously, he would arrive at the office in the evening with piles of sheets of paper, ready to fill them during the night, either with his sketches or with large-scale details drawn with the greatest possible accuracy. In the morning, he would be found exhausted and drunk, and the sheets of paper covered with drawings so perfect they might have been jewels.[10] But now the drink simply deepens his depressive block. Clients bring complaints to Keppie, threatening to take their work elsewhere.

In 1908 the world is crumbling. Glasgow Style designers fragment as Art Nouveau dissolves. Jessie King and E.A. Taylor leave Glasgow; Wärndorfer sells off his Vienna house, dispersing the contents of his magical music room; at the Art School Newbery is increasingly depressed and exhausted; Mackintosh's father dies at 70. At exactly the same moment, the McNairs, whose marriage is much less secure than their own, are back in Glasgow with their son Sylvan; eventually moving into the next street, but staying first with the Mackintoshes. Bertie McNair, out of work and money, having objected on

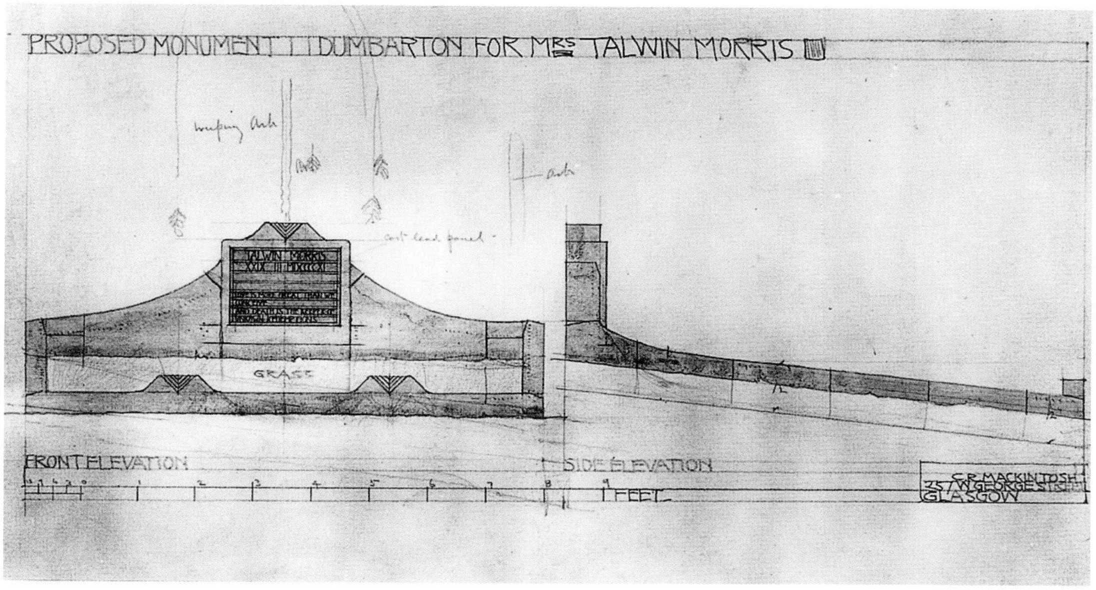


principle to the merger of Liverpool's art schools, and his father's business having collapsed, has taken to drink. Their trauma enters the precious, fragile space of the best friend and the inseparable sister they had left in 1899. Frances and Margaret never work together again, though Frances immediately starts teaching enamelling and embroidery at the School of Art (till 1911).[11]

Now Frances paints two couples and entitles it 'The Choice'. What is the story of this image? Which couple is which? Is the choice still, as it might seem, between the compromise of conventional success and the single-handed risk of the pursuit of Art? How different might their path have appeared, had the Mackintoshes had children?[12] Seeing Margaret's imagery in the period just before their marriage dissolve from emaciated and anguished women into sentimental cherubic infants and mothers, we only guess their hopes. Toshie clearly got on well with children, she seems more distant and stiff, more class-bound. Together they are left with their life as art, their art as their offspring – which, unlike children, do not break away unexpectedly, demanding affection and forcing change.

Change is extremely unsettling, yet if Toshie's work is to be a public art, it has to change and develop. His psyche resists the inevitable change with deep depression. His conversation can be intense and fiery; at other times he can offer simply brooding silence. Here is a visitor to their flat shortly before the move to the new house: 'Meet...the occupants of this house of white and violet. A gentleman, 35 years old, tall, dressed all in black, with long dark hair parted in the middle; the eyes slumber in their setting of bushy eyebrows but flame up from their gloom in occasional flashes of varicoloured spaces; the mouth betrays caution, perhaps timidity – perhaps mockery. The general appearance is of a clean-shaven American clergyman who is still pulsing with emotion and travail of his last metaphysical discourse but has succeeded, by powers of restraint, in preserving an impassivity and an unnatural silence.' It is a rare and wonderful portrait.[13]

**Design for a Gravestone to Talwin Morris, Dumbarton 1911**

When Talwin Morris dies, CRM designs a beautifully austere tombstone, simply enclosing a patch of gently sloping grass in front of the headstone. It has withdrawn entirely from any exuberance of natural forms to a sober quietude.

**Railings, Scotland Street School**
These decorative railings appear equally abstract, but can be seen to form a thistle shape, the emblem of Scotland, built up from the smaller rectangular shapes of thistle seeds.

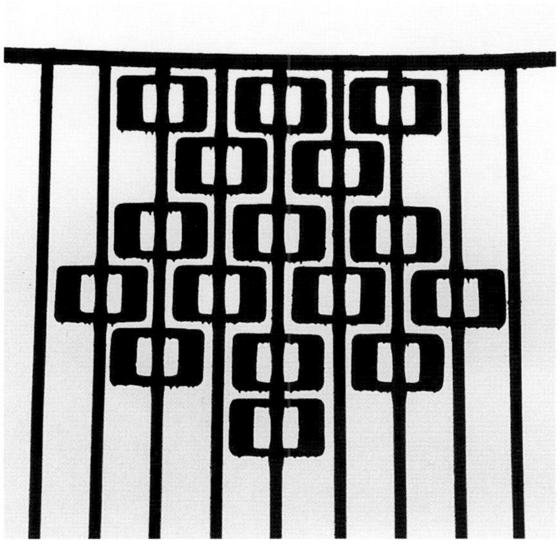

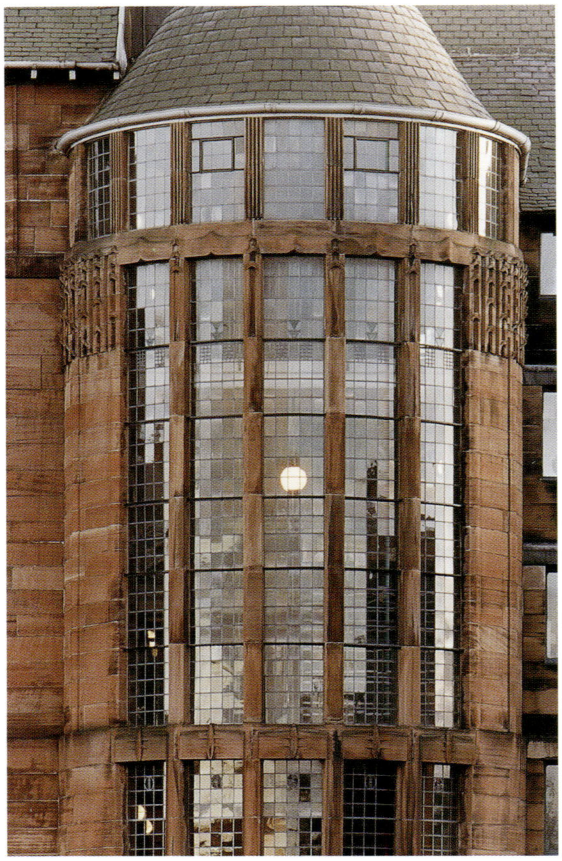

**Stair Tower, Scotland Street School**

CRM's last complete building, Scotland Street School, was designed in 1903 but was not completed until 1906. Outside, it is articulated with unexpected decoration, especially around the entrances and the stair-towers, with their extraordinary, daring precision of masonry and glass as they fly up towards their conical slate hats. These cylindrical forms don't hold spiral stairs, but traditional dog-leg stairs with a full-height void beyond the half-landings (p.90).

Depressive clouds darken around him. 'The bad rumour about Mackintosh appears to be true,' a Viennese Secessionist writes back to Hoffmann.[14] 'He seems like most Englishmen to drink too much, but he cannot be called a drunkard...at present he seems quite normal.' Howarth, who asked everyone he could find, met a 'conspiracy of silence' around Mackintosh's personal life. Mrs Newbery says heavy drinking was his serious problem; William Davidson that it was not. All this suggests that 'the enigma of his personality', as Harry Jefferson Barnes calls it, was incomprehensible even to those close to him. That his deepest feelings were deeply locked, yet the frustration in not being able to communicate them, resulted in his visible rages, depression and the solace of drink.

Some see him accepting the mantle of neglected genius without protest. In fact, it was critics (notably *The Studio* and Muthesius) who constructed this image first. Others suggest he almost shows a will to failure; that there is an element in him craving rejection; that he needs to be seen to fail to show his great artistry. Partly this does echo the Ruskinian moral crusade which so inspired his youth 'not to prefer mean victory to honourable defeat, not to lower the level of our aim, that we may the more surely enjoy the complacency of success.'[15] These critical tones suggest he brings it on himself, as if aware how self-destructive is the outspoken comment, the lack of contextual empathy, the unbending stance.

It must be difficult for Keppie to do business with this wilful, brilliant partner with whom he has nothing in common. The office must feel Mackintosh to be insufferable. Yet no one who had heard his 'Seemliness' talk should have been taken by surprise. Mackintosh spoke of the great struggle constantly waged on behalf of freedom of thought, personal expression and individuality against the forces of tradition and authority. These are the powerful men in the architectural profession 'who because of their imbecility, imagine they are conforming to a high convention of carrying on a laudable tradition, who imagine they are helping on the cause of art, whereas they are retarding it by feebly imitating some of the visible and superficial features of beautiful old works and neglecting the spirit, the intention, the soul that lies beneath...'. Without the work brought by Keppie even the busy years 1900-5 would have been very lean, but that didn't encourage moderation towards him from Mackintosh. Surely he does not mean to be obnoxious, is unaware of the insult caused by his comments. Certainly he is deeply depressed.

Mackintosh relied on a few patrons – Davidson (a businessman), Blackie (a publisher), Newbery (educationalist) and Cranston (restaurateur). His other interiors were for Margaret's and Jessie Newbery's parents; he had yet to meet Bassett-Lowke (industrialist). The key is that, at a time when most architects have clients – school boards to company boards, hospitals to churches, with their systems of contracting – Mackintosh has patrons. Does it link with the 'art-worker' architect whom he idealises, as against the 'business' he so demonises – because, unlike his father, he is no good at it? And in this, how much is at the encouragement of Margaret, battling on his behalf against the business world of Keppie? But the dreams and morbid romanticism, the Rossetti and Maeterlinck world, can go no further than the Willow's Room de Luxe. Maybe it is not just the trapped Mr Mackintosh who is his own worst enemy.

'Scottish artists who are wise leave their native land early in life in order to make their fortunes in London,' suggests a 1905 review of the Willow Tea Rooms in *Dekorative Kunst*. These were probably Muthesuis's words, and it is surely a warning. What keeps Mackintosh in alien Glasgow?

In 1908, he has disentangled himself from Auchenibert at Killearn. It has become unbearable simply to erect a building in which, by offering to design in any style required, he had debased himself. He has tried to keep up interest in the quality of workmanship, selecting stones on site, then detailing the casement windows and even designing a carpet, but entrusting much detail to Henderson. On his frequent site visits to Killearn, he far less frequently climbs the hill to the house; having a favourite seat outside the village pub from which he is only dislodged with great difficulty. The client objects to paying fees for this. Mackintosh again takes the line of least resistance; for the only time in his career, he resigns the job and other architects complete it.

Once the Art School is completed, he is clearly being carried by the office. His competition entry for Jordanhill College gets nowhere, his sketches unworkable by assistants. Henderson, under Keppie, takes it over and wins the competition. (Keppie will generously offer

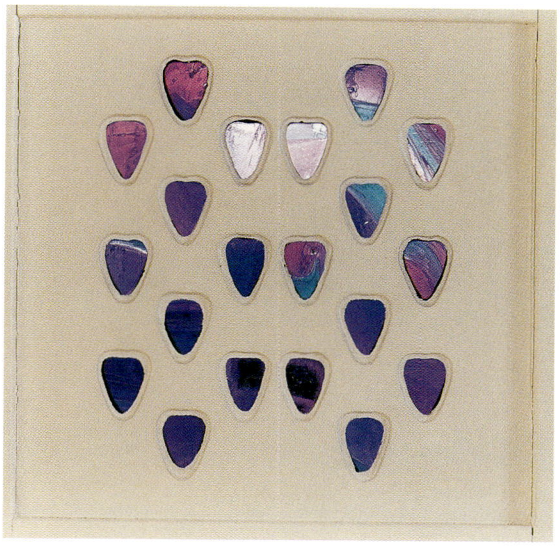

**Detail of Room Door in the Mackintoshes' House**

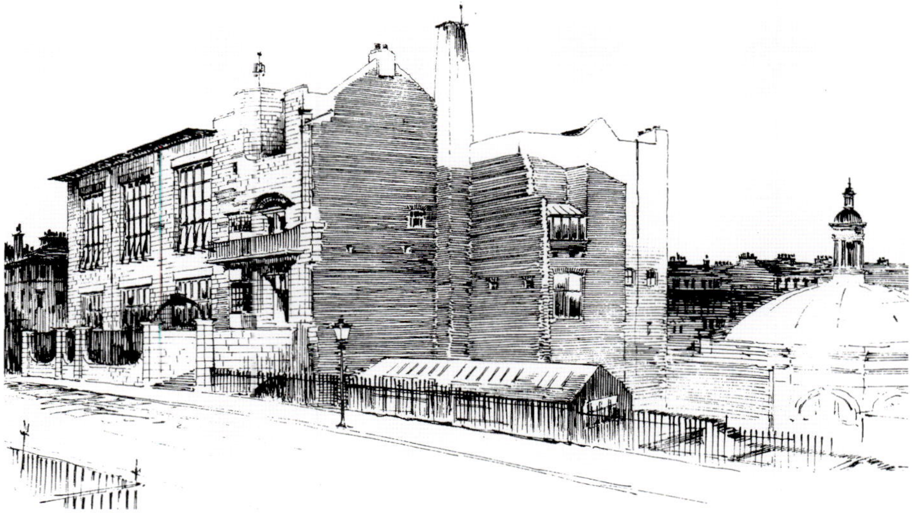

**Glasgow School of Art (Pre-second stage of building work)**

Having altered and redecorated his own terrace house in 1906 (detail above), CRM is finally appointed to complete the School of Art in 1907. Since opening in December 1899 it has stood as a half-built rump, as in this image from the 1907-8 Prospectus.

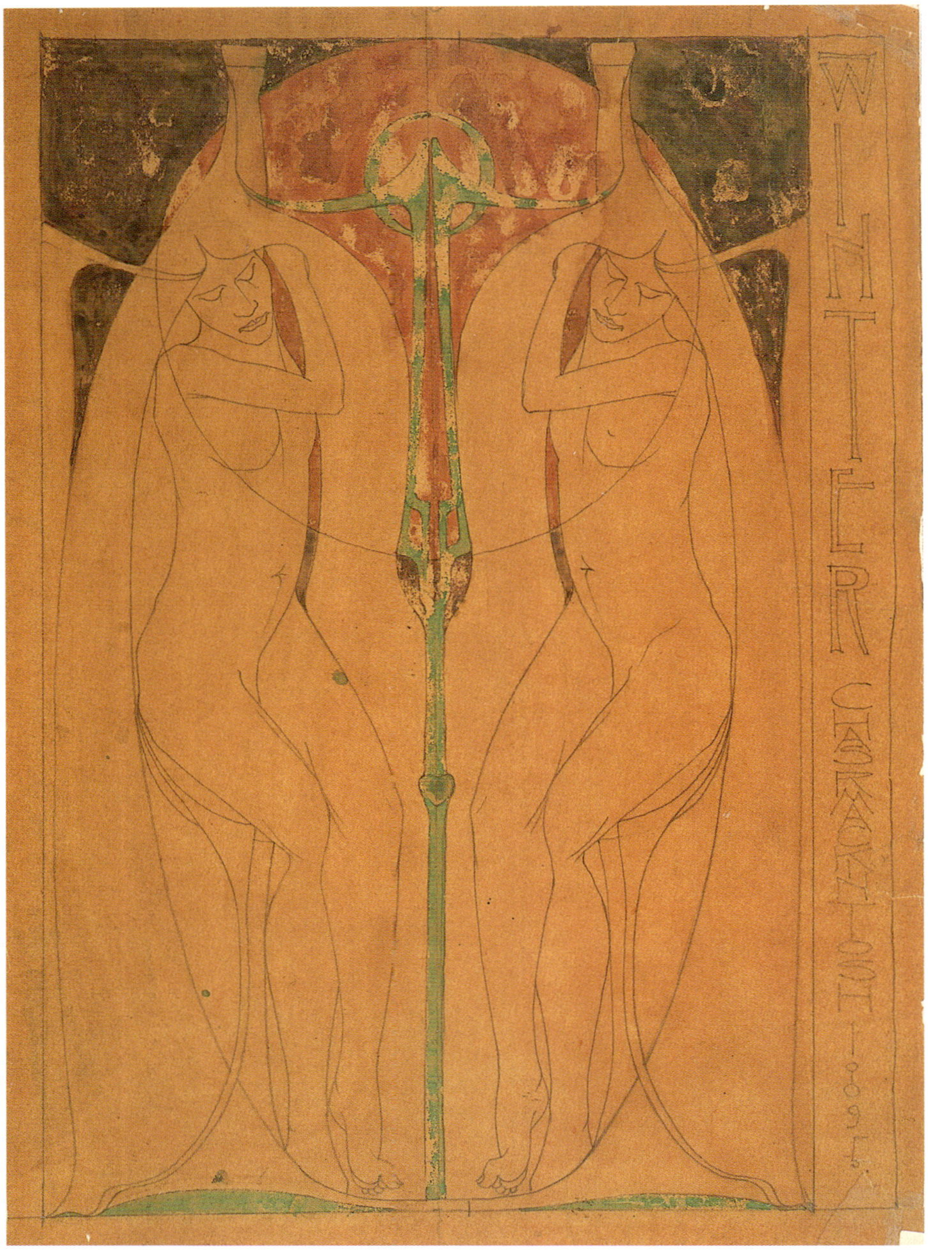


**Winter, 1895**

This symbolic sketch (of wh ch two versions remain) shows two full-bodied female figures asleep as if embryonic, awaiting their egg to hatch in spring, warmed by the (brown) male sun, up to which green shoots are already thrusting. What did CRM back in 1895 feel the -uture might be bringing?

Mackintosh the handsome sum of £250 as his share of the prize money; posting it, for by then they will have parted.)

In 1908, Mackintosh's 50 per cent of the office's profits comes to £918, but soon the total profits fall in 1910 and 1911 to £204 and £77. In his early years as a partner, Mackintosh drew regular monthly amounts from the office, almost as a salary. Now the withdrawals are very irregular, sometimes occurring daily, and for very small amounts, reflecting his lack of personal financial control.[16] Keppie, bureaucratic president of the Glasgow Institute of Architects, must show great tolerance towards his increasingly unhappy and unproductive partner. But again, to blame Mackintosh's financial incompetence on his present mood dismisses the reality of its being beyond his control.[17] 'Money, either paper or metal, slips through my hands in a way that would make a financier weep,' he writes to Margaret many years later. 'When you return you will take efficient control of all the funds and I for one will be relieved and glad.'

The professional ridicule in Glasgow is rubbed in when the School of Art is completed at the end of 1909. The magazine which Bourdon started (*The Magazine of the Glasgow School of Architecture Club*) 'wondered if Mr Mackintosh felt forlorn or relieved at having this child of his imagination off his hands. Of course that would depend on whether it was a child of joy or sorrow to him, a prodigy or a freak. In our opinion – but silence is the better part of discretion.' Such astonishingly snide ridicule, from Bourdon's dominant position in the Art School itself, is deeply painful. A century later, visitors are constantly reminded of this pain by the almost unbelievably crass urban manners of a building named after Bourdon thumped across Renfrew Street right against Mackintosh's building. This powerful ugly sister, built by Keppie Henderson in the 1970s, now contains the

Mackintosh School of Architecture.

Another critique in the previous issue of the same Architecture School Magazine, notes that 'the details of a repeated ornamental motif are never the same. Then it grows clear that the motif itself was selected in order that its internal arrangement might allow of endless different combinations, so that once the motif is selected, an office boy or trained cat can do the rest.' Here is the new generation. Sarcastic about craft work, dismissive of symbolism as a historical oddity, seeking U.S. steel-framed neoclassic skyscrapers (usually with repetitive and historicist ornament) as the way forward.

Mackintosh could never take this path. Of course his temperament doesn't help. His favourite elder sister calls him 'too proud and stubborn.' But then she disapproved of his becoming an architect in the first place.[18] He is tense, hypersensitive to criticism; morose, short-tempered. 'A satanic personality' says Jessie Newbery, in her struggle to understand.

Margaret continues trying to explore her being with a deep symbolic language, to preserve a sanity in her situation through artistic expression. Toshie has long since abandoned such therapeutic work. In 1911, she paints 'The Mysterious Garden': in an image of melancholy and suffering, a pair of birds hang upside down as if dead, between each of the faces at the top. Whatever can its complex story be stoically concealing? In 1913, she paints 'Pool of Silence'. A floating body; a woman standing with fingers to her lips. Calm, beautiful resignation. The rest is silence.

Now it really is the end. She organises their move to England for a holiday, but then, who knows what. They are on the edge of mid life, and this crisis must now be resolved. Mackintosh has been physically as well as psychically sick, and suffered from severe pneumonia in 1913. Finally splitting with Keppie, he sets up on his own back in 140 Bath Street, in Honeyman & Keppie's old office where he'd designed the Art School. But it is hopeless. With no capital and no clients, for who would employ him, it is quickly a dead end.

He is extremely exhausted and almost mute by the summer of 1914. Desperate, Margaret asks Walter Blackie, ever-stalwart patron, to visit. Blackie finds a man deeply depressed. He asks Toshie how he is keeping and what he is doing. There is no eye-contact and not a sound in reply. After a long silence, Mackintosh slowly and dolefully begins to talk. He has given up hope of architecture in Glasgow. His bags are packed, and he is ready to depart.

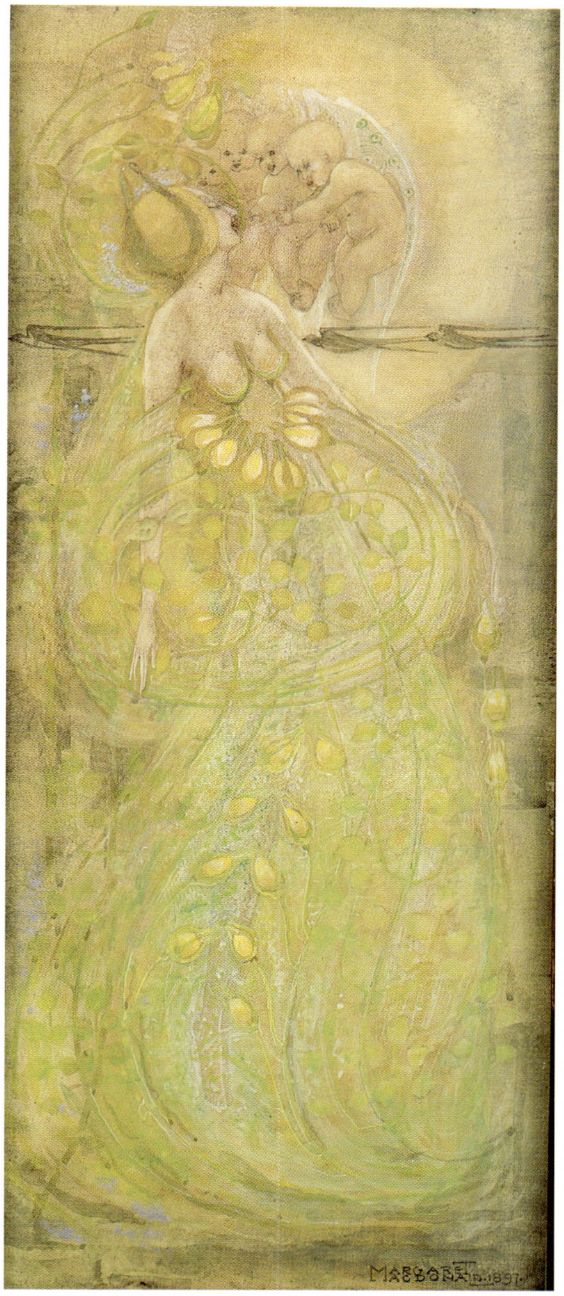

**Summer, MMM, 1897**

When Margaret Macdonald paints 'Summer', their relationship is assured. This astonishing image of fecundity, even reminiscent of the many-breasted Diana of Ephesus, is the almost cloying dream of a 33-year-old, still three years before their marriage. The swallows, almost as an arrow piercing her heart, carry their secret message which at that time could not speak its name, and which survived through all crises until death.

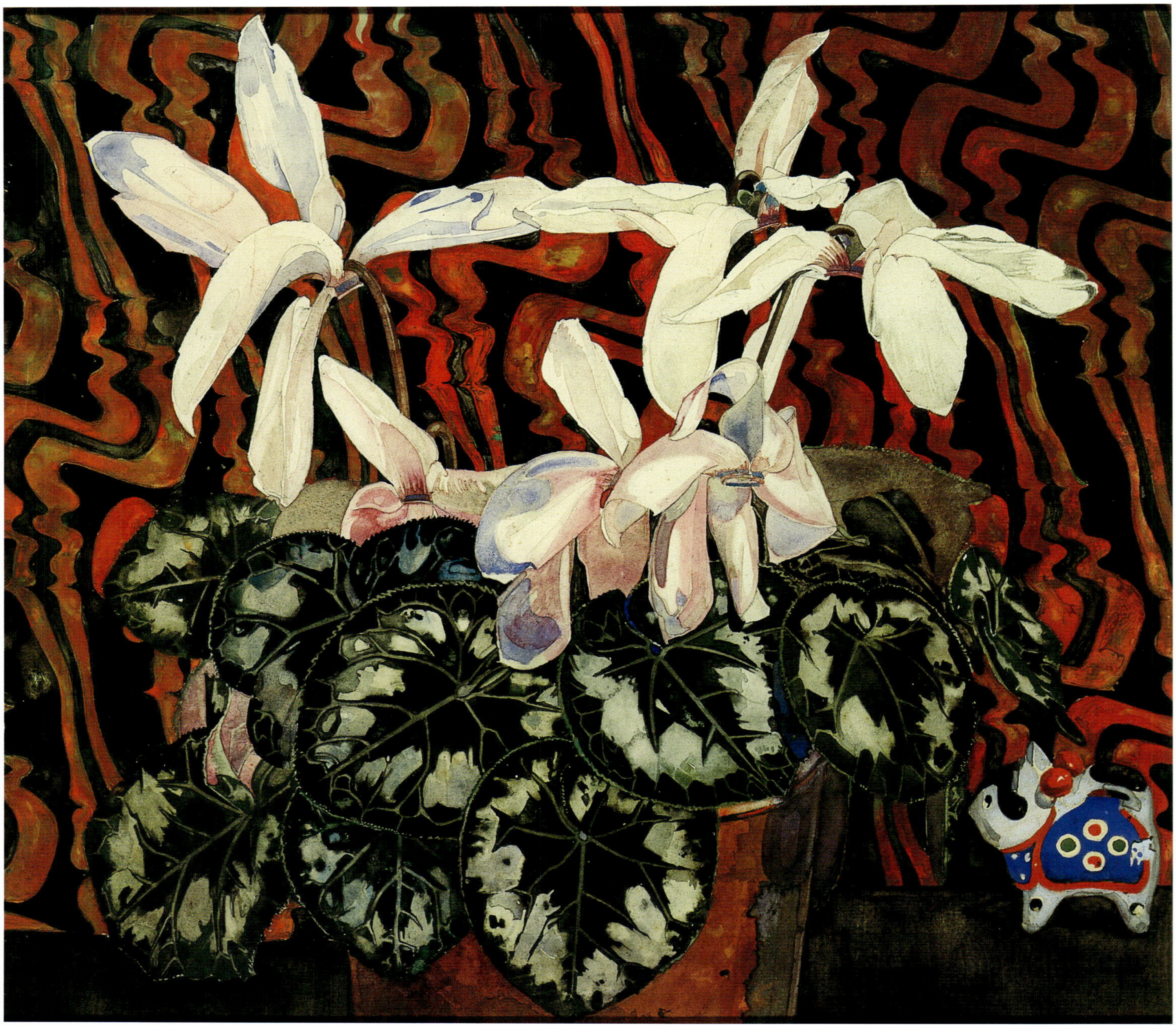

**Cyclamen**

In wartime London, CRM begins to merge his new pattern designs with a new subject, the paintings of cultivated flowers, to produce powerful graphic images. The background in 'Cyclamen' exists as a separate textile design. Flowers become increasingly abstracted, as the graphic 'Stylised dahlias', which he then uses as a repeating pattern, or in the even more 'Stylised Tulips', one of several similar variants for use on silk. Virtually none of his graphic and illustrative work can be dated more closely than to say they are done during these years in London.

# BOHEMIAN EXILE

In a dark nook of the *Blue Cockatoo* restaurant, the Mackintoshes sit at the most hidden table, their usual spot. This charmingly bohemian establishment, known neither for the quality of its cuisine nor the efficiency of its service, on the river front in Chelsea, remains ever-popular with artists. Right next door is the house of C.R. Ashbee, the Arts and Crafts designer,[1] who, like Mackintosh, had exhibited and been admired in Vienna back in 1900, and who became a lifelong friend and correspondent of Frank Lloyd Wright. (Ashbee built a street of seven houses here in Cheyne Walk, between 1893 and 1913.) Now the Great War is dragging to its end; and here the Mackintoshes come every evening.

In the informal atmosphere, in the candle-lit upper rooms, where artists meet and talk long into the night, they are at home. Here are their London friends: J.D. Fergusson, Glaswegian painter of wonderful, boldly coloured canvases, returned after years in France to London with his partner Margaret Morris, dancer and revolutionary dance teacher; E.W. Hoppé, photographer, for whom Mackintosh will convert a country cottage and who throughout these years is art editor of *Colour*, a magazine 'devoted to colour, strength and vitality in art', to which Paul Nash and Augustus John contribute; there are Eugene Goossens and Clifford Bax, musicians; James Pryde, Randolph Schwabe and George Sheringham, painters; George Bernard Shaw, playwright. Very much the same set can be seen at 32 Holland Park, which George Walton not long ago did up for his rich but wonderfully eccentric, anarchist-inclined patron George Davidson. All, that is, apart from the Mackintoshes, sticking quietly to the more bohemian atmosphere of Chelsea. They have shuffled off their bourgeois Glaswegian pretensions, in this new circle of younger artists – like painter Harold Squire, sculptor Francis Derwent Wood, and glass artist Arthur Blunt, each of whom is about to commission a studio from him. To Schwabe, painting tutor at the Royal College of Art, the Mackintosh he knows in London is 'not a great architect but a gifted eccentric and much loved friend.'[2]

Late at night, the Mackintoshes walk round to the Oakley Street bed-and-breakfast where they have one room. In the morning they walk the few paces to two adjacent rented studios in Glebe Place, his and hers, lofty and rather bleak spaces where, with their private connecting door, they live for eight

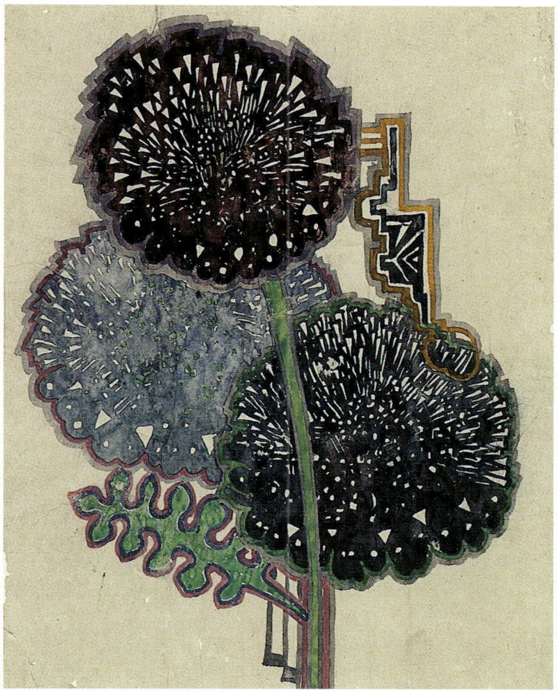

Stylised Dahlias

Stylised Tulips, textile design

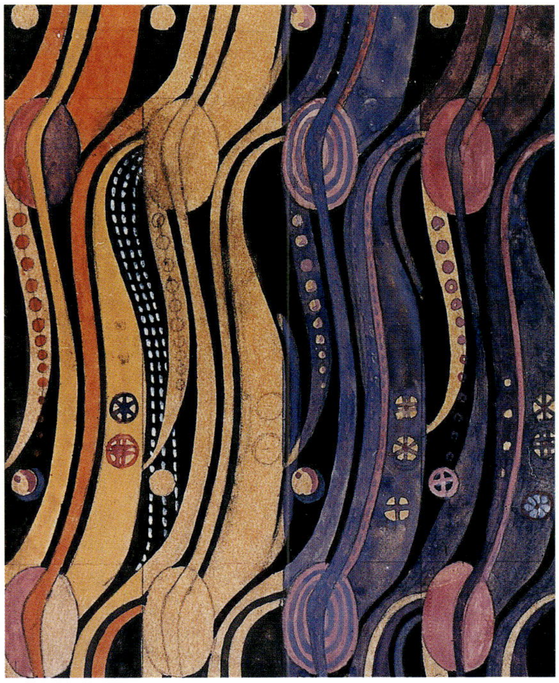

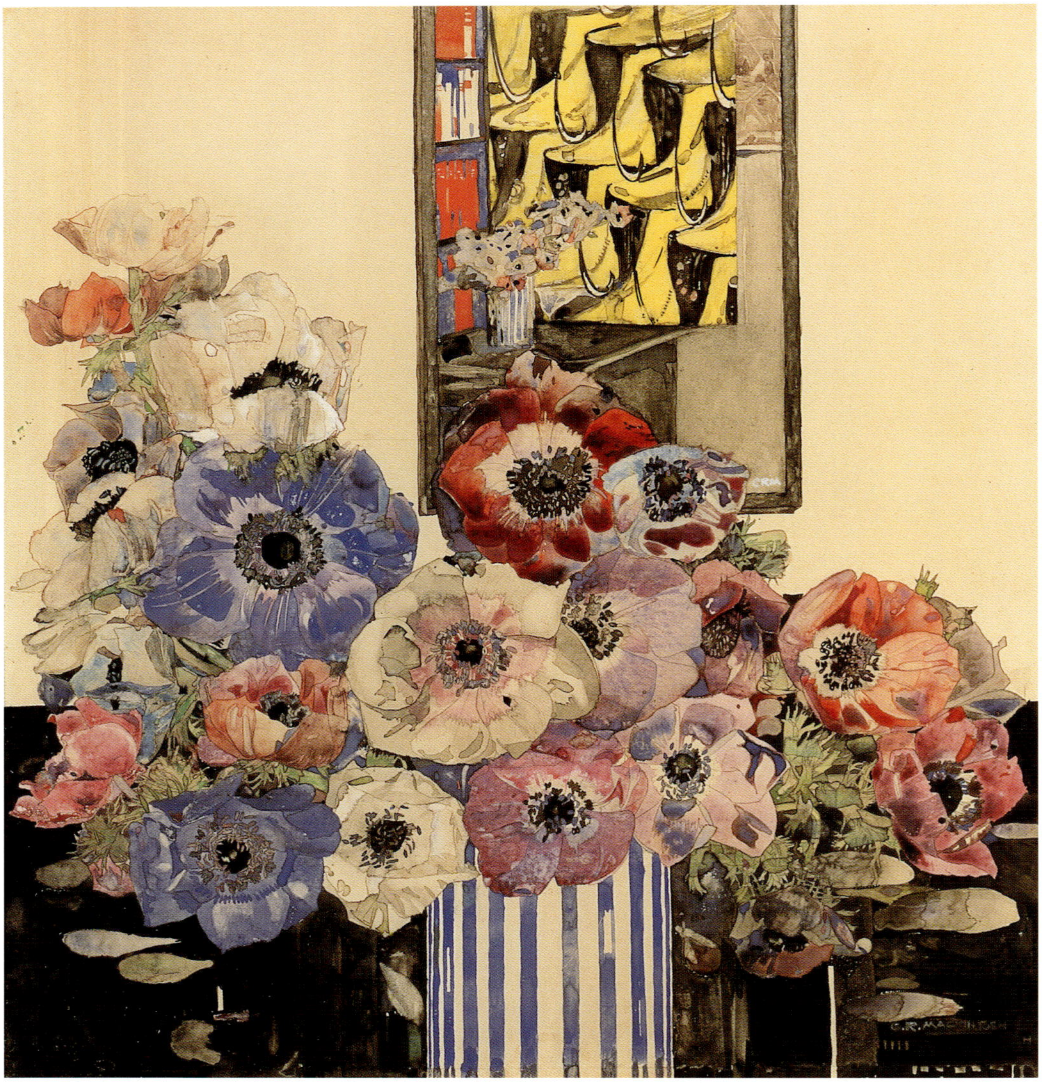

Anemones

Producing speculative designs is a quite new idea, but now encouraged by voices at *The Cockatoo* both Toshie and Margaret begin producing textile designs. Foxton of London and Sefton of Belfast take his designs for printed fabrics; paying from £5 to £20 for each. Mrs Sefton admires their work and arranges further useful introductions; they submit designs to Templeton's in Glasgow and Liberty's in London. The work is bright, charming and quite original. One of these lively designs is seen, in a mirror, in the background of 'Anemones'. This painting was exhibited at the International Society in 1916 but failed to sell (it was later bought by Walter Blackie).

years. Here they have been producing what little work they can, as the war drags on hardly seeming to touch them. Mackintosh is commissioned to refurbish and furnish a tiny terrace house in Northampton and to add another room under the Willow for Miss Cranston, but that is all that he can get built.

During the war he has started painting cut flowers in complex and spatially ambiguous contexts, but can find no market for them. Though these are sent to exhibitions, the best watercolours – 'Peonies', 'Anemones', 'Yellow Tulips', 'Grey Iris' – are not sold. Margaret has kept painting, but always far less than before their marriage; she exhibits occasional watercolours nearly every year. In 1916 they were invited to show work at the Arts & Crafts exhibition within the Royal Academy and, almost uniquely, produce a collaborative work. 'Voices of the Wood' seems to be two large oil panels, framed with candlesticks to light them. These panels, 'The Opera of the Sea' and 'The Opera of the Winds', are both closely based on tiny designs by Margaret used on Wärndorfer's piano in 1903. They are now transformed into startling and brightly decorative paintings, 'of wonderful colour but of doubtful meaning,' as *The Scotsman* reasonably put it.[3] (p.61) Toshie designs the candlesticks and, perhaps, some of the background design of the paintings. These two images will hang on the black basement walls he is currently digging out underneath the Willow Tea Rooms.

Though commissioned once more by Miss Cranston, it is not enough encouragement for him to revisit Glasgow, even to be welcomed by the Davidsons in his own old house. He never returns, never sees 'The Dugout'; nor does he ever visit Northampton to see his only other major work in progress, nor even, once it is completed, to sample his client's guest bedroom. He is not busy. And it is not just the war which keeps Mackintosh stuck in his safely narrowed Chelsea rituals.

Clearly there are times when he is deeply depressed; and the smell of alcohol is on his breath.[4] He is desperately short of money and twice in 1919 writes to William Davidson, at 78 Southpark Avenue, Glasgow W, asking him to buy paintings for £20 or £30, so that he can pay his overdue rent. (Faithful Davidson, as ever, sends the required cash.) At the war's end Mackintosh is surely hopeful for better times. He is 50 and architecture could still be his renewed future. But it is not to be. For many of his generation, the war has brought a sense of almost fatal disruption – Voysey and Walton, Harrison Townsend and Leonard Stokes vanish; Beresford Pike and Charles Holden change fundamentally. But it was not just Ashbee who had really lost direction much earlier, around 1908.

Fergusson ropes Mackintosh into organising a painting exhibition; both Toshie and Margaret become involved with a theatre club founded with their new friends, working on costumes and stage sets for at least two productions, one of them a Maeterlinck. And then, in May 1919, The Arts League of Service, a scheme for impoverished post-war artists, founded at Margaret Morris's studio theatre, proposes an ambitious block of studios, to be designed by Mackintosh.

He is alone as an architect in London, without contacts, and with neither inclination nor courage to join with others.[5] Yet around 1920, he must be convincing himself that he can make it. The friendly pub talk of the *Blue Cockatoo* builds up clouds of projects around a large vacant site nearby which they all know. One after another, three artists propose he designs them studios here, and finally a large block of studios for The Arts League is added to the scheme. He becomes convinced of the reality of this project, which is potentially massive. But it comes to nothing. Is it all in the pipe dreams of his friendly comrades in the warm alcoholic companionship of the *Blue Cockatoo*?

All that comes out is Squires's pathetically reduced studio, which finally and unmemorably is built, and his sketches for Margaret Morris's theatre seem a gormless deco number happily stillborn. What is he up to? His heart cannot be in it; yet his painting shows this new exuberance with form and bold colour seen in his wartime interiors and textile designs.[6] In the winters, they now travel to Dorset to stay with the Newberys who have retired to Corfe Castle. They ask the Schwabes to join them on holiday in Dorset; inspired by his friends, Mackintosh begins to

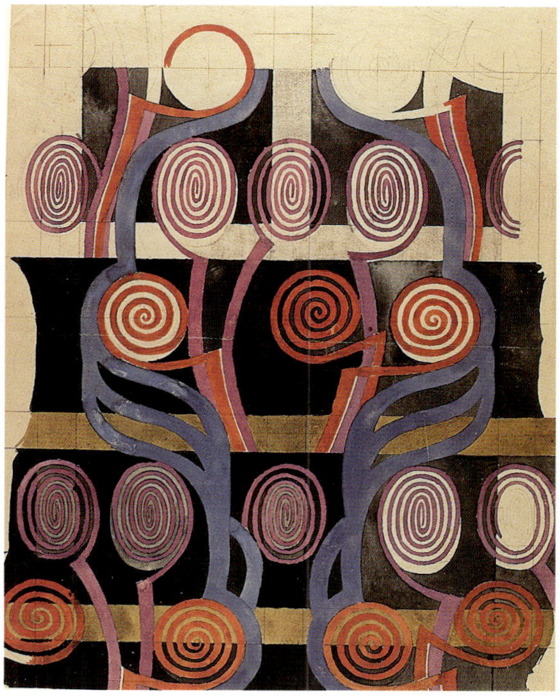

**Orange and Purple Spirals**

CRM's ever-inventive doodling moves from organic forms to abstract spirals. The example below is simply described by Mackintosh as 'furniture fabric'.

**Furniture Fabric: Blue, Black, Purple & White**

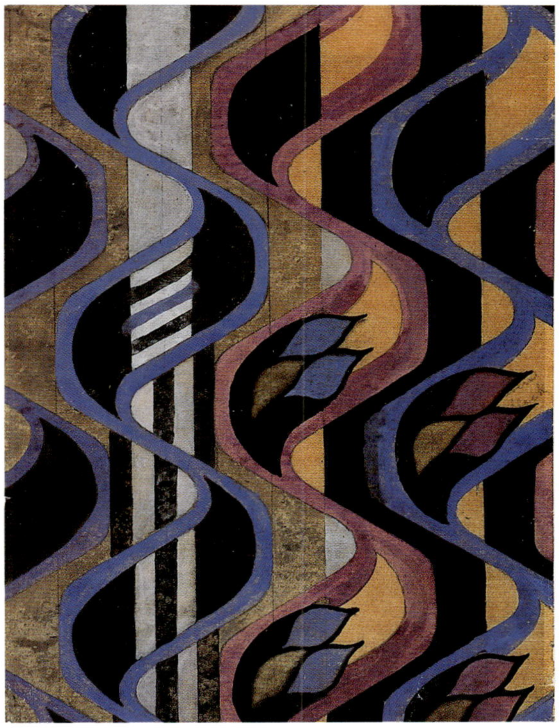

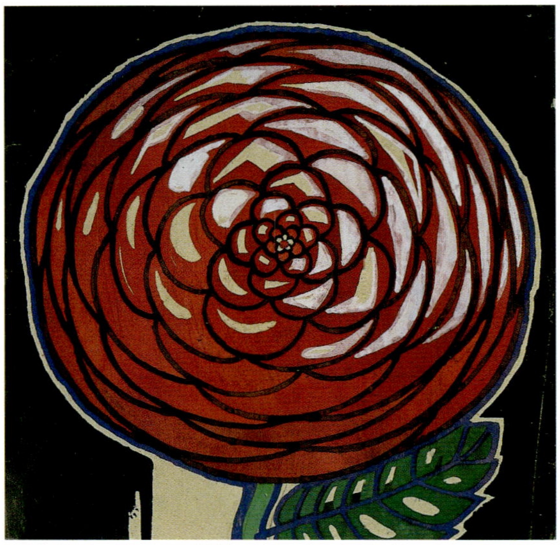

**Chrysanthemum**

One bold, formalised chrysanthemum can stand as an image on its own, or perhaps is to be built up into a large repeat fabric; whereas the 'Stylised Flowers on a Trellis' obviously is a repeat pattern.

**Stylised Flowers on a Trellis**

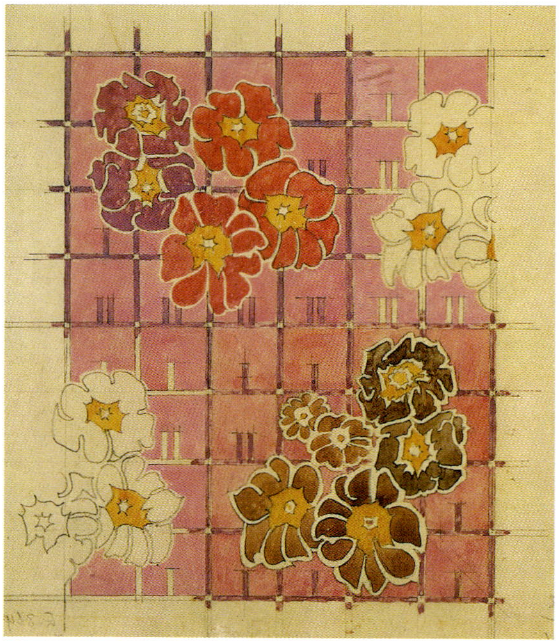

paint landscapes; mud and clay and greeny grey.

At an architectural exhibition at the RIBA, everyone else shows photographs of what they had built just before the Great War. Poor Mackintosh can only offer a couple of crudely collaged elevation drawings of an unrealised project in Chelsea. *The Architectural Review* calls it 'curiously old fashioned, recalling to mind the illustrations in early volumes of *The Studio*'.[7] But underneath the blanket of pity, however, is a project which is far from pathetic, which in its extraordinarily bold modelling would long outlast the empty pomp in those Edwardian photographs hanging alongside. The problem is not in the design. It is in the battling realism required to turn creative designing into built buildings.

Buoyed by his dreamily supportive friends, he certainly takes it seriously; he mugs up on London building regulations and finally submits a large scheme to the L.C.C. Perhaps Mackintosh believes that only bureaucracy is stopping the project; certainly his design sticks with the Surveyor to the Glebe of Chelsea for whom it is not 'architectural' enough. Another helpful bureaucrat adds swags and ornament to the elevations. Mackintosh refuses to give an inch. In the *Blue Cockatoo* he is heard to say that if they cannot allow this building he will give up architecture completely. The struggle to claw back into this public arena has been immense; getting a building built is indeed less like painting a picture than winning an election. And his electoral bandwagon is riding on an easily pricked bubble of confidence. By the time permissions are finally received, not another word is heard – other than in pity for the victim Mackintosh; Mary Newbery, for example, repeats that his ideas were 'too flat, too dull, too unaccommodating' for the authorities. This is too simple.

He retreats to working alone, without any of the mess of architectural procurement and all its required social and negotiating skills, he designs a few more silks, a few more book covers for Blackie which appear dull and old-fashioned, and yet more textile designs. And he continues to paint brashly cheery bouquets of stylised flowers to sell for a few pounds each.

In 1921, Frances Macdonald dies, perhaps by her own hand. Her sister is commissioned to paint a tiny watercolour for Lutyens' Queen's Doll's House project. Visitors remember her tea parties, as others had done in Glasgow; as ever it is the minute attention paid to every detail, the arrangement of tableware, the positions of chairs, the flowers. They never speak of their life in Glasgow, or of future plans. Margaret

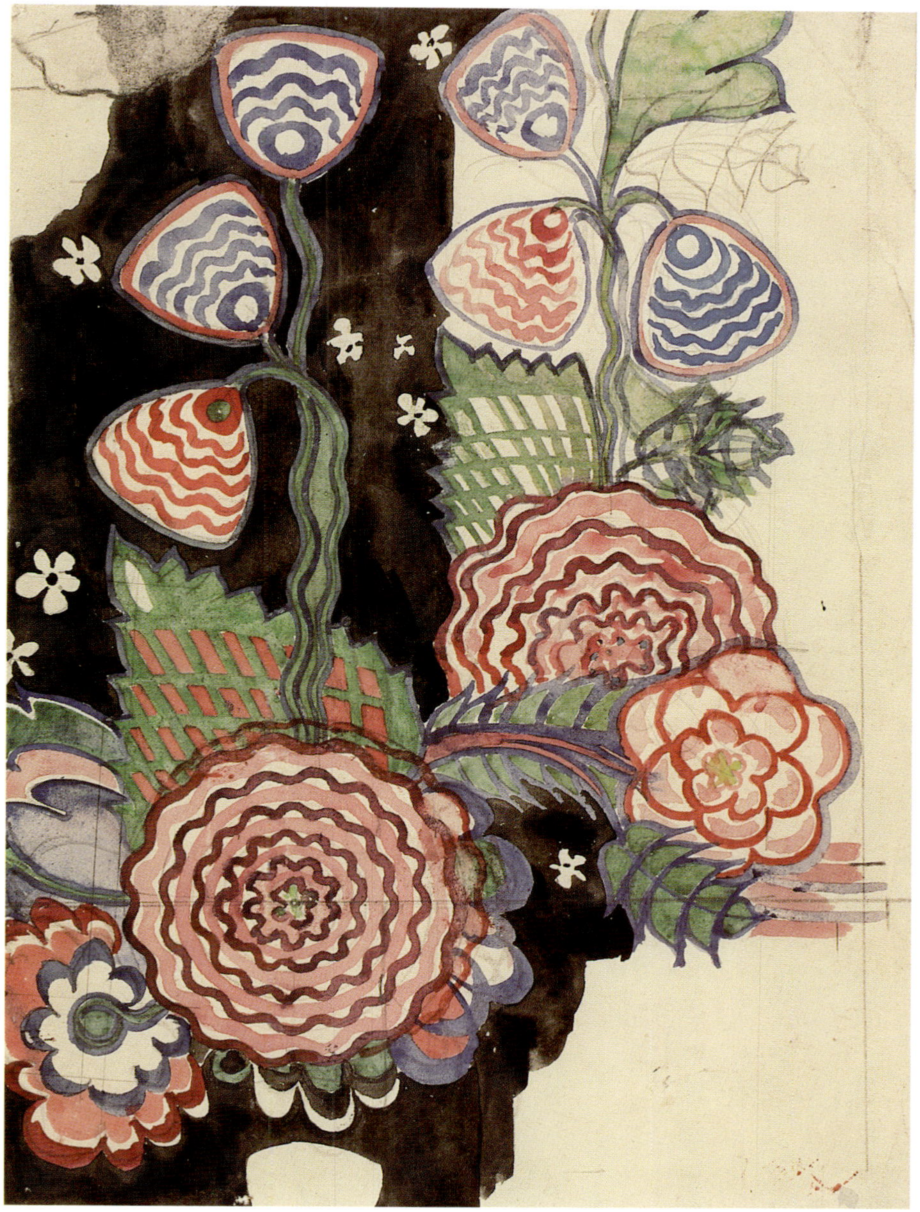

does one painting, a major work 'La Mort Parfumée', in response to her sister's death. It is a very graphic, dramatically coloured, extraordinary design obviously layered with meanings. As ever, what cannot be said in the symbolism of paint, cannot be said at all.

The sad face of Toshie looks out from Hoppé's photographic portraits (p.11) – barely recognisable as the young artist setting out from Annan's portraits 30 years earlier. As young Alice Schwabe remembers, Margaret does the talking, Toshie smiles. They keep their feelings to themselves. Quiet dignity. Much silence.

When *Ideal Home* prints an article on the Northampton house, although the text is ghosted by the client, Mackintosh is nowhere mentioned. That hardly helps.[8] But rumours that this client found the designer impossible to work with seem absurd. He kept returning for more designs and his own account of his next house, designed by Peter Behrens, begins: 'Mr Mackintosh was to have designed me a house for this site, but he went away to live in the Pyrenees and I lost touch with him'.[9]

A young Glaswegian architect, working in London for Burnet & Tait, arranges to visit Mackintosh hoping for a job. To his surprise, there is no office, and no job. Alone in his studio when the visitor arrives, Mackintosh is morose and depressed by the failure of his Chelsea projects. Margaret has to break the embarrassing silence. 'When you set up your office can you take me on?' the keen young man tries again. Finally Mackintosh replies that he is not setting up office. Their bags are packed.

J.D. Fergusson, who goes to the Mediterranean annually, has persuaded them to make the move. At the *Blue Cockatoo* they hear Edgar Hareford and Rudolph Ihlee, young Slade-trained painters, talk of their shortly going down to Collioure. The Mackintoshes quietly sublet and slip away once more. Cards with varied French postmarks occasionally arrive in England.

**Stylised Chrysanthemums**

Some fabric designs have their bases in organic forms: roses, corms, bulbs, tulips, or chrysanthemums. But there are also bold, abstract, geometric forms: 'jazz age' diamonds, triangles, squares, grids and lines in vivid colours, often on grey or black grounds. Made into dresses, upholstery or curtains, these must have been stunning. There are few hints as to his intention; occasional notes say chiffon, voile, or silk.

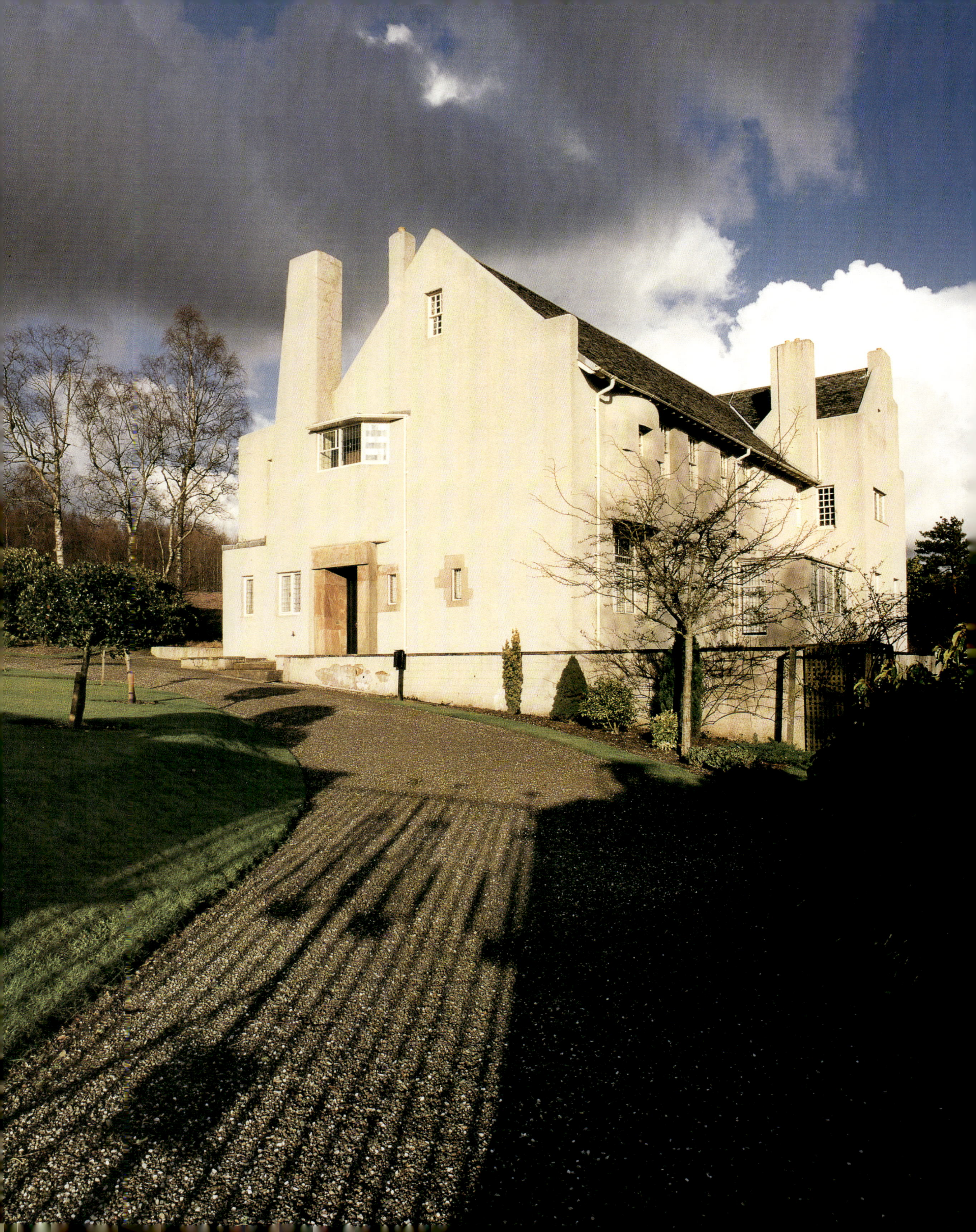

# DOMESTIC DREAMS

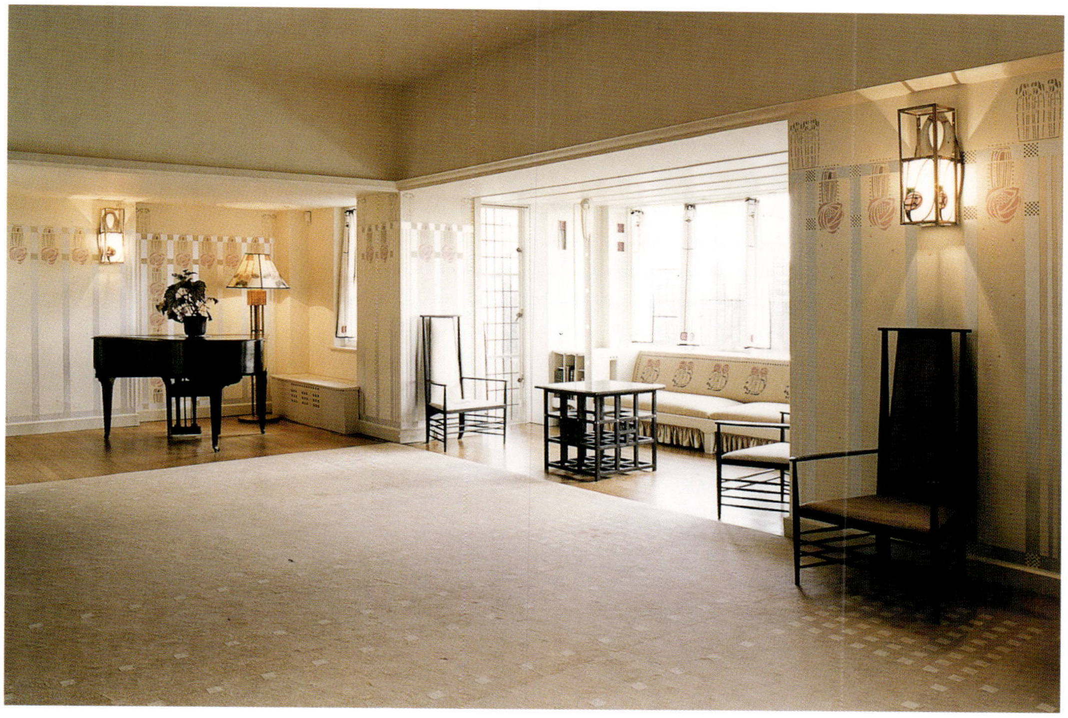

Mackintosh built his first house for a businessman who collected paintings by the Glasgow Boys, and who became his friend and life-long supporter. He had, earlier, worked in that client's family's house, and designed furniture and an occasional bedroom or drawing room for a few others in Glasgow. He then entered a competition for a fantasy 'house for an art lover' before designing his second new, and considerably larger, house for a leading publisher. Following these two commuter houses he extensively remodelled an old country house built exactly a century before. In the following years he was involved with two other new detached houses so unmemorable that neither is worth discussing. Then a decade later, in England, he briefly tried again, remodelling one small terrace house and producing various associated interior decoration and furniture designs.

This tiny list contains his career as a domestic designer. Compared with his successful Scottish contemporaries, Rowand Anderson or Robert Lorimer, Mackintosh's output is insignificant. Both these built up great practices, were based in Edinburgh, were knighted, and remained purveyors of quality revivalism to the gentry's tastes. Mackintosh never met the immensely rich patrons enjoyed by the likes of Horta in Brussels or Gaudi in Barcelona. It was not Glasgow magnates like Solvay, Stocklet or Guell, but the bourgeoisie who were his patrons. His largest house remains very modest in comparison to the southern English contemporary work of late Webb or early Lutyens. His one exercise at a real country-house scale was just an ideas project, without client or intention to build. Nor was he engaged with 'the smaller middle-class houses' for whose simple good design Barry Parker was so eloquently lecturing in the 1890s.[1]

**Drawing Room, The Hill House**

'The random scattering of stray rose petals and grasses which spread from the walls to proliferate throughout the furniture and fittings, looking just as if they have been carried in by the wind' (Anne Ellis).

**The Hill House (opposite) and Dining Room Light Detail (below)**

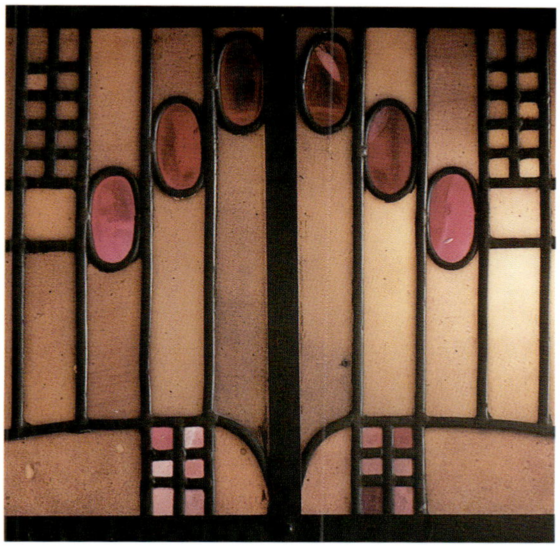

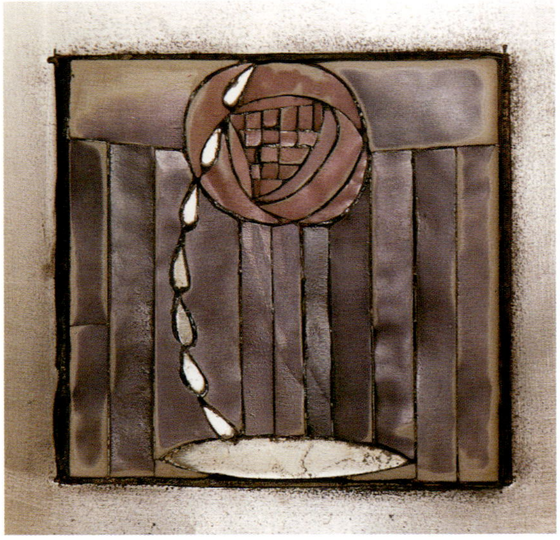

**Main Bedroom Details, The Hill House**

Decoration on the steel fireplace surround (above) and on the doors of the washstand (below).

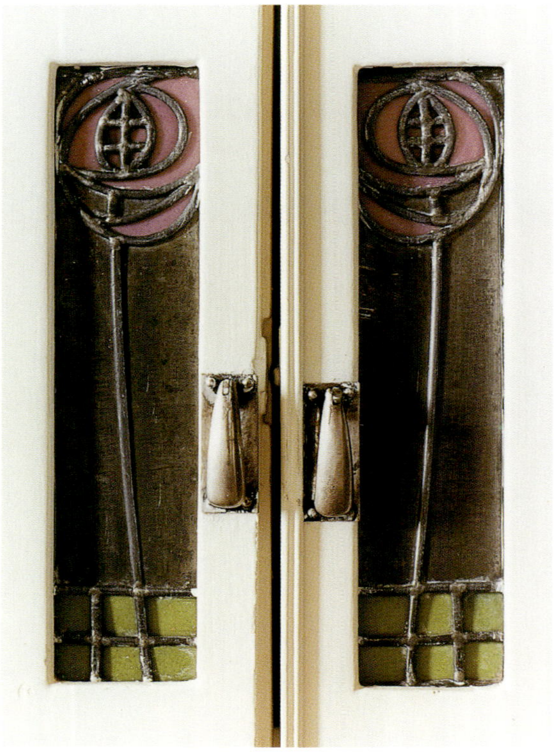

Windyhill for William Davidson, begun in 1899, and the Hill House for Walter Blackie three years later, both sit within large plots of detached suburban houses, above the Clyde coast villages of Kilmacolm and Helensburgh, which commuter trains were making particularly attractive retreats from the dirty city. All around, the new houses were mostly in sturdy stone, their designs largely diluted from the fashionable vernacular revival, asymmetrical, rural and often very English in image: the Hill House is surrounded by half-timbering and red tile roofs, and has a Baillie Scott house only two blocks away.

Mackintosh's houses do not declare their conspicuous good taste. His intentions are stronger, echoing the call in his lectures for a radical revitalisation of Scotland's architectural heritage. If Windyhill could be mistaken from a distance for a farmhouse, it certainly could not be mistaken for a house like Rowantreehill, built next door and at the same time by James Salmon. (This, with its extravagantly virtuosic verticality, and various projecting half-timbered bays, was published in Germany in 1900.[2])

Mackintosh stuck to traditional L-shaped plans for both houses, probably starting from a Lethaby exemplar which Windyhill closely resembles. Utterly conventionally, the bedrooms are above living rooms off the southern side of a long hall, the L formed by the service wing stretching north. The roofs are slated and the walls are all harled – protected with a layer of roughcast which covers all the surfaces, including window cills, as in traditional Scottish cottages. The arrays of varied window shapes (at Windyhill, there are four different pane sizes overlooking the courtyard), the forms of stairs and chimneys seem random, as if it is an 'honest' expression of what occurs in the rooms behind. But it is of course all carefully composed. This not only contradicts the classical tradition (and there was Rockland, a fine Alexander Thomson villa on the waterfront not far from the Hill House, to remind him of that approach); it was also unhistoric, particularly the horizontal windows, the great drawing-room bay and the wonderful second-floor children's room at the Hill House.

But the 'vernacular' appearance only withstands a first glance. Much of the modelling of the Hill House, as the entrance stair tower at Windyhill, forms quite abstract, elemental, formal compositions. The Hill House entrance facade is modelled graphically, in dynamically satisfying shapes of overlaying planes. Both houses have a grey, severe exterior, all the better to shelter, to conceal the family life within. Mackintosh recognised the distinct realms of the public world –

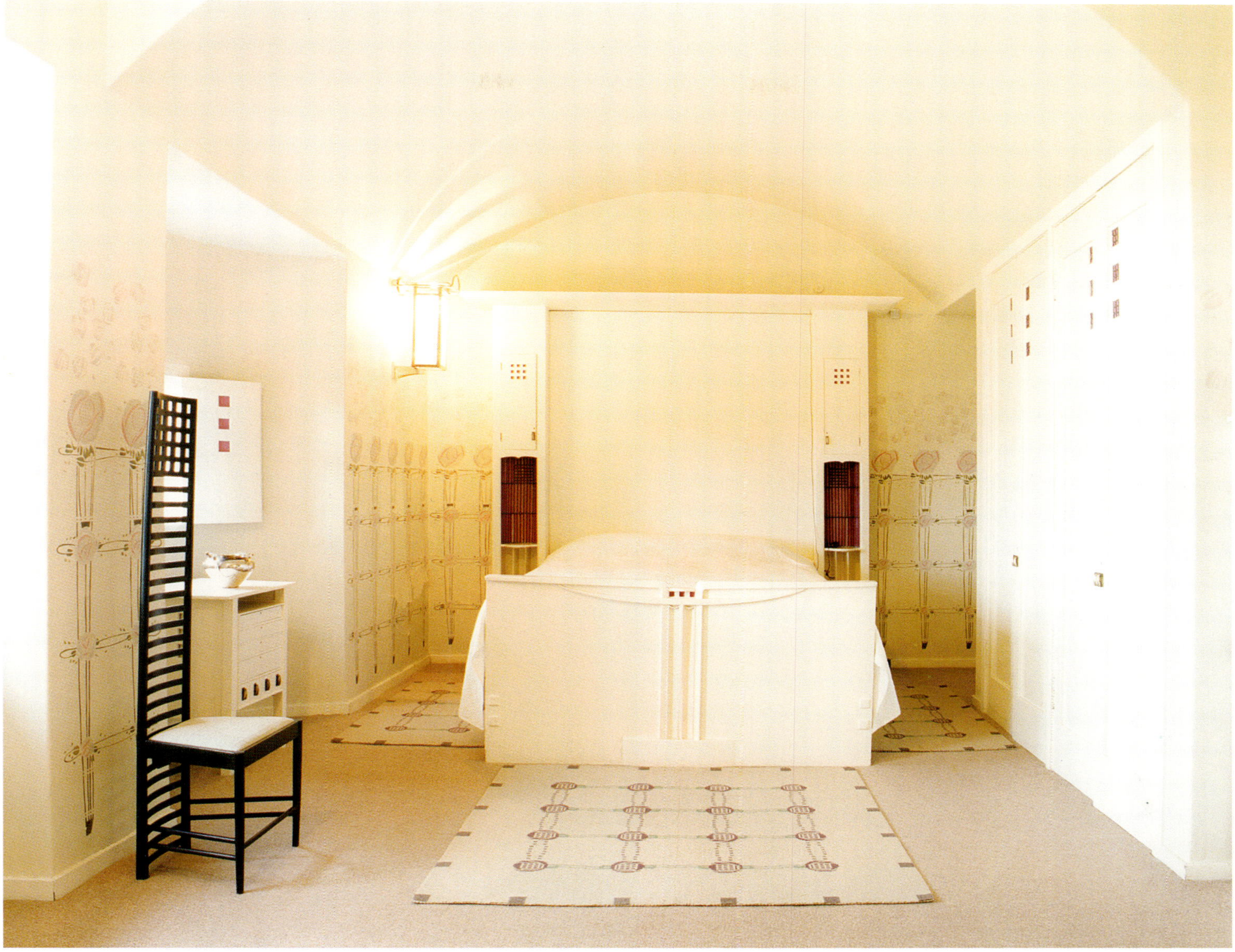

of the object in, if not of, the landscape – and the interior world of the domestic refuge.

Always supported by his brilliant design eye and facility in the minor arts – in graphics and in furniture, in design of cutlery, furnishing fabric or just the artistic arrangement of dried flowers – with these two houses his confidence as architect and as interior place-maker are finally matched. The interiors are not just fashionable fin-de-siècle decor as produced around Glasgow by various of his contemporaries; nor are they like the pragmatic, anti-symbolic work of his English contemporary, Voysey. Each space, and the succession of spaces, is based on precisely controlled underlying geometry, and an inventive symbolism which is always more or less audible.

Now he confidently, explicitly, plays with polarities of light and dark, holding the two extremes in dynamic equilibrium.

**The Hill House, Main Bedroom**

The vaulted bed area, initially to be enclosed behind leaded-glass screens and gossamer curtains designed by MMM, is a world of private sensuality; it has its own tiny bay window to the left, and the blown roses round the walls are loosened from their formal manners on the drawing room walls below.

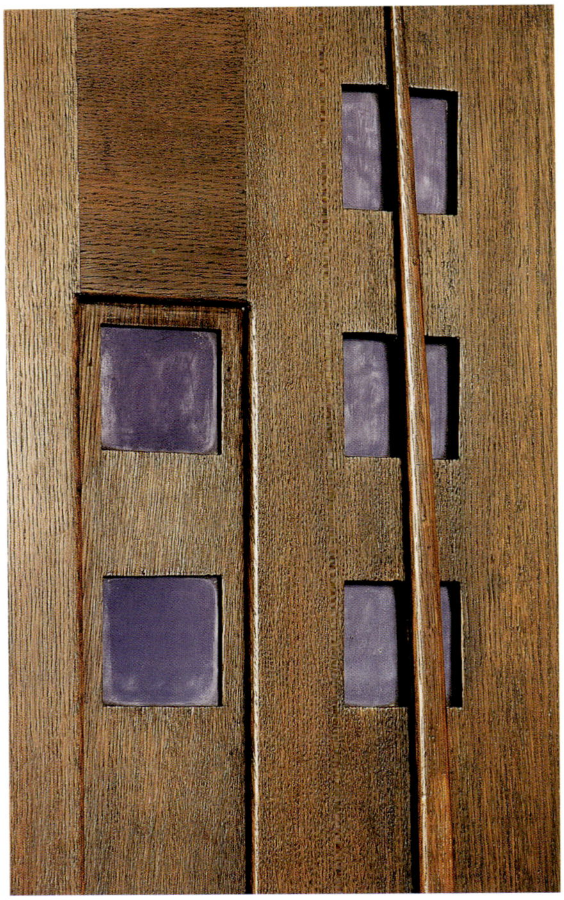

**The Hill House, Library Panel Detail (above) and Hall (opposite)**

The library, in dark oak and purple glass, is the male domain. Despite its formailty, as ever the organic reed bends the geometric form back towards nature. The mysterious forest of the hall is seen looking back towards the library and entrance. From the first half-land ng, visitors entering the hall below can be spied on from between the dark tree trunks unobserved.

At its most obvious, this is seen at the Hill House in the journey from the dark, protective, heavy entrance towards the softest, light, white spaces at the building's heart. At one extreme is the hard shell, characterised by the adjectives strong, sober, empiricist, objective. This is essentially a variant on the vernacular, on tradition. At the other end is the white interior, which attracts adjectives such as soft, decorated, idealist, fantastic, erotic; and this is essentially creative and modern. So the actual outside appears conservative to the glance. The deepest interior space, the main bedroom, appears progressive. The link between Eros and creativity is never deeply submerged.

Other main rooms play variations along the spectrum, the library at the Hill House tending to the dark (more traditional and more sober); the drawing rooms tend to the light. A black corridor door illuminated by sparks of deep ruby glass opens to reveal that it is painted white on the reverse where those glass spots now appear an opaque pink. Linking the extremes, symbolically but also literally, are hallways and stairs. These intermediate spaces are not just fascinating but perhaps – in performing a mediating role between the masculine, rather dour, tradition-conscious public world, and the feminine, almost dreamlike, fantastic and freely creative private world – they are (not just in the houses) his most important spatial creations.

The House for an Art Lover competition, brought to their attention when in Vienna at the end of 1900, was entered in March 1901. Of the 36 entries, none was judged of winning standard. Baillie Scott, receiving second prize, was admonished for his traditional exterior form. The Mackintoshes' entry was disqualified for not submitting the required interior studies in time; when they arrived, it was awarded a special prize (600, to Baillie Scott's 1800 marks). This portfolio of drawings allowed him to stretch his interior ideas, which are then developed in the more mundane medium of real spaces at the Hill House and then at his largest domestic refit project, Hous'hill.

The Art Lover project exaggerates the dark and light; the dining room is painfully austere, the music room a fairy kingdom. Judging from the few drawings there is little spatially exciting interior experience, other perhaps than the children's day room. Mackintosh's plain, 'modern' exterior was praised, but Baillie Scott's entry was seen as a more successful interior spatial design. Around the same time, Mackintosh drew, and published, 'An Artist's Cottage and Studio in the Country' and 'A Town House for an Artist', using the same language but on a minute and

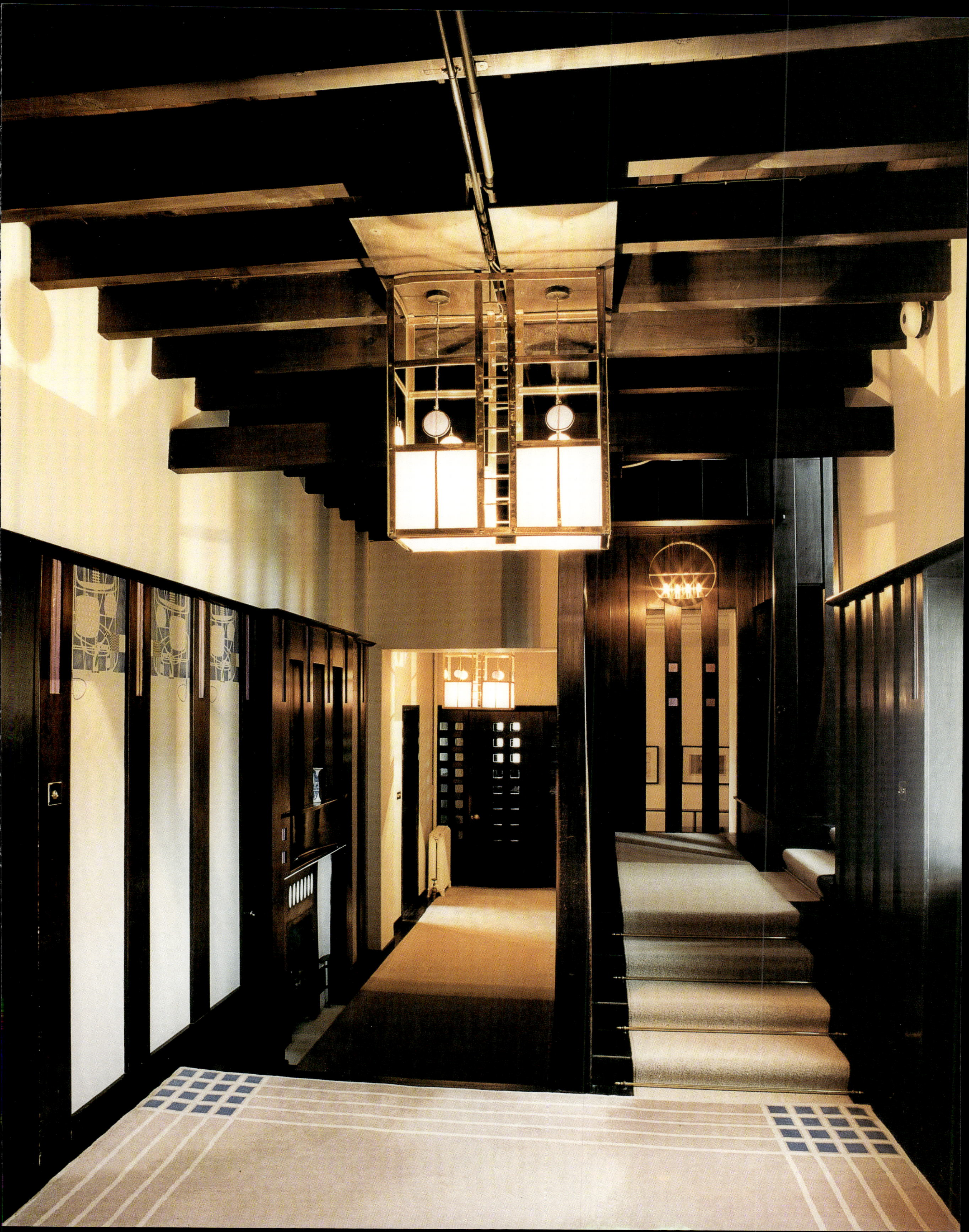

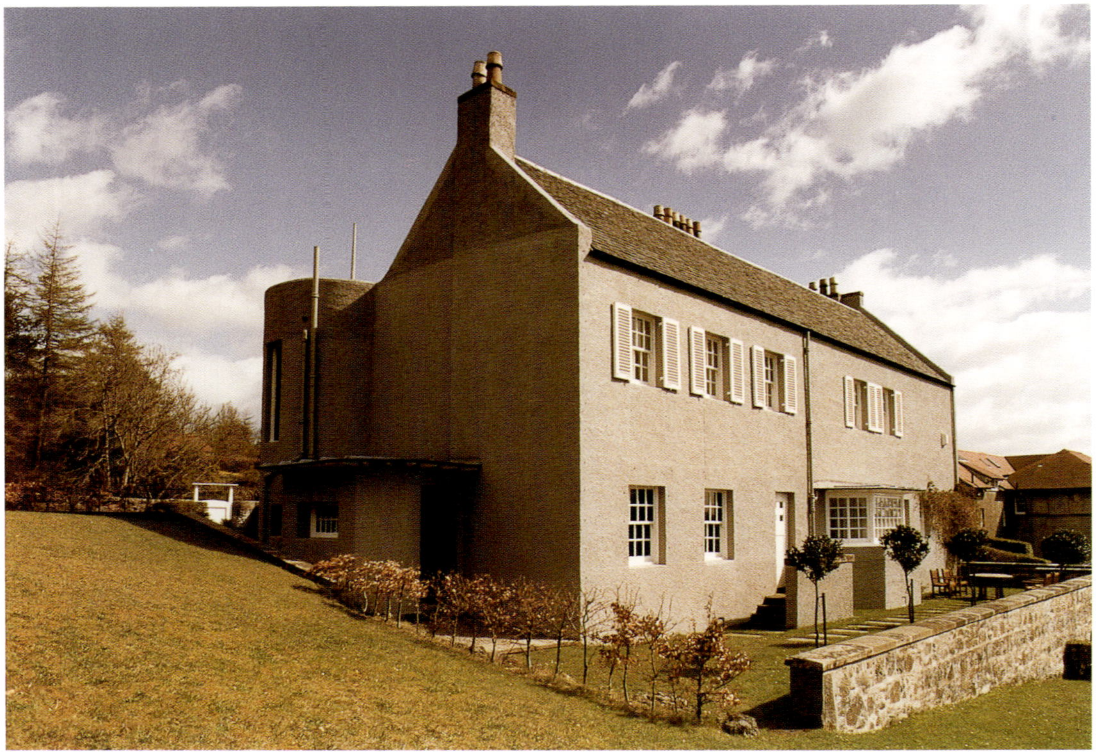

Windyhill, 1899-1901

charming scale. While spatially tight and exciting, each is an essay in architectural mass and form.

By this time, the Glasgow Style as interior settings was able to display its mainstream commercial acceptability – as was seen at Glasgow's 1901 International Exhibition.[3] The similarities quickly fade, as Mackintosh's domestic rooms become more coherent places than such stylistic makeovers. Clearly there were antecedents – Oscar Wilde talked of his Godwin interior as 'sonnets in ivory' – but around 1900 such complete spaces were rare. 'Evidently there are certain things in the air which affect our movement, in spite of all nationalism,' said *Dekorative Kunst* in the first published comment on Mackintosh and The Four (November 1898). It pointed out similarities between Mackintosh and an Obrist fabric, McNair and Koepping glasses, Van de Velde and McNair stained glass. It added: 'we are in a position to state that this [copying] cannot be the case because we saw the Scottish work when none of the other works had been published.' There can be no doubt that at the time of the 1900 Vienna exhibition, it was Mackintosh and the Scots who were the leaders, the Viennese artists the admiring followers.[4]

In that year, Josef Hoffmann designed a room round a piece of Mackintosh furniture.[5] At the exhibition, he bought an Ashbee salt cellar while Moser bought a Mackintosh chair. Hoffmann visited Mackintosh in 1902 and, while creating his own dining room for Wärndorfer, helped install Mackintosh's music room. Klimt's 'Watersnakes II' (of 1904-7) very obviously was linked with Margaret Macdonald's Wärndorfer imagery of 1903-4. If Hoffmann, Mackintosh and Kolo Moser were mutually influenced, every stylistic move by Mackintosh around 1900-2 seems followed by Olbrich one step later. Hoffmann's vast and opulent Stocklet house (1905) owed much to Mackintosh's Art Lover project but, letting unlimited funds go to

Windyhill Main Bedroom Detail

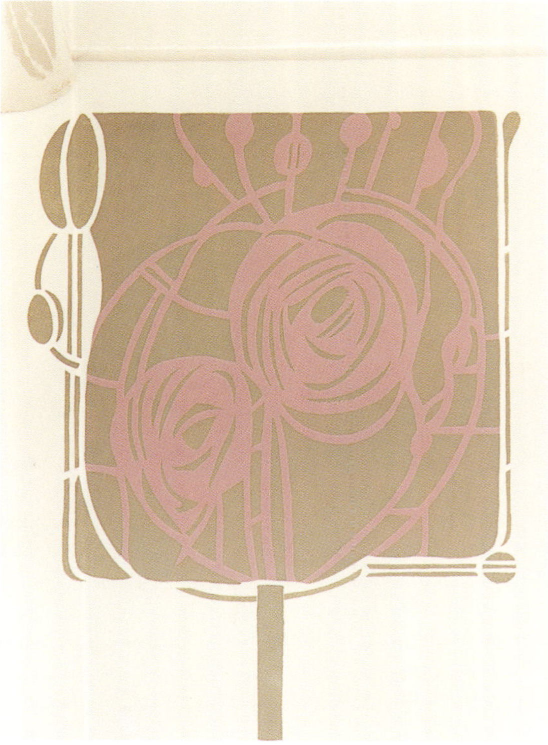

his head, the Viennese architect lost much of the Scot's tautness.

And other influence? Henri Van de Velde designed chairs remarkably similar to those he'd seen in illustrations of the Argyle Street tea rooms.[6] More interestingly, as it can't be based on published images, his Weimar Art School, though much more timid than Glasgow's, is certainly reminiscent of that building (e.g. in the studio window heads), and stair towers in a Weimar school are said to be based on Scotland Street.[7] *The Studio* spread the decorative style, and the Turin exhibition was widely influential – central, for example, to the metamorphosis of Peter Behrens whose work was soon to take new ways. Muthesius organised a tour of Britain for German architects, among them Behrens, who paid a glowing tribute to Glasgow and Mackintosh.

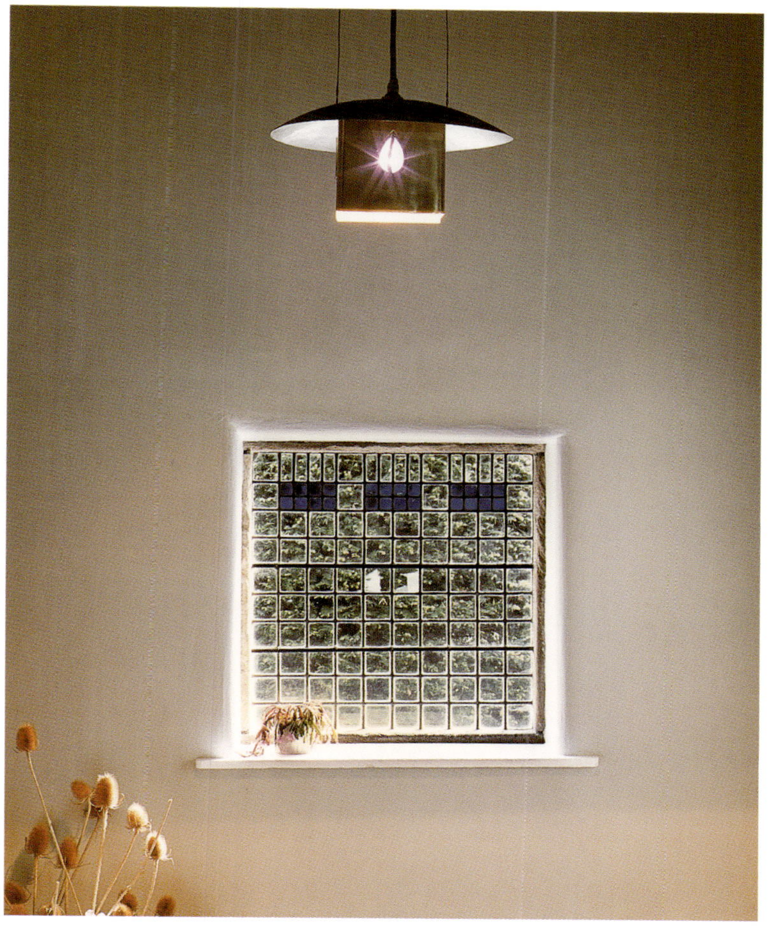

**Porch Window, Windyhill**

The purity, simplicity and subtle charm of the little drop pendant over the square porch window at Windyhill. Its 10 x 10 leaded squares have carefully placed colour and sub-division, while the wall curls softly into the window reveal, cottage style, echoing the harling on the outside.

And in the United States? *The Studio* was avidly read at Adler & Sullivan's, from where Frank Lloyd Wright had branched out in 1893; surely Wright read it, and perhaps also saw the Art Lover's House portfolio in 1901, although he later noted in a letter that 'the Mackintoshes of Glasgow' were at that time 'seen and heard only in Europe.' Wright himself was published in *House Beautiful* and *Ladies' Home Journal* in 1897, but surely these never reached Glasgow. Yet the barrel-vaulted playroom in his own 1895 house, with its low rectangular bays at the sides, are remarkably like those of the House for an Art Lover in proportion and in the shaping of the vault end. Could Mackintosh have seen the U.S. journals in Vienna when starting the design there in 1900?[8]

Visual images always migrate and transform with the ease of dreams, and no architect used elements from his memory bank more easily, and often playfully, than Mackintosh.

The completely unified interior is, as ever, an impossible dream. Mackintosh came near to it at Hill House, even though there was a financial crisis and Blackie couldn't commission as much furniture as he wished. Perhaps he came even closer at Hous'hill. This was not a new house but there was also less constraint on costs. Between 1903-5, elements from major spatial reconstruction to tiny objects effected a beautiful transformation in this house. Margaret designed curtains and napery, Toshie a little pen box inlaid with walnut squares and mother-of-pearl.

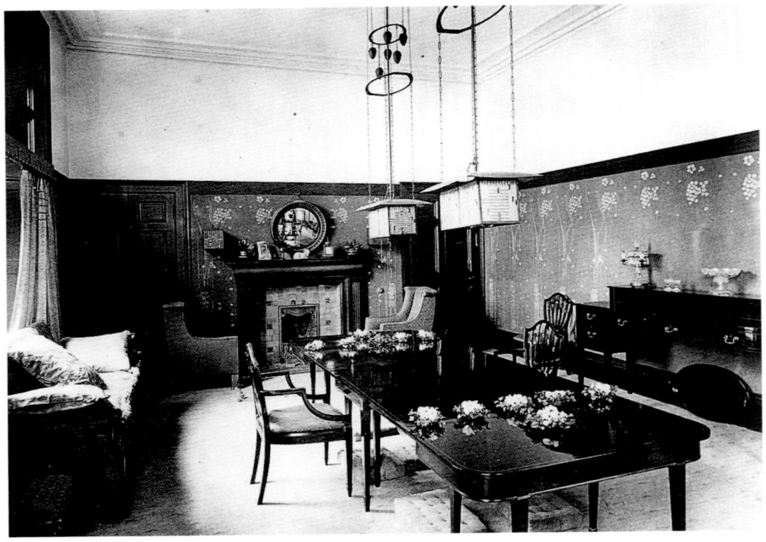

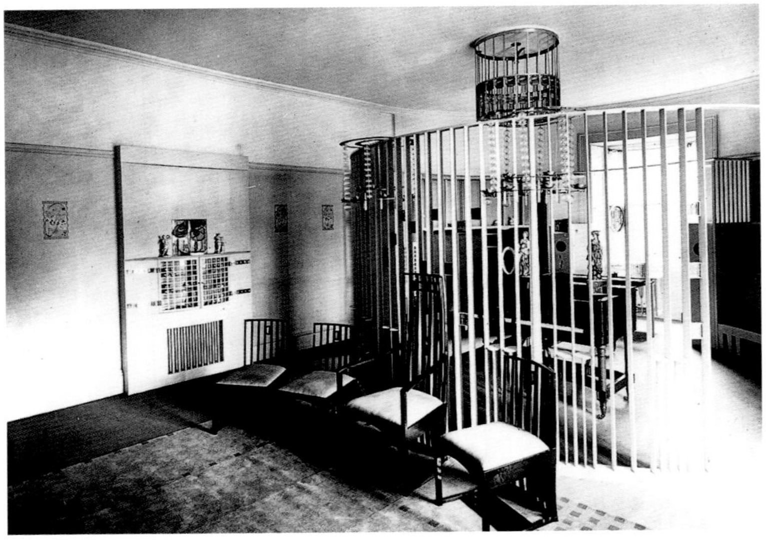

**Dining Room (top) and Drawing Room (below), Hous'hill, 1904**

Hous'hill, Cranston's home altered in 1904, was CRM's most extensive domestic commission, producing remarkable interiors and a wealth of beautiful and unique objects. It was poorly recorded (the extraordinary card room from 1909 not at all), was demolished and most of the objects lost (though many are now in museums worldwide). Meanwhile, the House for an Art Lover (dining room opposite) has been lovingly and laboriously realised from his few sketches of 1901.

**The House for an Art Lover, 1990s (opposite)**

The house, an old country estate now surrounded by south-west Glasgow, had been bought by Major Cochrane and his wife Kate Cranston. (They gave its name the strange spelling, perhaps trying to recapture its original sound. Although it was Househill through the nineteenth century – as the park remains – it had earlier been called Howsle, meaning 'a pretty dwelling and reasonable good house.'[9]) Here, sure of his client's confidence and purse, Mackintosh's inventiveness had freer rein than ever before, and the work was crafted to a high standard.

Some of the beautiful furniture remains, but unique fittings are only recalled in occasional memories. In the card room, for example, was a large fire surround made of thick plate glass sheets, broken in large pieces and set flat in mortared layers with a roughly straight edge projecting. It is said that this little room, with its walls of gold leaf, was the most admired in the house. Its fireplace must have been an extraordinary scintillating texture of shiny greens: not a surface to be stroked if you wanted to avoid lacerations, and surely undustable. According to Peter Wylie Davidson (who designed candlesticks for the house), 'when the sun shone on it, the mixed colourings of green, gold and violet were reflected from half-inch parallel rods of plate glass.'

The dining room was unified in Mackintosh's usual way, with a string cornice pulled tight, above an elegant wall pattern, whose erotic content here is subtly veiled. The scale of this very tall room is changed, just as he had developed first in their own flat: the cornice at door head never implies an Arts & Crafts cosy domesticity, but ties the structure and surface, door and windows together with minimal detailing. Unlike an Arts & Crafts room, with its dado rail, plain wall and then a deep frieze, Mackintosh has developed a decorated wall to the string at door head, and he lets it vanish above that (with no cornice or moulding at all if possible).

The major spatial effect at Hous'hill was in converting the bow-windowed drawing room directly over the dining room for music. Here the unifying string forms a circle of 20 ft (6 m) diameter, the semi-cylindrical bay being reflected in a lovely open screen of fins defining the space.

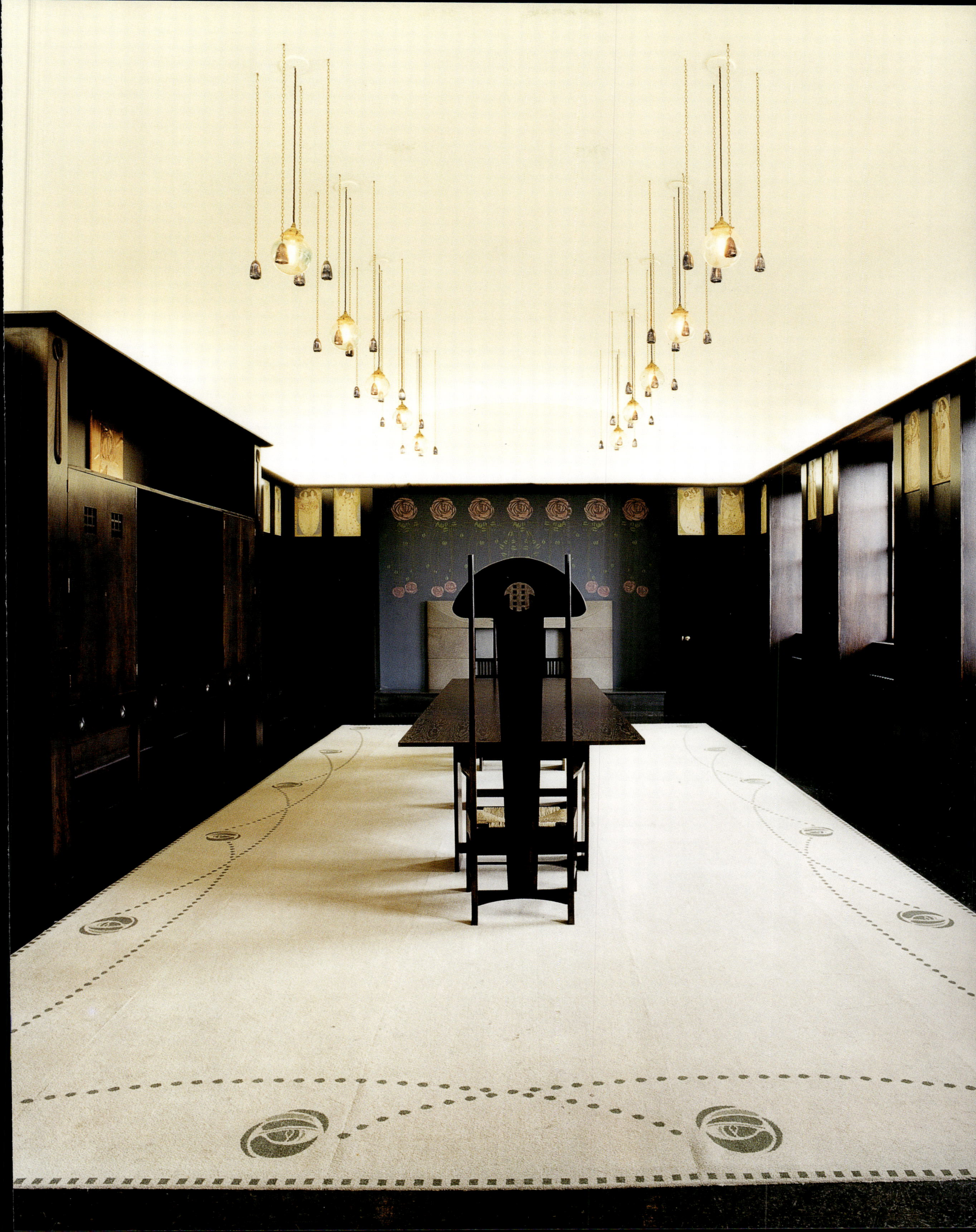

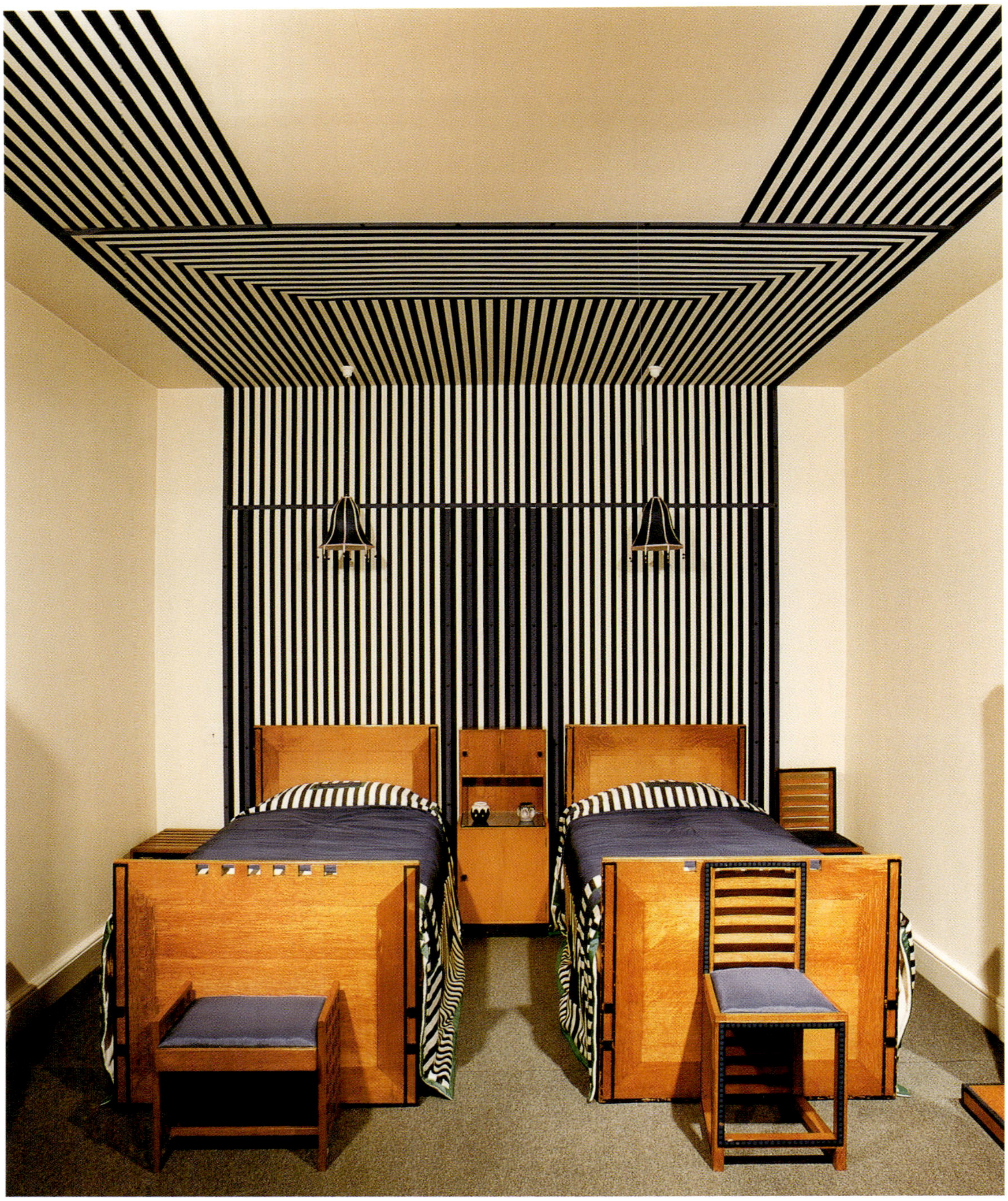

**Derngate Guest Bedroom, 1919**
**Reconstructed in The Hunterian Art Gallery**

In CRM's complete makeover of his earlier room, stripes ran from the bedspreads up the wall, over the ceiling and were taken up in the curtains opposite, almost turning the whole room into one four-poster bed. With the rectilinear light oak furniture, this was an extraordinary ensemble in a room barely 4 m square. The client described it, excitedly, as 'perhaps the most daring room in the house.' G.B. Shaw, when a guest here, claimed not to be disturbed by the migraine-inducing stripes above him, as he slept with his eyes shut. It was CRM's last interior scheme of any consequence.

# NEW WAYS

Mackintosh's architectural career in England was slight and patchy, as indeed is our knowledge of it. All his work was done very privately on his own from his Chelsea studio. By Christmas 1915, he was approached by a Northampton industrialist, Whynne Bassett-Lowke[1] to work on his poky and dark terrace house in Derngate. Bassett-Lowke was a model modernist: he understood and cared for precision engineering and for design quality; he was fascinated by gadgets and gizmos; he instinctively felt that link between design quality and social good which Germanic modernism had inherited from William Morris; he was an active Fabian, friend of G.B. Shaw and later became a prominent councillor, sponsoring municipal modernism in Northampton. He manufactured high-quality scaled replica machines and railways.

Impressed by the Paris 1900 exhibition as a young man, he soon had Viennese Secessionist stencil decoration in his office and, before 1914, he had contacts with the Deutsche Werkbund.[2] Now, at 39, he was getting married and, prohibited by war restrictions from building a new house, bought a tiny 1816 terrace property for £200. Talking with a friend on holiday, he was recommended 'the artist architect Mackintosh' (his words), whom he finally tracked down to London. What Mackintosh was asked to do, interestingly, is unclear. Not only was there a client with strong ideas of his own – Mackintosh had experienced that to his cost before, especially at Auchenibert – but here the ideas were progressive. Moreover the client controlled his own fabrication works, and valued Mackintosh as a progressive designer.

The basic architectural shell conversion, however, seems to have been the work of an accomplished local (ex-Glaswegian) architect A.E. Anderson, who submitted the drawings for all structural and services alterations for approval in June 1916.[3] Clearly the client – whose interest in hygiene, novelty and things nautical was almost as obsessive as Le Corbusier's – was closely involved: in the choice of the latest American fittings in the kitchen and tiny bathroom, in the en-suite bedroom wash facilities; in the fresh-air vents in bedroom doors, and in the new bedroom balcony.

In this really tight conversion there were two key

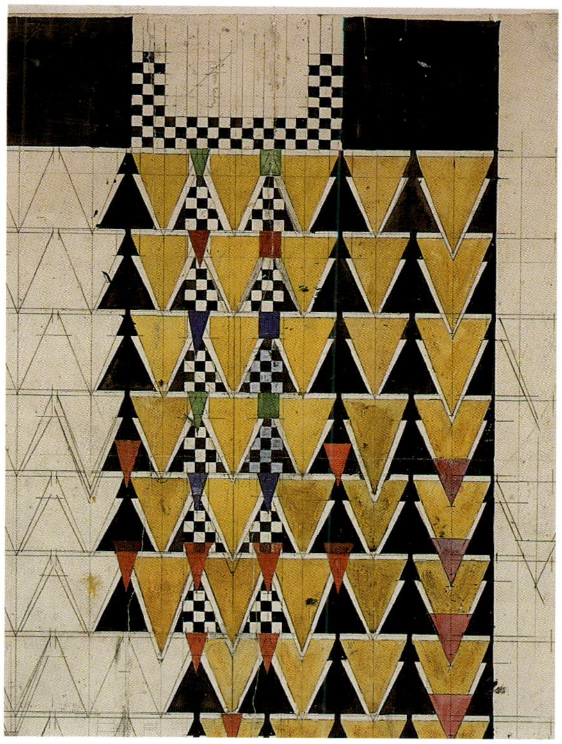

**Hall Design, 78 Derngate**

This tiny room (below) is only recorded in black and white, but CRM's design for the curtains and wall stencilling (above) gives a clue to its bold richness.

**Hall, Looking Towards Window, 78 Derngate, Northampton**

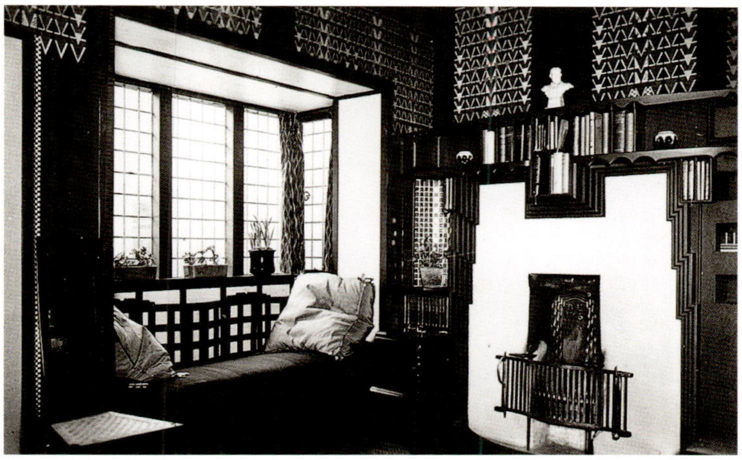

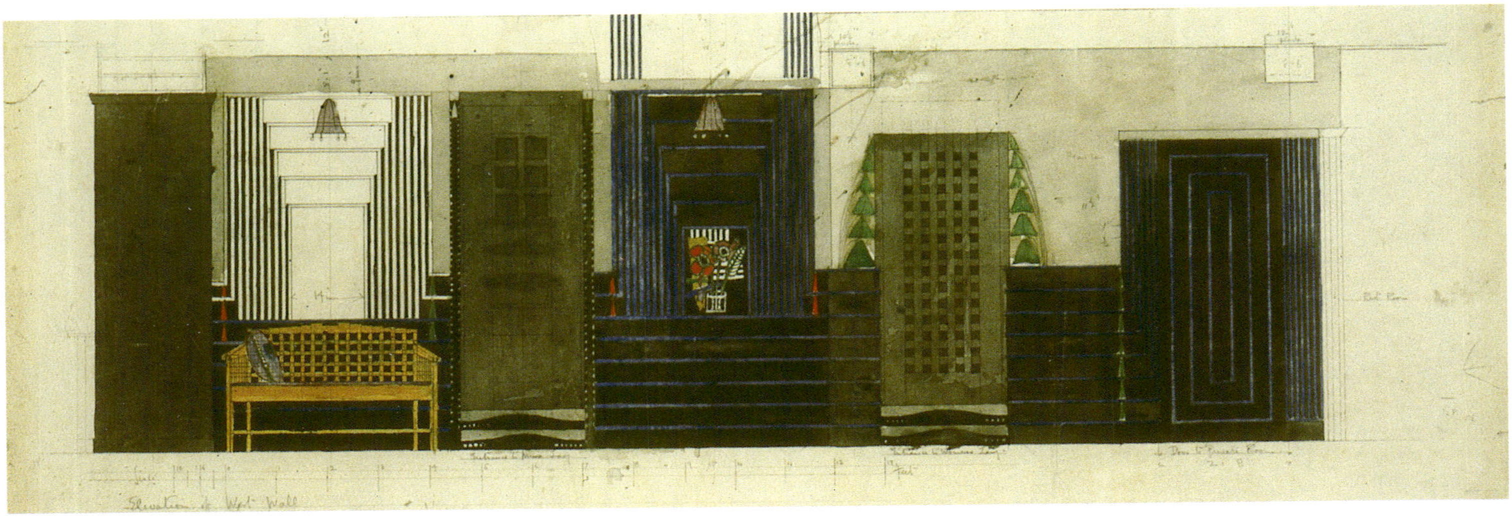

### Design for The Dugout

CRM's last work for Cranston is an astonishing idea, an ent rely artificially lit, basement tea room with a shiny black ceiling and centred on a memorial (below) to the ongoing slaughter. Little remains apart from the yellow settle and these drawings; the vestibule (above) centres on a flower drawing like those bouquets he was currently trying to sell in London.

### Design for the Memorial Fireplace in The Dugout

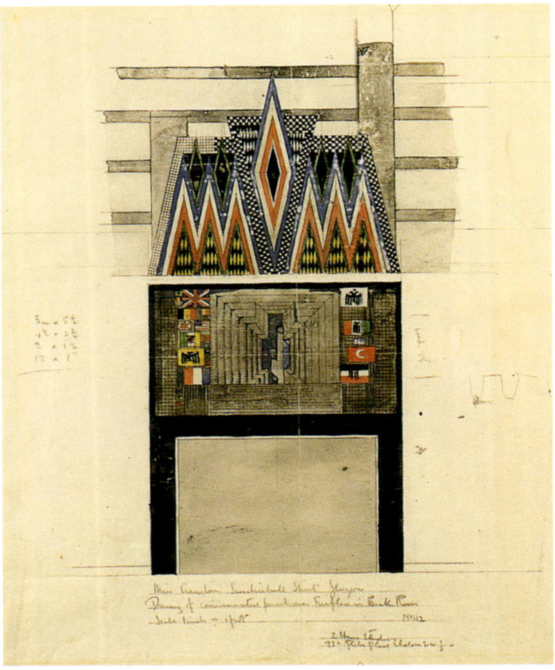

architectural moves. The first was to remove the hall partition and old stair, rebuilding it at right angles across the centre of the house, making a more habitable if still small main room. This room was further enhanced with a bay window to the street – though the street door now opened directly into the room. The second key move was at the garden side which stepped down a storey. Here a shallow reinforced concrete bay, just 5 ft (1.5 m) deep, was added. It enlarged and lightened the basement kitchen and gave the ground floor dining room a new bay with full width windows facing south. Higher up, the wall was not moved out but new French doors gave on to a framed bedroom verandah 'offering a most desirable venue for light breakfasts and suppers in the summertime,' as Bassett-Lowke put it; this supported an open balcony for the guest bedroom on top.

Mackintosh's interior contained two extraordinary spaces, releasing his pent-up design energy in a quite novel burst of inspiration. The first is the hall, where the prevailing colour was a velvety black on the walls, woodwork and panelling. The screen, with its carved newel spinning one up the stair, was a grid of squares which hid the treads from the room. Below the rising treads, the grid was infilled with a pattern of mirror and amber and clear glass which let light into the basement stair behind it.[4] A remarkable light fitting hung from a knobbled white square on the ceiling; a four-fold screen, of ebonised wood covered in petunia tapestry with yellow silk triangles, hid the door. The bay window seat, with its ebony finish and black moiré silk, had cushions of shot purple and yellow silk, edged with emerald-green ribbon. Rich, exotic and dark.

The second extraordinary makeover came a bit later. While the dining room and main bedroom were largely the work of (or indeed simply purchased by) the client, Mackintosh designed a

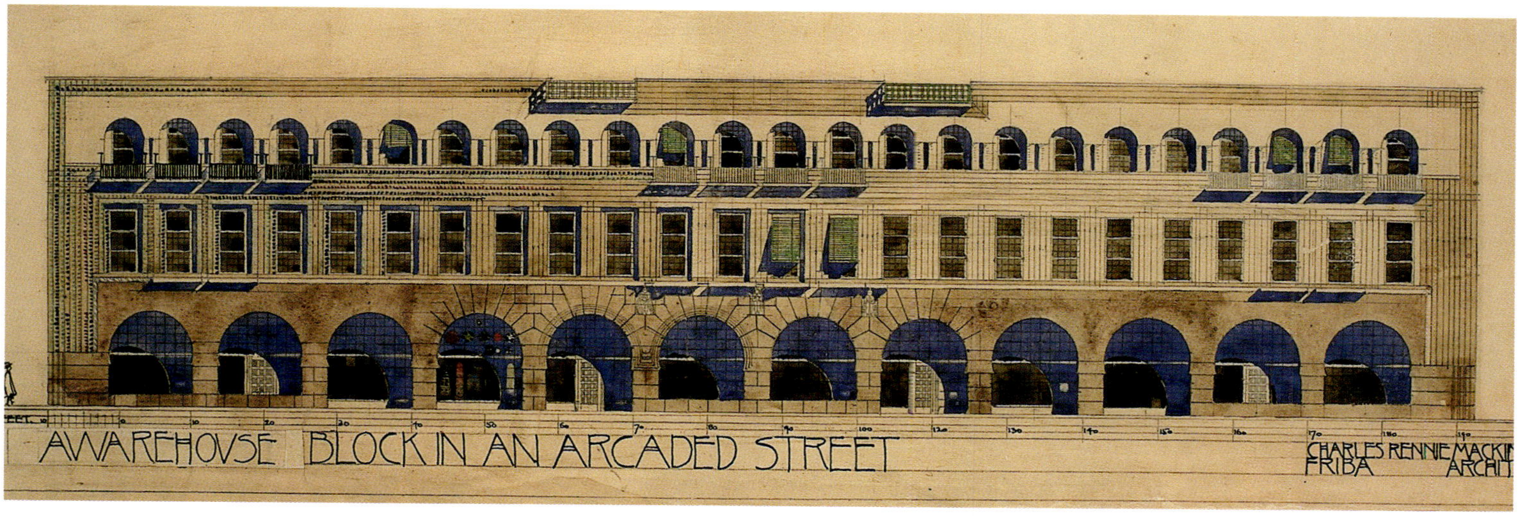


complete furniture suite for the spare bedroom.[5] These pieces, beautifully cool and geometric, in rich mahogany and inlaid with aluminium and mother-of-pearl, so impressed a friend of Bassett-Lowke's that he had a full duplicate set made.[6] However in 1919, the client asked Mackintosh to redo the room. This furniture was replaced with a new set, fitted within a dizzy decor of black and white stripes with ultramarine and touches of emerald green. This new furniture was even simpler than the first set. For example, the bedside chair was a light yellow oak with bold blue and black chequer decoration, upholstered in blue silk. It was bolder, less subtle than its predecessor; identical ladder spars run evenly up the back; with the earlier mahogany one it was graduated, the spars becoming thicker and closer towards the bottom.

Bassett-Lowke had used Mackintosh as a member of his team. It was a way of working Mackintosh never experienced before or since. The client, on a note about his folding screen to the front door, reminded him about the promise to design a cigarette box as soon as possible. He returned drawings with comments and his own sketches. He suggested materials, sending samples of coloured plastics for furniture inlay, of differently yellow silks for the hall screen, of grey hair cord samples for stair carpet – in each case wanting Mackintosh to make the choice. Mackintosh was respected, and was expected to respond: he designed a gramophone cabinet, sticky labels and a Christmas card as well as complete suites of furniture. But everything went to production not from the architect but through the client, who wrote of 'my cabinet maker'. This was a completely new sense of collaboration for Mackintosh. It was real patronage, but quite unlike any he'd known before. It seemed to suit his work marvellously. The furniture of this period is the best crafted of all Mackintosh's work; initially

**Design for a Warehouse Block in an Arcaded Street**

Recently arrived in London, CRM was spotted in 1915 briefly working for Patrick Geddes. Geddes was lecturing in London on cities, and about to travel to India. CRM's two fascinating, elegant and appropriately sun-shaded street elevations, of which this is one, are unique among his known works. (The other, more decorative, drawing shows a block of shops and offices.)

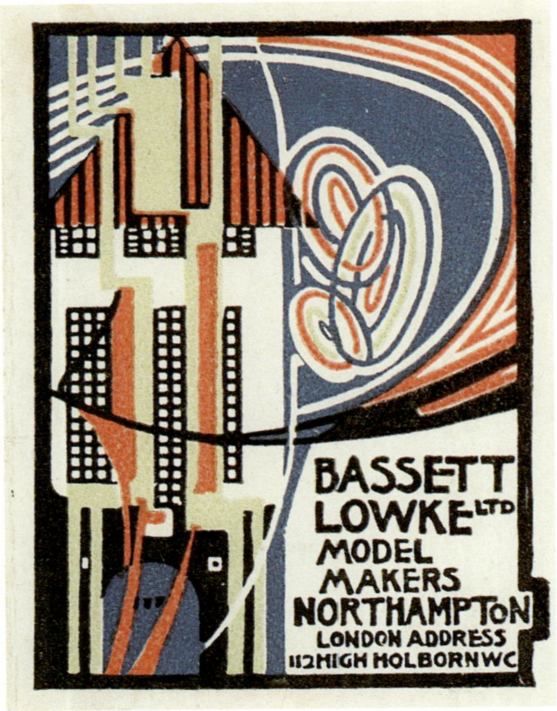


**Designs for an Advertising Label for Bassett-Lowke Ltd c.1919**

CRM also produced a wide range of ephemeral designs for him, down to a cigarette box and his 1922 Christmas card (p.160) and a number of these fascinating advertising graphics.

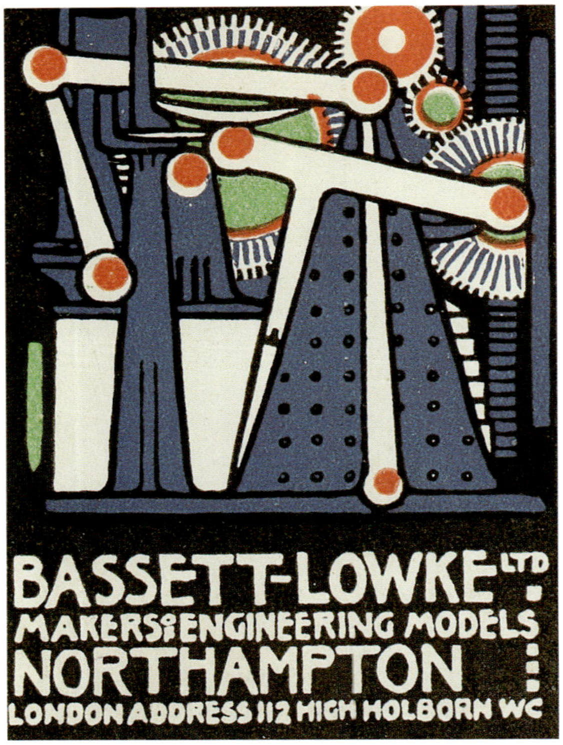


made in Bassett-Lowke's workshop, much of the best was by a London cabinet maker who, because of his German birth, had been interned on the Isle of Man as an enemy alien.[7]

Mackintosh had no overall architectural control, or perhaps even input. It seems he never visited Northampton, though the client regularly met him in London. Credit for the building can only be shared between Anderson, Mackintosh, the craftsmen involved and, centrally, Whynne Bassett-Lowke the client and general contractor. It resulted in an extraordinary mixture: the cool, white geometric back which appears so European, and certainly is unique in England at that time, and the Arts & Crafts modelling of the bay window at the front so typical of Anderson's other domestic work; the bulkhead lights and white tiles, and the woody panelled dining room with its Bassett-Lowke cupboards and their Mackintosh wall lanterns. The remarkable living room/hall, the stair screen and, two floors further up, the equally forceful spare bedroom.

Mackintosh extended a country house for Hoppé unmemorably, but the same circle of Chelsea friends gave him his main chance to build in England after the war. The large site of Cheyne House, its gardens coming very close to Mackintosh's studio, was for sale and various possible building plans were aired. Three houses were to be built in the garden, along Glebe Place, one for Derwent Wood, the next for Harold Squire and the third for Arthur Blunt. On the site of the old house itself, Mackintosh designed a block of 27 studio flats for artists. It suddenly looked in 1920 as if he might have an English architectural career. It was work for an office the size of Honeyman, Keppie & Mackintosh.

These were varied clients (the block was for the Arts League of Service), all artists whose dreams changed and never came close to reality; Mackintosh's drawings keep developing and are never totally resolved by the time it is abandoned. He had already produced various designs for the three studios when, on 31 March 1920, he took J.D. Fergusson and the dynamic Chilean founder of the League, Ana Berry, to visit the proposed site for the studio block. He recommended its purchase for £1850. They were positive and Mackintosh was instructed to prepare plans. It was to be a large complex of studio flats, run as a cooperative, with an attached theatre block for Margaret Morris.

The drawn schemes for the Cheyne House site are a marvellously modelled collection, a medley of varied forms.[8] It was, of course, very unlike Chelsea; although clearly influenced by Ashbee's built-up streetscape round the corner in Cheyne

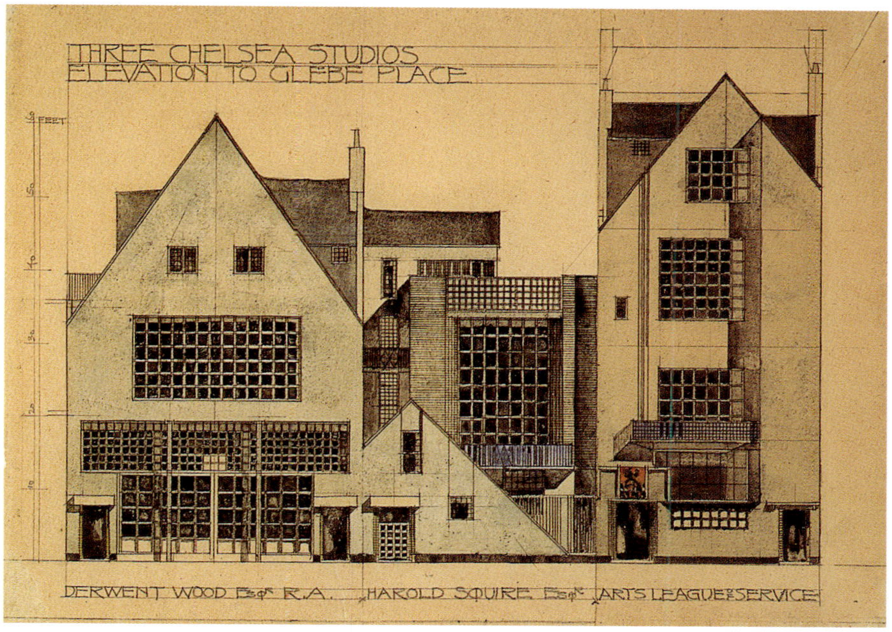


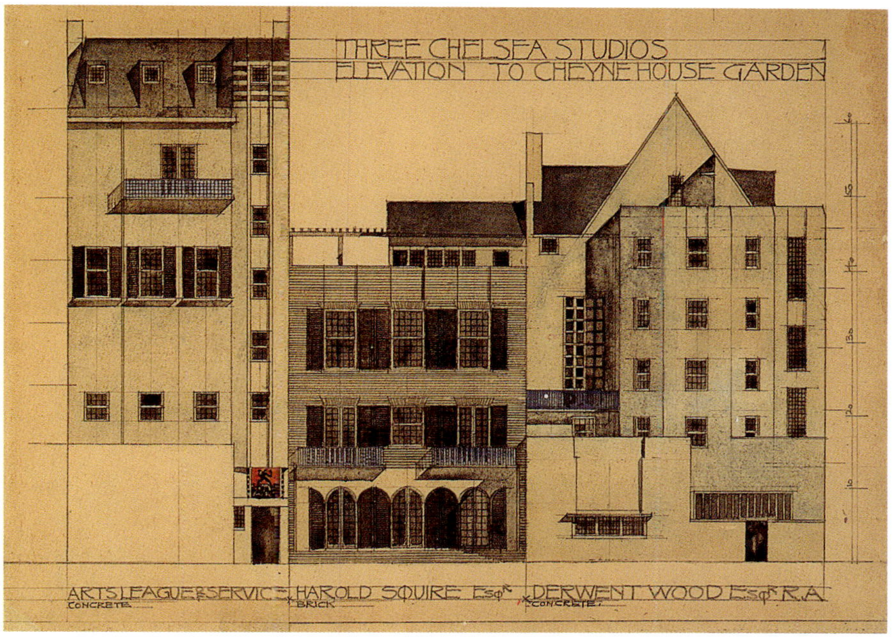


Walk, it might seem more at home in Geddes's Edinburgh, next to Ramsay Garden, and the tall old tenements stretching down the Royal Mile. We cannot guess how they would have developed into real places, but as graphic patterns they remain very powerful. Its never getting off the ground is one of London's great architectural losses of the twentieth century. Mackintosh never had the chance to prove he could design in a street, but this project (and, very differently, the uniform arcaded blocks designed in London for Geddes) leave powerful suggestions.

The Blunt project fades away in mid 1920, though Wood's studio developed and seems about to be built when it too falls silent. Drawings for the Arts League studios were submitted to the L.C.C, and builders' estimates received; it was said all the studios in the block were sold. There were official objections to the forcefully unornamented design, Mackintosh noting in his diary (22 June 1920) the complaint 'that my elevations are not architectural enough.' But authorities were finally satisfied and permission to build the huge studio block granted in December 1920. Yet it got no further. Nothing came of the whole development other than a much pared down studio for Squire which might not even be recognised as architect designed.

Bassett-Lowke said he couldn't find Mackintosh to design his new house. So Peter Behrens installed the Mackintosh furniture and fittings in his study as carefully as had Hoffmann in a Viennese study 25 years earlier. The study at New Ways has the cool rectilinear Mackintosh table, the clock unit all in black, the extraordinary light fitting from the Derngate hall and a radiator screen in vivid yellow, with stencilling in orange, red, blue and grey. Hopefully Behrens got the right yellow, the one Mackintosh used on the interior walls of his first house, Redclyffe, in 1890.

### The Chelsea Studios

There was a brick building between two concrete ones, and the vast studio block as the other arm of the L-shaped development, with its sweeping roof and Art School studio windows. Designs developed at varying times, but the collective composition was controlled, often, as in the view from Glebe Place, with great force. Suddenly the project vanishes. After his last office diary entry in January 1921, virtually no record exists of CRM for three years.

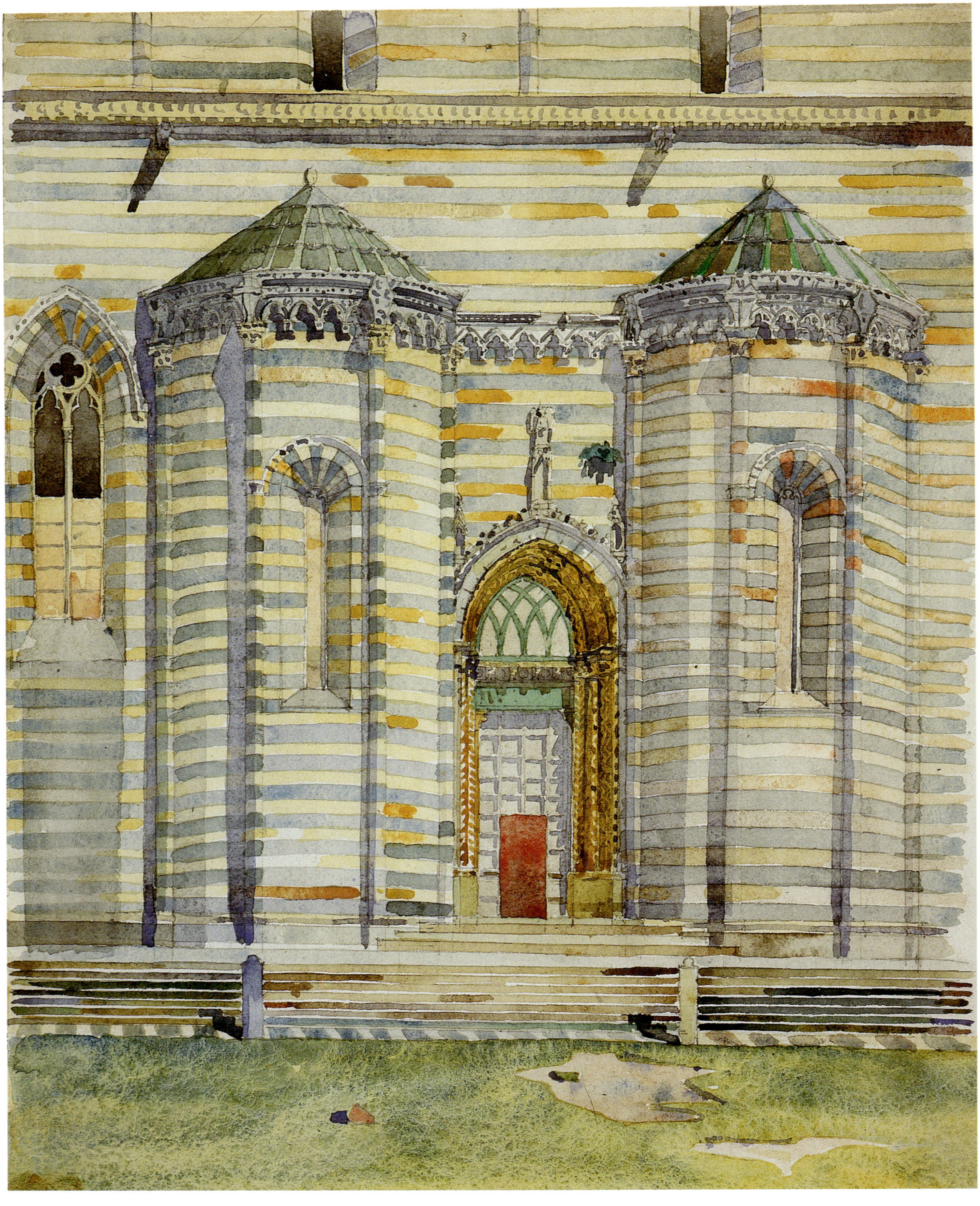

# THE SCOTTISH DRAUGHTSMAN

He pauses and looks. Walking through this Cotswold village in September, he sees a rose. He stops, studying its form with great concentration, and then draws it in firm HB pencil, as if carving it. The planes of packed, overlapping petals are firmly etched, hatched along their contours in precise parallel curving lines, different surfaces with differing intensities. Then beneath, carefully placed, he adds three lines: ROSE / CRM / 1894 and encloses this, for the first time, in a neat square. The young man has worked in architecture for a decade; a vital nourishment in that life is his sketching. But as he now crafts this rosebud life-size in his sketchbook, other possibilities, other thoughts, other futures come into mind.

His sketching trips are refreshing, of course, allowing that essential space; they let fresh oxygen break the stuffy office routine and sense of bureaucratic tyranny. But more important, they are a constant education; they constitute a study in which undertaking – in what he chooses to look at – is a statement of architectural position. His sketchbooks fill with the vernacular architecture of small towns and villages.

Up till now, with one exception, these have been Scottish trips, where images of castles or ruined abbeys predominate. Three years ago, in his first public lecture, he talked of how he would venture out 'not only under the balmy influence of summer, but along muddy roads and snowy paths, and with glowing heart but shivering hand to sketch the humble cottage, the more pretentious mansion or the mutilated though venerable castle, with feelings of the most indescribable delight...'.[1] The one exception is that he had already won the chance to visit Italy, and shortly after that talk, he had set off. He looked carefully at historic ornament and architectural detail, practising and improving his watercolour technique. It was all the quite typical production of a bright young architect; his heart hadn't seemed really in it.

Now, three years later, this is his first sketching trip in England and his heart clearly is here. For the next 20 years his jottings (as he calls them) will largely be in the English countryside. Sketching is part of the imaginative process, but (as he said in a talk last year) 'especially [of] the imagination that creates, not only the imagination that represents.'[2] He once said that he'd lost his first three sketchbooks – indicating how importantly he'd held on to all the others! It seems that one of

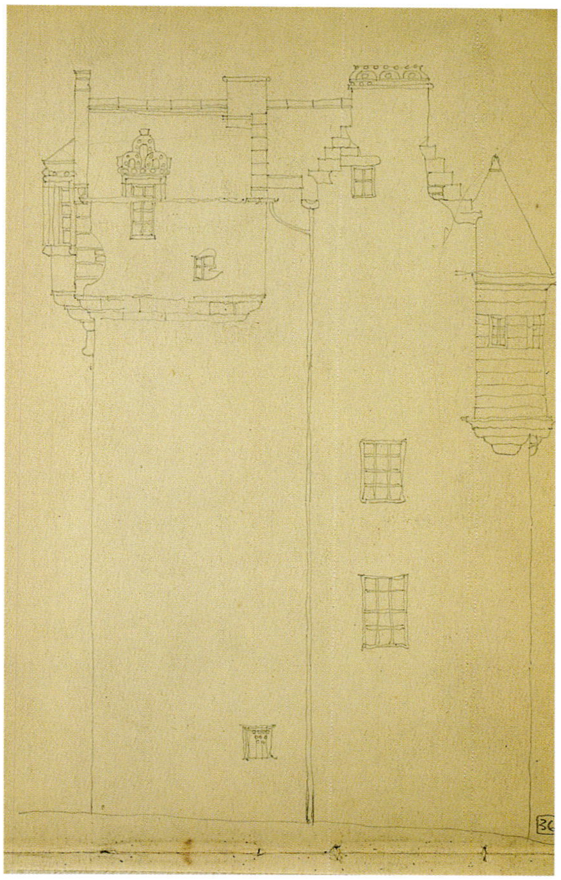

**Maybole Castle, 1897**

Lessons from Maybole, sketched near the Keppies' Ayrshire house, will be remembered in the Art School's east face.

**Orvieto Cathedral, North Elevation, 1891 (opposite)**

Orvieto is a competent student sketch on the grand tour. From Palermo and Naples he travels north to Rome and then Orvieto, Sienna, Florence, Pisa, Pistoia, Bologna, Ravenna, Venice, Padua, Vicenza, Verona, Mantova, Cremona, Brescia, Bergamo, Como, Milan and Pavia. He was up between 4.30 and 7.30 each morning, walking, looking, drawing; and adding lively, witty notes in his diary.

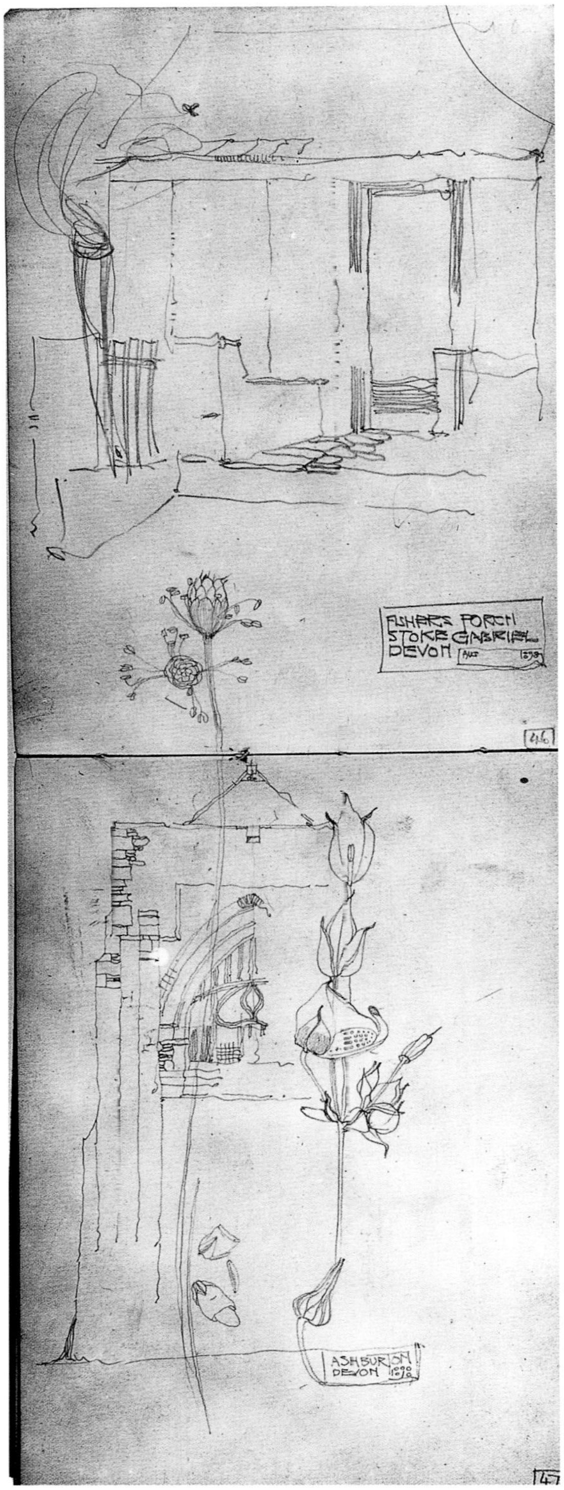


**Studies in Stoke Gabriel and Ashburton, 1898**

The sketchbook goes everywhere with him. He juxtaposes work ng details with lists of train times, doodles with diary notes and, in Devon (above), specimen flowers with a church.

them, perhaps the very first, and almost certainly from 1893, he lent to Jessie Keppie, who never returned it. After her death, an envelope of hers was found to contain this early sketchbook and six photographs of The Immortals.[3]

He has a brief holiday. Now, buoyed by Voysey's work in *The Studio* last year, is his first chance to learn from the English vernacular at first hand. Despite being so close to Birmingham, the Cotswold towns survive with their traditional forms and building techniques; an Arts & Crafts bastion against mechanisation. With hungry enthusiasm he arrives in the Vale of Evesham and virtually fills a complete sketchbook with images of forms. The sketchbook is small. Being bound along the short 4½ inches side, its 7 inch length can open double, so that he often draws tall images across the central gutter. He tried that out with some beautiful long flower drawings, a month earlier on weekend trips 'doon ra watter' to Bute and Arran. Using this double length for church towers here, he gets drawings 14 inches long (or 352 x 111 mm). Wandering from Evesham south to Winchcombe, he draws in Broadway, Chipping Campden, Buckland and Willersey: pub signs and shutters, ornate tombs and simple gravestones, doorways and knockers, gates and pinnacles, brackets and rainwater heads, oak panels and tables. (Often his misspelling, of places like 'Chippen Camden' and, later, 'Norwitch', of things like 'nockers' or plants like 'wich hazel' and 'jasimine', reminds us of his personality.) And he records the articulation of facades, the build up of wall and roof planes to shape the massing of a building, and of buildings in their street.

Drawing, copying, had been central to his evening classes for ten years, in an art school syllabus emphasising structure, whether the subject was natural or man-made, and focusing an analytical, almost scientific enquiry through the drawing. Ruskin's approach, which was more recently fighting for recognition in the school, is closer to his own: based on the observation of nature in its particularity rather than typicality; more empirical and intuitive. He can build the Ruskinian on the analytical foundation, combining strengths of both approaches, as he draws for use. As Louis Kahn has said, the painter draws to paint, the sculptor draws to sculpt, the architect draws to build. And he is an architect.

He can draw as a surveyor, from a decade of practised looking. He has learned both to render the church tower in perspective, sunshine and shadow, and also to record it in elevation and detail, perhaps only drawing in half to a centre line of its symmetrical shape. Just as architects have done since

Palladio first visited Rome in 1541, these differently scaled elements appear on the sheet together, the plan of an end wall, showing the depth and shape of its openings alongside its elevation. Unlike Palladio – or the typical survey drawing – he doesn't add dimensions, trusting his trained eye and hand to translate a moulding's proportions accurately into a sketch which shows its shape as if cut through.

And we can see immediate uses and derivations: brass handles on an old table in Buckland Church reappear on his own furniture designs within months; the divided window at Chipping Campden Church is remembered at Queen's Cross – as obviously is the tower of Merriot Church which he comes across next year in Somerset; the double-height bay window he also spots at Campden reappears in the Art School entrance bay.

Now, not one of these buildings he draws has even found its way into an architectural history book. He is learning from what Muthesius, in his Teutonic way, calls 'the guild masons' buildings' – in other words, from the local vernacular. This was a new approach to architecture, one which Muthesius saw as being England's great nineteenth-century contribution to modern architecture, exemplified in the work of Philip Webb, Eden Nesfield and Norman Shaw. 'The aim was freedom from the trammels of style, but not to the extent of scorning tradition,' is how Muthesius puts it.[4]

On this trip to England in 1894, the young architect's heroes are indeed not the great stylists, but the domestic and craft-centred followers of William Morris: Webb, Shaw, Lethaby, Macmurdo and Voysey.

Long after his architectural practice peters out, the sketches will continue. His very last architectural sketch will be of what Muthesius calls 'an old farmhouse on the east coast of England, Walberswick, Suffolk.' Drawn in extraordinarily different circumstances in 1914 it closes the circle on his concerns of exactly 20 years earlier. We have Muthesius's caption, because, by neat coincidence, he too illustrates it. In 1904, it opens *The English House*, the book which presents Windyhill and the Hill House to the public. Achievements which were the result, as Muthesius says, of 'that remarkable period, the mid 1890s in Scotland, during which so much that was new was seething and rumbling unseen as it struggled for expression.' Not least in this young man's sketchbooks.

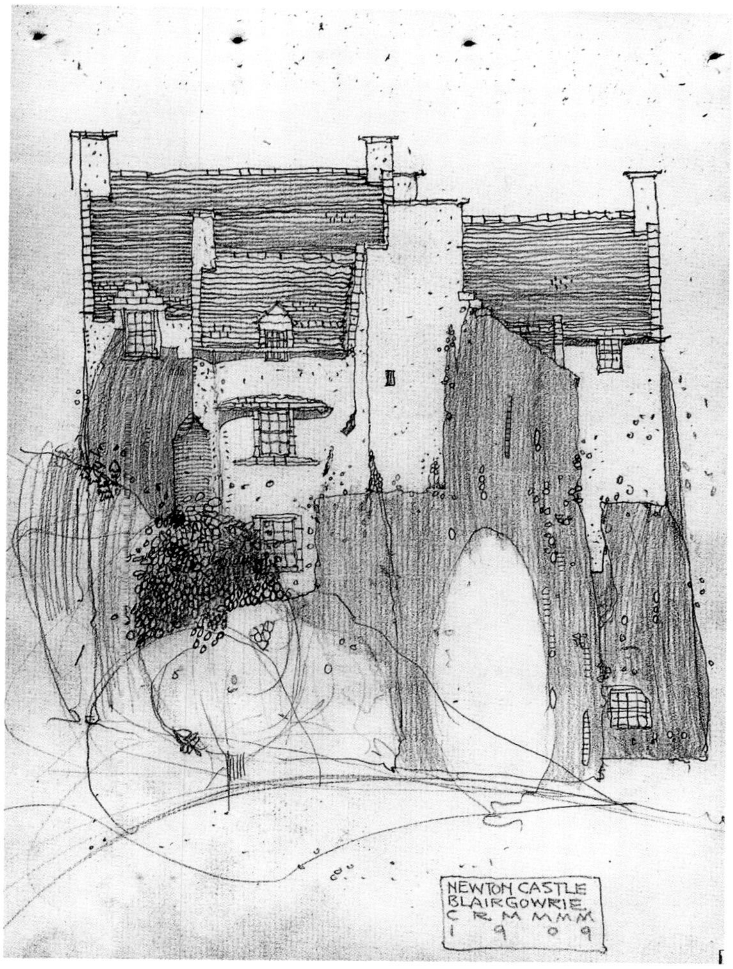


**Newton Castle, Blairgowrie, 1909**

The sketchbook records his penetrating look, his seeing more, adding to his store. In 1895, when working on the Medical School design, which is largely his surfaces over Keppie's form, he chances to look down the client's microscope and see a developing fish eye. He immediately draws it; later saying that it formed the basis for many fruitful decorative ideas. By 1909, when he draws 'Newton Castle', however, the sketch has become a composed picture itself.

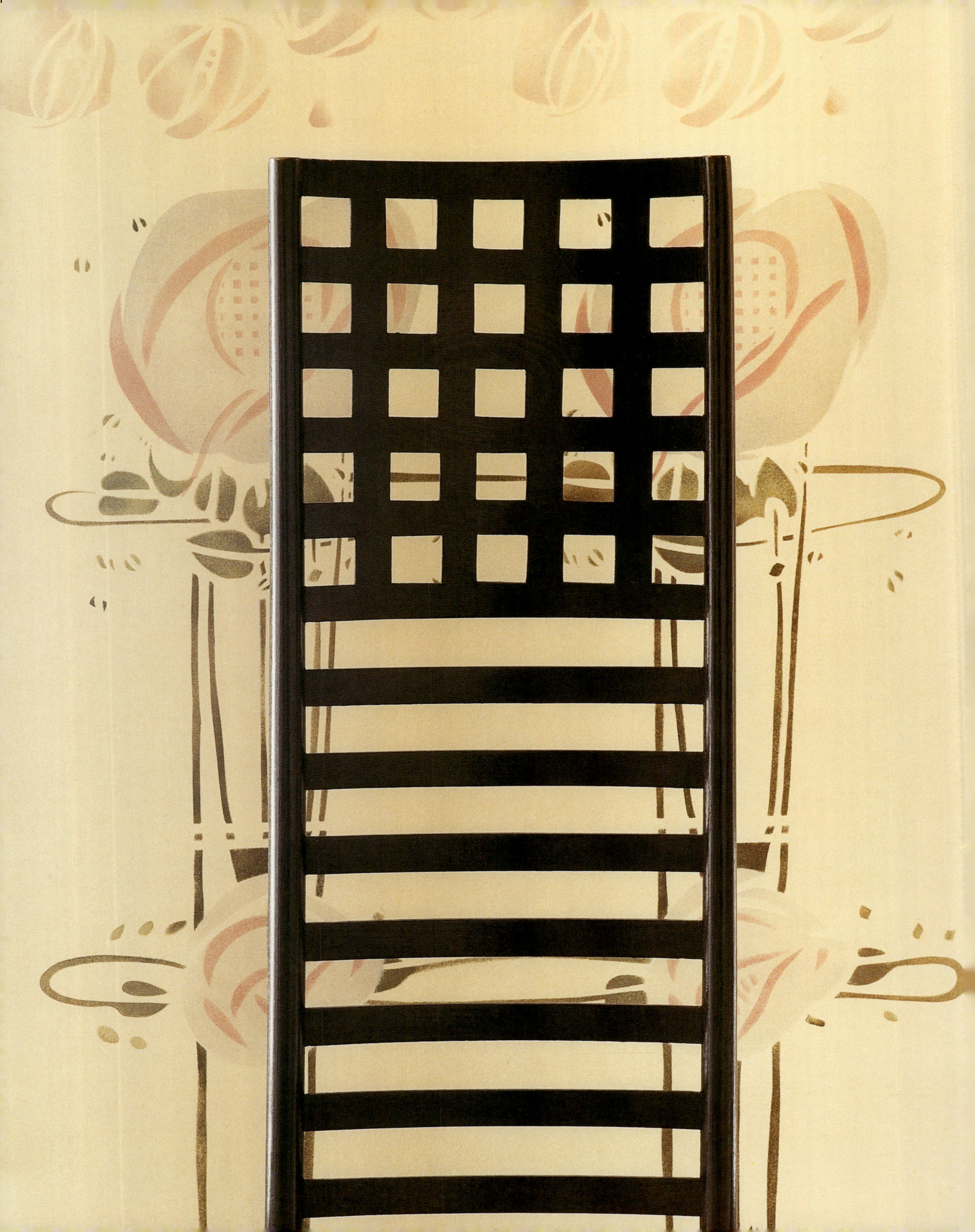

# MEANING IN ARCHITECTURE

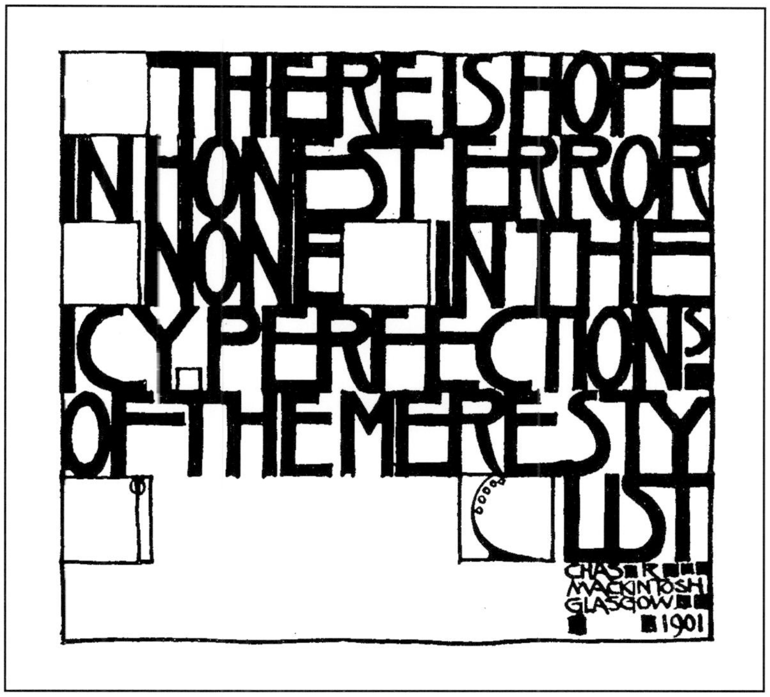


**'There is Hope in Honest Error...', 1901**

Mackintosh first took this Ruskinian phrase from Sedding (adding 'icy' to 'perfections') in a very Victorian design of 1892. He returns in 1901 to use it as quite a different image, the solid sculptural letters decorated only with a sprig of heather (the Macdonald emblem) and blaeberry (Mackintosh emblem).

**The Hill House, 1903 (opposite)**

Geometry and nature, the two navigational poles for the designer, his yin and yang, are glimpsed in the main bedroom at the Hill House.

Architecture, at the end of the nineteenth century, was in a terrible mess. Rampant eclecticism reduced the meaning of forms to trivial bombast. The typical late-century architect, complained John McKean Brydon in 1901, 'has worked in several styles – sometimes simultaneously – ringing the changes, as it were, in the search for novelty.' Another critic at the same moment talks of 'the cheerful eclecticism with which the designer today skips from century to century... an elasticity of appreciativeness.'[1] How could Mackintosh cut a path through this jungle?

'I care not the least for theories, for this or that dogma, so far as the practice of art is concerned, but take my stand on what I myself consider my personal ideal.' The 33-year-old architect was in full flight, addressing the Northern Art Workers' Guild in Manchester in the first few days of 1902.[2] Although he never spoke publicly again about architecture, he held onto his notes for this talk all his life. Handwritten with a deliberation, they are shaped for the page, spaced with long dashes and spaces. Yet clearly they are a flight of consciousness, a first draft which is highly articulate – like his drawings, there is a dynamism but no tentativeness. No words are scored out, no phrases rewritten. 'Shake off all the props – the props tradition and authority offer you – and go alone...'. It is an exhortation to individuality.

Mackintosh is well-read, with wide knowledge of architecture and art, but no scholar. He reads Ruskin and looks at the Arts & Crafts architects; he reads Maeterlinck – as much de rigeur as Ruskin in 1900 – and looks at the aesthetes. He talks about fitness for purpose and truth to materials, as if inevitably they will produce work which would be beautiful.[3] Yet the interiors at Hill House or the Willow de Luxe play with a much richer sense of function than this idea might suggest. He deeply loves the Scottish traditional architecture, yet he condemns those who copy – and in so saying, he copies the words of those whom he reveres.

These all suggest paradoxes. He rejects the Arts & Crafts line of 'taste' being a snobbish delusion, a distraction from their goal of rational appropriateness. He believes in the artist's

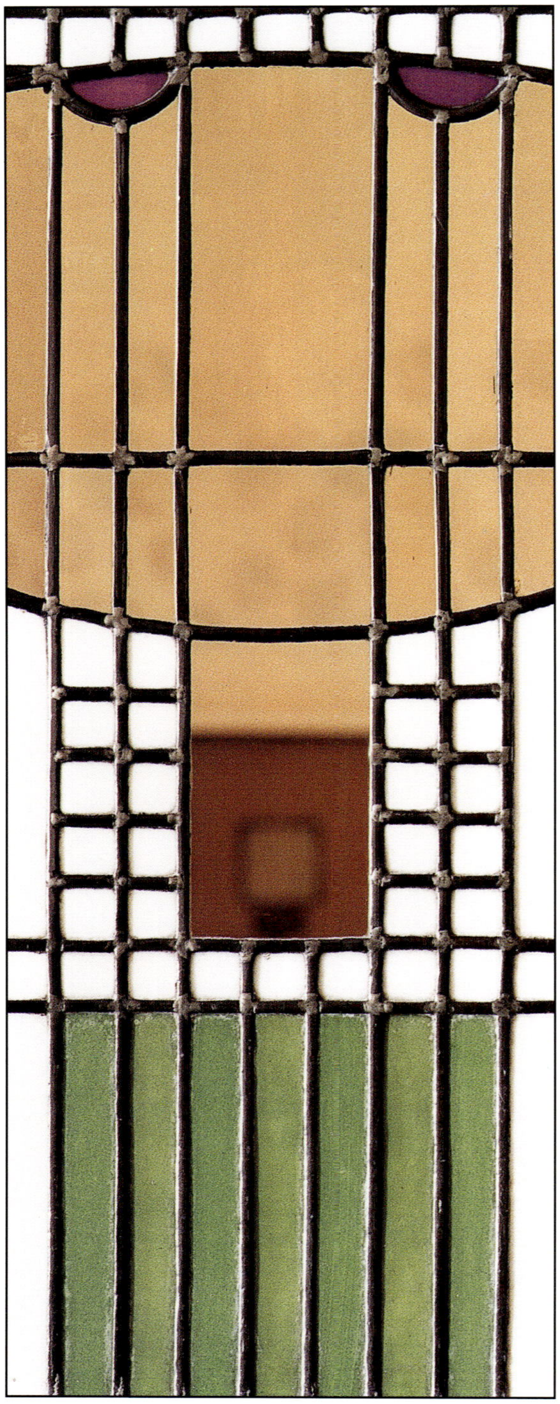

**The Hill House, Main Bedroom, Splash-back of Washstand, Detail**

Geometry and nature: the 'well-hidden geometric figure' of this lovely design has been deconstructed in a recent abstruse research paper which sees its design as a flower and also, interestingly, as 'a diagram of the human female reproductive system.'

individuality and in beauty. In that very first 1893 issue of *The Studio*, where Beardsley's imagery made such an impression on the Glaswegians, Voysey's work was also illustrated, but also his ideas: 'To go to Nature, is of course, to approach the fountainhead: if he does this [i.e. if the architect goes through an elaborate process of selection and analysis], although he has gone directly to nature, his work will not resemble his predecessors; he has become an inventor...Go to Nature direct for inspiration and guidance. Then we are at once relieved from restrictions of style and period, and can live and work in the present.' The champion of Nature was John Ruskin, its ideal student young Mackintosh. As with his transatlantic contemporary Frank Lloyd Wright, Ruskin was his first and most profound intellectual mentor. In 1893 he took *Stones of Venice* on his Italian study tour.

Ruskin's Arts & Crafts followers believed that art is not a special sauce applied to ordinary cooking; it is the cooking itself, if it is good. These words are Lethaby's, whose writing, especially on the symbolic meaning of architecture, so influenced Mackintosh. But, unlike Lethaby and Voysey, Mackintosh does not hold the position that appropriateness to purpose automatically creates beauty, the line which was to dominate 'functionalist' modernism.[4] He bypasses that potentially sterile track in the belief, shared with those who, like his client Fritz Wärndorfer, set up the Wiener Werkstätte, that 'every object must carry the mark of individuality, an active pursuit and not an inevitability of beauty...the indefinable sense of art.'[5] While William Morris was angrily frustrated to be 'ministering to the swinish luxury of the rich,'[6] Mackintosh accepts an elitist role for art, as does Hoffmann who comments 'it is absolutely no longer possible to convert the masses.'[7]

The ornamentation he sees on the new architecture around him seems meaningless and conventional. Unless some new content of nature and meaning is restored to it, it will die. Much is already dead. Lethaby (whose words these are) argues that ornamentation will pass more and more out of the building customs of the future.[8] Mackintosh, however, as the last Ruskinian, the last Victorian, is fighting against that; it is a tragic struggle against the force of history, billowing up in the imagination as the ranks of standardisation, modern business practice and the de-skilling of building sites, of functionalism as a social and democratic virtue, of industrial capitalism, as these all mass together under the banner of the modern world.

Burne-Jones had said that the more factory chimneys he saw,

the more angels he would paint. A generation later, in black industrial Glasgow, they steep themselves in myths and legends, in Egyptian as much as Christian and north European lore, and a deep sense that symbolic importance is more solid than stylistic imagery. By the 1890s there was a surge in things occult across Europe, from Rosecrucian, Theosophic and Spiritualist ideas to the Celtic revivalism which links them both to the Yates brothers in Ireland (the poet W.B., and the painter Jack who sends images for their *Magazine*) and Geddes's magazine *Evergreen* (which published all sorts biological, from 'The Moral Evolution of Sex' to the origins of Celtic imagery in its short life, 1895-6). Many new feelings, not least in social relations between men and women, struggling for expression. In this stew, real originality and cult trashiness mingle almost inextricably.[9] The symbolic world of the moment is well captured in Maeterlinck's *Pelléas*: a world of dream-like shadows where men and women speak in the most oblique terms, performing the most symbolic acts. There was a barely submerged primitive, even orgiastic eroticism: *Ver Sacrum* has a cover image of a volcano. Mahler's great eighth symphony of 1906-9 is a vast hymn to Eros as the source of creativity, a theme celebrated in Vienna at that moment also by Mann, Schnitzler, Wedekind, Klimt and Schiele. Entering that city, as a hero in a flower-decked carriage, must have intoxicated Mackintosh.

His world is soaked in symbolism. Layers and layers of reference can be peeled off their art works, and in no other form is its expression as complex as it is in architecture. For (as he says in 1893) 'the fairy tale which architecture embodies is told in an even more obscure and indirect manner than in painting, in literature or in music. Every form of an architectural composition, every feature, every detail will command your attention...'.[10] In his hunt for a language of meaningful symbolism with which to clothe his architecture, he was seduced by this spirit of the time. He struggles to embrace wider goals than those of the sober Lethabite empiricists in England – like Pearson, Bodley, Brooks and J.D. Sedding, the stars of Muthesius's 1901 book.[11]

His aim is to adorn his designs with living fancy, that is with meaningful rather than dead imagery – and it is not an issue of style.[12] Mackintosh here quotes Sedding who continues: there is hope in honest error, none in the perfections of the mere stylist.

He echoes Sedding's call for modern ideas to be clothed in modern dress; but what that means is not simple. For

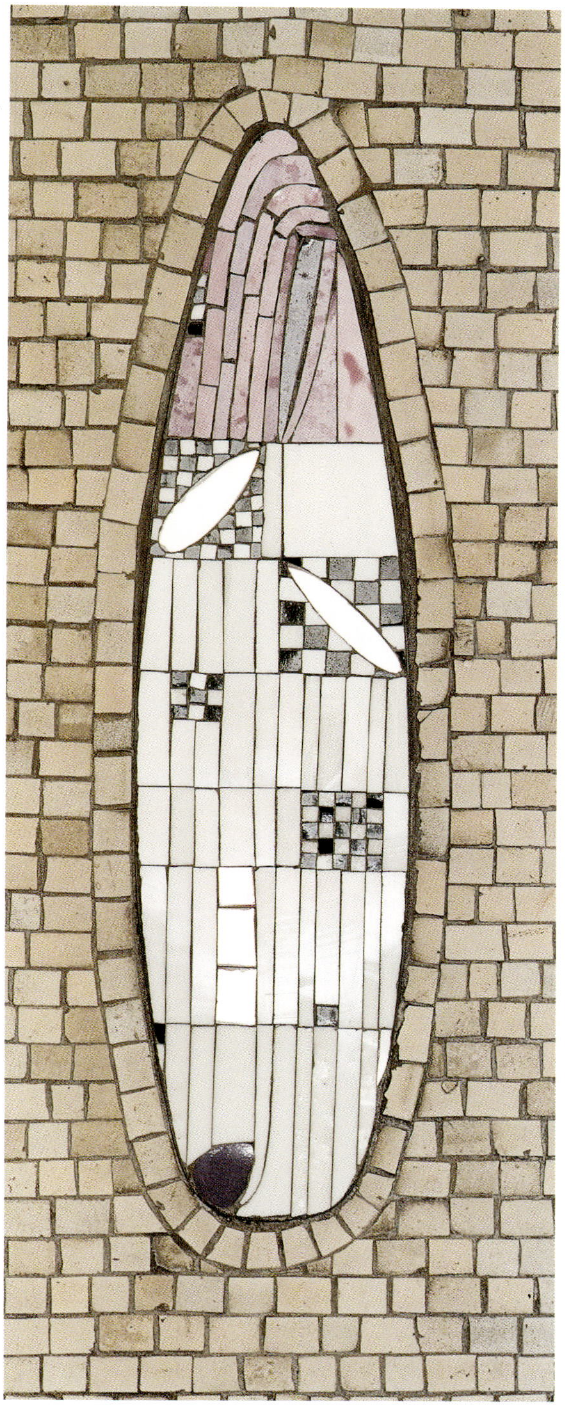

**The Hill House, Detail of Drawing Room Fireplace Mosaic**

One of five long wall panels set with mirror and glass within the mosaic of the fire surround.

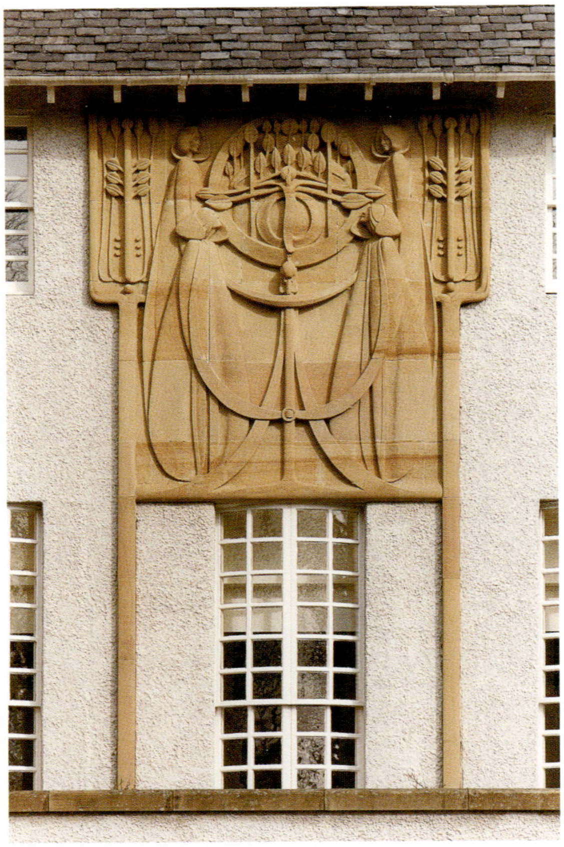

**The House for an Art Lover, 1990s, South Facade Detail**

CRM's sculptural stonework was never simply graphic, but told a veiled tale in symbols.

**Queen's Cross Church, 1897, Carving on a Column**

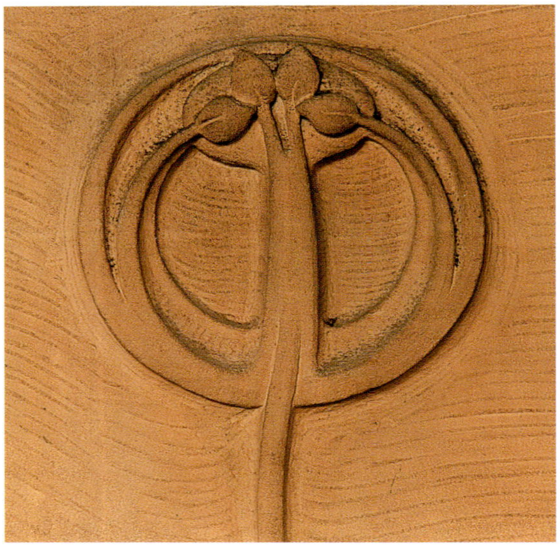

Mackintosh there must be more than this honest, direct, uncluttered response to site, materials and climate. While respecting these 'modern' followers of Morris, his concern in the 1890s is to staunch the outflow of meaning which drains architecture. (Sadly his mentors, only seeing his work framed with the Macdonald sisters' and McNair's at the Arts & Crafts exhibition in London in 1896, do not understand and therefore do not welcome him.)

He believes in the principles of beauty. These principles, however, can not be contained in historical aesthetic rules, particularly about proportion and order. Like Lethaby, he sees all that as outdated. He also senses it as a crutch, a convenience for mechanistic design, the use of modules, repetitive design, for Americanisation, standardisation and all that he abhors – and which, as the new century opens, he sees ever more clearly on the horizon.

Architecture should be more aware of native traditions and a little less cosmopolitan, as he says. His enthusiasm for Scottish traditional architecture, in a sensibility like Lethaby's or Voysey's for their English vernacular tradition, is a radical stance in classical Glasgow.[13] In the traditional Scots' architectural features, necessitated by material or climate or use, there is no sentimental historicism. He shows how their every difficulty is converted into a source of beauty, working with frankness and honesty and disdaining deception. It displays, he says, a principle which today is strangled in its infancy by undiscriminating and unsympathetic people who copy the ancient examples without trying to conform to modern requirements.

These outspoken complaints illustrate how the young architect wore his heart on his sleeve; perhaps unaware just how vulnerable a position that is. These precepts, however, imply an architecture rather different from that which he contrives to enter – with success – in student competitions.

However it is in moving beyond such vernacular realism, beyond a use of motifs with historical associations, and in stressing the symbolic nature of his work, that Mackintosh engages us. When asked how to judge architecture, he replies 'just as you judge painting or sculpture'. There is form, colour, proportion – all visual qualities – and the one great invisible quality in all art: soul. He quotes Ruskin to the effect that we cannot comprehend a building until we can place ourselves in the position of those it was built for, and fully understand the symbols and associations used by the designer 'as the words of

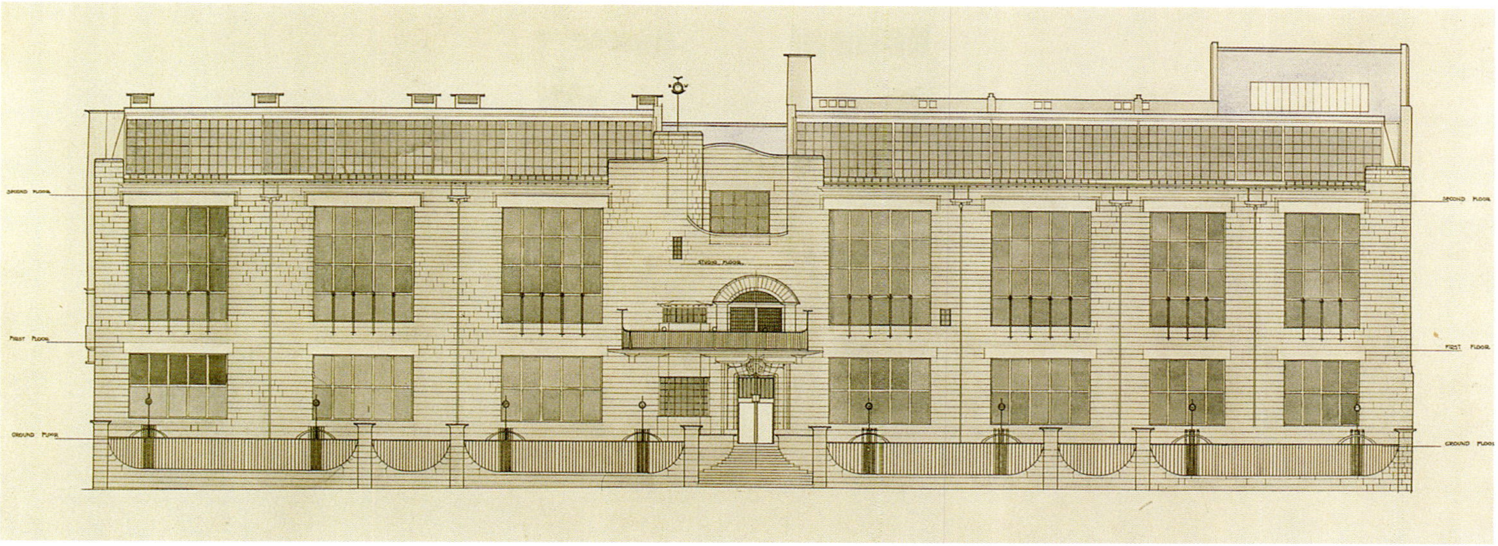

### Glasgow School of Art, North Elevation (with second-phase top storey)

The subtle dynamic balance of CRM's only urban facade, the north front of the Art School. Here four- and five-bay windows are juxtaposed in a way that is not immediately obvious. Even careful observers miss it: Sandy MacGibbon, perspectivist for Honeyman & Keppie, who later became Professor of Architecture in this actual building, drew all the studio windows equally sized and spaced. A student thesis describes it like this:'at first sight it appears perfectly symmetrical, then the asymmetry of the entrance block becomes evident, and after that one realizes that the entrance itself is not exactly central, this game continues...' (Angelos Widesan, Architectural Association, 1968). The key is that the entrance is precisely central. The railings on the street edge, in a regular beat against syncopated windows, lay a different grid across the image. Within the central element, bay windows are to the left and doors to the right; with the tower, little studio window and chimney each offset higher up, and only a first-floor balcony symmetrically binding the block together. Yet, though the main entrance is offset in that central composition, the symbolic timber column between the two little doors is at the exact centre.

his language'. If this is an impossible goal, Mackintosh talks of the 'fairy tale' which any real work of architecture embodies, though displaying it obscurely and indirectly.[14] If we visit the School of Art or the Hill House with this in mind, it is even more central to understanding the 'idiosyncrasies' of his only church.

It was said that 'Beardsley owned the most beautiful Japanese woodcuts one could see in all London, all of them of the most detailed eroticism. They were hanging in simple frames on delicately shaded wallpaper – all of them indecent, the wildest visions of Utramo. Seen from a distance, however, they appeared very dainty, clear and harmless'.[15] Without entering closely into Mackintosh's symbolic world, we only see him from a distance – dainty, clear and harmless. This is not to say that his detail is indecent or erotic; but that there is not a line drawn in Glasgow without symbolic purpose and rarely a single motif employed that has not some allegorical meaning. Many of which, surely, are erotic and sexually charged. The quality of any great work rests not in itself but in its ability to engage its viewers and users in creative dialogue. Symbolism always suggests rather than reveals; we have to make the imaginative link, to look carefully with our hearts and bodies.

By the end of the First World War, any thought of shared symbolic values had been shattered. While his wife may still have clung to her increasingly private symbolic world of the 1890s, Mackintosh's language had to be rebuilt, even his personal ideals refashioned. But his humane credo, stated in 1902, stands firm: 'reason informed by emotion, expressed in beauty, elevated by earnestness, heightened by humour – these are the ideals that should guide all artists.'

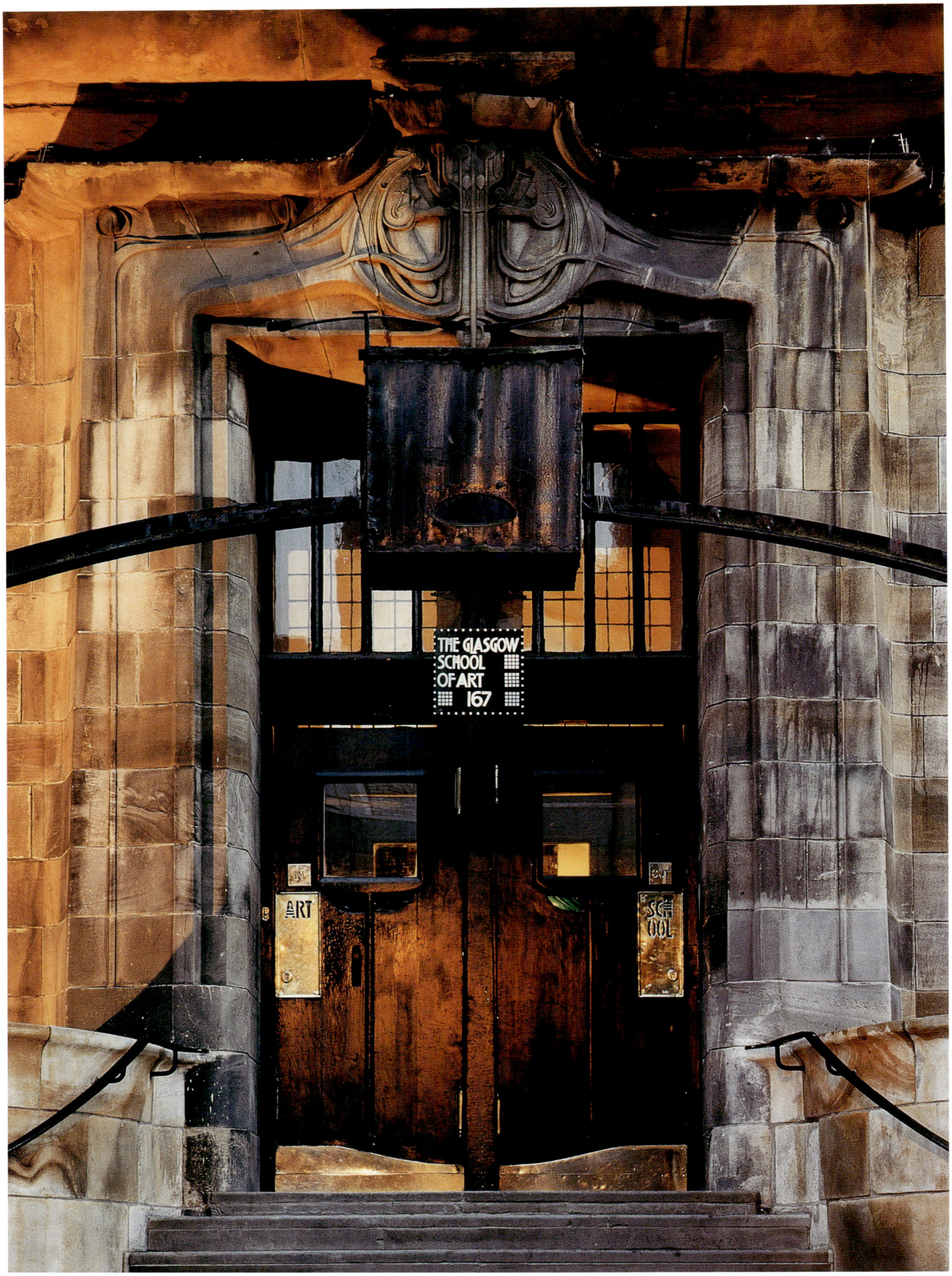
THE GLASGOW
SCHOOL
OF ART
167
IN
OUT
ART
SCH
OOL

# A SCHOOL OF ART

His real break comes in January 1897 when, aged 27, his entry wins the Glasgow School of Art competition. The governors, however, only have money for half, and it is years before they decide to finish the project. Mackintosh then completely revised a new western end which is finished exactly a decade after the first half, in December 1909 when he is 41. So this building, his masterpiece, is virtually his first and certainly his last building as architect. It has been called the most important building worldwide in that decade.[1]

As Mackintosh was detailing interiors and fitments in 1898-9, John Keppie ran the job on site, and also prepared to take credit for its design. But if Mackintosh is not credited widely with the design, there's no press coverage anyway. Just *The Glasgow Herald*'s note on the opening ceremony, which does not mention the designer's presence.[2] And it's nearly a century before Robert Venturi calls its street facade 'one of the greatest achievements of all time, comparable in scale and majesty to Michelangelo'. At the end of 1906 the School of Art governors are persuaded to complete their building; the original architects, Mackintosh's practice, is commissioned early in 1907. A changed design is inevitable: there are new requirements as well as new fire-escape regulations. There is also a new architect in the same skin. The west half, no longer the work of a precocious but derivative student, is bold, brilliant and entirely personal. And all so cleverly worked that the whole building is a brilliant unity. The library, behind great oriel windows and unprecedented wall forms, fitting into the same volume as one of the studios (on an 36 ft / 11 m square base), is the most original and complex interior space of his career.

The competition-winning layout, designed just two years after Mackintosh was himself a student there, responded directly to the utilitarian competition brief and to very tight finances. Possibly coming from a sketch by Honeyman, it is very straightforward: a central entrance on the main lower floor climbs straight into the heart of the building. There, directly ahead, the top-lit stair leads up to the 'museum', the school's hub, with the director's office above the entrance. Studios range to right and left on the two main floors, on the north side of long corridors; two lecture rooms, as required by the brief, are at opposite far ends, the north-east corner on the ground floor (which later became a studio) and south-west

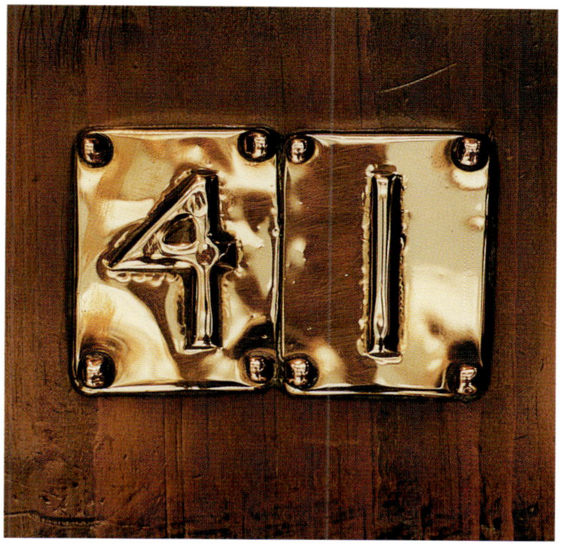


**Glasgow School of Art, 1898**

The main entrance (opposite) starts a wonderful spatial progression, under the great box light at the street, up narrowing steps to the tight front doors and into a compressed, vaulted entrance hall; then through to the light of the main stair ahead and up to the Director's office, directly above the entrance (whose door is detailed above). Over the entrance is the great knot, the symbolic women flanking a stylised rosebush, as the building's keystone – holding the key to CRM's views on art and life. The only decorative carving in the building, he modelled it himself in plaster.

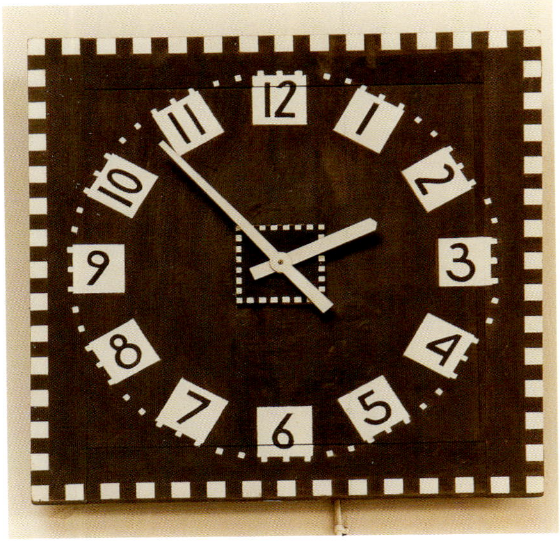


**Glasgow School of Art, Details**

The clocks are slaves from a centrally controlled electrical master, novel technology of which the school was proud. Above: a charming typical face – they vary slightly in design and size. Below: a typical interior door detail.

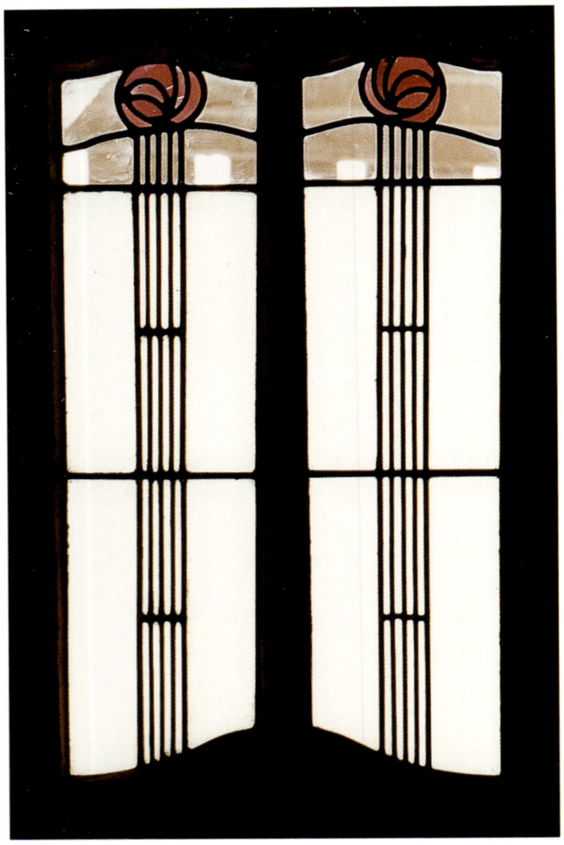

corner on the floor below (which remains in use). The land sloped steeply to the south allowing considerably more accommodation below the entrance level, although no windows were allowed on the enclosed site boundary which might be built up to by southern neighbours. The simple E-shape plan has top-lit basement studios filling the gaps in the E to the south.

Looking at the entrance from across the road, there is a secure logic to the subtle central massing of the forms being framed by the geometry of the austere studio windows on either side, each under the great brim of their cap. The appearance reflects the contrast. It's more than two art factories which hem in a lovable old castle. In the centre is the intricate, complex use of the hub (and the entrance, as in any building, is a subtle and multi-dimensional place which needs to be acknowledged); but also on top here is where the director sits – whose role and position is also complex and not entirely explicit. Spread alongside, we see the mono-dimensional, focused (and clear) activities of the studios. This is, therefore, not just a 'functional' expression, but an architecture which speaks, reflecting a deeper sense of what might be meant by 'honest' representation.

The east side, an asymmetrical composition with obviously picturesque baronial touches, remains as designed in the 1890s (apart from the attic peeping over the parapet). The lovely little tower's original excuse was that it took a tiny stair up to two attic rooms (a similar excuse to that on the front up to the director's studio). But in the second building phase which added an additional storey overall, it became simply a visual punctuation, topping the wonderfully articulated vertical strip, from its metal finial on the roof (barely visible from the ground) down the precisely cut rectangles of window to the basement door. To the right, the east walls of the studios, naturally, are blank (windows beside the basement door are later changes). To the left, the scale changes dramatically as it runs steeply down hill, here with its own symmetry of bow windows (for the board room) over the heavy rounded pediment of the staff room double window.

Ten years later, the west end, the great blank, uncoursed wall of dressed rubble (with its one romantic, tiny window), which flanks the north studio, remembers its ancient cousin, the opposite bookend. But now, layered onto this, is new masonry-work formed with the sharp skill Mackintosh had recently honed at Scotland Street School, here used with fearless incisiveness. Six identically cut ground-floor bays march across this wall; and from the southern three, oriels soar up, 60 ft

(19 m) to their triangular gable. All this is articulated in carefully coursed ashlar, held in an utterly precise geometry of solid articulated bays of stratified glass, masked with the small square net of its framing, and masonry courses, and the central three great library windows.

Down the hill, round the corner to the south, it is built up to the property line over which no projections were allowed. So while the west is modelled beyond the wall-plane, on the south it is all within the plane. Here the articulated bays continue, its symmetrical composition responding to that round the corner, but now sunk as if disappearing into the harled surface's quicksand.

It is not at all that these very different sides are discontinuous. Rather, their content, their meaning is remembered as we move round and the next side comes into view; they 'overlap', conceptually layer into each other, as all the corner views show so well. The sense of being able to hold difference without jarring, and with one layer not denying the last, is Mackintosh's genius in interior spaces; here is its masterly demonstration on an evolving and ultimately transformed exterior.

On the west flank is a remarkable basement door, so staggered and layered with the Mannerist reversals enjoyed by Mackintosh's formal games, suggesting a shadowy keystone. If we didn't know, we might wonder when it was built; and, more interesting than calling it 'proto Deco', wonder what all this layering of planes and lines might mean. It certainly worried the governors' sense of financial economy when, on a site visit with only the basement built, they looked uncomprehendingly at its complexity! In the second phase, the governors told the builders directly that they would not be responsible for paying for any work unless it was based on drawings signed and dated on their, the governors', behalf. On 7 February 1908 the governors complained loudly about work which they inspected on this porch and entrance in Scott Street being: 'carried out in an extravagant manner and not in accordance with the plans and estimates submitted and signed.' What did J. J. Burnet think, looking at this outrageous doorway? That is not recorded in the minute which said that Mackintosh was ill and unable to be present; perhaps Newbery

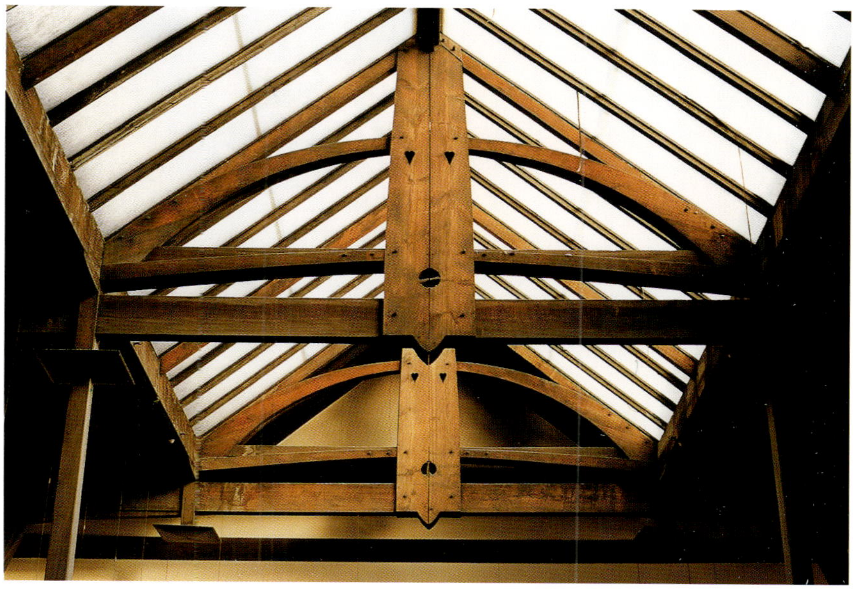

**Glasgow School of Art, The Museum, 1898**

The central gallery for exhibiting work (known then as the museum) is roof-lit over barn-like wooden trusses, softened with little hearts cut in their posts, after Voysey; the whole set within this modern structure of concrete and metal.

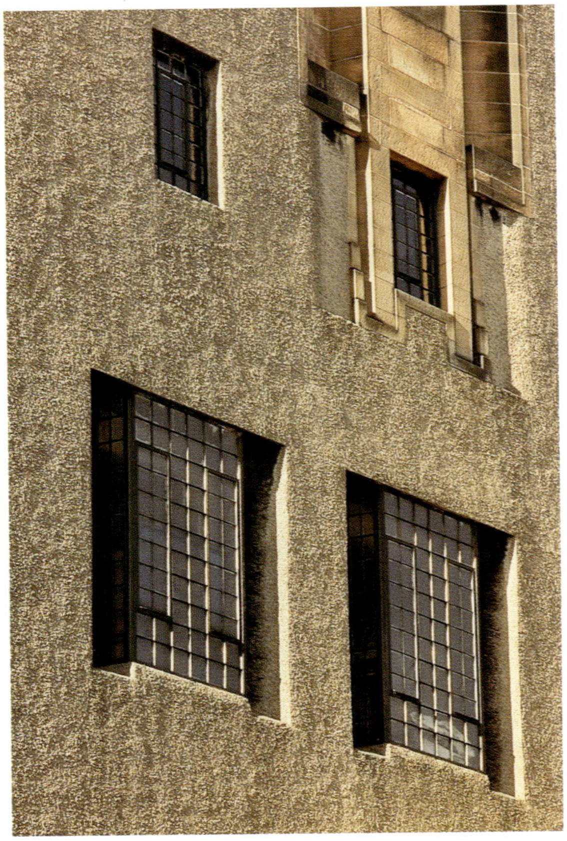

**Glasgow School of Art, South Face Details**

This is clearly the back, and it may have a cheaper, roughcast finish, but it is equally artfully composed (with perhaps ideas for sculpture in the tall ashlar niches flanking the library window).

**South elevation (detail), 1910**

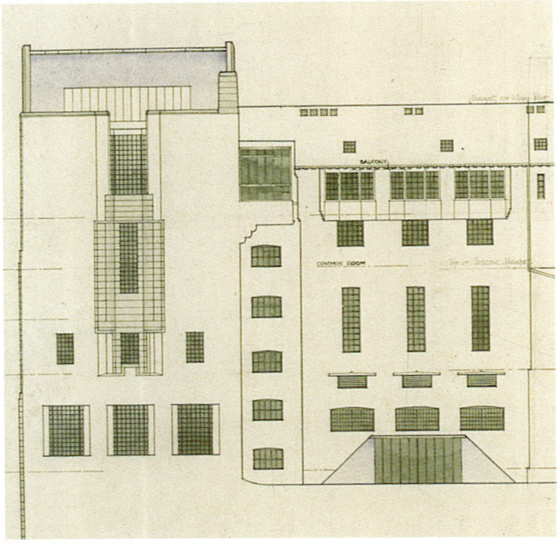

organised his judicious illness at that moment.

Robert Venturi's comparison with Michelangelo is not hyperbole. In his 1968 book *Complexity and Contradiction in Architecture*, Venturi was the first author after the era of Modernism to deal with the great Mannerist architects, from Michelangelo to Hawksmoor to Lutyens. (In his own more recent extension to the National Gallery in London, he tried similar games himself.) Mackintosh, in forming the skin of this west block, now had a fluent command of his language; in his reversals of the rules (hinted at in earlier projects), he is playing in this company.

Up the narrow steps and under the great stone knot – the building's literal key stone is the entrance. 'Portals must have guardians,' Mackintosh read in Lethaby. Here they are: the symbolic women flanking a stylised rose bush. The whole symbolic world developed by Mackintosh and his closest colleagues is distilled and solidified here. But is this, the only ornamented stonework on the building, intentionally hidden from the director above by the sharp cut of his balcony? And then, through the inner door, a different symmetry of the entrance hall is suddenly revealed, an odd squintness among squat columns as in a low crypt.

The stair rises straight ahead through this forest to the light of the 'museum', the school's central exhibition space. Here, in this steel and concrete building, is a timber cage of overlapping square balustrading and tall newels, some coming right up from the basement floor, others continuing up to the roof trusses flanking the stair-well. Further up, it is covered with almost barn-like wooden trusses – but for the Voysey-like little hearts cut into their posts. Those round the stair are carried on the timber columns; however, those to the sides have column caps simply floating in the space. Thus Mackintosh's mannerist games continue.

Over the entrance, the director's office is another world: bright yet enclosed. In here the cornice both holds the pure cube of the room (tying in the lovely concealed stair to his private studio above with storage and a W.C.), and breaks it, flowing gently into the deep window bay, its vault seeming scooped asymmetrically out of the thickness of the wall, like a castle window's deep embrasure.

From the centre, the great studios are strung along corridors of butt-jointed rough planked walls more to be expected in the shipyards and originally painted dark green. The great, working studios are direct, industrially formed machines for capturing

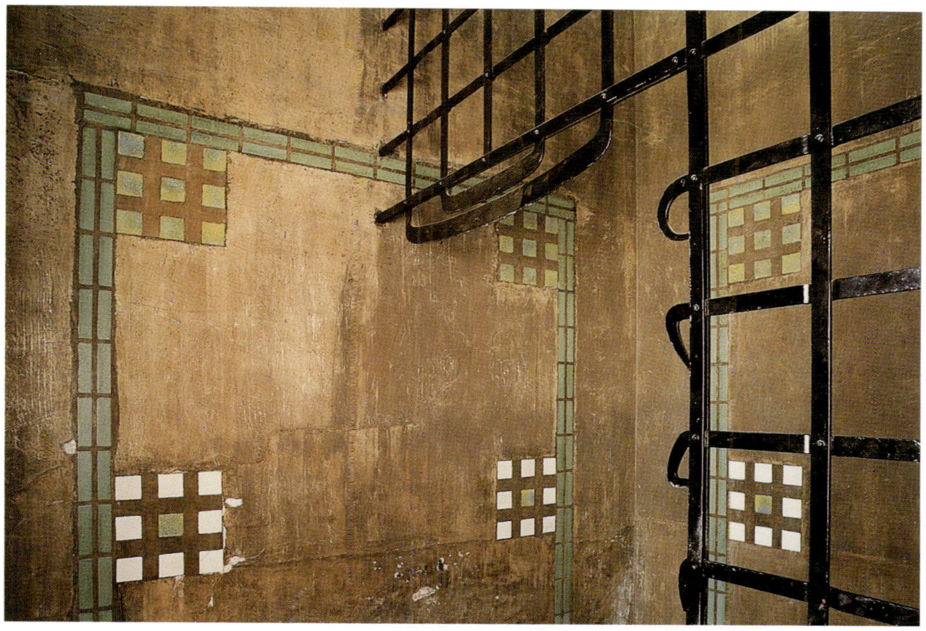

Glasgow School of Art, Staircase Detail

At each dark stairhead there are wrought-iron grilles, reminiscent of the yetts (or portcullis-like gates) barring entrance to a castle. Ends of the bars are curved amusingly where entrance to the top landing is 'cut' through. Two layers of horizontal grilles, moving against each other overhead, add dynamic visual interest for the climber.

and diffusing light. (These nearly 33 ft / 10 m tall spaces have from the start had hot-air central heating.)

End staircases were required in the second phase. To reach the eastern one a hole had to be broken through the existing south corridor wall, and it shows how Mackintosh reveals his adaptation. The new half-landing is carved into the old space, a curved concrete slab sitting on a steel beam which appears to be carried on timber posts flanking the opening. A typical Mackintosh material mix, always made for a rhetorical, visual point: the building as social document contains 'scars' telling of its changes. On these barest, almost medieval stairs with grey polished plaster walls, little squares of coloured tiles touch the eye and finger at each stop; every one is different. It is again the mix of sturdiness and delicacy, which he handles with unrivalled sureness – just like the tiny eyes of leaded coloured glass in the black doors and their rough corridors. And then at the top, a cage of metal flats under a circle veils the junction of masonry with timber roof. To link east and west when this additional top floor was added in phase two, Mackintosh didn't break into the existing central tower (the director's studio). Instead he cantilevered a glass-clad walkway past it (the 'hen-run') off its south wall. Simple, pragmatic, diagrammatic; and magical.

With the library at the other end, leaded-glass doors lead into its sacred grove of knowledge. The forest clearing, its trees silhouetted against the brightness beyond; the grouped lamps hanging on chains from darkness, with their jangling detail, folded structures of black and silver, hole-punched, metal flats around naked light bulbs, abstract, exotic birds with their touches of blue and pink glass, their dazzle veiling the dark canopy above. Never can the arrival at this moment of electricity in architecture have been better celebrated than in these fittings from 1909.

The central clearing is formed by eight wide trees, whose thick lower trunks are made up of three pieces; the outer two branch back to support the gallery, while the central trunk continues up, joining other thinner verticals from the gallery, to the forest canopy of crisscrossed branches. Underneath such

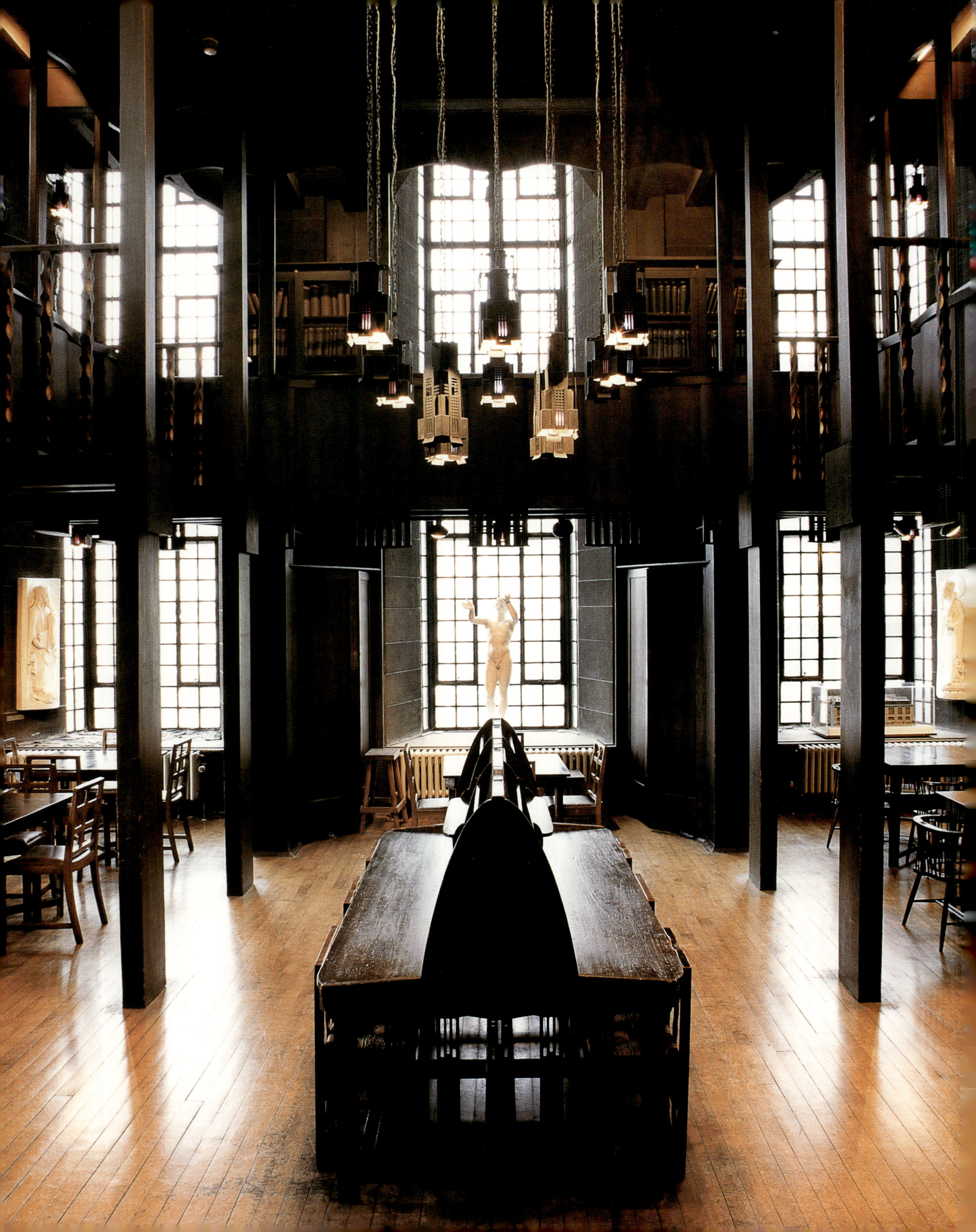

metaphors, just as under the decorated, scalloped almost frilled surfaces, the interior spatial geometry is precisely controlled and clearly articulated. And the structure all ties together; the columns (which stand on great steel joists in the floor) just touch the ceiling, as at the gallery of the Willow Tea Room, rather than support the roof, each being tied up to the twisted hangers from the higher steels in the storeroom above.

Never clear in photographs is its intimate scale – just 36 ft (11 m) square. The subtlest move was to set the balcony back from the columns, allowing a sense of spaciousness. Was the boldest move to carry the gallery across the windows? Throughout the second contract, the building committee protested at overspends, and J. J. Burnet ensured rigorously that it never sanctioned extras. In January 1909, they objected to a library gallery designed to cross the window wall; it would jeopardise the light inside. The architect members missed that committee meeting and Mackintosh, arguing that it would be more expensive now to change the design by removing it, won his balcony.

He said that getting it built was a daily battle, of which the board room contains hints.

The board, who so disliked the original tall white space they were given, found a new, stuffy, classical home, carved out of a ground-floor studio in 1906, even before the second half of the building was begun. Dark and enclosed, it is a most unusual room. The ceiling, a heavy mesh of layers of structure, has three extraordinary clusters of hammered copper light fittings in delicate wrought iron. Between its panelled walls are eight Ionic pilasters with capitals (each different) of which there is no like.[3]

Was this thoroughly claustrophobic, English-Tudor, classical room Mackintosh's ironic comment on the new orthodoxy of Edwardian academic architecture by the time the building was finished? Neither Keppie nor Burnet (both governors by then) would have been amused. Much of the unhappiness of the story can be read from Newbery's group portrait of the governors' building committee which hangs in this room. After it had been approved, Newbery added the architect at the left, on an additional strip of canvas. A defiant gesture to his pusillanimous Governors. It had been Newbery's idea to have a new building, and his diplomatic skill which made it happen. Although he was never 'client' – the Governors' building committee was ever powerful – Newbery insisted he wrote the brief; he was on the building committee and fought for his building every inch of the way. He understands his architect; in this portrait Mackintosh's expression is honestly captured.

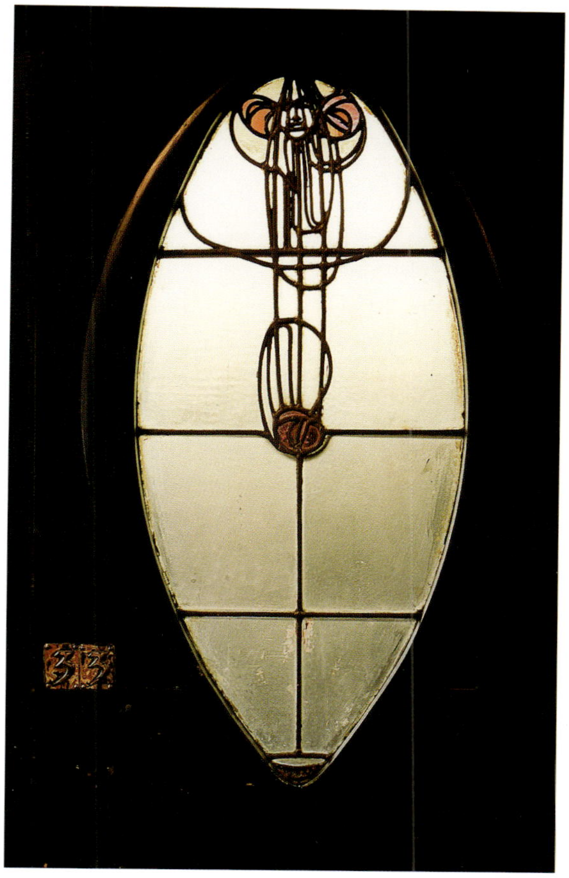

**Glasgow School of Art, Ladies' Cloakroom Door Detail, 1898**

**Glasgow School of Art, Library, 1908 (opposite)**

The central clearing is formed by eight wide trees, whose thick lower trunks are made up of three pieces; the outer two branch back to support the gallery, while the central trunk continues up, joining other thinner verticals from the gallery, to the forest canopy of crisscrossed branches. Underneath such metaphors, just as under the decorated, scalloped, almost frilled surfaces, the interior spatial geometry is precisely controlled and clearly articulated, and the structure all ties together.

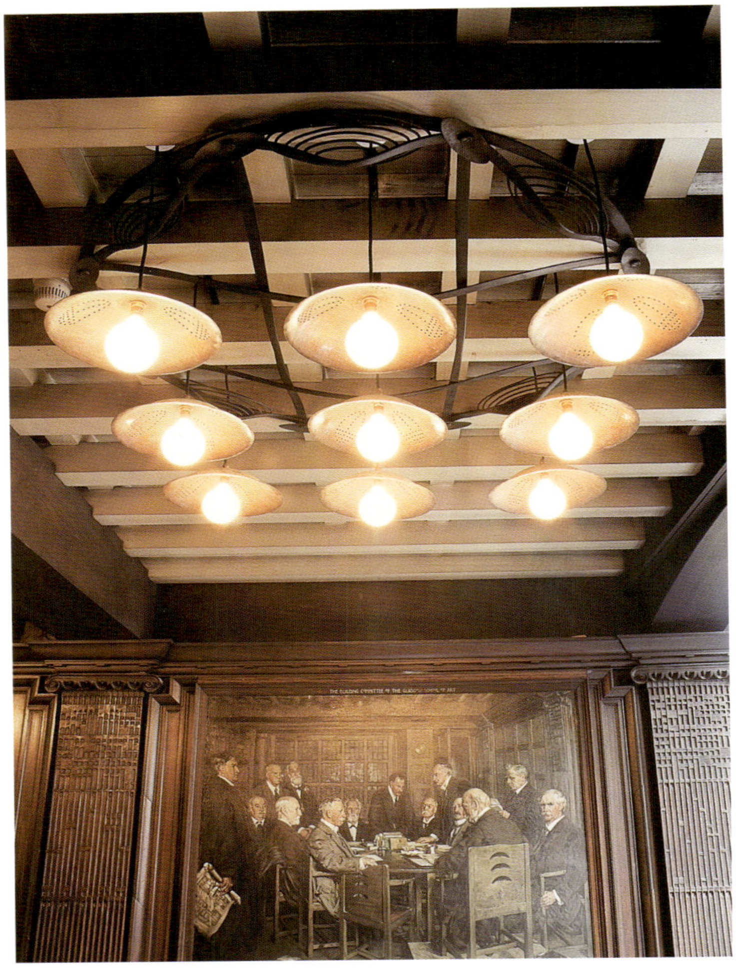

Glasgow School of Art, Board Room, 1906

Carved out of a large ground-floor studio, this tight, heavy and formal room is lit by three sets of nine lamps, in remarkable circular beaten and pierced copper shades. Underneath, hangs Newbery's portrait of the building committee, to which, at the left, CRM (holding drawing) has been stitched after the painting had been approved. A story of the strained relationships, apparent within that process, is clear in the expression of the architect.

The building brilliantly integrates overall architectural form and interior place-making, right down to the tiniest detail of door-handle, leaded-glass insert or nameplate. This range of concerns is balanced without any 'Modernist' worry about making them all the same. A tiny example: its clocks exemplify this essential theme of appropriateness rather than sameness: 'slave' units on an electric circuit with a 'master' clock are a novel idea; but they don't look machine-like, and each is an attractive graphic variant on chequerboard, square designs. A big example: filled with the latest technology – it is the first building in the world designed to have electric-powered air conditioning, yet it is also highly traditional in layout.

When Keppie joined Honeyman, one client he brought was Victoria Infirmary, on whose building he had worked for Sellars. He was well aware of its very successful 'plenum' system devised by William Key, and the Art School uses the same system.[4] Fresh, filtered and heated air, through a network of horizontal and vertical ducts, is supplied from a central fan room. The stale air is exhausted under pressure from the incoming, and discharged at roof level. The fans were made in Cincinnati by Sturtevant's, whose catalogue shows it by no means unique, though it is state-of-the-art technology. Research at the time was showing that health improved, in schools as well as hospitals, when such a system was introduced. Unlike the two buildings credited by Reyner Banham as being pioneers of air-handling – Frank Lloyd Wright's Larkin office building (a vertical stack of similar spaces) and the Royal Victoria Hospital in Belfast (a horizontal grouping of identical pavilions), there was much more complex shaping involved here. The ducts were very skilfully integrated, the air washed, its humidity and temperature regulated. It is therefore 'the first known building into which the technology for a form of true air-conditioning was incorporated at the initial stage and fully integrated into the construction.'[5] And clearly Keppie brought the right contacts.

This building lets us most clearly see how Mackintosh was not an Art Nouveau or 'Secessionist' architect, with their decorative intentions and traditional, handicraft methods. And how he was not one of the new scientific rationalists (seen clearly in Gropius and Meyer's 1914 factory in Cologne), being expressive of new materials and of 'function'. His aim was independent, adding ever more tactile and decorative layers onto the clarity and functional simplicity of structural necessity, services specialism and spatial geometry; thickening walls or hollowing them out into use which is also decorative (like the seats in bays outside the library), covering them with decoration which is also useful (like the great knots on the studio window stays). Neither just artist romantic nor architect rationalist, he has the ability to allow both and, to allow collage and contradiction, traditional and new mixing. The spatial experiments with the library window wall are as clear and pure as the functionalists; but they integrate here into a work of great art, a composition of truly original forms.

The Art School began as Mackintosh's masterpiece, in the old sense of the piece which ends an apprenticeship, honours mastery of the skill, and heralds a mature career. (It gained him his partnership, after all.) And it ends as his masterpiece, in the modern sense, because it developed after the 7-year gap of Mackintosh's career, into something quite different. It is also his masterpiece, as we so easily see in retrospect, because there simply weren't any others which followed. Robert Harbison commented 'there is more fruitful evolution in this building than in most architects' lifetimes.'[6] The awful realisation is that this building, its two halves opened only a decade apart, virtually was its architect's creative lifetime.

A year after its completion, Mackintosh's youthful mentor W.R. Lethaby wrote: 'Architecture, so far as at any given moment it deals with traditional needs, should be customary: so far as it has to meet changing conditions and ideals, it must be experimental...'.[7] This is exactly Mackintosh's achievement. Lethaby's architectural credo, formed in the 1890s, continued to develop amid the lonely classicism before and revivalism after the First World War. He faced up to industrialisation of building processes and materials, thoughtfully commenting on Le Corbusier's notion of a house as a mechanism for inhabitation. But by then his greatest, and unrecognised, follower was dead.

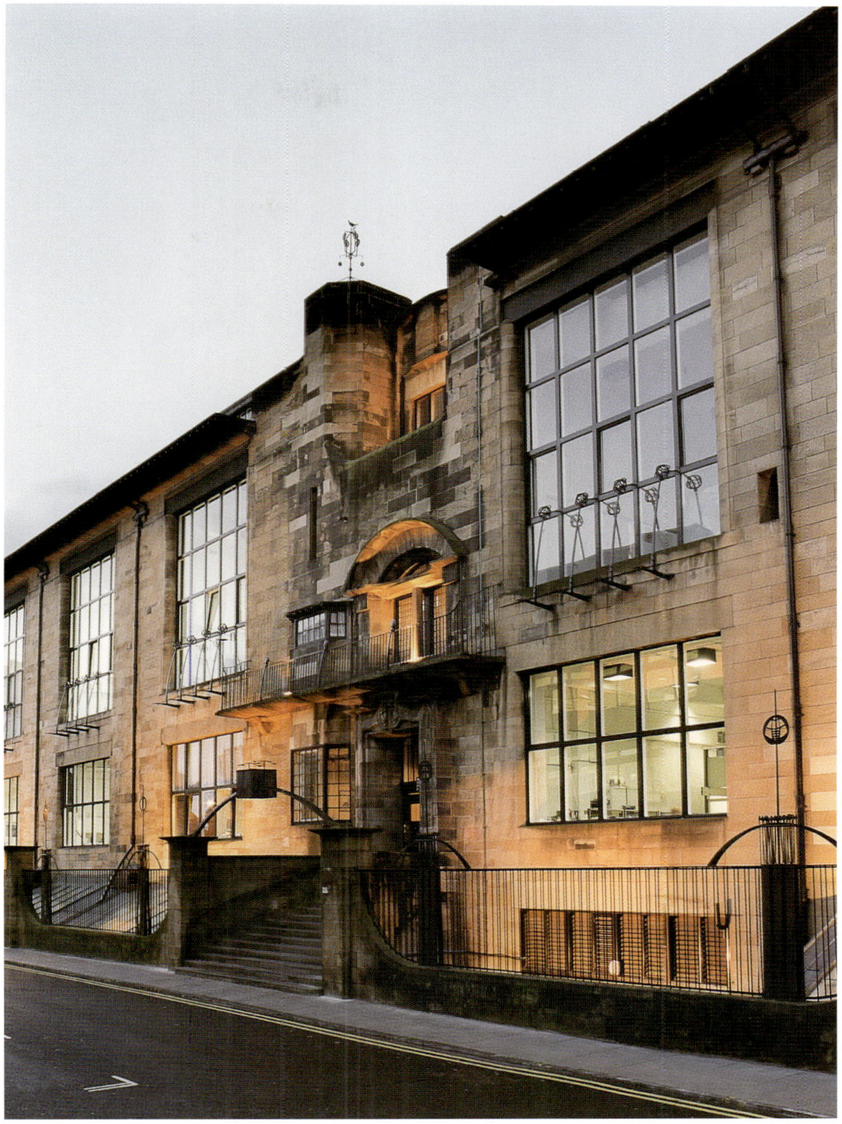

**Glasgow School of Art, North Facade**

The powerful entrance front worked out in 1897-8. It is an astonishing collage of great 'art factory' windows and romantic, sculptural, castellated entrance. But is it really, as the important American architect of 75 years later, Robert Venturi, asserts, 'One of the greatest achievements of all time comparable in scale and majesty to Michelangelo'?

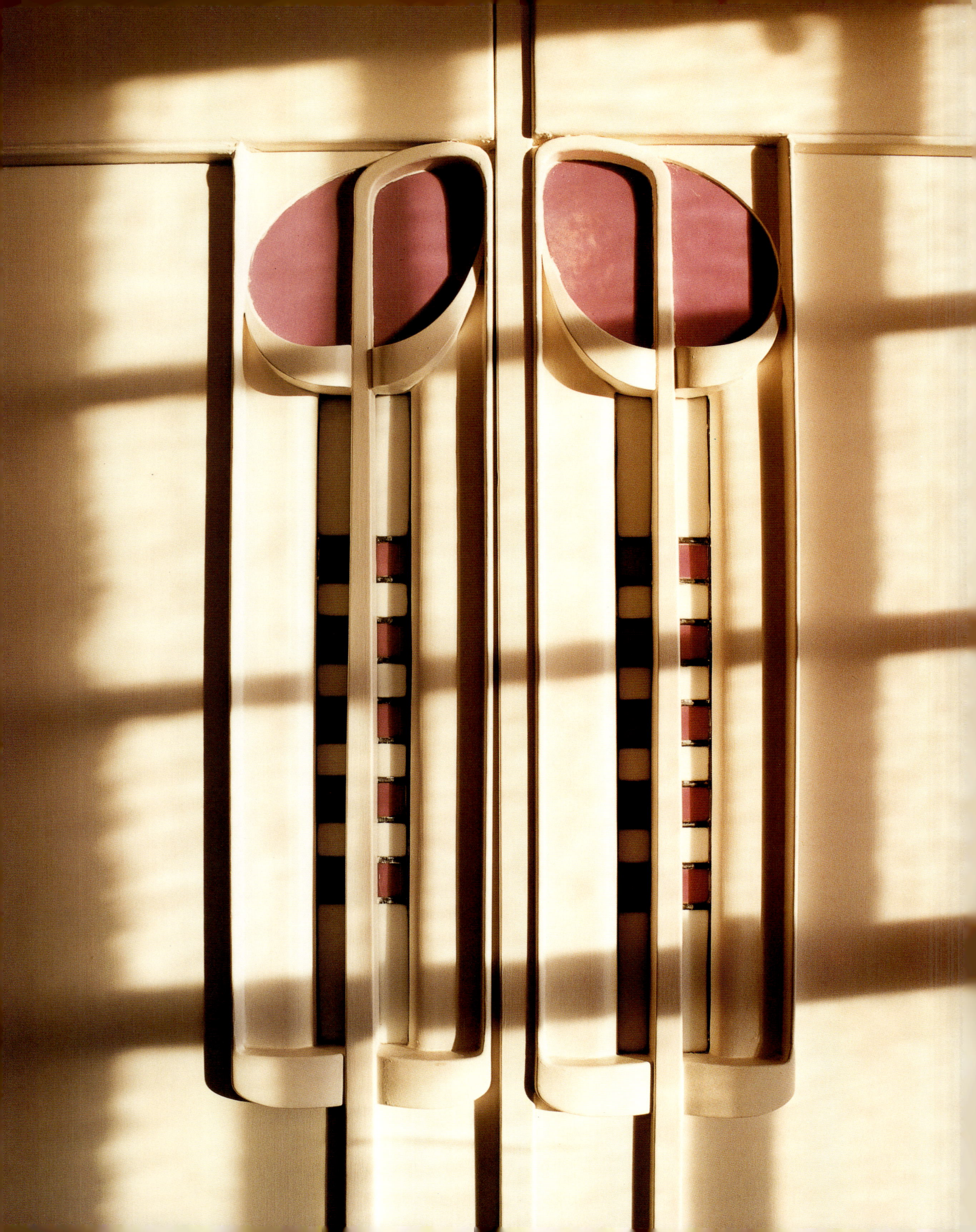

# ANOTHER FRAME

Whit kinna whigmaleerie
Let ye gie carte blanche tae yir accuser?
[Racine, *Phaedra*, in Edwin Morgan's Glaswegian translation]

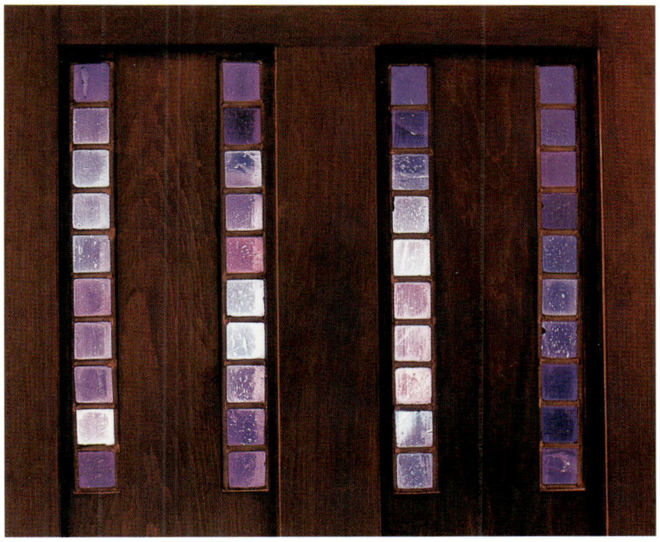

I was discussing Mackintosh's personality with a friend one evening. As I talked of how at times he seemed desperate to construct traps that he could fall into, she suddenly said 'you sound just like an Asperger's parent!' I am very grateful to her (a child psychologist used to making such diagnoses) for that little interruption. I read papers on the key Aspergers' website, and Tony Attwood's introductory book,[1] and it quickly made sense.

Asperger's Syndrome can be an extremely disabling condition, and it can be a very mild affliction. While it forms towards one end of the autistic spectrum, it is itself a continuum of expression, and 'becomes more a description of someone's personality than a clear developmental disorder,' (Attwood 1997). 'Many believe there is no clear boundary separating AS from those who are "normal but different".' (Bauer 1996).

I would suggest that Mackintosh exhibited traits associated with this condition. But I do so to help shape a more coherent picture of a personality than is often shown – by the memoirs of his acquaintances as much as biographers – and not to chart a pathology. I find this suggestion allows us to reframe Mackintosh; to see as a whole, aspects of him which on their own appear 'enigmatic' (the phrase of his friend Rudolph Schwabe's son-in-law), or incomprehensible, or just embarrassing (which may be why the Davidson family was so understandably keen not to let his private letters to Margaret be made public).

Asperger's Syndrome (AS) has only become a generally recognised condition in the past few years (although originally described by Hans Asperger in 1944). It is not uncommon in the male population – a Swedish study suggests 7 in 1000 show some degree of AS.

Today it is common that parents and teachers realise a child with AS is unusual but have no idea why. Before it is properly diagnosed, AS people are often seen as 'brilliant, eccentric, socially inept, a little awkward physically.' (L. Freisleben-Cook) And the major problem for those with whom they live is 'how to manage their anxiety and depression.' (Attwood, 1998) 'Their

**The Hill House**

Main Bedroom Wardrobe Detail (opposite), Cloakroom Door Detail (above), Drawing Room Window (below).

'Attention like this is a form of love, and one responds to it.' David Brett

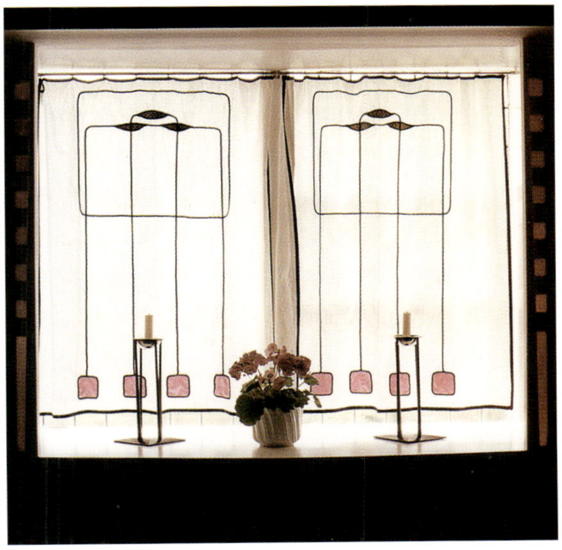

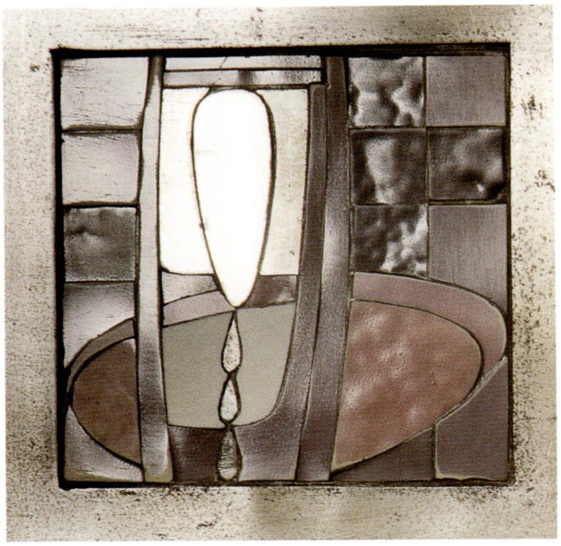

**Bedroom Fireplace Detail, The Hill House**

Nothing is ignored; a fire surround decorated, and a little attic door.

**Door Detail, Windyhill**

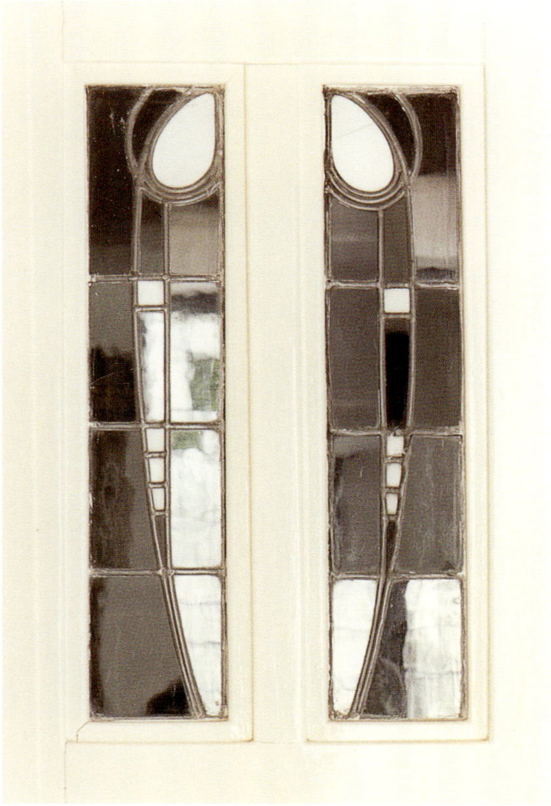

thinking is different, potentially highly original, often misunderstood, but is not defective... They are a bright thread in the rich tapestry of life.' (Attwood 1998). There is evidence that Ludwig Wittgenstein, Béla Bartók and the young Vincent Van Gogh had signs of AS. Does such a shape fit Mackintosh, even as a shadowy ghost?

Individuals with AS exhibit a range of characteristics, some of the most typical I list from the various diagnostic definitions in the literature. Many of these characteristics concern skills which the sufferer can, with difficulty, learn; and it is unusual to find someone with every one pronounced.

*They have a predominantly visual style of thinking.* CRM: this is obvious. *In school they usually focus on one or two subjects to the exclusion of all else.* CRM: he was only interested in drawing at school. *They often are dyslexic, and have organisational difficulties.* CRM: his writing, spelling and obvious disorganisation were well-known; poor financial control is documented both at home and in the office.

*They keep their own company; are loners even as children, avoid eye-contact.* CRM: drinking in Walberswick, always the shadiest corner table in their Chelsea restaurant. *Linked, they are solitary players, not collaborators; when they do work together, they demand to be in overall control.* CRM: even in the intensely cooperative and shared-work ethos in Glasgow in late 1890s, he never collaborates – and only uses MMM's detail work in his settings.

*They have clumsy body language; poor motor coordination; poor at sports.* CRM: his limp and intense physical self-consciousness; clumsiness at Christmas 1902 which nearly results in serious incident.

*They have higher than normal incidence of depression, and a genuine risk of suicide; depression may be expressed as alcoholism. Put another way, depressed people treated for alcoholism are not infrequently revealed to have AS. Alcoholism and AS display (biochemical and behavioural) similarities.* CRM: the depression and drink are well documented.

*They are seen as 'odd', unusual; sometimes with unusual tone of voice, 'foreign' accent.* CRM: the events up to his eviction from Suffolk builds clearly into this picture. *They are poor at empathising with others; have difficulty in reading others' social needs, difficulty with friendships/relationships and social awkwardness.* CRM: seen in the 1890s Jessie-Margaret years. (Is giving a jewel box to Jessie inappropriate, showing lack of empathy at their split?) How he is with visitors is documented.

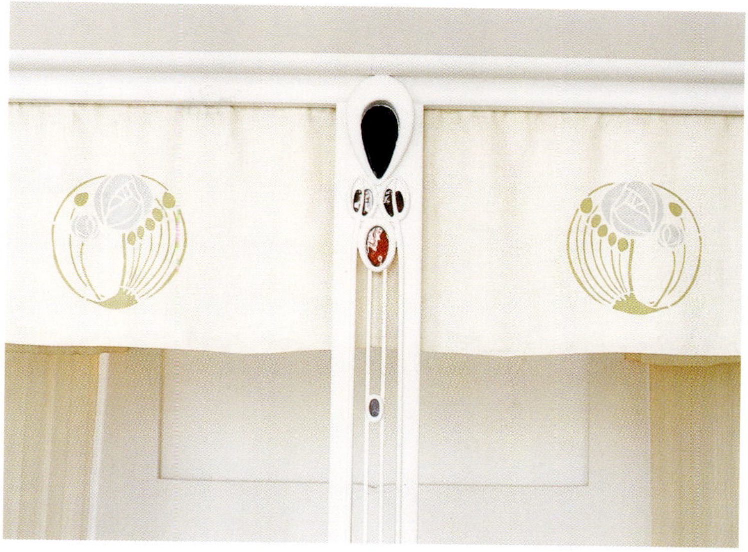

**Detail of the Marital Bed in The Mackintosh House, 1900**

CRM lived in his family of origin until he was 32. He then married into the perfect flat, which soon migrated into the house they owned from 1906; but they never had children to transform it into a family home. Leaving this place which had been a representation of their merged sensibility and creative being, they pulled up the anchor in 1914, never to return. And never again were they more rooted than to the vagaries of a bed-and-breakfast room, whether with Suffolk and London landladies or in little French hotels. And in the process, becoming increasingly mute, they also seemed increasingly content.

*They may not have a close and intimate relationship until much later than their peers.* CRM: aged 27 when relationship with Margaret really starts; 32 at marriage. *'A husband had difficulty knowing when and how to express his love for his wife. However, he could write her letters with an eloquence and passion that was unattainable using speech.' (Attwood).* CRM: the letters from France.

*They often are highly gifted, but deeply frustrated by their social difficulties, by their ineffective or inappropriate interactions. This can result in 'behavioural flare-ups, conflicts escalate, pressure may build up in such a child with little clue until he reacts in a dramatically inappropriate manner.... Outbursts of non-cooperation as a child.' (Bauer 1996).* CRM: childhood tantrums and inexplicable sudden rages are documented. *Linked to this, they 'wear their hearts on their sleeve', which is charming, vulnerable, but also shows unawareness of how personal comments can offend. 'The child with AS cannot, it seems, dissemble as we have learned to do.' (Bauer).* CRM: he offends by plain speaking, clearly documented and surely unintended is the scarcely veiled castigation of Keppie in a lecture.

*Their emotional response can be shocking and out of all proportion to situation; 'lack subtlety in retaliating...one incident becomes trigger that releases feelings that have long been suppressed...'. (Attwood).* CRM: the stored up fury about Reilly which explodes in France years later.

*They show indifference to peer pressure, dressing individually rather than following fashion.* CRM: individual creativity reinforces this (see next item below). But in his deerstalker and cape in Suffolk he seemed quite unaware of how this might be read as alien. *They show ritualised behaviour and need for order. (A typical AS sufferer is thrown into a tantrum by dust in the house).* CRM: the ritualised life is constructed in their flat and house: the utterly pure, white bedroom; the dark dining room, etc. Obsessiveness, eg of order and cleanliness, fits with this picture. It also fascinates outsiders, being a highly creative translation of this characteristic.

*They rely on regular pattern, responding best to a social routine handled by someone who can organise and order it, and need much reassurance at times of change.* CRM: he never lived alone, moving from living with family of origin to marriage. Clearly lost in France without Margaret, he invented a regular ritual of daily letter writing.

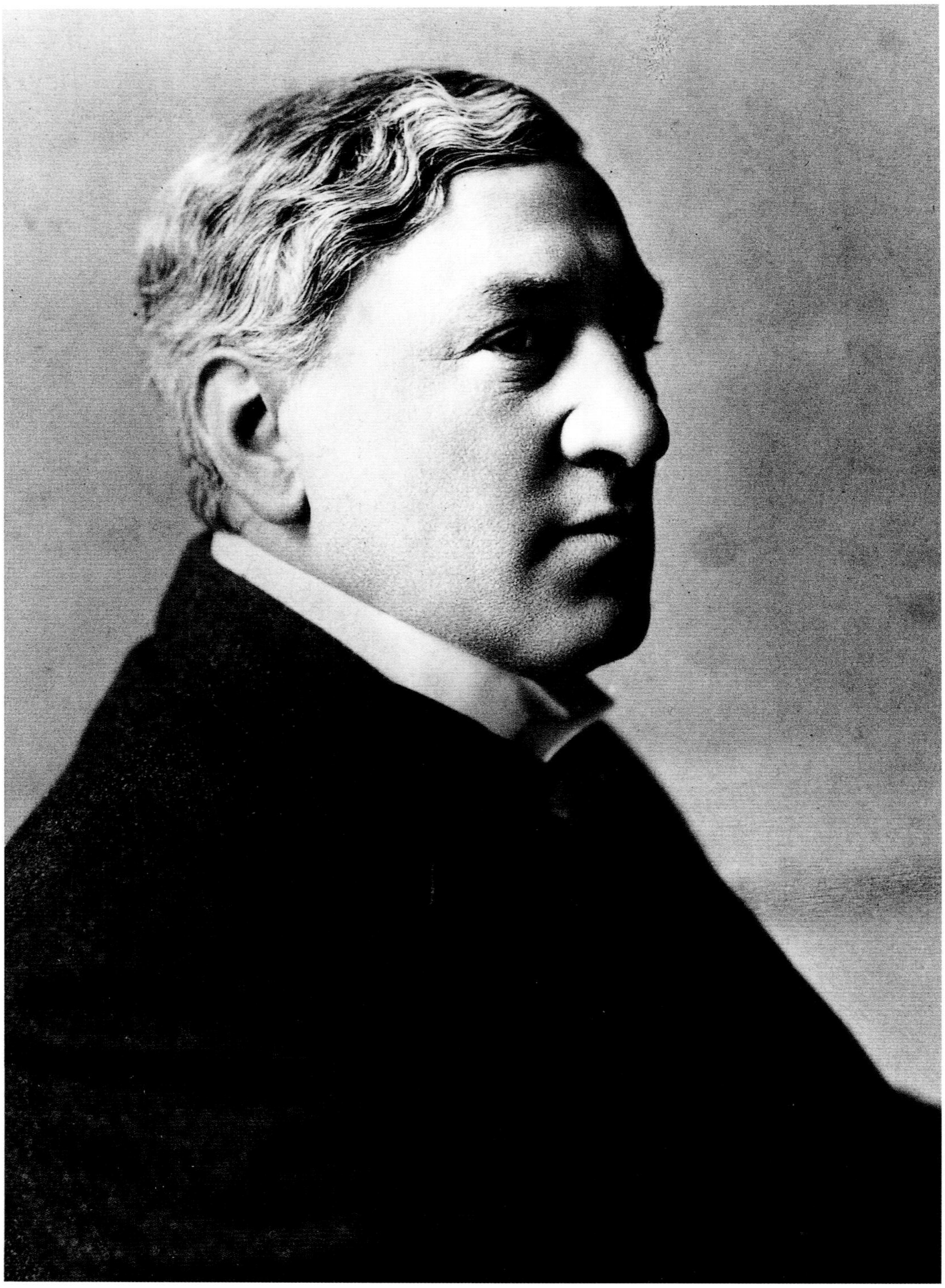

# BRAVE, TRUTHFUL AND WANTING TO GET THINGS PERFECT

There is a willow tree in the garden. He particularly asked for a garden with a tree, and there he sits. Silently thinking. Silent in the garden at Willow Road, for the surgery and radium treatment have left him unable to speak. Here, in the quiet Sauchiehall of Hampstead NW3, he is ceaselessly nursed by his wife. In Spring 1928, Alice Schwabe, during her school holidays, is in and out a lot, running errands for them, but mostly kept at a distance now from the speechless artist.[1] And always he is visited by Margaret Morris. Almost every day she brings distracting cheer, letting in some of the animated and colourful world outside; she starts to teach him to converse in a sign language.

He feels stronger, the blossoms are appearing, he is recovering. He tells Walter Blackie he will soon be back at work accepting the commission for a painting with a new surge of optimism. He feels a new wind in the sails, though not where the voyage will lead. 'Art has no end; only finite things have an end. Art is the highest way of life, and life is a quest, not a conquest.' These words written by Desmond Chapman-Huston, their London friend from Glasgow days, are now brought to mind by his visits.

The previous summer, he had known something was wrong when his tongue swelled up and was burned by his pipe-smoking. He had been increasingly lonely, sitting painting in Port-Vendres. His wife had gone to London to see a specialist for her heart condition, and to visit friends. 'Nothing could be more perfect than sitting where I was this morning,' he wanted to tell her, 'only you did not come to meet me at the end of the tunnel.' They had never been parted like this before. He couldn't telephone; he wrote daily. He told her he didn't know what to do. 'Without you,' he said, 'everything has a flatness. I feel as if I'm waiting for something all the time'. It is love, for sure. But also, he has always needed her ordered routine to keep him on an even keel. Without her, he seemed at a loss, unsure what to think, even how to be.

She carefully keeps all his letters, flowing with daily trivia and humorous observations, but animated by his love. 'This chronycle[2] seems to be full of fleeting impressions and disconnected sentences. But anyone who can read their meaning

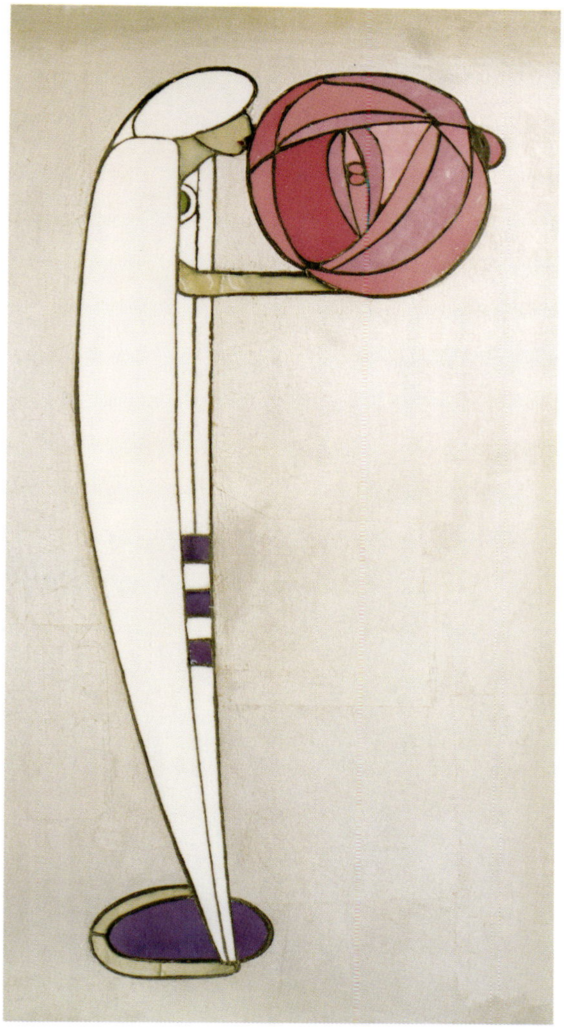

Cabinet Door. Silver Painted Wood Inlaid with Glass, in the Mackintoshes' own house, 1902

**Mackintosh around 1920 (opposite)**

There are no images of the artist after 1920, but already when photographed in London he seems to have lived many more than his just over 50 years.

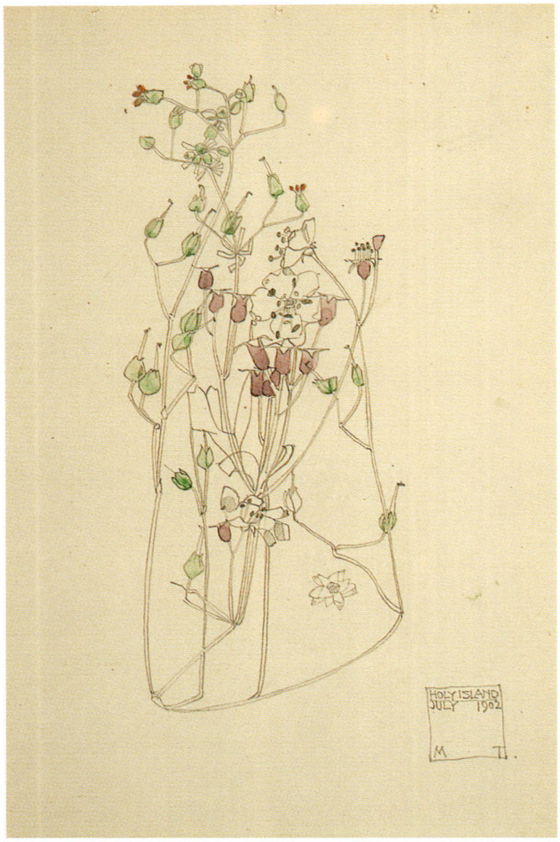


**Cranesbill, Holy Island, *c.* 1901**

CRM often retreated to the peace of Holy Island, drawing flowers there up to 1913. But after 1914, he never even returns to Glasgow, not to see friends or family (with whom he soon loses touch), not even to the Davidsons in his own house. He never sees his later interiors at all, neither The Dugout in Glasgow nor the house in Northampton. The Memorial Exhibition, in Glasgow in 1933, is an eye-opener to the range particularly of his later work; but it is amateurishly assembled, looking in Annan's photographic record like the jumbled booty in a newly opened Egyptian tomb, and considered too depressing to be illustrated here.

would find only three words: "I love you".'

And in his stillness, in the warm Mediterranean dusk, he had waited for her replies. 'On one side of the harbour green light, the other red light, but no letter from Margaret – silver light. Perhaps tomorrow morning a letter will come. I have only two interests – you first and then my work next.' All May and June she had been away, but finally, she was returning; he travelled to Perpignan where they met on 1 July, retreating to their private haven together. But by autumn 1927, his sore throat was no longer something he could keep to himself. Now his health was deteriorating and the local doctor urged that he saw a specialist. By the time he was prepared to journey to London, he was too ill to go alone – he couldn't even speak. With the 50 paintings still incomplete, he left Port-Vendres, with his good friend the painter Rudolphe Ihlee, long-time resident in Collioure, accompanying him to Dover. It was a very difficult journey.

Margaret sent an urgent telegram to the Newberys in Dorset, and Jessie Newbery met them at Victoria Station, guided them to a clinic, and the cancer was diagnosed. Students encircled his bed taking notes as the consultant explained the worst. The artist noticed their difficulty in accurately drawing the tongue and its tumour. He took the pencil and drew it with precision for them. Mary Newbury later said, it simply showed him as ever 'brave, truthful and wanting to get things perfect.'

Now in this Hampstead garden, the artist remembers his father's creating a new garden when he, Charlie, was 10; remembers back beyond his mother's death, just as his apprenticeship began, to more contented, accepted days before.

But complaints from the landlady intrude and they must move. Chapman-Huston lets them take his upper rooms in Bayswater, which at least overlook the gardens of Porchester Square. But through the summer of 1928 the artist becomes weaker rather than stronger; soon he cannot climb the stairs and spends his days in the ground-floor dining room. By the autumn he cannot even climb once a day to bed. He is gently moved round the corner to a nursing home in the square. On 10 December, he dies.

Where is his wife, his constant companion and support? As a ghostly automaton in unspeakable shock, she has been fading since the awful decision to take the train out of Port-Vendres a year ago, and by now she is simply his nurse, herself virtually invisible. Chapman-Huston takes over the funeral; she does not even attend. The day after he dies, he is quietly cremated in north London, leaving no grave.

He asked for his ashes to be scattered at Port-Vendres; within days his wife vanishes with them. She is seen in Port-Vendres occasionally and in conversation never talks about her late husband.

Apart from the Schwabes, Margaret Morris and J.D. Fergusson, and Chapman-Huston, the circle of his – their – friends seems to have shrivelled to the former patrons William Davidson and Walter Blackie and the Newberys. Four years later, back in London, his wife dies almost unnoticed. Six attend her funeral.

Jessie Newbery, on hearing of the death, writes to Mrs Schwabe: 'Margaret and Mackintosh have been our friends for 40 years – with never a rift between us...our lives were closely and affectionately interwoven...We had great pleasure and pride in watching the rise of their promising careers, great admiration for their gifts and characters. My husband always spoke of the cessation of the work of Mackintosh as a "National Calamity", Margaret's gifts were a great asset to Toshie – as adviser, appreciator, collaborateur.'[3] Fifty years later, her daughter, one of Toshie's closest younger friends, now an elderly woman herself, comments on his end: 'terribly, terribly sad waste. Perhaps he did all he was going to do. But I'd like to have seen his fiftieth house!'[4]

What is left? A terse letter from London valuers lists the contents of their Chelsea studios: furniture, large collection of sketches, architectural drawings and the 31 paintings 'practically of no value.' Including £1 for four of his own chairs, the total inventory is £88.16s.2d. William Davidson holds it all in trust for the residuary legatee Sylvan McNair, vanished to South Africa. With friends and other admirers, hoping to make some money on the sale to benefit Sylvan, he organises an exhibition in the McLellan Galleries, the old City Art Gallery, in the same block as the art school in which Mackintosh studied, on the not so sylvan street of the willows. Some items are sold, some given away, but the bulk goes back to the cellar of the Davidson office.

'The thing is,' says Mary Newbery, 'he was just, in a way, ordinary Glaswegian; and he didn't hook up with anybody.'

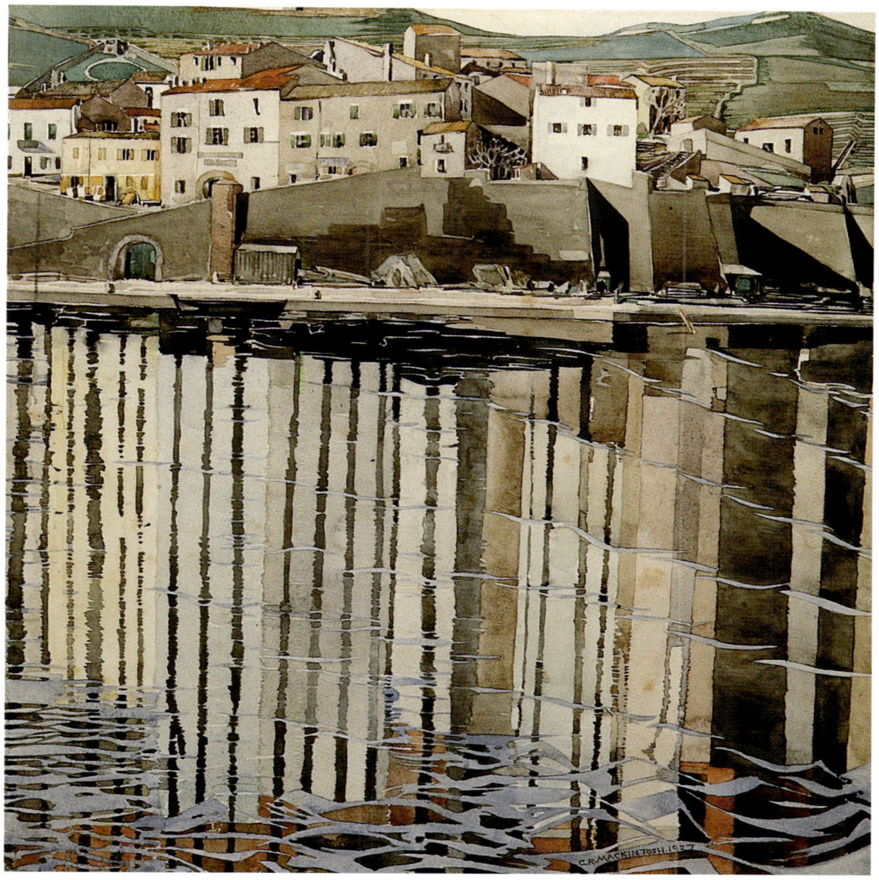


**La Rue du Soleil, 1926**

CRM strained to complete the 50 paintings he felt were required for a proper exhibition in London, but he just reached 40. 'I am struggling to paint in water colour. Soon I shall start in oils,' he wrote to Fra Newbery. But he never did manage to afford the oils, and had to remain, as he said, 'gey skint wi' the paint.' 'La Rue du Soleil' is one of the most dramatic and powerful of all his works. With its abstract linear pattern of the reflections, the whole composition is beautifully balanced by the waves at the bottom and sky at the top. It is one of only two paintings exhibited in London on their final return in 1928. (It was signed in 1928, and wrongly dated 1927, by the dying artist for Desmond Chapman-Huston who had bought it on exhibition.)

# NOTES

CRMSN: Charles Rennie Mackintosh Society Newsletter
CRM's lectures are published in Robertson, 1990.

PREFACE 1. Richards 1946, p 10

OVERTURE 1. Hoffmann asked him to submit jewellery to an exhibition in Vienna; 2. See Fleming 1933; 3. Goodhart-Rendel in Pevsner 1965, p 262; 4. Wigwam 1997; 5. Billcliffe 1979 6. The Artist's Townhouse, 1901 project, see CRMSN 66, 1995 pp 11–12; 7. Brett 1994; 8. CRM Seemliness 1902; 9. *The Magazine*, as they called it; four editions were produced by Agnes and Lucy Raeburn; No 1 in 1893, Nos 2 and 3 in 1894, No 4, belatedly in Spring 1896. They were found and given to the Glasgow School of Art; 10. These are held by the University of Glasgow under strict conditions; I only know of them through published extracts. 11. See Attwood 1998, p 126

THE FRENCH PAINTER 1. CRM letter to MMM, 1.6.27; 2. CRM letter to Newbery 28.12.25; 3. Colin Baxter, among others, has searched out his viewpoints and I am grateful for discussions on this; 4. CRM letter from Ille-sur-Têt to Fergusson, 1.2.1925; 5. CRM letter to MMM, 18.5.27; 6. CRM letter to MMM, 26.6.27; 7. CRM Architecture 1893; 8. CRM Seemliness 1902; 9. Morris 1881; 10. CRM as note 4; 11. CRM to MMM from Neat 1994; 12. Quoted in Spurling 1998; 13. Newbery 1977 and quoting her mother; 14. John Berger, afterword to Neat 1994; 15. CRM letter to MMM, Neat 1994; 16. Reilly became the professor of architecture in Liverpool in 1904 and later indirectly caused the dismissal of Herbert McNair, CRM's brother-in-law; 17. 'violent fits of rage' (Howarth 1977); it suggests the frustration of an Asperger's sufferer. 18. A few paintings, sent by his wife on her London forays, appear in the Chicago annual International Exhibition in 1922, '24 and '25; in an invited show in Paris in 1927 and in the Leicester Galleries, London in 1928.

PROFESSION OR ART, A TUG-O'-WAR 1. The obvious one is 'dyslexic'; a broader clinical sympathy might suggest a shadow of Aspergers Syndrome; 2. 1898, its cover by Talwin Morris; 3. Neat 1994:35; 4. But his first building on his own, a town house for relatives built in 1890 is completely unmemorable. Aspirations may be flying faster than experience and skill; 5. See Donnelly 1983; 6. He almost certainly helped detail a very late Honeyman church at Skelmorlie; the lamp at the church gate is almost precisely as CRM draws on his perspective of Martyrs' School; 7. From Bodley, Belcher, Stokes, and especially Sedding and his assistant Wilson, who uses asymmetrical compositions; 8. Neat 1994; 9. Honeyman retires 1.1.1901; the partnership is signed in October by Keppie and Mackintosh; however Honeyman remains much in evidence for the next few years; 10. The title of an important book of essays, Shaw (1892); 11. CRM Seemliness 1902

THE REAL THING 1. Ballantyne 1991-2; 2. Much of this from McGread, 1998; 3. Haddow 1975; 4. Manpower Services Commission's Job Creation Scheme paid for an architect and draughtsman; 5. CRMSN 17, Winter 1977–8; 6. William R. Martin (Edinburgh) sold more-or-less copies of CRM study dark oak chairs and tables, as well as a modified version of the Willow Tea Room tall clock. J. Garth Reynolds (Ludlow) sell oak chairs based on Ingram Street. A.H Mackintosh, furniture-maker of Kirkcaldy won awards in 1976 and '77 for their 'Cranston Collection.'; 7. Fabrics by The Hidden Road Company, 1984/5 ; 8. See Robbins 1990; 9. Ibid; 10. MacIntyre 1992; 11. The Horstmann furniture, copied from Derngate, is now in V&A, London; 12. Ellis 1994; 13. Agnes Blackie, in Moffat, 1989; 14. Derngate guest bedroom clock, 1919, taken from Otto Pritscher, published in 1908. 15. Articulated by E. E. Viollet-le-Duc in the 19th C; 15. Unlike Thonet (designers and manufacturers) and Hoffmann whose chairs were designed for quantity production, both of whose chairs exhibited in Vienna in 1900 were copied, along with CRM's, for the Austrian Embassy in Tokyo.

ART OF LIFE, A TUG-O'-WAR 1. Interview in Howarth 1952; 2. As a typical Gemini, says Neat 1994; 3. The furniture drawings are signed Chas R. Mackintosh, and neither Buchanan St nor Argyle St tea rooms appear in the books of Honeyman & Keppie (though some drawings are on office stationery); 4. Heinz Kohut's phrase for fin-de-siècle Vienna; 5. VolXX, 1896-7:32-3; 6. White 1897; 7. See Burkhauser 1992. Arte Decorativa Scozzese organised by Newbery showed the work of Mackintosh, McNair and John Guthrie and the Macdonald sisters, Jessie King and Jessie Newbery. 8. Beardsley died in 1898 aged only 25; all his illustrations date from 1891-5; 9. Their first joint work is Bruckmann's fireplace, panel by MMM.

THE DESIGNER AT WORK 1. CRM Seemliness 1902; 2. Gregh 1996; 3. Golden section is a division into two parts A and B where the ratio A:B is the same as B:A+B; this proportional relationship is confused continually with a numerical one like Fibonacci's in Gregh 1996; 4. 1925 drawing by MacGibbon, in GSA Calendar 1934-5; 5. Angelos Widesan, Architectural Association History Thesis, 1968; 6. As Peter Smithson, one of Britain's most original architects of the 1960s put it; 7. Ruskin 1848:5:5, perceptively quoted by Macleod in Robertson 1990; 8. The Hurst, Sutton Coldfield, 1894, by Lethaby is more or less repeated at Windyhill,1899, and thence developed at Hill House, 1902, as Robert Macleod pointed out to me; 9. 1902.19 Billcliffe 1979; 10. Since 1985/6 in Lewis Collection, Virginia Museum of Fine Arts, Richmond; 11. 1904.19A and 1902.1 in Billcliffe 1979; 12. White 1897:92

ONLY DREAMS ARE TRUE 1. Chapman-Huston 1910; 2. MMM letter to Muthesius, May 1903; 3. Chapman-Huston 1910 on their drawing room; 4. Olbrich's words; 5. CRM to Muthesius, July 1900; 6. Morton Shand; 7. Helland 1994; 8. CRM to Muthesius, July 1900; 9. Frances and Herbert McNair were also invited, but the recent birth of Sylvan prevents their travel; 10. Muthesius' words; the exhibition is laid out so that all visitors pass the Scottish exhibits; 11. Undated letter (*c.* 1910), Hoffmann archives Hdschr.I.Nr.162.137; 12. Ludwig Hevesi, 1905, quoted Howarth 1977; 13. Mackintosh designs a little Art School stand, for women bookbinders; 14. Mackintosh keeps up with the Hoffmann-Klimt group, linking into the Werkstätte with whom he exhibits in 1909; 15. *The Studio* 1902:96; 16. Muthesius (1904) 1979: 51; 17. Newbery 1977; 18. Kalas, *The Art of Glasgow*, 1905, reprinted in memorial catalogue 1933.

GLASGOW TEA CEREMONY 1. Muir 1901, p 172 (James Hamilton Muir is pseudonym for James Bone, his brother Muirhead Bone who also illustrates the book, and Archibald Hamilton Charteris); 2. He designed some interior fitments, now unknown, for a temporary exhibition restaurant in 1911 for which Margaret designed the menu; 3. CRM letter to Anna Muthesius, March 1903; 4. Muir 1901, p 172; 5. *The Studio*, 1906; 6. The anonymous *Dekorative Kunst* author was probably Muthesius; the 10-year-old was Margaret Morris 1963.

A WALK IN GLASGOW 1. Muir 1901, p 246.

AN ENGLISH ARTIST 1. Ruskin 1853, Vol I, xxx; 2. MMM letter to Anna Geddes, 14.1.15; 3. Quoted in Moffat 1989; 4. Ekhart Muthesius, foreword to Buchanan 1989. 5. Private letter, 1898; 6. Morris 1881; 7. Quoted in Moffat 1989; 8. Quoted Buchanan 1982 and Neat 1994; 9. CRM letter to William Davidson 18.6.1915; 10. What appears aloof and taciturn behaviour is possibly what is now known as a mild form of Asperger's Syndrome.

A DYING PRACTICE 1. Only a few, general, drawings were required; 2. Quoted Crawford 1995 p.137; 3. Letter to Francis Shand, in possession of CRM Society; 4. The cottage sometimes described as being at 'Cloak'; 5. See Walker 1981/2.

AUTHENTIC GLASGOW STYLE 1. CRM to Hoffmann, translated by Wärndorfer (?) and back by Howarth, Howarth 1977 ed, p xxxviii; 2. Daniel Robbins, in Kaplan 1996, p 66; 3. Brett 1992; 4. Reekie 1981-2; 5. White 1897, Part 1 p 90; 6. Mackintosh was not an Arts & Crafts 'honest' designer, but was concerned primarily with the finished appearance, cf Billcliffe 1979, p 9, 7. Newberry, 1973; 8. Helland 1994.

CRISIS 1. MMM letter to Anna Muthesius, Christmas 1904; 2. M.R. Dingwall, in Moffat, 1989; 3. She has added his name to her own, while her sister Frances more conventionally replaced Macdonald with McNair. 4. Letter, 5 January 1903; 5. MMM to Herman Muthesius, 27 March 1903; Quoted in Reekie 1981-2 as if a CRM letter; 6. MMM to Anna Muthesius, 1903; 7. *Our Homes and How to Beautify Them*, 1902 (sponsored by Waring & Gillow), text next to an interior of CRM's Art Lover's House; 8. He also learns from Keppie how to take credit, claiming he alone designed the Oval Room at Ingram Street; 9. Muthesius 1904; English translation p 61; 10. The charmingly worded report of Pevsner, 1950, who interviewed his former colleagues; reprinted in English in 1968, p 174; 11. Things get so bad that the Macdonald family presses McNair onto a boat to Canada with a one-way ticket. Though he returns, his in-laws never acknowledge him. Frances dies in 1921 aged 47, of cerebral haemorrhage or suicide. Herbert, shattered, abandons art, destroying all their work on which he can lay his hands. It seems likely she had a cerebral haemorrhage. We learn more about her, however, from the contemporary rumour of suicide; 12. Margaret sought gynaecological advice in an attempt to conceive (Mary Newbery in Neat 1994, p 152); 13. E.B. Kalas, *De La Tamise a la Spree*, 1905, quoted Macleod 1968; 14. Eduard Wimmer, member of the Secession, collecting material in the UK for exhibition in Vienna, met Mackintosh in Glasgow. Howarth, 1977, p xxxix; 15. Ruskin 1853, Book II, Ch VI; 16. The lack of management is also indicated in job records, where (as they are handwritten) the contrast with Keppie's is clear; 17. Dyslexics often show such difficulties; 18. M.R. Dingwall, in Moffat 1989.

BOHEMIAN EXILE 1. Ashbee left Cheyne Walk in 1917, but his mother and sisters remained there; 2. Quoted by his son-in-law, Barnes 1981; 3. *The Scotsman* 10.10.1916. At the next Arts & Crafts exhibition (1923), MMM and CRM are again invited, and send separate panels; 4. His work impresses, says Philip Mairet, but not his personality as 'his aura was suffused with alcoholic potations to which he was addicted,' letter to Murray Grigor, 2.3.1967; 5. His circle of artists seems to include not one architect; 6. 'Pinks', for example, which is published in *The Studio* in 1923 is brilliant, vital, colourful; 7. H.S. Goodhart-Rendel, *The Architectural Review*, Vol 53, 1923, p 31; 8. Bassett-Lowke is known, in the other areas of his life, for never being lavish in crediting collaborators. This omission doesn't mean he was unhappy with CRM; 9. A memoire, 1939;

DOMESTIC DREAMS 1. 'The Smaller Middle-Class House', lecture to architects, 1895, published in Parker & Unwin 1901; 2. *Dekorative Kunst*, III, 1900, p 97; 3. The Mac Four were not invited to exhibit, but some remnants of room settings can be seen inside Glasgow's Art Gallery; 4. Quoted precisely from Billcliffe & Vergo 1977, p.739; 5. A study for Dr Hugo Henneberg, Vienna; 6.*The Studio*, October 1906; 7. Shand 1935; 8. 'The works of men such as Morris, Philip Webb, Voysey. Mackintosh and Lorimer were well-known to American designers at the end of the 19th C.' Giffen 1995 – but I await his evidence; 9. Crawford, quoted Maclehose 1878, p.138.

NEW WAYS 1. Born in 1877 as Wenman J. B. Lowke, he changed his name to Bassett-Lowke in 1900 and was always known as Whynne; 2. He was an early member of the DIA, the Design and Industries Association founded on the model of the Werkbund; 3. His elder brother William had been CRM's predecessor as winner of the Thomson travelling scholarship; 4. Some squares concealed storage, one housed a barometer; 5. The main bedroom was painted delicate grey with mauve edging, the woodwork white and furniture grey sycamore, all, as the client said, 'particularly cool and refreshing'; 6. Now in the V&A Museum; 7. Bassett-Lowke's links with German craftsmen and manufacturers, some of whom were in this Knockaloe internment camp, led him to this workshop for internees for his furniture; 8. The corner studio in these drawings, for the Arts League, is not the same scheme which received permission.

THE SCOTTISH DRAUGHTSMAN 1. CRM Scotch Baronial Architecture 1891; 2. CRM, Architecture 1893; 3. Three early sketchbooks by CRM were recently discovered in the National Library of Ireland; 4. Muthesius 1904, English ed p 17.

MEANING IN ARCHITECTURE 1. Brydon 1901 and Street 1901; 2. No one really knows when or where CRM gave this paper Seemliness, but this seems the best guess, see John H G Archer 'Edgar Wood' in Nuttgens 1988; 3. Seemliness 1902; 4. The classical expression of architectural quality, from Vitruvius, has it made up of firmitas (constructional quality), utilitas (fitting to purpose) and venustas (beauty); Modernist functionalism would translate that into utilitas + firmitas = venustas; 5. CRM, Seemliness 1902; 6. Quoted Lethaby 1935, p 94; 7. Hoffmann, letter 23/2/1914, quoted Sekler, Ch VI, Note 61; 8. Lethaby 1892; 9. To quote Brett 1994 ; 10. CRM Architecture, 1893; 11. Muthesius1901; 12. 'For a man who has the gift will take up any style and will work in that, and be great in that, and make everything he does in it look fresh.' Ruskin 1848, Ch VIII ; 13. His talk Scotch Baronial Architecture (to 16 members and 2 guests of Glasgow Institute of Architects, 10 February 1891) on the native Scottish tradition he claims to be the first formal discussion of the subject among Glasgow architects; 14. CRM Architecture 1893; 15. Julius Meier-Graete, 1904.

A SCHOOL OF ART 1. Andy MacMillan; 2. *The Glasgow Herald* 21.12.1899; 3. It is a world away from his youthful classicism of earlier, as in details at Craigie Hall; 4. Key was then called to perform similar health-improving wonders in Belfast (as credited in Banham 1969) and Birmingham; 5. Cairns 1995, as is much of this paragraph; 6. Harbison 1989; 7. Lethaby 1910.

ANOTHER FRAME 1. The most accessible material is Tony Attwood's *Asperger's Syndrome* and OASIS (Online Asperger's Syndrome Information and Support) website. All quotations are from Attwood or from papers published on the OASIS website. The debate has developed further since this book's first publication.

BRAVE, TRUTHFUL AND WANTING TO GET THINGS PERFECT 1. Lady Alice Barnes in Moffat 1989; 2. CRM's word for the letters; 3. Her spellings, quoted in Barnes 1981 and Reekie 1981-2; 4. In Moffat 1989.

# BIBLIOGRAPHY


CRMSN: The Charles Rennie Mackintosh Society Newsletter

Agnoletti, F. (1905). 'The Hill-house Helensburgh'. *Deutsche Kunst und Dekoration* (March): 337-368.

Attwood, T. (1997). *Asperger's Syndrome*, London.

Ballantyne, I. (1991-2). 'Not up to standard!' CRMSN 57.

Banham, P. R. (1969). *The Architecture of the Well-Tempered Environment*, London.

Barnes, H. J. (1981). 'The Newberys.' CRMSN 30 (Autumn).

Bassett-Lowke, J. (1999). *Wenman Joseph Bassett-Lowke*, Chester.

Billcliffe, R. (1977). *Architectural Sketches and Flower Drawings by CRM*, London.

Billcliffe, R. (1978). *Mackintosh Watercolours*, Glasgow.

Billcliffe, R. (1979). *CRM: Complete Furniture, Furniture Drawings and Interior Design*, Guildford and London.

Billcliffe, R. (1981). 'Four Mackintosh tables.' CRMSN 28 (Winter).

Billcliffe, R. (1982). 'James Herbert MacNair.' CRMSN 33 (Autumn): 5–9.

Billcliffe, R. (1985). 'Mackintosh Textiles – another view.' CRMSN 41 (Autumn).

Billcliffe, R.(1993). 'Some thoughts on collecting Mackintosh.' CRMSN 61 (Spring).

Billcliffe, R. (1995). 'Note on current popularity of CRM.' CRMSN (Winter).

Billcliffe, R. & P. Vergo (1977). 'CRM and the Austrian Art Revival.' *The Burlington Magazine* CXIX: 739–744.

Bird, E. (1975). 'Glasgow's Response to 'The Spook School'.' *The Scottish Art Review* 14 (No 4):14–16, 28.

Blackie, W. (1968). 'Memories of CRM.' *The Scottish Art Review* XI (Special Number, No 4): 6–11.

Brett, D. (1988). 'The Eroticization of Domestic Space: A Mirror by CRM.' *The Journal of Decorative and Propaganda Arts*, Wolfson Foundation, Miami, Florida No 10 (Fall 1988).

Brett, D. (1992). *CRM: The Poetics of Workmanship*, London, 1992.

Brett, D. (1994). Review of Neat 1994. CRMSN 65 (Autumn 1994): 13–14.

Brydon, J. M. (1901). 'The 19th Century'. AA Notes, Vol XVI (January)167: 1–5,

Buchanan, W. (1980). 'Japanese Influence on Charles Rennie Mackintosh.' CRMSN 25 (Spring).

Buchanan, W. (1982). 'Mackintosh, John and Jessie Keppie.' CRMSN 32 (Mid-Summer): 3–10.

Buchanan, W. (1989). editor, *Mackintosh's Masterwork*, Glasgow.

Burkhauser, J. (1990). editor, *Glasgow Girls*, Edinburgh.

Burkhauser, J. (ed Howarth) (1992). ''Sala M' Arte Decorativa Scozzese.' CRMSN 58 (Spring 1992): 9–13.

Cairns, G. (1995). 'The Glasgow School of Art: The Missing Link of Environmental Systems History.' CRMSN 66 (Winter/Spring): 5–10.

Chapman-Huston, D. (1910). 'Dreamers in the Moon', A Creel of Peat: Stray Papers. London, reprinted in Neat 1994.

Chapman-Huston, D. (1930). 'CRM.' *Artwork* 1930 (no 21, Spring): 30.

Cinamon, G. (1991). 'The First Book Cover Designs by Mackintosh.' CRMSN 55 (Spring): 8–9.

Crawford, Alan, (1995). *CRM*. London.

Dekoratice Kunst (1899). 'Die Schottischenkunstler: MM, Frances Macdonald, CRM, Talwin Morris and J H MacNair.' *Dekorative Kunst* III: 48–9, 69–76.

*Dekorative Kunst* (1905). 'Ein Mackintosh Tee Haus in Glasgow.' *Dekorative Kunst* VIII (No 7): 257–73.

*Dekorative Kunst* (1905). *Willow Tearooms*. (April).

Donnelly, M. (1983). 'CRM and the Glasgow Herald.' CRMSN 84 (Spring).

Dresser, C. (1882). *Japan, Its Architecture, Art and Art Manufactures*.

Ellis, A. (1994). 'Recovery of the Original Drawing Room Scheme, The Hill House.' CRMSN 65 (Autumn): 5–7.

Fleming, A. A. (1933). Letter (CRM as ceramic designer). *The Studio* CVI: 41.

Gibbs, R. (1976). 'Mackintosh's Book Designs.' CRMSN 12 (Summer).

Giffen, D. H. (1995). (Professor of Interior Design, Kent State, Ohio) note in CRMSN 67 (Summer)

Gordon, J. (1979). *Decadent Spaces: Notes for a Phenomenology of the Fin de Siècle. Decadence and the 1890s*. I London.

Gregh, E. (1996). 'The Hill House', *Architectural Research Quarterly*, 1, 3 (Spring).

Grigor, M. and R. Murphy (1995). *The Architect's Architect: CRM*. Glasgow.

Haddow, R. (1975). 'Ingram Street interiors future.' CRMSN 8 (Summer).

Harbison, R. (1989) 'The Glasgow School of Art: Master of Building', *The Architects' Journal*, 14 June.

Helland, J. (1994). 'The Critics and the Arts and Crafts: The Instance of Margaret Macdonald and C R Mackintosh.' *Art History* 17( Summer): 209–227.

Hillier, H. (1959). 'Willow should be restored.' *The Scottish Arts Review* 1959.

Howarth, T. (1952). *CRM and the Modern Movement*, London (revised 1977).

Kaplan, W. (1996), editor. *CRM*, New York/Glasgow.

Kimura, H. (1982). CRM: Architectural Drawings Catalogue and Design Analytical Catalogue, Glasgow.

Kinchin, P. (1991). *Tea and Taste: The Glasgow Tea Rooms, 1875–1975*, Oxford.

Kinghorn, J. (1990). 'The Redevelopment of the Argyle Street Tea Rooms.' CRMSN 54 (Autumn): 10–13.

Larner, G. & C. (1979). *The Glasgow Style*, Edinburgh.

Lethaby, W. R. (1892). *Architecture, Mysticism and Myth*, London

Lethaby, W. R. (1910). 'Architecture of Adventure', RIBA lecture, *RIBA Journal*, Vol 17, 467

Lethaby, W.R. (1935). *Philip Webb and His Work*, Oxford.

Levy, N. (1985). 'W J Bassett-Lowke as Architectural Patron' in *The Bassett-Lowke Story*, London.

McGread, C. (1998). 'GSA and the Campaign to save Ingram Street Tea Rooms.' CRMSN 73 (Summer): 6–7.

MacIntyre, R. H. (1992). 'An Artist's Cottage and Studio CRM 1900 for Dr & Mrs Tovell, 1990.' CRMSN 58.

Maclehose, R. (publisher) (1878). *The Old Country Houses of the Old Glasgow Gentry*, Glasgow.

McKean, C. (1985). 'The Influence of Mackintosh in the 1930s.' CRMSN 47 (Autumn).

McKean, C. (1992). 'The debut.' CRMSN 60 (Winter): 6–8.

Macleod, R. (1968). *Charles Rennie Mackintosh*, London.

Macleod, R. (1996). Review of C & P Fiell on CRM. CRMSN 69 (Spring).

*Machine Minding*, (early 1920s). 'The problem of choosing a magazine cover.' 1 (part 5): 94.

Moffat, A. (1989). *Remembering CRM*, Lanark.

Morris, M. (1963). Letter. *The Glasgow Herald*.

Morris, W. (1881). 'Art and The Beauty of the Earth', lecture in *Collected Works*, Vol 22, p.155

Morse, E.S. (1885) *Japanese Homes and their Surroundings*, reprinted 1961, New York.

Muir, J.H. (1901) *Glasgow in 1901*, Glasgow & Edinburgh.

Munro, N. (1931) *The Brave Days*.

Muthesius, H. (1901). *Die Neuere Kirkchkiche Baukunst in England*, Berlin.

Muthesius, H. (1904).*The English House, 1904 onwards*; English edition, London 1979

Neat, T. (1994). *Part Seen Part Imagined, Meaning and Symbolism in the work of CRM and MM*. Edinburgh.

Newbery, F. (1922). Letter to J Q Pringle, quoted in Barnes (1981).

Newbery, J. R. (1933). 'A Memory of Mackintosh' Mackintosh Memorial Exhibition 1933 Catalogue.

Newbery, M. (1973) Interviewed by I Davis and J Bedford in *The Connoisseur* 183 (738):280-8

Nuttgens, P. (1995). Review of Grigor &Murphy 1995. CRMSN 67 (Summer): 12.

Nuttgens, P. (1988), editor, *Mackintosh and his contemporaries*, London.

Parker, B. & Unwin, R. (1901). The Art of Building a House, London.

Paterson, I. (1995). 'William McIntosh.' CRMSN 67 (Summer): 5–8.

Pevsner, N. (1950). *CRM*, Milano, Il Balcone. (English translation, in *Studies in Art, Architecture and Design*, London, 1968)

Pevsner, N. (1965) 'Goodhart-Rendel's Roll Call', *The Architectural Review*, October, 262

Raeburn, L. (1893). 'Round the Studios.' *The Magazine* (of the GSA students) 1893 (October).

Rawson, G. (1993). 'Mackintosh, Jessie Keppie and the Immortals; some new material.' CRMSN 62 (Summer).

Reekie (Robertson), P. (1981-2). 'MMM.' CRMSN 31 (Winter/Spring).

Richards, J.M. (1946). *An Introduction to Modern Architecture*, Harmondsworth.

Robbins, D. (1990). CRMSN 54, Autumn 1990

Robertson, P. (1995). *CRM: Art is the flower*, London.

Robertson, P. (n.d. 1998?). *The Mackintosh House*, Glasgow.

Robertson, P. (1990), editor. *CRM: The architectural papers*, Wendlebury.

Robertson, P. (1999), editor. *CRM: Architectural sketches*, Glasgow.

Ruskin, J. (1848). *The Seven Lamps of Architecture*, London.

Ruskin, J. (1853). *The Stones of Venice*, London.

Schorske, C. E. (1981). *Fin-de-siècle Vienna*, Cambridge.

Sekler, E.F. (1982). *Joseph Hoffman, Das architectoniske werk*, Salzburg/Wien.

Selby, F. (1975). 'Queens Cross Church.' CRMSN 7 (Spring).

Service, A.(1975). editor, *Edwardian Architecture and Its Origins*. London.

Shand, P. M. (1935). 'Glasgow Interlude', *The Architectural Review* Vol LXXV11.

Shaw, R. N. (1892) and T.G. Jackson, *Architecture: A Profession or an art?* London.

Spurling, H. (1988). *The Unknown Matisse*, London.

Steele, J. (1994). *CRM Synthesis in form*, London.

Street, A. E. (1901). *The Architectural Review* (quoted from Dennis Sharp, introduction to Muthesius 1904 English edition).

*The Studio*. (1893a). 'Beardsley.' (April).

*The Studio*. (1893b). 'Toorop's The Three Bridges.' (September).

*The Studio*. (1900). 'Glasgow School of Art.' XIX: 53–55.

*The Studio*. (1901). Article on CRM. Special Number on Modern British Domestic Architecture: 112–115.

*The Studio* (1902). 'The International Exhibition of Modern Decorative Art at Turin: Scottish.' XXVI (July): 91–104.

*The Studio*. (1906). 'Modern decorative Art at Glasgow.' (October): 31–36.

Taylor (1906). 'The Argyle Street Tearooms, Glasgow.' XXXIX: 31–36.

Vergo, P. (1973). 'Gustav Kilmt's Beethoven Frieze.' The Burlington Magazine CXV: 109–113.

Walker, D. (1968). 'The Early Work of CRM.' *The Architectural Review* (November).

Walker, D. (1975). 'Mackintosh' in Service 1975. 219 et seq.

Walker, F. A. (1981-82). 'The Mysterious Affair of Cloak.' CRMSN 31 (Winter/ Spring)

White, G. (1897). 'Some Glasgow Designers and Their Work.' *The Studio* (a) XI parts 1 and 2,(b) XII: (a) 86–100, 225–236, (b) 47–51

Wigwam (1997). *CRM Art Architecture and Design*, CD-ROM, Bellshill, Wigwam Digital.

Wimpenny, G. (1979–1980). 'Reconstructing the Willow.' CRMSN 24 (Winter).

Young, A.M. (1968). *Charles Rennie Mackintosh 1868–1928*, Edinburgh Intl. Festival.



Text written by John McKean. The moral right of John McKean as author has been asserted.



Colin Baxter: front cover, 2, 4, 8 (above), 10, 26-8, 30 (below), 31-6, 40-43, 46-7, 62, 65-73, 76-81, 90-91, 94, 95 (top), 96, 98-9, 103 (below), 104, 105 (top), 114-121, 123-4, 134, 136-8, 140-144 (above), 145-153, 155.

Aberdeen Art Gallery and Museums: 87 (below)
The Annan Gallery: 6, 63, 74, 75 (above).
Roger Billcliffe: 18, 23, 108
The British Museum: 16, 19, 39, 129
The Fine Art Society, London, UK / Bridgeman Art Library: 57, back cover (below)
Glasgow Museums: Art Gallery and Museum, Kelvingrove: 14, 20, 55, 97, 101, 107
Glasgow School of Art: 11, 17, 21, 25, 48, 49, 50, 52-4, 100, 105, 126, 139, 144 (below), 154, back cover (above)
Ken Grierson, Beaten Path Studio: 39
The Hessisches Landesmuseum, Darmstadt: 61
Private Collection – Photograph by Permission of the Fine Art Society, London: 110
The Scottish National Gallery of Modern Art: 13
Tate Gallery, London: 12
University of Glasgow (The Hunterian Art Gallery, Mackintosh Collection): 1, 7, 8 (below), 9, 13 (above), 15, 18 (above), 22, 24, 27, 29, 30 (above), 37, 38, 44, 45, 51, 56, 58-60, 64, 75 (below), 82-86, 87 (above) 88, 89, 92, 93, 95 (below), 97, 102, 103 (above), 106, 109, 111, 112 (above), 113, 122, 125, 127, 128, 130-3, 135, 156, 157, 160
The V&A Picture Library, London: 112 (below)

Colin Baxter Photography would like to thank the following for access to their properties and permission to reproduce images in this book:
The CRM Society: 32-35, 138 (below)
Mrs Fisher: 95 (above), 120-121, 152 (below)
The Glasgow School of Art: 4, 10, 98, 141-148
Henderson's the Jewellers: 72, 73, 77
The House For An Art Lover: 46-7, 123, 138 (above)
Martyrs' School 30 (below), 31
Anne Mulhern 76
The National Trust for Scotland (The Hill House, Helensburgh): 8 (above), 36, 43, 114-119, 134, 136-7, 150-51
Graham Roxburgh 26-28
Scotland Street School: 90-91, 103-4
University of Glasgow (The Mackintosh House, Reconstructed in the Hunterian Art Gallery): 62, 65-70, 94, 96, 99, 105, 124, 153, 155
Hans and Ria van Kessel: 40-41


Captions:
Front Cover Photograph: Detail, Washstand (1903), Main Bedroom, The Hill House.
p.1 Cuckoo Flower, Chiddingstone, 1910
p.2 South-east corner, Glasgow School of Art
p.4 Detail of a bookcase now in Glasgow School of Art but originally designed for Windyhill, Kilmacolm
p.160 Greetings Card for Mr & Mrs W.J. Bassett-Lowke
Back Cover Photographs: (above) Hill House – south-west elevation (below) Blue and pink tobacco flowers, design by Charles Rennie Mackintosh (1868-1928).

# INDEX



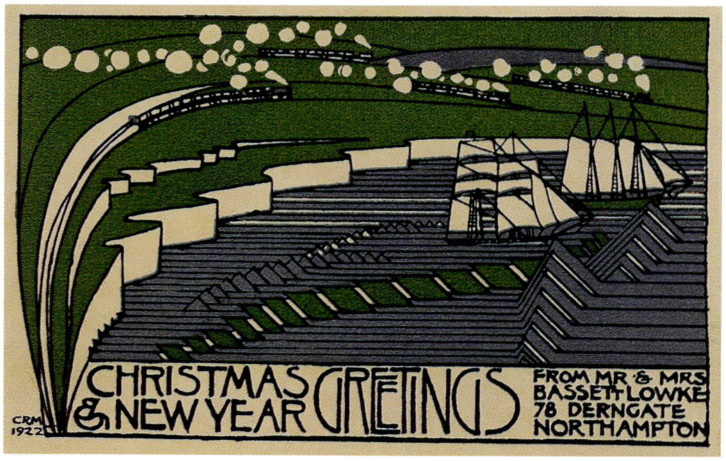





First published in Great Britain in 2000 by Lomond Books Ltd
14 Freskyn Place, East Mains Industrial Estate, Broxburn EH52 5NF
www.lomondbooks.com
Reprinted 2001, 2003, 2004, 2005, 2008, 2012

Produced by Colin Baxter Photography Ltd
See copyright information on page 159.



A CIP Catalogue record for this book is available from the British Library.

ISBN 978-1-84204-137-6 Printed in China